G6

Constitutional Acceleration within the European Union and Beyond

Modern constitutionalism as an idea and practice is facing great uncertainty in current times. Scholarly debates focus predominantly on constitutions beyond the state, while the predicament of domestic constitutionalism is much less considered. This volume contributes to a theoretically informed analysis of the key challenges and changes affecting domestic constitutionalism in Europe and beyond, departing from the idea of 'constitutional acceleration' or the increased propensity of different actors to engage in (formal) reform of the constitutional order. The volume points to a fundamental change in the function of constitutions in that constitutions themselves are increasingly subjects of political contestation rather than framing political debates.

The collection of essays addresses a range of critical challenges – including societal acceleration, depoliticization, civic engagement, multi-faceted constituent power, modernization, populism and nationalism, and transnationalization. The volume includes a variety of disciplinary, and in some cases interdisciplinary, approaches, including (political) sociology, political science, constitutional law, and constitutional and legal theory, and will be of interest to researchers and students in any of these areas. Case studies focus on the EU and the wider European context, and include highly relevant but little known or ill-understood cases, such as the recent constitutional events in Iceland, Italy, or Romania, and cases of democratic reversal, such as Hungary, while also engaging with traditional but rapidly changing cases of constitutional interest, such as the UK.

Paul Blokker is Associate Professor and Jean Monnet Chair at the Institute of Sociological Studies, Charles University, Prague. His publications include *New Democracies in Crisis? A Comparative Constitutional Study of the Czech Republic, Hungary, Poland, Romania and Slovakia*, Routledge (2013); 'EU Democratic Oversight and Domestic Deviation from the Rule of Law: Sociological Reflections', in: C. Closa and D. Kochenov (eds), *Reinforcing the Rule of Law Oversight in the European Union*, CUP (2016); and, co-edited with Chris Thornhill, *Sociological Constitutionalism*, CUP (forthcoming, 2017).

Routledge Research in Constitutional Law

This series features thought-provoking and original scholarship on constitutional law and theory. Books explore key topics, themes, and questions in the field with a particular emphasis on comparative studies. Where relevant, titles will engage with political and social theory, philosophy, and history in order to offer a rounded analysis of constitutions and constitutional law. Series Editor: David Marrani

Available titles in this series include:

The Legal Philosophy and Influence of Jeremy Bentham
Essays on 'Of the Limits of the Penal Branch of Jurisprudence'
Edited by Guillaume Tusseau

Constitutionalism in the Global Realm
A Sociological Approach
Poul F. Kjaer

The Accountability Gap in EU law
Marios Costa

Equal Citizenship, Civil Rights, and the Constitution
The Original Sense of the Privileges or Immunities Clause
Christopher R. Green

Democracy and the Human Rights Act
Republican Analysis of Citizen Power
Dennis Dixon

Constitution-making and Human Rights in the Sudans
Edited by Mohamed Abdelsalam and Lutz Oette

Constitutional Acceleration within the European Union and Beyond
Paul Blokker

Constitutional Acceleration within the European Union and Beyond

Edited by Paul Blokker

Routledge
Taylor & Francis Group
LONDON AND NEW YORK

First published 2018
by Routledge

2 Park Square, Milton Park, Abingdon, Oxfordshire OX14 4RN
52 Vanderbilt Avenue, New York, NY 10017

Routledge is an imprint of the Taylor & Francis Group, an informa business

First issued in paperback 2019

British Library Cataloguing-in-Publication Data
A catalogue record for this book is available from the British Library

Library of Congress Cataloging-in-Publication Data
Names: Blokker, Paul, editor.
Title: Constitutional acceleration within the European Union and beyond / edited by Paul Blokker.
Description: New York, NY : Routledge, 2017. | Includes bibliographical references and index.
Identifiers: LCCN 2017021885| ISBN 9781138211070 (hardback) | ISBN 9781315453644 (adobe reader) | ISBN 9781315453637 (epub) | ISBN 9781315453620 (mobipocket)
Subjects: LCSH: Constitutional law—European Union countries. | European Union.
Classification: LCC KJE4445 .C6585 2017 | DDC 342.24—dc23
LC record available at https://lccn.loc.gov/2017021885

ISBN: 978-1-138-21107-0 (hbk)
ISBN: 978-0-367-87666-1 (pbk)

Typeset in ITC Galliard Std
by Swales & Willis Ltd, Exeter, Devon, UK

Contents

Contributors

Andrew Arato is the Dorothy Hart Hirshon Professor in Political and Social Theory at the New School for Social Research in New York. He has taught at L'École des hautes études and Sciences Po in Paris, as well as at the Central European University in Budapest. He had a Fulbright teaching grant to Montevideo in 1991, and was Distinguished Fulbright Professor at the Goethe University in Frankfurt, Germany. Professor Arato has served as a consultant for the Hungarian Parliament on constitutional issues (1996–1997) and as US State Department Democracy Lecturer and Consultant (on constitutional issues) on Nepal (2007). He was reappointed by the State Department in the same capacity for Zimbabwe (November of 2010), where he had discussions with civil society activists and political leaders in charge of the constitution-making process. He was invited Professor at the College de France (Spring 2012). Professor Arato's scholarly research is widely recognized, and conferences and sessions have been organized around his work at University of Glasgow Law School (Spring 2009) and Koc University, Istanbul (December 2009), as well as at the Faculty of Law, University of the Witwatersrand, Johannesburg, South Africa (August 2010). Arato was appointed Honorary Professor and Bram Fischer Visiting Scholar at the School of Law, University of the Witwatersrand, Johannesburg (June 2010–June 2011).

Baldvin Thor Bergsson is a political scientist at the University of Iceland, and a reporter at the Icelandic National Broadcasting Service (RUV). Between 2013 and 2015, Bergsson held a research fellowship at the University of Trento, Italy. His research includes a focus on social movements and changing power relations in the aftermath of the Icelandic financial crisis in 2008. He holds an MSc in International Political Theory from the University of Edinburgh. He has worked as a reporter and assistant editor for the Icelandic National Television and Radio (RUV) since 2002, and covered both politics and the economy extensively. He has hosted several live political debates and election nights and is currently the host of the TV news magazine Kastljós.

Paul Blokker is Associate Professor at the Department of Sociology, Institute of Sociological Studies, Charles University and Jean Monnet Chair in European Political Sociology. His current research is on constitutional change, constitutional politics, a sociology of constitutions, multiple democracies, critique and dissent, and democratic participation. His recent publications include: *Sociological Constitutionalism* (edited with Chris Thornhill, Cambridge University Press, 2017); *New Democracies in Crisis? A Comparative Constitutional Study of the Czech Republic, Hungary, Poland, Romania and Slovakia* (Routledge, 2013). He is an International Editorial Board Member of the *European Journal of Social Theory* and Co-Editor of the new journal *Social Imaginaries*.

David M. Farrell is a member of the Royal Irish Academy. He is a specialist in the study of parties, elections, electoral systems, and members of parliament. His current research focuses on the role of deliberation in constitutional reform processes. In 2012, he was elected as President of the Political Studies Association of Ireland. In 2013, he was elected as Speaker of the Council of the European Consortium for Political Research; a position he was re-elected to in 2016. Professor Farrell is founding Co-Editor of *Party Politics*. David is Head of the School of Politics and International Relations, at University College Dublin. Prior to his move to Dublin, Professor Farrell was Professor and Head of Social Sciences at the University of Manchester.

Gábor Halmai is Professor of Law and Chair of Constitutional Law at the European University Institute in Florence. His primary research interests are comparative constitutional law and international human rights. He has published several books and articles, as well as edited volumes on these topics in English, German, and Hungarian. His most recent book, *Perspectives on Global Constitutionalism* deals with the use of foreign and international law by domestic courts (published by Eleven International Publishing in 2014). He joined the EUI after a teaching and research career (at the Eötvös Loránd University in Hungary, at Princeton University in the US, and at the European Masters Program in Human Rights and Democratisation in Italy) as well as years in a professional career as Chief Advisor to the President of the Hungarian Constitutional Court, member of the EU Fundamental Rights Agency's Management Board, and numerous other civic activities.

Clodagh Harris is Senior Lecturer in the Department of Government, University College Cork. Her research interests include: democratic theory and practice (particularly deliberative and participatory democracy); democratic innovations; citizen engagement and community education; and the scholarship of teaching and learning in political science.

Bogdan Iancu is Associate Professor (Comparative Constitutional Law, Constitutional Theory) at the Faculty of Political Science, University of Bucharest. He holds a doctorate in law (summa cum laude) from the Central European University (2006), and has researched at the faculties of law of the University of Toronto and McGill University, the Yale Law School, and the Wissenschaftskolleg zu Berlin. Iancu has lectured at McGill University and Université de Montréal and held a Boulton Fellowship at

McGill (2002–2004), Alexander von Humboldt Research Fellowship at the University of Bremen Faculty of Law, and at the Faculty of Law of the Humboldt University in Berlin (2008–2010).

Kriszta Kovács is Associate Professor of Comparative Constitutional Law at the UNESCO Chair on Human Rights and Peace at ELTE University Faculty of Social Sciences, Budapest. She is also a former Vice Dean at the Faculty, a former Senior Adviser of the Hungarian Constitutional Court, and former Co-President of the Joint Council on Constitutional Justice (Venice Commission, Council of Europe). She holds a PhD in Law from ELTE University, Budapest and has held fellowships at the Human Rights Institute of the Columbia Law School, New York, at the University of Trento, Italy, at the University of Birmingham, UK, and from the UK Foreign Office and the Zeit Stiftung. She is the author of *Towards Equality: From the Ban on Non-discrimination to Affirmative Action* (L'Harmattan, 2012) and the co-author of *Constitution for a Disunited Nation: Hungary's 2011 Fundamental Law* (CEU Press, 2011). Her recent book chapters include 'Hungary's Post-Communist Administrative Law Regimes' (with Kim Lane Scheppele, in *Comparative Administrative Law*, eds. S.R. Ackermann and P.L. Lindseth, Elgar, 2017). Lately, she has presented papers on constitutional transformations at various universities, such as the University of Oxford, Yale University, Queens University, and Humboldt University.

Zoran Oklopcic is Associate Professor at Carleton University's Department of Law and Legal Studies. In the past, he was MacCormick Visiting Fellow at the Edinburgh Law School, as well as a Visiting Scholar at the University of Pompeu Fabra, Department of Political Science. He holds an LLM from the Central European University, and earned his SJD from the University of Toronto Faculty of Law. He has published in the areas of constitutional theory, comparative constitutional law, and public international law. His work on constituent power, self-determination, secession, and constitutional pluralism has appeared in journals such as *Constellations*, *Leiden Journal of International Law*, *Canadian Journal of Law and Jurisprudence*, *Global Constitutionalism*, and *Transnational Legal Theory*. His current research focuses on the mutation of self-determination discourse in Catalonia, as well as on the 'duty to negotiate federalization' as a potential component in early-conflict constitution making. He also works on a larger book project, tentatively called 'After the People: Provincializing Constitutional Theory.'

Francesco Palermo is Professor for Comparative Constitutional Law at the School of Law, University of Verona, and Director of the Institute for Comparative Federalism at Eurac Research in Bolzano/Bozen. From 2007 to 2010, he served as Senior Legal Adviser to the OSCE High Commissioner on National Minorities. From 2007 to 2016, he was member of the Council of Europe's Advisory Committee on the Framework Convention for the Protection of National Minorities, of which he was the President from 2014 to 2016. Since March 2013, he has served as a non-party member of the Italian Senate, working in the constitutional committee and in the human rights committee. Since 2016, he has been the President of the International Association of Centres for Federal Studies (IACFS). He authored over 300 publications, including 9 monographs, and 31 edited volumes.

Jane Suiter is Associate Professor at the School of Communications, Dublin City University. She is currently co-Principal Investigator on an EPA project on climate change coverage in Irish media and is Communications Director of a COST project on populist political communication with an emphasis on media and social media. She is Deputy Research Director of the Irish Constitutional Convention, a member of the ECPR standing group on Democratic Innovations, and Co-Convener of the PSAI specialist group Voters, Parties, and Elections. Jane has recently co-edited the volume *Constitutional Deliberative Democracy in Europe* with Min Reuchamps (ECPR Press, 2016).

Silvia Suteu is a Lecturer in Public Law at University College London. She was previously a doctoral researcher, tutor, and ESRC research fellow at the University of Edinburgh, where she also co-founded the Constitutional Law Discussion Group and acted as Associate Director for Research Engagement of the Edinburgh Centre for Constitutional Law. Silvia's current research interests are in constitutional theory and comparative constitutional law. She is especially interested in the theory and practice of participatory constitutional change, constitutional entrenchment and democratic theory, transitional constitutionalism, and gender-sensitive constitution-making.

Gábor Attila Tóth is Alexander von Humboldt research fellow at the Humboldt University, Berlin. He is also Associate Professor of Constitutional Law and International Human Rights at the University of Debrecen. Previously, he gained visiting fellowships to the New School for Social Research, New York, a research fellowship to the Humboldt University, and an Oxford scholarship from the British Council. He has served as consultant to constitutional issues to the Constitutional Court of Moldova and expert for the Freedom House. Between 2000 and 2010 he worked as adviser to the Constitutional Court of Hungary. He was founder of the Hungarian Civil Liberties Union. He is author of numerous articles and eight books, including the edited volumes, *Constitution for a Disunited Nation* (CEU Press, 2013) and *Human Rights* (Osiris, 2003).

Acknowledgements

The idea of the edited book originated in the comparative, three-year research project 'Constitutional Politics in Post-Westphalian Europe' (CoPolis), funded with a *Unità di Ricerca* 2011 grant of the Provincia Autonoma di Trento, Italy. The research project was based at the Department of Sociology, University of Trento. I am very grateful for the financial support. The CoPolis project organized three conferences, one at the Central European University, Budapest, March 2014, one at the University of Oxford, October 2014, and a final conference at the University of Trento, May 2015. Some contributions to this volume have been presented and debated – in much earlier versions – at these events.

I would like to thank the CoPolis project members Kriszta Kovács and Baldvin Thor Bergsson for their outstanding scholarly work and contributions to the volume, as well as the contributors to the volume in general for their highly inspiring and engaging chapters, and willingness to revise, rethink, and refine their arguments. I would finally like to thank Elena, Elio, and Duccio for their inestimable human support.

Introduction

Constitutional challenges, reform, and acceleration

Paul Blokker

Constitutional reform is high on the political agenda in European Union member states and Europe at large,[1] as well as beyond the European context, in other parts of the world. In the last two to three decades, some countries in Europe – including so-called established as well as more recently established democracies – have experienced a relatively frequent number of attempts at changing their constitutional law(s). From a more general, global perspective, Elkins and Melton observe that constitutional amendment has become more frequent since the 1950s, and, in particular, from the 1990s onwards.[2]

Powerful tendencies of transformation of modern constitutionalism (as a largely domestic, state-based framework), and even its demise, are observed,[3] not least having to do with the emergence of structures and institutions with constitutional relevance beyond the domestic context. This is most clearly evident in the process of European integration. An Italian constitutionalist, Gaetano Azzariti, recently observed that constitutionalists currently experience a 'situation of inquietude, determined by an insecurity with regard to their self-identity, and by the perception of an ever larger gap that separates traditional knowledge, necessary to interpret and hence represent the world, from the reality of the represented'.[4] The gap between a represented reality and the reality of the represented is equally observed from a sociological perspective, in terms of the process of 'social acceleration'. The latter is highly relevant for a discussion of modern constitutionalism, in that social acceleration requires increasingly rapid and frequent intervention into established institutions, including the constitutional framework. Indeed, one could argue that '[c]onstitutions will remain necessary, but more improbable'.[5]

The chapters in this volume address a variety of crucial constitutional challenges as well as modes of change, analysed as dimensions of a more general tendency towards 'constitutional acceleration', that is, the increased propensity of different actors to engage in (formal) reform of the constitutional order.[6] In this introduction, constitutional change and acceleration are the main object of discussion, in that some of the main motivations for and triggers of constitutional reform in contemporary times will be looked into (§1), the idea of constitutional acceleration further explored (§2), different modes and instruments of revision and amendment outlined (§3), as well as different subjective approaches to constitutions ('constitutional mindsets') delineated (§4). In the final part (§5), the different sections and chapters of the book will be briefly introduced.

1. Motivations for, and triggers of, constitutional reform

In current times, constitutional reform is upfront in public, political debates for a number of significant reasons (often found in a combination in distinctive constitutional realities), including *economic reasons*, not least related to the recent economic and financial crisis; reasons of *modernization*, stemming from the observation that existing constitutional orders are out of touch with the necessities of current times; reasons of *redefinition of political units*, in particular due to calls for extensive autonomy of distinctive regions; reasons of *identity and national self-rule*, relating to calls for a more upfront reflection of national identity in constitutional orders and the emergence of populist constitutional projects, allegedly defending national sovereignty, interests, and culture; reasons of *participation and popular sovereignty*, in which calls are made for allowing for more robust participation of citizens in constitutional reform and democratic politics; and reasons of *post-sovereignty*, in which calls are made for adaptation of constitutions to realities of shared sovereignty and/or the increased prominence of international and supranational legal regimes in national contexts.

Financial and economic crisis

One significant way in which the financial and economic crisis has affected constitutional orders is by importantly informing calls and mobilization for constitutional reform. This has been the case (in highly different ways) in, for instance, Hungary, Iceland, Ireland, and Italy. The crisis in financial and subsequently economic terms was in some cases translated into a crisis of political and even moral values (as most clearly occurred in Iceland in 2008/9).[7] Contiades and Fotiadou speak of a 'frenzy about constitutional reform'[8] in the immediate wake of the financial crisis. In a number of European countries, the crisis formed an external trigger for latent or ongoing political projects for constitutional reform. The specific reactions to and implication of the crisis for domestic constitutional orders have been variegated,[9] and have included the adoption of a new constitution,[10] attempts to draft and ratify a new constitution,[11] more modest formal attempts at constitutional revision,[12] forms of informal amendment, as well as important changes in the procedural underpinnings of processes of constitutional reform (see below).

Modernization

A related and in some cases significant motivation for reform is the observation that existing constitutional orders are obsolete or outdated. This observation has taken different forms in specific countries. A good example is Iceland, where the constitution is open to critique on the basis of its externally imposed nature, in that the existing constitution dates back to 1920, when Iceland obtained independence within the monarchy of Denmark and adopted its own constitution, which was, however, nearly identical to the Danish constitution.[13] When Iceland declared independence from Denmark in 1944, it basically replaced references to the king with references to the president in the constitutional document, leaving the Icelandic constitution open to the charge that it had not been adopted in an internal constituent process.[14] A further dimension of constitutional modernization is a drive to efficiency and the understanding of the constitution as an instrument for enhancing speed and efficiency in government.[15] This dimension was perhaps most clearly observable in the attempt at reform of the Italian constitution, strongly informed by the idea of 'governabilità' (governability) of the Italian state, and the view that the perfect bicameralism of the Italian parliament obstructs efficient government.[16]

Pluri-national states

A complex and potentially highly conflictive dimension of constitutional reform is in the case of pluri-national states and substate calls for decentralization, autonomy, and in some cases even independence.[17] Significant cases in Europe include pluri-national states such as the United Kingdom, where, in particular, Scotland has been pushing for greater autonomy and independence as well as Spain (the Basque Country and Catalonia). But calls for more substantial forms of autonomy are also made elsewhere, such as in Italy. The constitutional aspirations of substate nations involve calls for autonomy, representation, and/or recognition.[18] In important ways, subnational constitutional aspirations call into question taken-for-granted liberal notions of constitutionalism that tend to equate a constitutional settlement with a majority nation. Indeed, the notion of recognition implies the idea of explicit reference to the pluri-national nature of the state and of co-authorship of constitutional rules by substate nations: the 'demand is that the constitution should, in its own description of the nature of the state, reflect, declare, and symbolize the reality of that state's national pluralism'.[19] An interesting example is article 68(1) of the (former) Hungarian Constitution of 1989: '(1) The national and ethnic minorities living in the Republic of Hungary participate in the sovereign power of the people: they represent a constituent part of the State'.

A particularly relevant case is that of post-Brexit United Kingdom. As the chapter by Silvia Suteu attests, the constitutional settlement of the UK is put strongly to the test in the aftermath of the Scottish independence referendum (September 2014), which led to calls for a UK constitutional convention, and subsequently the Brexit referendum, which strongly questioned the relations between the different units of the UK. Relations between the national state and regional levels are equally at stake elsewhere, as, for instance, in a recent attempt at constitutional reform in Italy.[20]

Identity and national self-rule

The centripetal forces affecting pluri-national states also point to a separate, but at the same time related, phenomenon: the emphasis on majority nationalism in projects of constitutional reform.[21] In Europe, nationalism and its relation to constitutionalism should be understood from a complex perspective of European integration, divided sovereignty, substate autonomy, and the increased diversity of societies, not least due to the recent upsurge in migration. The phenomenon of the endorsement of the national majority in constitutional reform is most clearly visible in the adoption of the new Fundamental Law in Hungary in 2011,[22] but increasingly plays a role elsewhere too (e.g., manifesting itself in different ways in Poland and the UK). The rationale of constitutional change in some of these cases is the idea that the national majority and its culture needs protection.[23] This type of constitutionalism, which could be referred to as communitarian constitutionalism, emphasizes national majority interests and the active promotion of a particular vision of communal life. The political vision is one of individuals embedded in and owing allegiance to a given community, and constitutionalism is understood as a means to protect a distinct community, its ethos, and its traditions. A communitarian view understands the individual as a 'socially embedded' self and the community as highly important in forming the individual.[24]

Populism

Constitutional nationalism can be related to (right-wing) populist forms and understandings of constitutionalism.[25] This peculiar, and in many ways worrying, engagement with processes of constitution-making and constitutional reform is explicitly present in the constitutional developments in countries such as Hungary and Poland. The relation between populism and constitutionalism is generally understood as one of deep tension. As Jan-Werner Müller has recently put it, 'populism is inherently hostile to the mechanisms, and ultimately, the values commonly associated with constitutionalism: constraints on the will of the majority, checks and balances, protections for minorities, and even fundamental rights'.[26] According to Nadia Urbinati, populists seek to 'implement an agenda whose main and recognizable character is hostility against liberalism and the principles of constitutional democracy, from minority rights, division of powers, and pluriparty system'.[27] Populists are seen as impatient with procedures and institutions, and loath of intermediary bodies, as they prefer unmediated, direct relations between the populist ruler and the people. But it equally needs to be recognized that populism as a political phenomenon cannot be reduced to a form of anti-establishment critique and disdain for legal rules and formal procedures, as it equally contains a theory of power.[28] Recent developments in Poland and Hungary in particular have shown distinctive projects of getting hold of state power, with an explicit and extensive attention for, and engagement with, constitutional matters and constitutional reform. Populists tend to legitimate such engagement by reference to popular sovereignty and the national political community or the people. In this, populist constitutionalism causes significant tensions in the European Union, which is grounded in the fundamental values of democracy, the rule of law, and human rights (art. 2, Treaty on European Union). In this, the populist-constitutional phenomenon has resulted in intense debates on both democratic backsliding and illiberal democracy in Europe, the effectiveness of conditionality, and the possibility of supranational monitoring of democracy.[29]

Participation and democracy

In strong contrast to the populist understanding of engagement with popular sovereignty is a tendency towards actual citizen participation in constitutional reform. Such reform is often informed by the perception that liberal, representative democracy is facing declining legitimacy. The insight is that in order to safeguard democracy, (constitutional) reform is necessary in order to strengthen and innovate democratic systems. Such a reasoning of democratization is visible in a range of constitutional projects throughout Europe in the last two decades or so, including the so-called Charter 88 movement in the UK, experiments with deliberative fora in, for instance, Belgium, the Netherlands, Iceland, Ireland, and Romania, and an attempt to grassroots constitution-making in Iceland in 2011. Two dimensions that stand out are that of constitutional design (introducing new forms of democratic participation in the constitution) and procedures of constitutional reform (introducing civic participation in reform processes). There appears to be a growing trend towards 'increasing public participation in the constitutional design process',[30] which may include public ratifications through referendums as well as referendums on constitutional matters, participation in the formulation of constitutional rules (in particular through deliberative processes), and the election of citizens in constituent fora.

Sovereignty and post-sovereignty

Domestic constitutionalism is increasingly affected by the development of transnational forms of constitution-like structures.[31] This phenomenon of 'constitutional pluralism' not only relativizes in important ways the status of national constitutions,[32] but it equally leads to forms of reaction and adaptation by nation-states, including in terms of constitutional revision or reform.

In the specific context of the EU, constitutional reform is frequently related to the integration process itself. This was perhaps most visible in the run-up to enlargement in the early 2000s, when various accession states engaged in constitutional reform in order to adapt to EU membership.[33] In this context, some have suggested the idea that a transnational constitutional template is being imposed on national states,[34] while others have questioned this.[35] Be that as it may, forms of adaptation to supranational law are clearly of wider significance, as recently attested by the constitutionalization of the so-called 'golden rule' in the context of EU austerity policy. The Court of Justice of the European Union evidently plays a crucial role, in that it engages in reviewing domestic law in the context of EU law. In a similar manner, the European Court of Human Rights (ECtHR) is equally a significant international player with regard to reviewing state constitutions on the basis of the European Convention on Human Rights (ECHR).[36]

Beyond international and transnational legal regimes, and national interaction with and adaptation to these regimes, the increased prominence of international advisory bodies should be acknowledged.[37] In the European context, one of the most prominent bodies is the so-called Venice Commission or European Commission for Democracy through Law, originally established to assist the post-communist countries in the early 1990s.[38] The Venice Commission particularly operates through its Opinions on constitutional reform, drafted by its experts, and requested by member states, but also by the Council of Europe itself or other international organizations. Conspicuous cases of such Opinions have in recent years included Hungary, Iceland, Poland, and Romania.

What is striking, though, in the European context, is that the idea of a national sovereign order within which constitutionalism operates has not disappeared, but that rather a dual interpretation or coexistence of a European constitutional order and national constitutional orders has emerged, expressed in the term divided or pooled sovereignty,[39] in terms of a 'self-limitation of nation state sovereignty'.[40] This also means that both a form of constitutional collaboration between the supranational and national constitutional orders has emerged (e.g., in the form of a judicial dialogue), but equally that the European constitutional context is characterized by enduring tensions, not least over definitions of sovereignty and democracy. The latter takes the form of judicial interpretations and legitimations, as most prominently in the famous series of *Solange* judgments of the German Constitutional Court, but it now increasingly also involves explicit political 'disobedience' and defiance on the part of some the EU member states (in particular, Hungary and Poland), and even an (attempted) breakaway, as in the case of Brexit. In the latter case, resistance is not only directed against the European Union and the primacy of EU law, but also against the ECtHR and the ECHR. The latter institution and convention are equally contested in other European states.[41]

Finally, a significant but as yet understudied phenomenon is that of international diffusion and emulation of constitutional reform. In particular, the cases of Iceland and Ireland seem to have had a wider European impact, and have become part of domestic discussions on constitutional reform.[42] In this respect, a prominent example is equally, even if in a very different manner, the case of Hungary and its new Fundamental Law. The latter seems to have particularly influenced recent, and highly problematic, constitutional politics in Poland, while other countries might follow suit.

2. Constitutional acceleration

Constitutional acceleration has been defined as the 'intensification of the recourse to revision to update the constitution'.[43] Modern constitutionalism has always been characterized by the tension between its (various degrees of) rigidity and promise of endurance, if not eternity, on one hand, and the need for change and reform, not least informed by understandings of self-rule,[44] on the other.

Constitutional acceleration can – at least in part – be understood as a reaction to a wider, societal form of acceleration or 'high-speed society'.[45] In other words, in particular in relation to dynamics of globalization, modern societies are increasingly subject to phenomena of change, leading to increased perceptions of uncertainty and exposure to risk. Prandini has defined social acceleration as an 'increase in the decay rates of the reliability of experiences and expectations, and by the contraction of time spans definable as the present'.[46] Social acceleration can be understood as consisting of technological acceleration and innovation, social change or transformation, as well as a heightened tempo of everyday life.[47] This multifaceted acceleration is significant from a modern constitutional point of view, in that constitutional law should be understood as not merely a meta-framework or superstructure of, but equally as deeply imbued in, social relations. Various forms of acceleration in society are bound to have major effects on the constitutional framework of society.

Modern constitutions involve attempts to freeze time, or to institutionalize and stabilize important characteristics of present society into the future.[48] High-speed society would lead, in this perspective, to an increased distance between (rapidly changing) society and institutionalized constitutional norms. In other words, modern constitutions are increasingly exposed to 'constitutional obsolescence'.[49] The idea of a sacred and unalterable constitution, grounded in the modern imaginary of order and stability or mastery,[50] is increasingly out of touch with rapidly changing societal circumstances, not least with regard to international and transnational phenomena.

The gap between the instituted and the to-be-instituted that potentially results from relatively rigid constitutional frameworks that lag behind rapidly changing societal circumstances may be identified as *constitutional anomie*.[51] Constitutional anomie emerges because of the discrepancy between the formal-institutional dimension of constitutional orders and wider societal relations, forms of interaction, and related norms. Emile Durkheim's understanding of anomie is relevant here in that it – in one of its meanings – relates to the absence of regulation regarding (novel) social phenomena. In a Durkheimian view, anomie emerges in a situation of an absence of regulation of social relationships, resulting in declining social solidarity.[52] Anomie is about a disjunction between the legal and the social.[53] As Besnard argues, 'Anomie, in this work [Durkheim's *The Division of Labour in Society*, Paul Blokker's insertion], is conceived as the absence or the defect of a social regulation capable of insuring cooperation between specialized functions'.[54]

The idea that societal acceleration informs constitutional acceleration is useful, not least in the attempt to understand ongoing transformations of constitutionalism in the European context. As argued by William Scheuerman,[55] in a kind of Schmittian manner, social and economic acceleration tends to inform the strengthening of executive power in matters of constitutional amendment, not least in order to bypass slow parliamentary, deliberative processes (the recent Italian attempt at reform is a case in point). Executives are deemed more rapid in their response to accelerated social and economic life, but a predominance of executive, constituent power brings with it various thorny problems. Popularly endorsed, executive constitutional action is likely to forego issues of wider consensus and political pluralism, and, as a *uni-vocal* institution, tends to reduce constituent power to a partisan instrument.[56]

A relation of constitutional acceleration to societal acceleration also brings to the fore the issue of crisis. In many cases discussed in the book, crisis (of an economic, political, or even moral kind) is indeed a prominent factor in pushing for constitutional reform, and a crisis rhetoric often calls for 'rapid-fire *agere*' to the detriment of 'slow-going *deliberare*'.[57] In general, crisis-informed constitutional change seems to contribute to a less clear distinction between constitutional and normal politics, and a growing impatience with formal amendment procedures. As observed by Palermo, constitutional acceleration relates to a 'common tendency of intolerance with regard to formal revision and with regard to its intrinsic limits, accompanied by the necessity to experiment additional solutions'.[58]

In this, the impatience mentioned above takes a more upfront manifestation in a tendency towards what could be called 'populist constitutionalism', that is, an engagement in constitutional reform and constitution-making by political forces that articulate clear forms of legal skepticism and instrumentalism, and tend to have a predilection for majoritarian or even single-leader driven forms of engagement with constitutions (the most dramatic examples are that of Hungary and Poland).

3. Modes of constitution-making and constitutional reform

It is not unfair to argue that even if there is persistent and growing attention to constitution-making and constitutional reform in scholarly debates, there is an absence of comprehensive, comparative assessments of modes of constitutional amendment and reform, and the types of actors involved (including international actors).[59] This seems particularly true with regard to recent innovations and participatory forms. In particular the latter processes are often set up outside or in parallel to existing formal amendment rules (such as in the cases of Iceland and Ireland), and in some cases consist of complex, multi-stage processes. Constitutional reform processes involve different 'modes of representation', based on either elite appointment, direct election, or indirect selection of constitutional reform bodies.[60] Modes of representation can be related to different understandings of democracy (see below) and tend to increasingly also involve direct citizen participation. In a rudimentary sense, processes of reform can be understood as either open or closed, that is, open (and pluralistic) when citizens and/or other actors have the right, and are allowed, to participate, and closed when the reform is taking place 'behind-closed-doors'.[61] A further consideration can be made regarding modes of legitimacy, including 'elite adoption', when it is politicians ratifying a reform, 'institutional ratification', when institutions such as Parliament or the Constitutional Court are involved, and popular ratification, when a reform is finalized with a constitutional referendum.[62]

What is central is evidently the role of constitutional amendment rules, which stipulate who can initiate amendment, what procedures are to be followed, which parts of the constitution are immune to change, and how an amendment is to be adopted and ratified.[63] Richard Albert distinguishes between foundations, frameworks, and specifications. The foundational dimension of formal amendment concerns a distinction between amendment and revision, the former indicating a change in the constitution within the existing framework, the latter indicating a more fundamental change, which might touch upon the constitutional framework.[64] Such a distinction may be made clearly (such as in the case of the Austrian Constitution), or may not be (such as in the case of the Italian rule, art. 138 or art. 9 in the Czech Constitution). Often, in addition, an essential or non-changeable part of the constitution is indicated (for instance, the republican form). Frameworks pertain to the procedures of change, and whether these are single-track or multi-track, and the scope of amendment (comprehensive, restricted, exceptional). Multi-track involves (potentially) different procedures, for instance, majority votes in two houses of parliament, and the possibility (e.g., in case of the lack of a supermajority) of a final confirmatory popular referendum. Finally, specifications relate to operational restrictions on amendment in the form of, for instance, voting thresholds and quora, restrictions on subject matter, and deliberation requirements.[65]

Formal constitutional reform is predominantly initiated by specific *political actors*, that is, the parliament, the president, and in some cases even by a number of citizens (e.g., Romania). This seems to put the role of the *judiciary* in the background, but it should not be overlooked that also in formal change the judiciary often plays a prominent role. In some traditions, this is much more self-evident, as in common law systems, but increasingly also in civil law systems, the judiciary is upfront, not least by means, as is the case in some countries (again, Romania is an example), of constitutional review of constitutional amendments themselves.[66] In particular in the European context, the role of the judiciary is increasingly important not least because of the growing standing of inter- and transnational legal regimes, with a (quasi-)constitutional status, such as EU law or the ECHR. Regarding the role of *citizens* in constitutional reform, in political science and comparative constitutionalism literature, only very recently a sustained interest in modes and practices of constitutional reform and civic engagement in reform has emerged.[67] As comparative research and case studies, however, show, different modes of constitutional revision and of inclusion of the citizenry are available and have been used in different reforms. For comparative purposes, it is useful to start from a diversification proposed by James Fishkin. Fishkin is one of the few scholars who has attempted to look at constitutional reform from a perspective of different democratic models. Fishkin's models provide analytical hold over formal constitutional reform, while equally shedding light on the place and form of citizen engagement in reform processes. Fishkin elaborates four relevant models: competitive democracy, elite deliberation, deliberative democracy, and participatory democracy[68] (see Table 0.1).

Fishkin's first two models, that of competitive democracy and of elite deliberation, put an emphasis on representation and elite-driven constitutional processes, in this allowing for an indirect role of citizens in constitutional reform. *Competitive democracy* emphasizes the role of elected representatives and the

Table 0.1 Citizen involvement in constitution-making

Form of citizen involvement	*Democratic models*	
Indirect representation	**Elite deliberation**	**Competitive democracy**
	Governmental committees Conventions (delegates) Expert committees	Constituent assemblies
	Parliamentary committees	
Direct participation	**Participatory democracy**	**Deliberative democracy**
	Confirmatory referenda Constitutional initiatives	Citizen assemblies Citizen conventions

Source: Fishkin, *When the People Speak* (n. 67); Fishkin, 'Deliberative Democracy' (n. 67); Renwick (n. 41); own elaboration.

competitive struggle between parties. In this model, citizen participation is valued little and in general politics is about competition over votes, rather than deliberation or participation.[69] Constitutional reform from the perspective of competitive democracy may take the form of the constituent assembly, with elected members from a range of political forces, as in the case of the Italian Constituent Assembly of 1946–1948. Ordinary citizens are represented by political elites, and have no direct say in the constitutional deliberative process, as citizens are seen as unable to deal with the complex issues of constitutional reform.[70]

Elite deliberation prioritizes public reason of a high cognitive standard and favours small elite bodies that deliberate on matters of justice and the common good on behalf of the people. In constitutional reform, the deliberative elite is in charge of the 'refinement' or 'filtering' of public views, so that it is able to unearth 'what the public *would* think if it were able to consider the issue in the way the representatives can in a deliberative body'.[71] In constitutional reform, small elite bodies are bestowed with a mandate (or claim to have one) to deliberate on a new constitution or far-going constitutional changes. A clear-cut example is the Philadelphia Convention of 1787, the members of which were appointed by state legislatures.[72] Further examples of elite-driven reform are expert commissions and negotiations between political leaders.[73] A hybrid example of constitutional reform following both the ideals of competitive democracy and elite deliberation is that of parliamentary committees. Special-purpose committees, consisting of representatives from different political parties, and with *distinctive expertise*, deliberate on constitutional reforms and produce reform bills for the parliament to vote on *in plenum*.

Fishkin's participatory and deliberative models include innovative and experimental forms of constitution-making that foresee a more direct involvement of citizens in constitutional revisions.[74] Participatory democracy is frequently understood in terms of the referendum instrument, which aggregates individual votes into a majority. In case of constitutional revision, referenda often take the form of *ex post*, confirmatory referenda on a finalized proposition for constitutional reform.

Stephen Tierney has pointed to three main problems or dangers with the referendum instrument, in particular in the context of constitutional reform:[75] the elite control syndrome (the danger of elite manipulation of referenda), the deliberation deficit (the 'mere aggregation of individual wills'), and the majoritarian danger (the marginalization of dissenting individuals and minorities). A general danger is that political leaders turn directly to the voters for approval, claiming in this a more sincere form of democracy, but without providing effective voice to citizens.[76] Participatory democracy can, however, equally be designed in more engaging ways, not least in the form of legislative (constitutional) initiatives, which allow citizens to mobilize in favour of a self-designed constitutional amendment.

Much of the experimentation in recent constitutional reform regards deliberative democracy[77] and frequently takes the form of citizens' assemblies. Such assemblies form deliberative fora, which may include citizens alongside political representatives (as in the case of the Irish Constitutional Convention, 2012–2013, where citizens were randomly selected), citizens and experts or scholars (as in the Romanian Forum Constitutional in 2013), or may even consist exclusively of citizens (as in the case of Iceland in 2011). Citizens' assemblies ordinarily have a consultative function. In both participatory and deliberative democracy, active and direct citizen engagement in constitutional politics is prioritized.

If we turn to some of the more significant examples of citizen involvement in constitutional reform, we find combinations of the models discussed in action. In the case of the constitutional reform attempt in Iceland (2010–2012), both civil society associations and the Socialist Party pushed for comprehensive, citizen-driven constitutional reform. Two one-day deliberative fora were set up, in which circa 1,000 citizens participated, while a Constitutional Council, consisting of 25 independent citizens elected at the end of 2010, was responsible for producing a draft constitutional revision in four months (April–July 2011). The draft produced, consisting of a fully new constitution, emphasized, amongst others, a range of important participatory institutions, while the drafting itself has often been hailed as highly innovative in its usage of social media in soliciting comments and suggestions from citizens. In the fall of 2012, a referendum with six questions was put to the population.[78] In the case of Ireland, on one hand, two major political parties – Fine Gael and the Labour Party – endorsed inclusive constitutional reform, and on the other, academics as well as civil associations pushed for participatory and deliberative reform, in particular through the organization We the Citizens. At the end of 2011, a one-year Constitutional Convention was started in which 66 citizens (selected by lot) deliberated together with 33 politicians over constitutional reforms. One of the results of this process was the (successful) May 2015 referendum on same sex marriage. In Romania, a Forum Constituţional was set up (March–July 2013), a collaboration between the civic organization Asociaţia Pro Democraţia (APD) and the Romanian Parliament (a similar endeavour took place in 2002). The forum consisted of deliberative events, including citizens, scholars, and politicians, organized in major Romanian cities as well as the gathering of citizens' comments on an online platform.[79]

4. Constitutional 'mindsets'

Constitutional change is often discussed in terms of norms, procedures, circumstances, and outcomes, but it has to be emphasized that legal change is the result of a variety of social agents engaging in legal, political, and social action. In the words of Hauke Brunkhorst, 'modern law does not follow a developmental *telos* of ever more rational, inclusive, and liberal formation, but faces social conflicts *and* struggles between social groups and classes, which are always struggles over material and ideological interests'.[80] Constitutional change hence involves the 'mindsets' of actors that endorse or resist change. By doing so, these 'constitutional subjects' (most prominently politicians, judges, and scholars) continuously shape and reshape the meanings of constitutional concepts and principles. Empirical constitutional reality, in this view, is characterized by an 'ongoing political struggle over who defines concepts and how'.[81] Such mindsets can be related to different tendencies in constitutional change, understood as an instrument to deal with societal acceleration. One of the tendencies discussed in this volume, participatory constitutionalism, relates to a constitutional mindset that stresses democratic self-legislation. In specific ways, it could also be argued that populist constitutionalism appeals to the rule of a democratic people. But other tendencies, not least on an emphasis on legal constitutionalism and court-driven change, draws on a different mindset, particularly endorsed by experts and professionals, and promotes incremental change and order.[82]

Hauke Brunkhorst, following Martti Koskenniemi, has helpfully engaged in the delineation of two principal 'constitutional mindsets' that inform constitutional subjects: the Kantian and the managerial mindsets. Whereas the Kantian mindset invokes autonomy, egalitarian self-determination, representative government, and universal rights, the managerial mindset endorses the rule of law, judicial review, possessive individualism, and competition.[83] The Kantian constitutional mindset is 'not just the rule of law – but the *emancipation from any law that is not the law to which we have given our agreement*'.[84] Whereas the Kantian mindset can be related to revolutionary change and the *pouvoir constituant*, the managerial mindset pursues negotiation, diplomacy, and compromise. The managerial constitutional mindset is 'designed to *preserve* the evolutionary advances of the structural coupling of law and other functional systems'.[85] In this, the Kantian mindset speaks of universal language, while the managerial mindset is the language of technocrats, and political and economic elites.[86]

The two constitutional mindsets are informed by a dual imperative dimension that is at the basis of modern constitutionalism. On one hand, modern constitutionalism is strongly informed by the idea of the division, order, and constraining of power. In this respect, constitutionalism is marked by the idea of order and stability, and it reflects a largely negative idea of constitutional law as a medium that constrains rulers and prevents the abuse of political power. On the other hand, modern constitutionalism is equally strongly oriented towards the idea of popular sovereignty, and it expresses the view that 'governmental power ultimately is generated from the "consent of the people"'.[87] Martin Loughlin has reformulated this dual imperative as a 'modern constitutional imagination', which understands the modern constitution as 'a document drafted in the name of the people to establish and regulate the powers of the main institutions of government, to specify the relationship between government and citizen, and to take effect as fundamental law'.[88]

The dual mindsets provide the observer with an important frame to explore and analyze more specific instances of constitutional change and reform, exposing an inherent tension in order-based and technocratic discourses, on the one hand, and democracy and emancipatory discourses, on the other. But the distinction also reveals the ultimate connection between the two discourses and ideas; that is, without the managerial approach to constitutionalism, the realization of the democratic, Kantian project would not be possible.[89]

5. Overview of the volume

The chapters in the volume all address, even if in very different ways, (some of) the above-mentioned issues, tendencies, complexities, and conflicts regarding constitutional reform, change, and transformation in contemporary times. The first part opens the volume with a number of theoretical and empirical reflections on constitutional reform and change, and significant tendencies affecting constitutionalism, in the contemporary context.

Francesco Palermo's chapter provides an in-depth discussion of the phenomenon of participatory forms of constitutional revision from the perspective of pluralism. Throughout Europe (and beyond), there is an increasing interest in forms of constitution-making which prominently involve citizens in a variety of ways, and beyond the limited involvement that characterizes the ex-post referendum, present in many European constitutional systems (e.g., Ireland, Italy, Romania). In Palermo's account, the widespread attention for civic participation should be understood against the backcloth of representative democracy, which is increasingly facing problems of legitimation and representation, growing claims for voice on the part of (groups of) citizens and other societal actors, as well as an increasing complexity of decision-making. In his contribution to the theorization of participatory processes in constitution-making (so far not available), Palermo discusses a number of recent, paradigmatic, and intriguing cases in Europe: the EU, Germany, Austria, Ukraine, Ireland, Iceland, and Italy.

Zoran Oklopcic's chapter explores new ground in a highly stimulating and critical discussion of peoplehood. The people, demos, ethnos, plebs, or populus is the work of imagination, and as such an imaginary (Oklopcic recalls in this the idea of Benedict Anderson). But rather than arguing that we should remain stuck with the idea of the people as some form of collective figure that provides unity, Oklopcic calls for a triple role that peoplehood plays in political and social discourse and practice, that is, as arbiter, warden, and manager. The people as an imaginary functions as a selective mechanism in political, legal, and moral choices, as a form of investment in distinctive collective projects, and as a constituent force. Oklopcic's discussion is of a constitutional or foundational nature in that he argues that the social imaginary of peoplehood is constituent, it shapes the substance as well as the outer limits of any discussion of the possibility for constitutional democracy. This imaginary takes a radical, Sieyèsian form in calls for a radically sovereign people in radical democracy or the more modest role of rebellion in the ultimate instance – against great oppression – in the Lockean view. It is the latter that leads to the binary view of radical change (revolution) or incremental change (amendment). Oklopcic argues, however, that ultimately the Sieyèsian and the Lockean view share an important dimension: the investment in the vocabulary of peoplehood. The liberal-democratic constituent imagination provides an orderly view of democratic society and invents its people as patient, as being reasonable and willing to wait for incremental change (apathetic). The radical-democratic constituent imagination invents its people as the opposite, the people as active and engaged, as always willing to challenge the instituted order. Both imaginaries, however, obscure legitimate demands for either comprehensive and responsive change in the name of significant minorities. The chapter takes a highly original turn in the final part, in which Oklopcic stages an imaginary conversation between four characters, named Chatterjee, Pettit, Lefort, and Rosanvallon.

The chapter by Andrew Arato and Gábor Attila Tóth offers a compelling analysis of the role of international actors in processes of constitution-making. Such an analysis is most relevant given the variegated roles of international actors in the making of new constitutions, but also increasingly in processes of constitutional amendment and revision. The latter is particularly evident in the interventions of the Venice Commission in countries such as Iceland, Hungary, Poland, and Romania. Arato and Tóth provide a rich discussion of different types of constitutional regime change, in particular counterposing the 'classical' revolutionary form (the United States, France) with what they see as a novel, post-sovereign form of constitution-making.[90] The analysis raises intriguing questions regarding the democratic nature of constitution-making and of constituent power, the locus of sovereignty, and different forms of constitutional legitimacy (normative, sociological). Arato and Tóth argue in favour of a multi-actor, post-sovereign type of constitution-making, inter alia, as it allows for a wider inclusion of different actors, which positively effects the legitimacy of the process and the constitutional outcome, and as it manages to operate within legality. Constitutions need to live up to procedural legitimacy (allowing different actors and groups to participate), a more structural sociological form of legitimacy (longer term support of social actors on the ground), and normative legitimacy (universalistically understood norms and rights). In particular, with regard to the last point, normative legitimacy, the role of international actors seems warranted, embedding constitutions in a wider, international web of juridical and constitutional regimes.

The second part of the volume discusses singular and highly significant case studies in 'established' democracies in Western Europe, exploring and analyzing recent processes of constitutional reform.

The chapter by Paul Blokker engages with the Italian 'season of constitutional reform', focusing in particular on the recent attempt (2013–2016) at a comprehensive reform of the second, organizational part of the Italian Constitution of 1948. The political-sociological approach focuses on constitutional conflict and analyzes various constitutional subjects involved, including civil society, as well as major shifts in constitutional discourse as well as practice (in the form of constitutional instrumentalism) that became prominent from the early 1990s onwards. The postwar narrative of constitutionalism as an anti-totalitarian and democratic compromise among the major (victorious) political forces, upheld by a form of constitutional veneration by wider society, has during the 1990s increasingly become the target of claims for comprehensive reform, often on the basis of the observation that the 1948 Constitution is in some of its parts obsolete and obstructs an efficient form of 'governabilità'. In this, Italy forms a case study of shifts in understandings of constitutionalism away from a post-war 'constitutional veneration' and towards instrumentalist, majoritarian views of the constitution, populist endorsements of popular involvement (not least by means of referenda), and a direct relation between the leader/executive and the people. But the chapter also describes a pattern of constitutional resistance from below, against what is seen as an assault on the 1948 Constitution, in the attempt at establishing a decisionist, plebiscitarian, and executive-driven democracy. Such constitutional resistance has (once again) led to a rejection of the recent attempt at comprehensive reform, the project of the Renzi government, in a referendum held in December 2016.

The chapter by Silvia Suteu deals with the case of the United Kingdom from a perspective of participatory constitution-making. The UK is a key example of constitutional acceleration in the last 25 years or so, with significant changes introduced by the Labour government in the 1990s, including the adoption of the Human Rights Act in 1998, the process of evolution, and the usage of the referendum instrument. The constitutional order of the UK has not, however, settled, and, as Suteu argues, the constitutional question remains on the agenda, in particular after the radical break introduced by the Brexit referendum. Suteu's chapter is focused on the idea of a constitutional convention in the UK, stemming from the idea that in-depth change ought to involve the citizens. Suteu outlines the main proposals for such a convention and asks thorny questions regarding the effectiveness of a participatory process related to the convention's legitimacy, its mandate, and the involvement of political institutions. Suteu concludes that the setting up of a constitutional convention in the UK should be done with caution, and drawing on comparative insights from the Icelandic and Irish cases suggests the need for paying close attention to a convention's inclusiveness, the clarity of its mandate, and inclusiveness towards political actors and institutions.

The chapter by Jane Suiter, David Farrell, and Clodagh Harris discusses the Irish experience with constitutional reform in recent years. The Irish case is one in which constitutional acceleration is particularly visible, as the pace of constitutional revision in recent years has sped up, with five amendments being approved since 2010, while demands for further constitutional change are frequent (not least in political party manifestos). The formal route to constitutional change in Ireland is via referendums.[91] Suiter et al. introduce a useful distinction regarding the substance of revisions, distinguishing between EU-Treaty related matters, institutional change, and social change/modernization issues. In the second part of the chapter, Suiter et al. pay detailed attention to the 2012–2014 Constitution

Convention, a much-discussed and unprecedented event (inspired by citizens' assemblies in British Columbia and the Netherlands) in which citizens were selected randomly to participate in various deliberative meetings regarding constitutional amendment in the timeframe of 14 months. The Irish case is clearly relevant with regard to the trend towards participatory forms of constitutional revision (see also the chapters of Palermo and Suteu), and, while not providing a clear-cut case of success, it does shed light on the potential and the future relevance of the Irish 'Convention method'.

Baldvin Thor Bergsson's chapter analyses the often-discussed but ill-understood case of constitutional revision in Iceland. Bergsson discusses the constitutional revision process in a thorough and detailed manner, paying due attention to the societal mobilization around constitutional change that emerged in the mass protests in 2008/9, the cumbersome set-up of the so-called Constitutional Council in 2011, the proceedings of the council and the production of a constitutional draft, and the holding of a referendum on the draft in October 2012. Bergsson brings to the fore the significant hurdles the citizen-based council faced in its role of constitutional revision, not least in the form of the annulment of the elections of the council by the Supreme Court due to alleged irregularities. Bergsson importantly argues that the label of 'crowd-sourced' constitution is misplaced, and emphasizes the diminishing interest of voters in constitutional change, coming through in general elections as well as in public opinion polls. The sorts of the constitutional draft of the Constitutional Council remain uncertain, even if some proposals in parliament have been made regarding specific amendments. The most recent general elections in October 2016 seemed to indicate some potential new interest in constitutional revision (not least in the form of the Pirate Party's general adhesion to the process), but no structural outcome can be observed so far.

The third, and final, part of the volume discusses distinctive, problematic case studies in 'new' democracies in East-Central Europe, analyzing constitutional reform and revision in the context of recently established democratic-constitutional regimes.

The chapter by Bogdan Iancu on constitutional reform in Romania provides an in-depth discussion of constitutional change in the post-1989 period, and is a perfect example of partisan attempts at constitutional engineering by both the political centre-right and centre-left, in particular since 2007. Iancu gives a comprehensive account of the constitution-making process in the early 1990s, arrives at the conclusion that it was a majoritarian process, without extensive involvement of the wider public nor of the political opposition, and in which inexperience and a somewhat uncritical borrowing from foreign experiences ('ludic experimentation') resulted in a rigid constitution, of which the endurance, according to Iancu, has been inversely proportional to its capacity to integrate Romanian society and perhaps even to provide legal stability. In this, the semi-presidential model is highly unstable and has frequently led to protracted conflict between the president and governmental forces. The strengthening of the Constitutional Court since 2003, in particular by increasing its independence and by providing it with the final say over constitutionality of law, has led to the rise of an additional power centre with, however, a very mixed track record. Iancu concludes importantly by arguing against what he sees as academic fads (such as both the recent 'participatory' and 'deliberative' turn and the global standard of 'new constitutionalism') and by endorsing an approach in constitutional law that is cautionary and contextually sensitive.

Kriszta Kovács' chapter on constitutional identity and its relation to constitutional amendment offers both a conceptual discussion and an analysis of the case of Hungary. In general terms, Kovács discusses the idea of constitutionalism in the context of change, and the limits of change in terms of unamendable parts (often in the form of 'eternity clauses') or provisions of constitutions, and complex, often aggravated amendment procedures, present in many but not all European countries. What is particularly intriguing is how formal amendment, which follows the existing amendment rules, appears at times to be in contrast to the basic principles of a constitution or its 'basic structure'. This is where Kovács introduces the notion of constitutional identity, which she understands as referring to the 'constitutional essence' of a constitutional order, relating to the essence of a particular political community. Such a constitutional essence is frequently to be guarded by constitutional courts by means of reviewing constitutional amendments. In Kovács' view, in the Hungarian case of post-communist democracy, constitutional identity has changed twice by means of amendment, first in 1989 and then in 2011, and in both cases important tensions with the idea of constitutionalism are present. The recent 2011 change in constitutional identity has, however, not, as it promised to, led to a resolution of problems inherent in the constitutional change of 1989 (in particular with regard to legitimacy problems) but has actually exacerbated legitimatory matters, and as a consequence compromised constitutionalism in Hungary.

In the final chapter, Gábor Halmai further discusses the highly significant case of Hungary, which has drastically moved away from its position as the democratic frontrunner amongst post-communist societies in the 1990s to an increasingly illiberal democratic regime in the 2010s. The Hungarian transition from communism to constitutional democracy has been understood as a process of post-sovereign constitution-making[92] in that several societal forces, rather than one force (the parliament as singular representative of the people) produced the new constitutional order. In Halmai's view, the adoption of the Fundamental Law in 2011 constituted a move against the practice of post-sovereign constitution-making, as the new Law had been drafted and adopted by the parliamentary majority. Halmai provides a comprehensive set of reasons for the Hungarian 'backsliding to illiberal democracy'. These reasons include a lack of historical experience with democratic rule as well as the development of a sense of national victimhood as a result of historical defeats or 'fiascos', a socialist legacy of socio-economic expectations and state paternalism, a predominance of a legalistic, judicial control of democratic politics and a concomitant lack of development of societal forces (civil society), and the design failures of the democratic system (the electoral system as well as the amendment rule). Halmai ends with a discussion of the democratic prospects for the Hungarian state. He characterizes contemporary Hungary as a hybrid regime, an illiberal democracy, which is somewhere between full-fledged democracy and dictatorship. The future of Hungarian democracy is problematic in that the illiberal assault on democratic constitutions faces little resistance from wider society, as a political and constitutional culture has not robustly developed. Furthermore, a political trend away from liberal democracy can be detected, while important institutions that endorse liberal democracy in Europe (notably the EU) do not seem to be able to forcefully impose this model amongst EU member states.

Notes

1 J. Wheatley and F. Mendez, *Patterns of Constitutional Design: The Role of Citizens and Elites in Constitution-Making* (Routledge, 2007); F. Palermo, *La manutenzione costituzionale* (CEDAM, 2007); X. Contiades (ed.), *Engineering Constitutional Change: A Comparative Perspective on Europe, Canada and the USA* (Routledge, 2012); X. Contiades and A. Fotiadou (eds.), *Participatory Constitutional Change: The People as Amenders of the Constitution* (Routledge, 2016); E. Bos and K. Pocza (eds.), *Verfassunggebung in konsolidierten Demokratien: Neubeginn oder Verfall eines politischen Systems?* (Nomos, 2014); D. Oliver and C. Fusaro (eds.), *How Constitutions Change: A Comparative Study* (Hart Publishers, 2011).
2 See T. Ginsburg and J. Melton, 'Does the Constitutional Amendment Rule Matter at All? Amendment Cultures and the Challenges of Measuring Amendment Difficulty' (2015) 13:3 *International Journal of Constitutional Law* 686–713, figure 1.
3 G. Azzariti, *Il costituzionalismo moderno può sopravvivere?* (Laterza, 2013); M. Loughlin and P. Dobner (eds.), *The Twilight of Constitutionalism?* (Oxford University Press, 2010); C. Mac Amhlaigh, C. Michelon, and N. Walker (eds.), *After Public Law* (Oxford University Press, 2013).
4 Azzariti (n. 3) vii.
5 R. Prandini, 'The Future of Societal Constitutionalism in the Age of Acceleration' (2013) 20:2 *Indiana Journal of Global Legal Studies* 731–76, 737.
6 The emphasis in the volume is largely on formal, political projects of constitutional reform, while informal change – through judiciary interpretation, legislative action, or political practice – are less of an explicit focus.
7 B. Bergsson and P. Blokker, 'The Constitutional Experiment in Iceland', in E. Bos and K. Pocza (eds.), *Verfassunggebung konsolidierten Demokratien: Neubeginn oder Verfall eines politischen Systems* (Nomos Verlag, 2014); see the chapter by Bergsson.
8 X. Contiades and A. Fotiadou, 'How Constitutions Reacted to the Financial Crisis', in X. Contiades (ed.), *Constitutions in the Global Financial Crisis: A Comparative Analysis* (Routledge, 2013) 9–62, 22.
9 Contiades and Fotiadou (n. 8).
10 For the case of Hungary, see the chapters by Kovács and Halmai in this volume.
11 For the case of Iceland, see the chapter by Bergsson in this volume.
12 For the case of Ireland, see the chapter by Suiter, Farrell, and Harris; for the case of Italy, see the chapter by Blokker in this volume.
13 A. Th. Arnason, 'A Review of the Icelandic Constitution: Popular Sovereignty or Political Confusion' (2011) *Tijdschrift voor Constitutioneel Recht* 342, 343.
14 Arnason (n. 13) 345.
15 Contiades and Fotiadou (n. 8) 23.
16 See Blokker's chapter on Italy in this volume.
17 Cf. J. Lluch, 'Introduction: The Multiple Dimensions of the Politics of Accommodation in Multinational Democracies', in *Constitutionalism and the Politics of Accommodation*

in Multinational Democracies (Palgrave Macmillan UK, 2014) 1–18; S. Tierney, *Constitutional Law and National Pluralism* (Oxford University Press, 2005).

18 S. Tierney, 'Flexible Accommodation: Another Case of British Exceptionalism?' in J. Lluch (ed.), *Constitutionalism and the Politics of Accommodation in Multinational Democracies* (Palgrave Macmillan UK, 2014) 159–79, 160.

19 Tierney (n. 17) 162.

20 See the chapters by Blokker and Palermo in this volume.

21 B. Kissane and N. Sitter, 'The Marriage of State and Nation in European Constitution' (2010) 16:1 *Nations and Nationalism*, 49–67.

22 See the chapters by Kovács and Halmai in this volume.

23 Cf. L. Orgad, *The Cultural Defense of Nations: A Liberal Theory of Majority Rights* (Oxford University Press, 2015).

24 Cf. L. Thio, 'Constitutionalism in Illiberal Polities', in M. Rosenfeld and A. Sajo (eds.), *The Oxford Handbook of Comparative Constitutional Law* (Oxford University Press, 2012) 133.

25 C. Mudde, 'Are Populists Friends or Foes of Constitutionalism?' Policy Brief, The Social and Political Foundations of Constitutions (Oxford University, 2013); C.R. Kaltwasser, 'Populism vs. Constitutionalism? Comparative Perspectives on Contemporary Western Europe, Latin America, and the United States', Policy Brief, The Social and Political Foundations of Constitutions (Oxford University, 2013).

26 J.W. Mueller, *What Is Populism?* (University of Pennsylvania Press, 2016) 68.

27 N. Urbinati, *Democracy Disfigured* (Harvard University Press, 2014) 129.

28 Urbinati (n. 27); Mueller (n. 26).

29 Cf. C. Closa and D. Kochenov, *Reinforcing Rule of Law Oversight in the European Union* (Cambridge University Press, 2016).

30 J. Blount, 'Participation in Constitutional Design' in T. Ginsburg and R. Dixon (eds.), *Comparative Constitutional Law* (Edward Elgar, 2011) 38–56, 38; cf. X. Contiades and A. Fotiadou (eds.), *Participatory Constitutional Change: The People as Amenders of the Constitution* (Routledge, 2016); T. Bustamante and B.G. Fernandes (eds.), *Democratizing Constitutional Law* (Springer, 2016); M. Reuchamps and J. Suiter, *Constitutional Deliberative Democracy in Europe* (ECPR Press, 2016).

31 G. Teubner, *Constitutional Fragments: Societal Constitutionalism and Globalization* (Oxford University Press, 2012); J. Přibáň, *Sovereignty in Post-sovereign Society: A Systems Theory of European Constitutionalism* (Routledge, 2016).

32 Cf. P. Holmes, 'The Politics of Law and the Laws of Politics: The Political Paradoxes of Transnational Constitutionalism' (2014) 21:2 *Indiana Journal of Global Legal Studies* 553–83.

33 Cf. A. Albi, *EU Enlargement and the Constitutions of Central and Eastern Europe* (Cambridge University Press, 2005); C. Karlsson and K. Galic, 'Constitutional Change in Light of European Union Membership: Trends and Trajectories in the New Member States' (2016) 32:4 *East European Politics* 446–65.

34 Cf. C. Parau, 'Explaining Judiciary Governance in Central and Eastern Europe: External Incentives, Transnational Elites and Parliament Inaction' (2013) 2 *Europe-Asia Studies*.

35 See, e.g., the chapter by Iancu in this volume.

36 Cf. M. Madsen, 'International Human Rights and the Transformation of European Society: From "Free Europe" to the Europe of Human Rights', in M. Madsen and C. Thornhill (eds.), *Law and the Formation of Modern Europe: Perspectives from the Historical Sociology of Law* (Cambridge University Press, 2014) 245–74; A. von Bogdandy and P. Sonnevend (eds.), *Constitutional Crisis in the European Constitutional Area* (Nomos, 2015).

37 See Arató and Tóth in this volume.

38 For a critical view, see M. De Visser, 'A Critical Assessment of the Role of the Venice Commission in Processes of Domestic Constitutional Reform' (2015) 63:4 *American Journal of Comparative Law* 963–1008. See further P. Craig, 'Transnational

Constitution-Making: The Contribution of the Venice Commission on Law and Democracy' (forthcoming) *UCI Journal of International, Transnational and Comparative Law*; J. Nergelius, 'The Role of the Venice Commission in Maintaining the Rule of Law', in A. von Bogdandy and P. Sonnevend (eds.), *Constitutional Crisis in the European Constitutional Area* (Nomos, 2015) 291–310.

39 Cf. J. Priban, *Sovereignty in Post-Sovereign Society: A Systems Theory of European Constitutionalism* (Routledge, 2015) 21.

40 Priban (n. 39) 22.

41 For the example of the Netherlands, see B.M. Oomen, 'A Serious Case of Strasbourg-Bashing? An Evaluation of the Debates on the Legitimacy of the European Court of Human Rights in the Netherlands' (2016) 20:3 *The International Journal of Human Rights* 407–25.

42 Cf. Alan Renwick, *After the Referendum: Options for a Constitutional Convention* (The Constitution Society, 2014).

43 Palermo (n. 1) 15.

44 Cf. Prandini (n. 5).

45 H. Rosa and W.E. Scheuerman, *High-Speed Society: Social Acceleration, Power, and Modernity* (Penn State University Press, 2009).

46 Prandini (n. 5) 733.

47 W.E. Scheuerman, 'Constitutionalism in an Age of Speed' (2002) 19 *Constitutional Commentary* 359–60, 353.

48 Prandini (n. 5).

49 Scheuerman (n. 47) 361.

50 Cf. P. Blokker, 'The Imaginary Constitution of Constitutions' (2017) 3:1 *Social Imaginaries*.

51 P. Blokker, 'Constitutionalism and Constitutional Anomie in the New Europe' (2010) Quaderno 53 (Department of Sociology and Social Research, University of Trento).

52 E. Durkheim, *The Division of Labour in Society* (The Free Press, 1997).

53 D. Augenstein and J. Hendry, 'The "Fertile Dilemma of Law": Legal Integration and Legal Cultures in the European Union' (Tilburg Institute of Comparative and Transnational Law) Working Paper 2009/06, fn. 24.

54 P. Besnard, 'The True Nature of Anomie' (1988) 6:1 *Sociological Theory* 91–95, 92.

55 Scheuerman (n. 47).

56 Cf. Scheuerman (n. 47) 383.

57 Scheuerman (n. 47) 384.

58 Palermo (n. 1) 14.

59 Cf. D.S. Lutz, 'Toward a Theory of Constitutional Amendment', in S. Levinson (ed.), *Responding to Imperfection: The Theory and Practice of Constitutional Amendment* (Princeton University Press, 1995) 237–74.

60 J. Wheatley and F. Mendez (eds.), *Patterns of Constitutional Design: The Role of Citizens and Elites in Constitution-Making* (Routledge, 2007) chapters 1 and 2.

61 Wheatley and Mendez (n. 59).

62 Wheatley and Mendez (n. 59).

63 Cf. R. Albert, 'The Structure of Constitutional Amendment Rules' (2014) 49 *Wake Forest Law Review* 913.

64 Albert (n. 63) 929.

65 Albert (n. 63) 948–49.

66 Cf. Contiades and Fotiadou (n. 8).

67 Bustamante and Fernandes (n. 30); Contiades and Fotiadou (n. 30); Reuchamps and Suiter (n. 30).

68 J. Fishkin, *When the People Speak: Deliberative Democracy and Public Opinion* (Oxford University Press, 2009). J. Fishkin, 'Deliberative Democracy and Constitutions' (2011) 28:1 *Social Philosophy and Policy* 242.

69 Fishkin, *When the People Speak* (n. 67).

70 Fishkin, *When the People Speak* (n. 68) 68.
71 Fishkin, *When the People Speak* (n. 68) 72; italics in original.
72 Fishkin, 'Deliberative Democracy' (n. 68).
73 Renwick (n. 42).
74 See also Reuchamps and Suiter (n. 30); C.F. Zurn, 'Democratic Constitutional Change: Assessing Institutional Possibilities', in T. Bustamante and B. Gonçalves Fernandes (eds.), *Democratizing Constitutional Law* (Springer International Publishing, 2016).
75 S. Tierney, *Constitutional Referendums: The Theory and Practice of Republican Deliberation* (Oxford University Press, 2012) 23–42.
76 Urbinati (n. 27) 171.
77 Renwick (n. 42) 24; Reuchamps and Suiter (n. 30); Zurn (n. 74).
78 Cf. Bergsson and Blokker (n. 7); Z. Elkins, T. Ginsburg, and J. Melton, 'A Review of Iceland's Draft Constitution' (2012), available at: https://webspace.utexas.edu/elkinszs/web/CCP%20Iceland%20Report.pdf.
79 Cf. P. Blokker, *New Democracies in Crisis?: A Comparative Constitutional Study of the Czech Republic, Hungary, Poland, Romania and Slovakia* (Routledge, 2013).
80 H. Brunkhorst, 'Constituent Power and Constitutionalization in Europe' (2016) 14:3 *International Journal of Constitutional Law* 680–96, 681.
81 A. Jakab, *European Constitutional Language* (Cambridge University Press, 2016) 2.
82 H. Brunkhorst, 'European Constitutionalization Between Capitalism and Democracy' (2016) 23:1 *Constellations* 15–26, 15.
83 H. Brunkhorst, *Critical Theory of Legal Revolutions: Evolutionary Perspectives* (Bloomsbury Publishing USA, 2014); Brunkhorst, 'Constituent Power' (n. 78) 682.
84 Brunkhorst (n. 83) 46; italics in original.
85 Brunkhorst (n. 83) 46; italics in original.
86 Brunkhorst, 'Constituent Power' (n. 80) 683.
87 M. Loughlin and N. Walker, *The Paradox of Constitutionalism: Constituent Power and Constitutional Form* (Oxford University Press, 2007) 1; Cf. Blokker (n. 50).
88 M. Loughlin, 'The Constitutional Imagination' (2015) 78:1 *The Modern Law Review* 1–25, 2.
89 Brunkhorst, 'European Constitutionalization' (n. 82) 16.
90 See also A. Arato, *Post Sovereign Constitution Making: Learning and Legitimacy* (Oxford University Press, 2016).
91 As according to article 46 of the Irish Constitution. Article 46.2 states that 'every proposal for an amendment of this constitution shall be initiated in dáil Éireann as a Bill, and shall upon having been passed or deemed to have been passed by both houses of the oireachtas, be submitted by referendum to the decision of the people in accordance with the law for the time being in force relating to the referendum'.
92 Arato (n. 90).

Part I

Reflections on constitutional change in times of acceleration

1 Towards participatory constitutionalism?

Comparative European lessons

Francesco Palermo

1. The crisis of decision-making and the challenge of participation

The advent of constitutionalism brought about substantial simplification with regard to the status of individuals by inventing citizenship as a unifying factor. Conversely, as far as decision-making is concerned, constitutionalism has unequivocally meant more complexity due to the adoption of pluralism as the very foundation of the democratic government: unlike in the pre-constitutional era, decisions were no longer taken by one but by many, according to pre-defined rules and controlled by the judiciary. Institutional pluralism was developed both horizontally—division of powers among different bodies and organs—and vertically, i.e., between different levels of government.

Democratic decision-making is the backbone of constitutionalism. Decisions are legitimate only if taken by bodies, and according to procedures, directly or indirectly accountable to the people. Such accountability has normally taken the form of direct or representative democracy, whereby the latter has progressively prevailed alongside the development of ever more sophisticated institutional arrangements.

In more recent times, two factors have begun to cast this simple scheme into question. First, the growing number of people, their better education, and the resulting growth of the will to actively participate among a majority of individuals and interest groups has made the traditional forms of representative and direct democracy ever more unsatisfactory to an ever larger number of people. Elected assemblies are perceived as less and less representative and, in fact, they were conceived of at a time when a very small number of persons were allowed to turn to the ballots and in which assemblies served as platforms to reach compromises between a small elite of aristocrats and the bourgeoisie. At the same time, direct democratic tools such as referenda and popular initiatives prove to be rudimental instruments, often in the hands of mobilized minorities, and greatly unfit to regulate increasingly complex issues, ones which often require deep specialized knowledge and that can rarely be reduced to a 'yes' or a 'no'. Disaffection with politics, the decreasing role of political parties, increasingly recurring protests, and several other symptoms of popular discontent vis-à-vis the political process are, therefore, the outcome of structural and systemic factors rather than of the lower quality of political elites. The latter phenomenon—to the extent it exists—is a consequence rather than the cause of growing heterogeneity, more independent thinking, and a greater democratic consciousness of people.

Second, contemporary constitutionalism has required institutions and procedures to become ever more complex and sophisticated. While necessary to adapt a relatively simple institutional and procedural machinery—such as that based on the separation of legislative, executive, and judicial power—to growing challenges, such complexity inevitably makes democratic control more difficult, adds layers of government and decisional instances, sometimes mixes up the realms of the various powers, and dilutes accountability.[1] Such phenomena are not necessarily negative; occasionally, convoluted decisions can in fact be more transparent and accountable.[2] In any event, such complexity is inherent to the complexity of society (one may think, for instance, of the technical norms on a number of indeed highly complicated and specialized issues), and even to the very basic democratic need to control and limit power: examples can range from the establishment and the progressive development of the judicial review of legislation to the role of supranational institutions.[3]

Such developments—occurring extremely quickly in the course of the last few decades and which seem to be speeding up more and more as time passes—raise the question as to whether traditional decision-making, based on either direct or representative democracy, is reaching its limits, and thus requires new and more sophisticated tools in order to come to legitimized decisions.

In contemporary societies, decision-making has become an extremely complicated task. This is due to a number of reasons, the most significant being the phenomenon of legal pluralism[4] and its spread in modern constitutionalism. Decisions are made by a growing number of actors vested with different legitimacies beyond the mere political/electoral one. These actors are arrayed both vertically (levels of government) and horizontally (parliaments, governments, agencies, courts, administrations, interest groups). Numerous norm suppliers coexist and shape decision-making and implementation in each subject area, and, at each level, a plethora of actors access institutions in both formal and informal ways to make their claims heard and possibly influence legal norms. Subject matters become more articulated the more society and technology evolve. Thus, jurisdictions tend to overlap as no field can be clearly separated from others, and the legal and administrative regulation of each competence matter is regulated by an entanglement of norms and procedures produced by several authorities at different levels, often in an uncoordinated manner.[5] At the same time, there seems to be no alternative to the evolution of governance towards greater complexity and pluralism, not only because societies are simply becoming more intricate, but also because democracy requires that many voices be heard and included in decision-making processes, especially in order to increase the social acceptance of norms.

Vast complexity requires efficient procedures that allow actors and levels to interact without duplication and to make decisions cooperatively without blocking one other. Thus, one of the most significant challenges faced by constitutional law and political science is how to combine pluralism with good and effective governance. Put another way: how is it possible to make decisions in a manner that is democratic, transparent, inclusive, and effective, taking into account different claims, different interests, and different legitimacies? From the outset, it looks like a titanic endeavor, but, as difficult as this might be in practice, the solution can be found in the adoption of appropriate methods of coordination among actors. Growing complexity is simply part of the natural and inevitable evolution of contemporary societies; consequently, institutions and procedures must become increasingly articulated and sophisticated.

2. Bicycles and dams: Participation and the lack of a constitutional theory

At present, democratic decision-making resembles the very first bicycles of the late 19th century: the small rear wheel is direct democracy, the big one is representative democracy, and on it sits the driver (the executive). Such a bike was a revolutionary innovation at the time it was invented, but for contemporary standards it is far too slow.

In more recent times, frustration with regard to the lack of effective participation through the representative bodies and the structural limits of direct democracy created what can be described as a 'dam effect': like a river blocked by a dam, the water tends to flow in alternative, sometimes unnatural ways.[6] Alternative flowing channels need therefore to be built, in order not to waste the water: such a dispersion of water not only dissipates it with all its negative consequences, but it also makes the dam itself useless. Contemporary democracies cannot pretend that the dam does not exist, nor can they claim that it will be destroyed by the flooding water: rather, they are faced with the challenge of developing effective additional channels for the water and possibly to make the best use of the water encapsulated by the dam.

Starting in the 1980s and accelerating in more recent years, especially at the local level, several spontaneous practices have been initiated in order to overcome some of the structural deficits of classical decision-making. The different forms of such experimental practices and instruments have been commonly classified by scholars into two main groups: participatory and deliberative democracy,[7] though some include also a third genus, associative democracy.[8] Rather than engaging in terminological and definitional issues, it seems more useful to consider deliberative and participatory exercises as a common phenomenon, aiming at complementing (rather than substituting) the classical forms of representative and direct democracy. In essence, what matters is the development of complementary forms that are trying to overcome or at least to integrate and dilute the main feature common to both representative and direct democracy: the majority principle. Participatory and deliberative democracy (which can be labelled as alternative or complementary decision-making tools) aim at enlarging the number of involved actors, at anticipating and preventing conflicts, as well as at including relevant stakeholders and collective knowledge as early as possible in the decision-making process.

The aim is to avoid, prevent, or at least prepare—to the extent possible—majority decisions and, consequently, to limit opposition to the decision eventually taken, by absorbing such opposition at the earliest possible stage, establishing a more pluralistic and participative decisional process. In fact, this is a natural evolution of the very essence of pluralism and stems directly from constitutionalism. It is an enlargement of the established decision-making techniques following the exhaustion of structural limits of traditional instruments.

While legal, political, and sociological literature has begun to pay increasing attention to such new forms of decision-making, it has not yet developed a consistent theoretical framework to classify and explain this phenomenon. The persistent lack of a sound theory makes the analysis of such practices descriptive rather than normative, at least from the point of view of a possible classification and thus for comparative investigation. This is the reason why several definitions put forward in the literature—but quite often also by the legislators themselves—consider that participatory instruments include or perhaps even coincide with tools that are typical of direct democracy, such as referenda, popular initiatives, and consultations. It would be pointless to suggest here one more definition of participatory and/or deliberative democracy based on a futile attempt to include all possible comparative experiences different from more traditional representative democracy. We propose, instead, to identify one criterion that characterizes all decision-making processes of this kind. Such criterion is the abandonment of the majority principle, or at least the inclusion of participatory practices prior to a majority decision. Relevant for this research are all decision-making processes that depart from or at least complement and anticipate the majority rule and adopt different rationales to come up with a decision. This decision can, in the end, still be made by the majority (in an elected assembly or in a referendum), but is at least initiated, prepared, and discussed by involving a variety of actors and taking different perspectives into account.

A lot more could be said on this. A thorough and comprehensive analysis would include, *inter alia*, the role of political parties, the theory of democracy, the not necessarily democratic nature of citizens' initiatives and NGOs, the different impact of such instruments in cooperative and confrontational democracies (including along ethnic lines), as well as studies on the efficiency and performance of governments and administrations, partially in order to better clarify that more participation does not necessarily mean, per se, better and more efficient democracy. To the contrary, it can make the system more cumbersome and in the end even less democratic. The theoretical point to be made here, however, is more humble. It just considers the phenomena described above and the existence of a variety of instruments that have been pragmatically, rather than systematically, developed in comparative practice and tries to consider how this can add to a contemporary understanding of constitutional pluralism. In other words, the aim is not to develop a theoretical framework for alternative/complementary and non-majority-based decision-making procedures, but simply to provide a small contribution to the development of such a theory by looking at a few paradigmatic examples in the constitutional sphere.

3. Some cases of (somewhat) participatory constitutional processes

It is often contended that participatory practices are possible only at a local level. There is of course some truth in such contention, the more obvious one being that size matters: the smaller the community involved, the easier is participatory decision-making.[9] At a closer look, however, such a statement needs to be at least partly relativized. First, the same holds true for whatever organization and deliberative processes: also representative and direct democracy are easier to be set up on a smaller scale.[10] Second, the degree of success of participatory practices is not much higher on a smaller than on a bigger scale.[11]

In fact, participatory procedures are being experimented with at a constitutional level too, and while their outcomes have not been immediately successful, they are changing some of the long-held views regarding the constitution drafting or amending processes.[12] Some recent European examples seem to support this conclusion and will be briefly examined in the following pages.[13] The national cases have been selected and examined following a 'scale of intensity' of participation, from rather political bodies with just some small expert participation (Germany, Austria) to international assistance (Ukraine) to more proper participatory forms, from a maximum of non-party-political involvement (Iceland) to mixed bodies (Ireland), ending with a failed attempt to split expert and political levels (Italy). As the constitutional level is, however, not only national, but also supranational and subnational, also the supranational case of the EU and some recent subnational experiments (based on the Italian case) are analysed to round up the analysis.

3.1. The EU and the convention method

The issue of the constitutionalization of the EU is causing a never-ending debate among lawyers. Supporters of a more formalistic view, according to which the EU is still an international organization regulated by 'normal' international treaties, tend to deny the existence of a European constitution due to the lack of the formal and substantial elements of a constitution. Supporters of a substantive view, on the other hand, maintain that the EU already has a constitution in functional terms.[14] In any event, it is undisputed that the EU has a constitutional law even without a formal constitution, and that the relationship between domestic and European law needs to be understood in constitutional terms.

For the purposes of this chapter, it suffices to point out that the EU constitution-building process is quite relevant for a number of reasons. First, constitution-building at the level of the EU is clearly separated from any sort of state and nation-building. Second, this process is being realized through a series of (legally and logically) connected acts and facts of constitutional relevance,[15] that spread out over an extremely long time, making it impossible to separate the one from the other, to such an extent that it gives rise to endless debates between those who support the idea that a European constitution has already been established and those who support the opposite view. Third, this process is being realized through a progressive stratification of constitutionally relevant acts (particularly through the case-law of the courts), which tend to functionally substitute formal moments of a constitutional 'big-bang'. Fourth, even though the treaty amending process is still deeply anchored in international (thus inter-governmental) law, significant participatory elements have recently been added to that process.[16]

In such a context, the Cologne European summit of 1999 decided for the first time to set up a special and unprecedented procedure in order to draft a very significant constitutional document for the EU: the Charter of Fundamental Rights of the European Union. Instead of following the traditional procedure of an intergovernmental conference, it was decided to establish an ad hoc European 'Convention', composed of 15 representatives of the Heads of State and Government, 30 representatives of the national parliaments, 16 representatives of the European Parliament, and 1 representative of the Commission, plus a number of observers representing the Court of Justice, the Council of Europe, and other bodies. This example was followed and further developed by the 2001 Laeken summit, when a second Convention ('Convention for the Future of Europe') was established in order to prepare a draft 'Constitution for Europe'. This body was composed of 102 members drawn from the national parliaments of member states and candidate countries, the European Parliament, the European Commission, and representatives of heads of state and government. Not only did the Convention deliberate in public, but it also adopted a participatory working method, including by establishing an open forum for debate, where proposals were posted and each European citizen could provide comments and suggestions.[17]

Both conventions produced tangible results: the first adopted the Charter of Fundamental Rights of the EU, which is now an integral part of the EU treaties,[18] and the second drafted the so-called Constitutional Treaty, which was not adopted after being rejected by referenda in France and the Netherlands in 2005. Nonetheless, its substantive provisions were included in the Treaty of Lisbon and in the resulting Treaty on the Functioning of the European Union (TFEU).

More importantly, after amendments introduced by the Lisbon treaty, art. 48 TEU now provides that the establishment of a Convention be the ordinary way to amend the EU treaties. While nothing is said as to the working methods of the Convention, the participatory practice established by the work of the second Convention would seem difficult to disregard. Thus, while still not very formalized, participatory procedures are gaining a foothold also at the constitutional level of a sizeable organization like the European Union. This is further confirmed by a number of provisions inserted in the treaties, such as art. 10.3 TUE (right to participate), art. 15 TFEU (participation and transparency), and others, although their concrete impact has so far been very limited.[19]

3.2. The national level and its nuances

National experiences with participatory bodies for the purpose of constitutional amendment show substantial differences in terms of aim, composition, timing, and working method of the respective body, as well as political 'seriousness'. Common to all processes is, however, some addition to the formally prescribed procedures for constitutional amendment and the fact that the numbers and forms of such 'additions' are spreading out throughout the European continent in recent times.[20] Based on procedural differences, such processes can be classified on a scale that ranges from merely technical, expert advice to political bodies (Austria, Germany) to international support (Ukraine) to more properly participatory bodies, which vary from a completely non-party-political organ (Iceland) to mixed institutions (Ireland) to an attempt to divorce the political and the expert component (Italy).

3.2.1. Expert advice to political bodies: Germany and Austria

At the beginning of the millennium, in both Austria and Germany special bodies have been set up with a view to amending some parts of the respective federal constitution.[21] In Germany it was just a selected group of representatives of the federal Parliament (*Bundestag*) and of the federal Council (*Bundesrat*), which was joined and supported by experts on constitutional and financial issues. The purpose was to come up with a technically valid and politically acceptable reform proposal on the division of powers between the Federation and the *Länder* as well as on the financial relations in the German federal system. The drafts were subsequently adopted as the so-called 'federalism reform I' (2006, on the division of powers) and 'federalism reform II' (2009, on financial relations). The participatory element was thus extremely limited and essentially based on technical expertise.

Austria went a little step further as it established a formal body, called convention, which worked between June 2003 and January 2005 and was tasked with formulating constitutional amendments, as well as with the 'unification' of federal constitutional law.[22] The core of the convention was the so-called founding committee, a very institutional/political body composed by the federal chancellor and vice-chancellor, the speakers of the upper and the lower chamber, the heads of the political groups in Parliament, the regional governors, and representatives of the mayors. The committee subsequently appointed 18 experts (mainly in law) and representatives of the civil society, who were nevertheless proposed by the political parties proportional to the respective strength in Parliament.[23] The convention adopted a wide-ranging report that was eventually submitted to Parliament. As the convention reflected party-political cleavages, its proposals faced the very same political obstacles in Parliament and very little of its report was adopted at the end of its mandate. However, the proposals produced were taken up by a committee of experts established by different federal governments in 2007 and in 2008, and important issues such as the establishment of the administrative courts in the *Länder* were eventually taken up and transposed in constitutional amendments that were subsequently adopted.

3.2.2. International support: The case of Ukraine

The issue of international conditionality may raise several questions as to its relation with participation. In fact, it is certainly not a form of popular participation, rather the contrary, as some conditions are imposed on a political or even technocratic level. However, the forms of international involvement in constitution drafting or amending processes are relevant to this study, as they nevertheless represent a segment of pluralism beyond the (domestic) political process.

Among the various possible examples of international conditionality, suffice here to mention a recent and relatively soft form of international support in constitution-reforming processes in Europe, the 2015 constitutional commission in Ukraine.[24] Established by presidential decree in March 2015 and headed by the (then) speaker of Parliament, the commission was composed of 55 national members, most of whom were from the dominant political parties and some from the 'civil society', especially academia. In addition, the commission was supplemented by some international 'observers', mostly from the Council of Europe but also from the OSCE, who had the right to participate in the plenary and in the working group meetings, although with no right to vote. In addition, it was agreed that the text of the wide-ranging draft constitutional amendments be submitted to the Venice Commission, the Council of Europe's advisory body on constitutional issues, for an opinion. Such opinion was given in June 2015, although on a very short notice.[25]

The subsequent political developments slowed the process of approval of the constitutional amendments. In early 2016, Ukraine plunged into a major political crisis that paralyzed both the executive and the legislative branches. The governing reform coalition that came to power in 2014 came apart, and the president of Parliament (as well as chairman of the constitutional committee), Mr. Groysman, was installed as Ukraine's new prime minister in April. Meanwhile, a contested ruling by the constitutional court interpreted broadly the procedure for constitutional amendment,[26] stating that the Parliament's ability to pass constitutional amendments (with support from at least 226 votes in the first reading and at least 300 in the second) is no longer limited to two consecutive sessions. Previously, the two readings had to be held in sequential parliamentary sessions.[27] This allowed parliament to continue its review of the package of decentralization amendments that passed a first reading in the first session of 2015 but were not approved in the second session.

3.2.3. Ireland and the conventional method

In Ireland, a constitutional convention more similar to 'established' conventional/participatory assemblies was set up in 2012 and worked from 1 December 2012 until 31 March 2014. It was composed of 100 members: one chairman, 29 MPs, 4 representatives of the Northern Irish political parties, and 66 randomly selected citizens. The selection was done by a polling company and ensured to be respectful of gender, age, and geographical distribution, and the citizens remained largely anonymous, as only their names were made public.

The convention had a specific mandate. Eight thematic issues were identified in the motion establishing the body, and the convention had thus to provide proposals for each of such questions. These regarded the following issues: 1) reducing the presidential term of office to five years; 2) reducing the voting age to 17; 3) partly reviewing the electoral system; 4) conferring the right to vote in presidential elections to citizens residing abroad; 5) the constitutional guarantee of same-sex marriage; 6) removing from the constitution the clause of 'woman in the house'; 7) increase political participation of women; 8) remove the offence of blasphemy from the constitution.

The topics had been largely discussed in politics, academia, and society for a long time and were considered to be ripe for deliberation, but before adopting decisions on controversial issues, the decision was made to submit them to public deliberation in a specialized body such as the convention.[28] The working method reflected this idea, as each of the 10 sessions held over weekends was introduced by the presentation of an expert paper (circulated before), then the debate took place between advocates and opponents of the proposal contained in the paper, and the day after the discussion was reconsidered and eventually the issue was put to a vote.[29]

Considering the wide support in politics and society for the issues, one could have expected a speedy adoption of the proposals of the convention. However, this was not the case. The government's response was delayed and when it came only 2 out of 18 recommendations of the convention were put to a referendum (notably the constitutional recognition of same-sex marriages, which was approved by a large majority in May 2015), while others have been endorsed in principle and will be put to a referendum at a later stage. While at first glance the result may seem limited, the Irish approach deliberately included time as one of the fundamental variables of the constitution-amending process, diluting and 'digesting' the changes over a longer period of time.

3.2.4. Iceland and the temptation to do without politics

The Icelandic Constitution was adopted in 1944, when the island unilaterally declared independence from Nazi-occupied Denmark. Since then, the Parliament was under the obligation to overhaul the provisional constitution, but it failed to deliver, primarily because of the perceived lack of urgency. This changed when Iceland's financial system collapsed in 2008. Following the economic crisis and its dramatic effects, Icelandic society called for a political and moral renewal, one which should include a new constitutional document.[30] In 2009 the first grassroots movements of intellectuals and civic organizations were started, calling for a national 'brainstorming session' christened the National Assembly. This gathering identified core values and a number of issues particularly interesting for Iceland, such as education, economy, environment, etc. The government, led by Ms. Sigurdadottir, in power since 2009, adopted the assembly's idea of a broad and participatory constitutional reform. In June 2010 the Act on the Constitutional Assembly was adopted. It provided not only for the election of a Constitutional Council composed of 25 members but also for a crowd-sourcing gathering on constitutional matters, a one-day civic/participatory event to be held before the elections for the Council and to be prepared by a constitutional committee composed of seven experts.[31] The constitutional gathering, from which members of political parties were excluded, took place on 6 November 2010: a total of 950 randomly selected Icelanders participated in 128 different roundtables.[32] The outcome was the identification of eight main themes for the Icelandic constitution, which became one of the bases of deliberation of the Constitutional Council, which was elected on 27 November from among 522 self-selected candidates by a proportional, single transferrable vote system. Members of parliament were excluded from candidature. The turnout was very disappointing: only 27 percent of the electorate went to the polls, which is less than half of the normal turnout in a political election. Furthermore, there were major problems with the voting and following some claims of irregularities the Supreme Court suggested annulling the elections. The Act on the Constitutional Assembly was eventually repealed and the Constitutional Council was installed by means of parliamentary appointment.[33]

The Council started its work in April 2011. It based its work on the conclusions of the national gathering as well as on the report of the constitutional committee and adopted a very transparent working method, including an active website where draft proposals were posted and citizens could provide comments and suggestions. The draft constitution was adopted by consensus by the Constitutional Council, and was then sent to the Icelandic Parliament in July 2011. It was then submitted to an evaluation by a group of international experts[34] and by the European Commission for Democracy through Law (Venice Commission), an expert body of the Council of Europe dealing with constitutional issues.[35] Both groups expressed some criticism of the draft.

As the text was then stalled in parliament, it was decided to hold a nonbinding (consultative) referendum on 20 October 2012. The referendum asked six questions, one on the reform as such[36] and five on specific proposed contents.[37] The turnout was 49 percent and all questions were answered with a clear majority in the affirmative. The political parties were split on how to follow up on the nonbinding referendum; debates were held in parliament but no final vote took place on the text adopted by the Constitutional Council. Instead, a different bill was presented that postponed the discussion until after the 2013 elections, providing further that a reform should take place before April 2017 and be adopted by at least a two-third majority in parliament and subsequently confirmed by a majority of voters in a referendum with at least 40 percent turnout. This amendment was passed by the Althingi in July 2013, right after the general elections. A constitutional committee was set up in November 2013 to deal with the follow up of the referendum, although in the view of many the real objective of the government's move was to water down or disregard the results of the 2012 referendum.[38] The committee was composed of political representatives only, and only from the parties that lost the referendum. It seems clear, now that the emergency situation following the financial crisis in 2008 has been overcome, the unique process that Iceland experimented with will be abandoned, even though the process is formally continuing and may any time be resumed, also considering the fluctuating political climate in the country and the frequent elections in recent times.

Also, the strong popular pressure for a participatory constitutional reform gradually decreased with the passing of time and the Parliament took over again.[39] Despite the vanishing enthusiasm[40]—resulting also from the speedy recovery after the economic crisis—the process does represent a unique experience of participatory constitutional reform. Whatever happens in terms of constitutional change in Iceland, from now on, it will be politically difficult not to include forms of participation and the experience will remain as a milestone in the still rather spontaneous process of developing instruments and procedures for participatory democracy, including at the constitutional level. The interest that the Icelandic experience attracted far beyond the little populated island shows that this process might have a significant comparative impact also in the future.

The small population of Iceland might raise the objection that what has been an experiment to extend participatory democracy to the national constitutional level was in fact nothing else than a confirmation of the fact that such instruments are better suited for the local level, since Iceland's population corresponds to that of a medium-small town in most larger countries. Notwithstanding, also the geographical size and the distance should be taken into account, as these are—especially in extreme geographic conditions like in Iceland—potential obstacles to effective participation. In any event, the experimentation with participatory procedures at the national constitutional level needs to be extended to bigger countries in order to prove the approach's value.

3.2.5. Italy: The widest consultation, the smallest result?

The call for constitutional reforms has been a pressing one in Italy for about three decades. The main deficits of the constitution are widely identified in the academic and in the political discourse as revolving around two aspects. The first is the decision-making process at the national level, which arises also due to the crisis of political parties. This has made it extremely difficult to form stable political majorities and thus to pursue a clear governing agenda, not least due to a very cumbersome legislative process, with two quite sizeable chambers vested with essentially the same powers including the vote of confidence for the government. The second area in need of profound reforms is that of the vertical relationship between the state, the regions, and the municipalities, a sector in which a number of overlaps, conflicts, and inefficiencies have arisen.[41] Although such relations have been deeply reformed through a number of significant constitutional amendments adopted between 1999 and 2001,[42] the problems have not been solved and the intergovernmental conflict has even increased.

It was 1983 when the first ad hoc parliamentary committee was set up and tasked to work out a constitutional reform bill. This committee was followed by several other parliamentary and governmental committees, especially during the 1990s: each of them produced valuable proposals but none was turned into a constitutional amendment.[43] Thirty years after the first efforts, in 2013, a new process for constitutional reform was started. In the beginning, the idea was to set up a constitutional convention, a mixed body composed of a certain number of members of parliament and an equal number of experts. The idea was soon abandoned due to sharp criticism of the differing legitimacy of the members of such a body, half elected and half appointed. Therefore, a special procedure was started, according to which a special committee composed of 42 members of both chambers of parliament would be appointed to work out a proposal to then be approved by qualified majority in Parliament and subsequently submitted to confirmative referendum irrespective of the majority in Parliament.[44] In parallel, an expert panel consisting of an equal number of academics (42) was set up as a consultative body to the President of the Republic, tasked with the preparation of some drafts that were to then be submitted to Parliament for its sovereign deliberation.

Parallel to this process, the government organized the widest public consultation[45] ever to take place in Europe. It set up an internet platform where a number of questions related to the constitutional reform were asked to those who desired to participate.[46] The questions were grouped in three main areas: system of government, direct democracy, and territorial setup of the country.

The outcome was quite significant: in three months[47] and despite very little (if any) attention by the media, more than 203,000 people completed the online questionnaire.[48] They confirmed that the main priorities for reform are the bicameral system and the territorial setting of the country, but while the overwhelming majority was in favour of providing only one chamber of Parliament with the vote of confidence to the government and budgetary power, most citizens opposed the idea of reducing the powers of the regions by centralizing competences, despite the fact that this was suggested by the expert group and advocated by most political parties. The final report was prepared and made public by the government.[49]

In terms of practical follow-up to this initiative, quite little happened. The government changed in February 2014 (from Mr. Letta to Mr. Renzi) and the different political climate led to a discontinuation of the envisaged reform process: the constitutional law derogating the ordinary constitution-amending procedure (by establishing a special parliamentary committee and providing for a compulsory final referendum) was abandoned and a new process was started, following a purely institutional way. The new government presented a draft reform text in late March 2014 and parliament examined it according to the traditional procedure. No further consultation was started on this text, which was eventually adopted by Parliament in May 2016 and subsequently put to referendum in December of the same year. The referendum rejected by clear majority the constitutional reform, which thus could not enter into force.

However, it is worth noting that the online platform that was originally established in order to carry out the consultation on the constitutional reform was not discontinued and became the official site for public consultations on several other legislative proposals by the government on a number of key issues, such as the reform of the public administration, fiscal policy, and others. While the particular (and first) consultation on constitutional reforms was eventually stalled, public consultation did establish itself as a method of government.

3.3. The subnational level: Selected cases from Italian regions

Since the start of the new millennium, an impressive amount of participatory experiences has spread out at all levels (including the subnational one) and in several areas (including the constitutional amending process). Some of these processes became paramount and widely studied examples, in some occasions even prototypes (such as in British Columbia, in Vorarlberg, in Catalonia, and others), although a detailed comparative analysis of such cases still does not exist and would no doubt help identify common traits and rationales of the several differences.[50]

Italy is an interesting case in point in this regard. While the second wave of autonomy statutes, following the constitutional reform in 2001, which granted considerable new powers to the regions, was completed by the 15 normal regions between 2004 and 2012, none of the five special regions[51] amended its statute.[52] Four of them, however, somehow started participatory processes in order to elaborate new autonomy statutes.[53] The approaches have been quite different from one another and while none was completed successfully in terms of adopting a new statute, all attempts have been marked by a participatory approach.

The first special region to experiment with a participatory method for elaborating a new autonomy regime, and the one that came closer to a success, was the northeastern region of Friuli Venezia Giulia, which established a constitutional convention in 2004. The regional law[54] set up a 'regional convention', tasked with the elaboration of a new special autonomy statute. The idea to create a specialized body was based on the assumption that the elected regional parliament was not in a position to effectively debate on the issue nor to guarantee wide participation in the reform process. The convention was composed of an equal number of elected representatives (of the political parties represented in the regional assembly and of the municipalities) and of members from the 'civil society', such as, *inter alia*, representatives of the universities of the region, of the social sector, of the trade unions, and of the linguistic minorities settled in the region (Friulian, Slovenian, and German speakers). The convention did work for some six months in a participatory way, including by granting access to all interested citizens, and presented a new draft autonomy statute composed of 80 articles, each of them supplemented by a few alternative formulations reflecting the various options discussed in the convention. The text was submitted to the regional assembly, which quickly adopted a new autonomy statute and which largely confirmed the proposals put forward by the convention. The text, however, was not supported in the national parliament and could therefore never be passed.

A similar path was followed in the small northwestern, alpine region of Aosta Valley, which created an analogous convention in 2006.[55] The body reflected the same rationale in its composition and also produced a text after one year of participatory work.[56] The text was submitted to the regional assembly in 2008, which however never properly debated it, due to political change that meanwhile occurred both at the regional and national level, and subsequent assemblies never resumed the convention's work.

Sardinia took a different and more radical approach. In 2012 a set of 10 referendums (5 consultative, 5 abrogative) were put to a popular vote.[57] One of the consultative referendums asked the voters whether or not they wanted the regional assembly to call for a constitutional assembly, directly elected by the citizens, tasked to drafting a new autonomy statute. While the turnout was relatively low (35.5 percent), the quorum of 33 percent was met and the votes were thus valid. In the particular case of the referendum on the election of a constitutional assembly, the overwhelming majority of those who participated in the vote (94.2 percent) supported the proposal. Five years after, however, the referendum has not been implemented, due to changes in the regional political arena, where a new political majority was formed, and the constitutional assembly has not been yet elected, nor will it probably ever be.

The latest attempt to amend the special autonomy statute was started in the most complex region, the one in which the presence of national minorities makes every balance much more complex and difficult: Trentino-South Tyrol. In April 2015 a provincial law in South Tyrol was passed[58] establishing a convention for the reform of the autonomy statute. The approach chosen was almost identical to the one implemented in the Aosta Valley, including a preparatory phase during which the whole population will be consulted through open meetings and a forum of 100 people, representing all segments of society, will be established to accompany the work of the convention. In February 2016, the second autonomous province composing the region (the province of Trento) adopted its law to set up a similar body.[59] Both bodies began their work in the second half of 2016 and produced proposals in the second half of 2017. The proposals elaborated in South Tyrol, however, have been very controversial and no consensus could be reached, including among the language groups. Furthermore, as the autonomy statute is for the whole region, an additional challenge will be how to merge the proposals into a unified text, also considering that the views on certain issues are quite different in the two provinces.

4. Concluding remarks

4.1. Poor performance?

While deeply diverging in composition and approach, all the mentioned experiences show that legislators are increasingly aware of the claim for participation emerging in pluralistic societies and that classic representative democracy mirrored in elected assemblies is no longer perceived as properly reflecting the complexity of society. A possible additional explanation has to do with the weakness of politics (and consequently of representative assemblies) in a growing number of countries, i.e., the decreasing legitimacy of elected representatives in the popular perception and growing contestation of the perceived elites. Such a phenomenon forces political elites to seek broader participation in order to make decisions more widely accepted by the citizens. Such an explanation might be supported by the fact that most of such participatory experiments take place in countries where disaffection vis-à-vis politics is growing, while it is much more limited in countries in which such feeling is less common. Be that as it may, it is a fact that the number of participatory processes, including in constitution-amending, is growing.

While increasingly popular, however, such processes have so far produced little results in terms of the number of reforms adopted. One may therefore argue that the overall performance of participatory instruments is relatively poor, at least at a first glance. Undeniably, either the influence of non-political members of such bodies is quite limited (such as in the case of Germany, Austria, Ukraine), or the texts adopted by such bodies are rarely and only partly transposed in legal norms (see the mentioned cases of Iceland, Ireland, Austria, and Italy, both at national and subnational level, as well as the peculiar case of the EU).

At a closer look, however, some elements have to be taken into account. First, it is not so much the participatory bodies themselves (that normally do produce proposals) but rather the political process that is not particularly receptive. This possibly has to do with the fact that participatory institutions normally work over a time span which usually crosses political elections. Therefore, their ability to achieve positive results might be impaired by political changes and by the creation of new political majorities in the assemblies. The relatively extended duration of these processes can also result in producing proposals when some of the initial pushing factors have been (or are perceived as having been) overcome, as the case of Iceland seems to prove: no more financial crisis, no more new constitution.

Secondly, the balance between political representatives and other members is difficult to achieve and should be tailored to each specific situation. Too much political representation replicates the dynamics of elected assemblies that participatory bodies are aimed at overcoming, but too little of such representation might disconnect such bodies from the political reality of the assemblies that are ultimately called to eventually adopt the texts. Furthermore, as the experience of the Italian special regions shows, the more numerous the actors and levels that take part in the decision-making, and the more complex the procedures, the more difficult the obstacles to be overcome by texts prepared by participatory bodies. This does not mean, however, that federal/multilevel systems are less suited than unitary countries to experiment with and further develop participatory practices. Rather, the opposite seems to be true, as the next section tries to demonstrate.

In the end, the issue of the performance of such bodies is rather nuanced and cannot be tackled in a simplistic way. At the same time, as participatory processes are still in an embryonic stage, their performance and, more generally, the effectiveness of their link with the political-representative decision-making still require substantial fine-tuning.

4.2. Federalism as a matrix?

While very different in terms of structure, composition, role, functions, context (most of the mentioned countries are not federal), and level of government, all experiences analysed in this chapter present interesting participatory features at the level of the constitutional process. Furthermore, should the conclusion be reached that in federal systems participatory democracy is less likely to be implemented at central and/or at subnational levels, this would mean that in federal countries participatory claims are less pressing and, therefore, that federalism is as such already compensating for some pluralist claims. Above all, the point here is to try to address the aforementioned deficit, i.e., the lack of a sound constitutional theory on participatory and deliberative forms of democracy, complementary to representative and direct forms based solely on the majority principle. Thus, the question is whether and to what extent federalism can help in this regard. It is contended here that it can.

Federalism is an institutional principle, i.e., it is a mode of organizing state structures in a way that preserves the plurality of levels of government and their decisional autonomy.[60] As such, it does not per se include citizens in decision-making any more than other systems, even though in a federal system a citizen is involved more often, if nothing else then at least through various levels of election. Moreover, the wider subnational and local autonomy, the more these levels of government can experiment with forms of participatory democracy. But as such, participation is certainly a different phenomenon than federalism.

Federalism is, however, the most powerful and so far the most experimented with tool for institutional pluralism. It does exactly what is at the core of this study: by multiplying it, it attenuates and complements the majority principle; deciding by majority—but at different levels—fragments and dilutes the majority principle and thus produces a counter-majoritarian effect. For this reason, it can be argued that federalism is the oldest instrument for dividing and de-concentrating power, even though others have followed, such as judicial review of legislation. Federalism is the most developed form of institutional pluralism. In their common innate connection with pluralism lies the link between federalism and participatory democracy: the latter is a contemporary manifestation of the claim for pluralism, of which federalism is perhaps the oldest. In other words, federalism can be identified as the institutional side of pluralism, similarly to what participatory democracy is on the societal or even on the individual side. Both are expressions of pluralism: institutional and societal respectively.

Federalism and its by-products (such as regionalism, devolution, and the like) developed at a time when the claims for pluralism were limited to the institutional sphere. It was not the individual nor organized 'civil society' that claimed a share in power and the right to effectively participate in decision-making, but existing institutions. Conversely, participatory forms of democracy are demanded in a time when institutional pluralism is no longer sufficient, the interests in society cannot all be channelled through institutions and the claim is therefore extended to a direct form of participation, no longer mediated by institutions—such as subnational units, for instance.

If such analogy is correct, it can be concluded that federalism—with its institutions, procedures, structured relations, and mechanisms for the prevention and resolution of conflicts—can provide inspiration for the development of a theory and (more importantly) procedural solutions for the growing demands for participatory democracy.[61] As the older brother of complementary decision-making processes,[62] the history and the machinery of federalism could be looked at in order to identify how instruments and procedures for participation could be designed and to foresee what the development of such participatory instruments might look like. Consequently, as it has always been the case for federalism, there will be times when participatory instruments will be used more or less often, depending in part also on the priorities of the country concerned, on the time available, on the reasonability of participatory claims, and on the policy fields in which participation is called for.

Furthermore, in federalism, inter-governmental relations are institutionalized and regulated by procedures and it is safe to predict that participatory instruments will also become more procedural in form: the instruments for participation will tend to be procedural, regulated in a way that looks similar to administrative procedures, where discretion is more limited as compared to legislation. Federalism makes it impossible for one level of government to arbitrarily decide to use a power, as division of powers is clearly laid down in the constitution and legislation. Similarly, the decision to participate, the limits on access to participation, the degree of influence, and so on, will increasingly be determined by rules on the participatory procedure.

Very importantly, federalism largely developed and established itself through judicial litigation and it is well known that judicial review originally was born in order to guarantee the hierarchy of norms. Similarly, it is safe to expect a growing role of judges in determining the specific content of participatory processes. Primarily it will be the administrative judges (at least in the continental systems where they exist), but the more the legislation on participation develops, the more the role of ordinary or even constitutional judges in guaranteeing the right to participate can be expected to increase.

4.3. Issues rather than levels?

As Dahrendorf once put it, there is no other future for democracy than pluralism as the constitutional means to institutionalize social conflicts.[63] Unlike non-democratic and partisan constitutions,[64] democratic constitutions are not meant to meld social divisions into an artificial unity, but to establish the formal and substantive prerequisites for political competition.[65] Participation is and will increasingly be a key element of pluralist constitutionalism. While federalism has been a key factor for developing institutional and ideological pluralism, participatory and deliberative instruments will be critical to develop additional and supplementary forms of decision-making, thus increasing the degree of pluralism and the overall legitimacy of contemporary constitutions.

Participation and other forms of deliberation are in fact key elements of pluralism, as the latter clearly requires broad inclusion of the various segments of society far beyond mere electoral or direct democratic rights. At the same time, federalism can represent a possible (perhaps the most developed) matrix for institutional participation, showing how participatory and deliberative elements can be included in and complement traditional decision-making processes.

Besides the theoretical aspects that participatory/deliberative democracy is raising and the possible link with comparative federalism, this chapter has focused on some initial, embryonic experiments in introducing participatory procedures into constitutional drafting or amending processes. The mentioned examples are very different in terms of scope, modes, and range of participatory procedures, and perhaps even with regard to the aims and the very understanding of participatory and deliberative processes. The practical outcomes have been quite limited, as participation has for the most part been marginal, the institutional actors have kept overall control, and in the end the processes did not produce significant constitutional changes. For these and other reasons, the aforementioned experiences are far from constituting the basis for a possible theory of participation and deliberation in constitutional processes. However, they show that participation is not necessarily confined to local issues nor to small-scale projects, but is fit to cover also the very foundations of societies.

It is not so much the size, but rather the issue at stake that determines the success or failure of new forms of deliberation, complementary to the traditional representative or direct democratic ones. To be effective, participation needs to be carried out with some passion, to be moving and even exciting for people, motivating them to engage. Therefore, participation is more likely to happen on issues going to the heart of the interests of people. These issues are normally either very local, or very foundational, such as constitutional questions. There is, by contrast, less likelihood of mobilizing people on either very technical or extremely dry issues, such as those typically decided by the majority of legislation that is normally adopted at national or subnational level.

A lot more (and more systematic) research is needed in this field, including by lawyers, before a sound, structural theory can challenge consolidated, but now clearly insufficient, dogmatic categories. Only more thorough research and the further development of the practice of participation, including judicial adjudication of some emerging challenges, will reveal whether the initial, tentative hypotheses sketched out in this paper are meaningful or not.

Notes

1 Thus the phenomena of 'blame shifting', i.e., the opportunity for decision-makers to avoid accountability for decisions influenced by other governments, as described by R.K. Weaver, 'The Politics of Blame Avoidance', *Journal of Public Policy* (1986) 371–98. Another frequent consequence is that of overlapping and interlocking jurisdictions, making it difficult to identify and divide political responsibility clearly, a widespread problem first identified by Fritz Scharpf (see F.W. Scharpf et al. (eds.), *Politikverflechtung* (Kronberg/Ts Scriptor Verl., 1976), 1976–1979). At the European level, see critically F.W. Scharpf, 'Die Politikverflechtungsfalle: Europäische Integration und deutscher Föderalismus im Vergleich', *Politische Vierteljahresschrift* 26:4 (1985) 323–56; and J. Zielonka, *Is the EU Doomed?* (Polity Press, 2014).

2 When more actors participate, the chance that transparency increases is greater. Each level is subject to controls because it is, to some extent, interested in keeping its constituency informed. Therefore, each level does not want other levels to take non-transparent decisions against its interests.

3 One may think of some of the legislation adopted at various levels, including the supranational one, where texts are drafted by small and closed groups of unknown and not legitimized people, often based on informal and nontransparent consultations, and leading to texts that are either difficult to interpret or extremely technical in nature. One may consider if such pre-legislative activities can be made more transparent and accountable and even whether some legislation is at all necessary. For sure, there is room for improvement in this regard.

4 *Inter alia*, N. Krisch, *Beyond Constitutionalism: The Pluralist Structure of Postnational Law* (Oxford University Press, 2012); R. Michaels, 'Global Legal Pluralism', *Annual Review of Law & Social Science* 5 (2009) 243–62; B.Z. Tamanaha, 'Understanding Legal Pluralism: Past to Present, Local to Global', *Sydney Law Review* 30 (2008) 375–411; and J. Griffith, 'What is Legal Pluralism?', *Journal of Legal Pluralism* 24 (1986) 1–55 (also available at www.jus.uio.no/smr/english/research/areas/diversity/Docs/griffiths_what-is-legal-pluralism-1986.pdf).

5 This might also involve the relationship between public and private spheres, thus going beyond the public law sphere to imply the possibility and even the opportunity to create functional jurisdictions populated by private actors competing with or substituting for the public service providers. See B.S. Frey, 'Functional, Overlapping, Competing Jurisdictions: Redrawing the Geographic Borders of Administration', *European Journal of Law Reform*, V 3/4 (1997) 543–55.

6 Other effects are produced that do not take the form of deliberative or participative procedures, such as, in particular, technocratic-bureaucratic decision-making. Such a tendency towards technocratic governments, for example, has been quite evident in several Southern European countries during times of financial crisis.

7 In a nutshell, *participatory* democracy is linked especially to several experiments seen in South America, is more practice oriented, and often originates from protest movements. A typical example of such an approach is participatory budgeting. *Deliberative* democracy, by contrast, has its roots in Europe and North America, and takes forms such as citizens' assemblies and other bodies complementing rather than substituting for elected assemblies or referenda. See the seminal work by J. Steiner, *The Foundations of Deliberative Democracy: Empirical Research and Normative Implications* (Cambridge Univ. Press, 2012).

8 Whereby power is decentralized and partly transferred to voluntary civic associations such as citizens' initiatives, NGOs, interest groups, etc. See the seminal work by P. Hirst, *Associative Democracy* (Cambridge Univ. Press, 1995); and more recently P. Hirst and V. Bader, *Associative Democracy: The Real Third Way* (Frank Cass, 2005).

9 U. Allegretti, 'Participatory Democracy in Multi-Level States', in C. Fraenkel-Haeberle et al. (eds.), *Citizen Participation in Multi-Level Democracies* (Brill Nijhoff, 2015) 211.

10 N. Steytler, 'Comparative Conclusions', in N. Steytler (ed.), *Local Government and Metropolitan Regions in Federal Systems*, Vol. VI, A Global Dialogue on Federalism (McGill-Queen's University Press, 2009) 417.

11 As can be inferred from B. Peters, 'Die Leistungsfähigkeit heutiger Öffentlichkeit: Einige theoretische Kontroversen', in H. Weßler (ed.), *Bernhard Peters – Der Sinn von Öffentlichkeit* (Suhrkamp, 2007) 187ff.

12 See A. Arato, 'Conventions, Constituent Assemblies, and Round Tables: Models, Principles and Elements of Democratic Constitution-Making', in *Global Constitutionalism* (2012) 1.01, 173ff.

13 For a survey and analysis of non-European experiences of participatory constitution-making, focusing especially on Africa, see A. Saati, *The Participation Myth: Outcomes of Participatory Constitution Building Processes on Democracy*, Umea Univ., Research Report (2015) 1, available at http://umu.diva-portal.org/.

14 The two approaches are reflected by, on the one hand, the German judicial saga from the 'Maastricht' (BVerfGE 89, 155 (1993)) to the 'Lisbon' (BVerfGE 123, 267 (2009)) rulings, when the court repeatedly pointed out that without a State there

cannot be a constitution, and without a people there cannot be a State. On the other hand, the Court of Justice of the European Union not only affirmed the principle of supremacy of EU law, but since 1986 defined the (then) European Community as 'a community based on the rule of law, inasmuch as neither its member States nor its institutions can avoid a review of the question whether the measures adopted by them are in conformity with the *basic constitutional charter, the Treaty*' (ECJ, 23-4-1986, case 294/83, *Parti ecologiste 'Les Verts'*, ECR, 1339 at 23, emphasis added).

15 In addition to the founding treaties, in the last two decades there has been an overflow of constitutional documents, adopted at ever closer intervals: from the Single European Act (1986) to the treaties of Maastricht (1992), Amsterdam (1997), and Nice (2000), the Charter of Fundamental Rights of the EU (2000), the Treaty establishing a Constitution for Europe (2004), and the Lisbon treaty (2009). These constitutional developments have been followed by significant constitutional amendments in almost all Member States. Also, the 2016 'Brexit' referendum partly fits into this constitutional path for its undeniable constitutional impact.

16 B. de Witte, 'The Closest Thing to a Constitutional Conversation in Europe: The Semi-Permanent Treaty Revision Process', in P. Beaumont, C. Lyons, and N. Walker (eds.), *Convergence and Divergence in European Public Law* (Hart, 2002) 137–60.

17 Statistics on the work of the Convention and on the number of active engagements by citizens are available at: http://european-convention.europa.eu/EN/bienvenue/bienvenue2352.html?lang=EN. After the closure of the Convention's page the platform was transformed into a new interactive site where citizens, associations, and organizations can follow and participate in the debate on the future of Europe: http://ec.europa.eu/archives/institutional_reform/.

18 Article 6 Treaty Establishing the European Union (TEU).

19 More on the reasons, A. Lollini and F. Palermo, 'Comparative Law and the 'Proceduralization' of Constitution-Building Processes', in J. Raue and P. Sutter (eds.), *Facets and Practices of State-Building* (Martinus Nijhoff, 2009) 301–26.

20 Which makes a certain selection necessary. An additional interesting case in point is the experience of Romania, which set up twice (in 2002 and in 2013) a 'constitutional forum', which organized public debates in various cities throughout the country and offered the opportunity to submit proposals for constitutional revision on the forum's website. The final outcome consisted of a report presented to the parliamentary commission, which produced a constitutional revision draft in late 2013 and submitted it to the Constitutional Court (which according to art. 146a Const. must review amendment proposals) and to the Venice Commission in February 2014. Both bodies expressed several doubts on the proposal. See further P. Blokker, 'Constitutional Reform in Europe and Recourse to the People', in X. Contiades and A. Fotiadou (eds.), *Participatory Constitutional Change: The People as Amenders of the Constitution* (Routledge, 2016). The author classifies the Romanian case as 'populist-majoritarian constitution-making', i.e., in his words, 'a problematic variant of political constitutionalism'.

21 G. Avolio and C. Zwilling, 'Percorsi alternativi di revisione costituzionale in Germania ed Austria. Il rischio dell'empasse tra bilancio e progetto', in *Diritto Pubblico Comparato ed Europeo*, 2006-I, 3–19.

22 Constitutional provisions in Austria are scattered throughout the legislation. Besides the federal constitution (B-VG, 1920) and specific constitutional laws (such as the financial constitutional law F-VG, 1948, and the law on the fundamental rights, 1867), there are several hundreds of provisions with constitutional rank within ordinary legislation, i.e., individual provisions adopted with constitutional majority that are therefore more entrenched than the rest of the legislation they are contained in. Nearly every government includes unification and systematization of such provisions and the establishment of a unified body of federal constitutional law in its political platform, but this has not been achieved so far.

23 See Beschluss des Gründungskomitees vom 2. Mai 2003, at www.konvent.gv.at.
24 On the process and on the role of the international community see A. Arato, 'International Role in State-Making in Ukraine: The Promise of a Two-Stage Constituent Process', 16 *German Law Journal* (2015), available at www.germanlawjournal.com/index.php?pageID=11&artID=1692.
25 Venice Commission preliminary opinion on proposed decentralization in Ukraine, CDL-PN(2015)006.
26 Справа № 1-21/2016.
27 More specifically, the Court (addressed by Parliament) ruled that amendments to the constitution related to the judicial system (the first part of the constitutional reform package) meet the requirements of Articles 157 and 158 of the Constitution. Such articles establish that the Constitution cannot be changed, if amendments abolish or restrict rights and freedoms, or if they are aimed at eliminating the independence or violating the territorial integrity of Ukraine; the Constitution cannot be amended in wartime or in state of emergency; a draft law to amend the Constitution may be submitted to Parliament no sooner than one year after the date when a decision regarding the draft law has been issued, and the Parliament cannot amend twice the same provisions of the Constitution of Ukraine during the same term.
28 S. Suteu, 'Constitutional Conventions in the Digital Era: Lessons from Iceland and Ireland', in 38 *B.C. Int'l & Comp. L. Rev.* (2015), http://lawdigitalcommons.bc.edu/iclr/vol38/iss2/4.
29 See www.constitution.ie.
30 For a detailed illustration of the whole process and additional literature see B.T. Bergsson and P. Blokker, 'The Constitutional Experiment in Iceland', in K. Pocza (ed.), *Verfassunggebung in konsolidierten Demokratien: Neubeginn oder Verfall eines Systems?* (Nomos Verlag, 2014), also available at http://papers.ssrn.com/sol3/papers.cfm?abstract_id=2320748.
31 See the TED video presentation by Gudrun Petrusdottir, chairperson of the constitutional committee, at www.youtube.com/watch?v=AiO9oNbpN14&feature=relmfu.
32 http://agora.is.
33 A.T. Árnason, *A Review of the Icelandic Constitution—Popular Sovereignty or Political Confusion*, Tijdschrift voor Constitutioneel Recht, 2:3 (2001) 342–51.
34 www.venice.coe.int/webforms/documents/default.aspx?pdffile=CDL-REF(2013)010-e.
35 Opinion no. 702/2013, CDL-AD(2013)010, at www.venice.coe.int/webforms/documents/?pdf=CDL-AD(2013)010-e.
36 Do you want the Constitutional Council's proposal to be adopted as the basis of a new draft constitution?
37 1. In the new constitution, do you want natural resources that are not privately owned to be declared national property? 2. Do you want to insert in the constitution provisions on an established (national) Church of Iceland? 3. Do you want a provision authorizing the election of particular individuals to the Althing? 4. Do you wish a provision giving equal weight to votes cast in all parts of the country? 5. Do you wish a provision stating that a certain proportion of the electorate is able to demand that issues be put to a referendum?
38 T. Gylfason, *Chain of Legitimacy: Constitution Making in Iceland*, CESifo Working Papers No. 6018, July 2016.
39 T. Gylfason, *Iceland's Citizen Constitution: The Window Remains Wide Open* (6 Apr 2016) verfassungsblog.de/icelands-citizen-constitution-the-window-remains-wide-open/.
40 For example, the very active and interesting web portal agora.is is no longer maintained or updated.

41 See F. Palermo, 'Italy: A Federal Country without Federalism?', in M. Burgess and G.A. Tarr (eds.), *Constitutional Dynamics in Federal Systems. Sub-national Perspectives* (Montreal & Kingston, 2012) 237–54.
42 Const. laws no. 1/1999, 2/2001, and 3/2001. Furthermore, a new reform was adopted by parliament in late 2005 but did not enter into force, as it was rejected by popular vote in a confirmative referendum in June 2006.
43 Ironically, the reforms that were in fact adopted by Parliament in 1999 and 2001 as well as in 2005 were produced by the Parliament itself and were not the product of special parliamentary, governmental, or expert committees.
44 This would have implied an ad hoc derogation to the constitution-amending procedure laid down in art. 138 of the constitution, which provides that if a constitutional law is adopted by two-thirds or more in each Chamber in the second reading then no referendum need take place.
45 While not binding and not necessarily representative of public opinion, a public consultation is far more than just an online poll, as it is a structured process based on a consolidated methodology. This very consultation was supported by a scientific committee and by the National Institute for Statistics (ISTAT).
46 The platform was called 'partecipa' (www.partecipa.gov.it) and it required registration in order to avoid the possibility of one single person participating more than once.
47 The consultation was open between 8 July and 8 October 2013, i.e., it included the month of August, which is normally the holiday month in Italy.
48 Disaggregated data are even more interesting. Out of the 203,000 who filled out the whole questionnaire, more than two-thirds were male, their education was higher than average, and most of them (60 percent) were (active or retired) civil servants.
49 Full text at www.riformecostituzionali.partecipa.gov.it/assets/PARTECIPA_Rapporto_Finale.pdf.
50 For a theoretical framing see A. Gamper, 'Forms of Democratic Participation in Multi-Level Systems', in C. Fraenkel-Haeberle et al. (eds.), *Citizen Participation in Multi-Level Democracies* (Brill, 2015) 67–84.
51 On the functioning of the system see recently F. Palermo, 'Autonomy and Asymmetry in the Italian Legal System: The Case of the Autonomous Province of Bolzano/Bozen', in G. Pola (ed.), *Principles and Practices of Fiscal Autonomy* (Routledge, 2015) 227–41.
52 The procedure is different: the normal regions adopt their own regional constitutions by qualified majority and the national government can challenge them to the constitutional court if it considers it violates the national constitution (as it happened in a handful of cases), while the autonomy statutes of the special regions are adopted by constitutional law of the national parliament. This way, the special statutes result from a bilateral, negotiated procedure, are more entrenched but also more difficult to amend.
53 The only one that was not active was Sicily.
54 Regional law no. 12/2004.
55 Regional law no. 35/2006. All texts and documents are available at www.consiglio.vda.it/convenzione_autonomia/documentazione_i.asp.
56 The only relevant difference with Friuli Venezia Giulia was that the convention in the Aosta Valley established a forum, an additional body of all interested citizens, to monitor and support the work of the convention.
57 Decree of the President of the Region no. n. 18/2012.
58 Provincial law no. 3/2015. This poses an additional problem since the autonomy statute is regional (i.e., it includes both autonomous provinces of Trento and Bolzano/Bozen).
59 Provincial Law no. 1/2016. The body set up in Trentino is slightly smaller than the one established in South Tyrol (25 members as opposed to 33 + 100 making up the participatory forum) and is relying more on the cooperation between political representatives and experts: most of the nonpolitical representatives, including those

appointed by many sectors of civil society (trade unions, linguistic minorities, etc.) come from the local university. In South Tyrol the approach and the composition is rather different.

60 It is not for this contribution to engage in exploring the relationship between federalism and democracy. This is done by A. Benz and J. Sonnicksen and partly by S. Kropp in the same volume. See also the work by A. Stepan, 'Federalism and Democracy: Beyond the US Model', in *Journal of Democracy*, 10 (1999) 19–34.

61 See F. Palermo and K. Kössler, *Comparative Federalism* (Hart, 2017) 111–21.

62 The German scholar Peter Häberle once famously described regionalism as the younger brother of federalism (P. Häberle, *Europäische Rechtskultur* (Suhrkamp 1997) 233). Federalism might have more little brothers than just regionalism.

63 R. Dahrendorf, *The Modern Social Conflict: An Essay on the Politics of Liberty* (Weidenfeld and Nicholson, 1988) 107.

64 See M. Dani, *The 'Partisan Constitution' and the Corrosion of European Constitutional Culture*, LSE paper series, LEQS paper 68/2013, Nov. 2013, available at www.lse.ac.uk/europeaninstitute/leqs/leqspaper68.pdf.

65 M. Loughlin, *Sword and Scales: An Examination of the Relationship between Law and Politics* (Hart, 2000) 189.

2 (Not) fast and (not) furious?

(Un)constitutional responsiveness and the boundaries of constituent imagination

Zoran Oklopcic

1. Beyond the liberal-democratic and radical-democratic conjurations of peoplehood

The theoretical trench warfare about the meaning of 'the people'—its sovereignty, ultimate authority, constituent power, and the right to self-determination—rages on. It does so, seemingly, with unabated enthusiasm. Is 'the people' a demos or an ethnos? Is 'the people' another name for *plebs*—all those downtrodden—or is it just another name for a demos, all those affected by the exercise of political power? Can its identity be known in advance, or must it remain mysterious until the point when we identify it, but only in retrospect? When, how, and where is 'the people' when it exercises its constituent power? Can it do so only when exhausted from suffering? Are we to find it in local assemblies, which then send their delegates to the Constituent Assembly, or can we identify its visage in mass demonstrations in city squares? When 'the people' claims its right to self-determination, how should we understand its rightful location—as a predetermined territory, or as the land, which it materially improved over time? Busy with giving it meaning, all such arguments seem to have forgotten—or have considered irrelevant (it's hard to tell)—one simple but non-trivial truth. Irrespective of which one among the questions above we chose to answer, the answer will be a figure, which cannot but be the work of *imagination*. Once seen in this light, it becomes harder to believe that its identity is *really* that of a demos, ethnos, plebs, *populus*, or something else altogether. Instead, once seen in that light, 'the people' will appear in its three-fold roles that it has played all along, beneath each and every particular mask of peoplehood. As the product of the practice of theoretical imaginations 'the people' is better seen as the *arbiter*, *warden*, and *manager*.

Irrespective of the perspective from which it is approached—be it ontological, normative, phenomenological, systems-theoretical, or historico-sociological—it adjudicates the legality, morality, sensibility, and intelligibility of our expectations. As it does so, it makes sure that our expectations will be invested in pre-approved collective purposes. You may, for example, expect that your struggle for self-determination results in the formation of a nation-state, or that your exercise of constituent power deposes a dictator, or that your participation in a constitution-making process results in a framework for ongoing open-ended collective self-government. What you cannot expect, however, is to establish a polity, which doesn't serve the collective good of 'the people', but rather some other-regarding political project, such as the establishment of world proletarian federation or the global caliphate. Serving in the role of the warden of your expectations, 'the people' will quickly hunt down your fugitive imagination and bring it back to its rightful place. Finally, when invoked in the field of struggle, 'the people' manages not only our emotions, but also the expectant emotions of our adversaries. To invoke its sovereignty, rights, or authority is to render the conversation about concrete hopes either pointless or irrelevant: the sovereign people has a right to hope whatever it wants, and their specific content is none of 'the people's' enemies' business. By the same token, to invoke the name of 'the people' is to make fears dissolve into diffuse anxiety, to be able to broadcast resoluteness, not doubt. In that context, to speak of its 'will' is to sublimate our unruly desires into a 'demand': imagined at the same time as legitimate, reasonable, and definitive. Those who summon this 'people' into existence are not simply theorists, jurisprudents, sociologists, and philosophers—they are also modern equivalents of what Ernst Cassirer called *homines magi*.[1] They are the practitioners of imagination, which is not only theoretical and constitutional, but also constituent.

In interpreting the meaning of peoplehood in various propositions in which it finds itself either as the subject or, much more rarely, as the predicate, these practitioners intervene in 'the ways people imagine their social existence, how they fit together with others, how things go on between them and their fellows, the expectations that are normally met, and the deeper normative notions and images that underlie these expectations'.[2] Since their interpretations culminate in the imagery of 'the people' as the holder, bearer, or protagonist of constitutional acts that culminate in the formation of constitutional orders, their theoretical imagination could be called *constitutional*. As it intervenes in the social imaginary of peoplehood, however, this imagination is much more than that. It is *constituent*. Its work shapes the anticipatory consciousness of all who invest their expectations in the vocabulary of peoplehood. As the practitioners of constituent imagination, they are the conjurers of peoplehood. By summoning 'the people' as the arbiter, warden, and manager of popular expectations into existence, they broadcast the encouragement or the discouragement of oftentimes fuzzy, but nonetheless identifiable *propositional attitudes*. Put differently, every time a theorist offers his or her ontological, normative, doctrinal, systems-theoretical, or historico-sociological interpretation of a proposition of peoplehood, he or she is always also emitting a set of messages at a lower frequency: assume that here, *hope* for this now, don't *desire* that there in the future, *worry* about that in *this* struggle, or I wouldn't *bet* on this *there* if I were you.

From the ideological point of view, three classes of conjurers—radical democrats, liberal democrats, and deliberative democrats—exert an inordinate influence over the visions of 'the people' within a wider *Eurocentric* social imaginary, on both sides of the Atlantic. In this chapter, my aim is not to arbitrate between their radically opposed conjurations. Instead, my first aim is to explore the implications of that which unites them: their role in the hope-, purpose-, anxiety-, and desire-management of all those who invest their expectations in the vocabulary of peoplehood in the struggles on the ground. Instead, this chapter is interested in a more specific question: what is it in those conjurations that discourages us from reconsidering the dominant attitudes towards constitutional responsiveness, which, at the moment, exhibit no patience for impatience, no understanding for the need for speed, and no consideration for minoritarian aspiration, beyond the already existing vehicles of contemporary constitutionalism.

2. Figurations of peoplehood: Two sovereign deciders and one community of equals

The radical-democratic conjuration of peoplehood is essentially Schmittian. 'The people' that emerges from such Schmittian imagination is not just a collective self-governing body, but also a god-like sovereign, who appears on the scene, and constitutes a constitutional order *ex nihilo*. Thus understood, such people is a sovereign decider: accountable to no one, always ready to rightfully rupture existing constitutional order and create a new one. For radical democrats who implicitly or explicitly subscribe to this view, this is all we need to know when it comes to this decider's personality traits. In contrast, liberal-democratic conjuration of peoplehood is Lockean. While the Schmittian vision doesn't concern itself with 'the people's' character or temperament, Lockean vision portrays 'the people' as a fallible, but ultimately *reasonable person*. 'The people', memorably described by some theorists as Ulysses, binds itself to the mast of a constitution, in order to fend off the seductive call of populist Sirens.[3] In order for such people to exercise its constituent power, liberal democrats first imagine it as slow to engage in radical political action, thoroughly exhausted with suffering grave oppression before it exercises its revolutionary constituent power. Such view of 'the people's' character gives rise to a *revolution/amendment [R/A] binary*: 'the people' either radically re-constitutes constitutional order as a result of oppression, or otherwise changes it through regular constitutional channels.

From that perspective, radical democratic accounts are not so different from the liberal democratic accounts of peoplehood, after all. As they seek to persuade us that 'the people' spontaneously irrupts, seizes the initiative, self-constitutes, or risks tragedy, radical democratic conjurers don't bother forewarning us that they are in the same business of hope-, purpose-, anxiety-, and desire-management, as are their liberal-democratic fellow conjurers. Though they radically disagree with liberal democrats about what kind of political lessons ought to be conveyed by a particular proposition of peoplehood, what unites them is their common aversion towards two particular tropes. The two tropes of *not-yet* and *good-enough* undergird most popular expectations of those on the ground, and can only be properly appreciated once we estrange ourselves from the way in which 'the people' manages our anticipatory consciousness. What worries a liberal-democrat is the potential of these tropes to make *impatience* not only intelligible, but also legitimate. Once we remind ourselves that popular expectations always entail an attitude towards those two tropes, it becomes possible to ask *Why not yet?*; as well as to conclude, *Not good enough!*

In order to evade being confronted with these utterances directly, liberal-democrats invent 'the people'—a reasonable, *patient*, collective actor—and imaginatively organize the exercise of its 'will' around well-known binaries: public–private; norm–exception; people–minority; revolution–amendment; majoritarian–counter-majoritarian. With the tropes of not-yet and good-enough displaced from liberal-democratic constituent imagination, the oppressed are relegated to reminding the oppressor of their ongoing reasonableness in confronting the ignominy with which they were faced. As Martin Luther King Jr. wrote from his Birmingham jail cell: 'I hope, sirs, you can understand our legitimate and unavoidable impatience',[4] because the time has come 'when the cup of endurance runs over, and men are no longer willing to be plunged into the abyss of despair'.[5] With the help of a liberal-democratic 'people' and the ecosystem of the conceptual binaries built around it becomes possible to counter the logic of those who claim their exhaustion with patience with the demands for more patience. What remains unintelligible from the perspective of a liberal-democrat is a sentiment echoed by Jesse Williams, commenting on the enduring police brutality against African-Americans. Instead of embracing Martin Luther King Jr.'s famous claim, Williams exclaimed, 'Freedom is always coming in the hereafter. But you know what, though, "the hereafter" is a hustle. We want it now'.[6]

One would think that radical democratic imaginations of peoplehood exhibit more sensitivity towards the phenomenon of minority impatience. That, however, is not the case. While liberal democrats fear 'Why not yet!' and 'Not good enough!', radical democrats fear the opposite: 'It is good enough . . . (because) it could be worse', or, 'It's good enough . . . for now'. While the former worry about impatience, the latter worry about diminished expectations, and the complacency, servility, or false consciousness of its bearers. As a result, radical democrats conjure collective subjects whose members don't concern themselves with making judgments about what is good enough and when, before they 'irrupt', 'seize initiative', or 'co-institute' a new order together. So when it comes to imagining faster pace, and a greater extent of institutional responsiveness towards impatient constitutional demands made out of turn, the position of liberal democratic and radical democratic constitutionalists are not as far apart as may seem otherwise. While the causes of their aversion towards such responsiveness are different, they metabolize it similarly—by evoking the figure of a willful sovereign decider. For Lockean liberal democrats, that sovereign decider is a reasonable and self-aware Ulysses. From his perspective, impatient constitutional demands *for more and sooner* are foolish, and can only lead to a constitutional shipwreck. For Schmittian radical democrats, a sovereign decider is a god-like omnipotent creator. For those who approach constitutional demands from his perspective, the problem with impatient constitutional demands—'Sooner!', 'More!' Only me!—is different.

Rather than imprudent (childish, shortsighted, or impulsive) they are illogical, and thus inconsequential: the only way to achieve the success of such demands is for a sovereign decider to exercise its constituent power anew and create a constitutional order *ex nihilo*. Either as unwise or as inconsequential: that is how democratic impatience appears in the eyes of liberal and radical democrats. *Unadvisable but possible as orderly* (i.e., through a pre-entrenched constitutional referendum) or *always possible but only as approaching the speed of light* (through a sudden burst of people's constituent power) this is their image of an accelerated constitutional change. *Already taken care of* (through the guarantees of fundamental rights) or *logically impossible* (since 'the people' can only legislate for itself): that is their respective response to the question of forthcoming responsiveness towards minoritarian constitutional aspirations.

In addition to the two figures of a sovereign decider, there is another figuration of a sovereign people that discourages us from rethinking the affective, temporal, and personal dimensions of constitutional responsiveness. In contrast to reasonable Ulysses and a god-like Schmittian sovereign, this people is not an embodied willful individual. In this incarnation it is more obviously a figure of speech, more vividly represented in theoretical imagination than in actual political struggle. In this incarnation, 'the people' is a *demos*—a legitimate political community of co-equal fellow citizens. As an idealized description of a polity in which fellow citizens treat each other with equal respect and consideration, this demos is a superior, idealized alternative to its pathological other: ethnos. In the imagination of constitutional and democratic theorists, ethnos is a pre-political community bound by language, culture, sympathies, and shared memories, all of which prevent it from constituting itself as a polity governed by the ideal of political equality and the rule of law. Seen from the perspective of this binary, impatient constitutional demands are worse than just unwise or inconsequential: since they can only come from the side of an ethnos, they are vicious and atavistic. In this case, our attitudes towards the demands for more agile and discriminating institutional responsiveness will be destined to take a sharp turn for the worst, as well. Approached through the lens of a demos as a political community of co-equals it will be seen 'not simply as unadvisable or as (almost) impossible, but also as unfair, and thus illegitimate.

3. From Athens to Flint: Morphologies of disrespect beyond 'the people'

The persuasiveness of these conclusions will depend on the persuasiveness of the conceptual binary that makes them intelligible: the dichotomy between demos and ethnos. The sensibility of that binary, however, is contextual. Upholding it is more intuitive in some constitutional conflicts than in others. In ethnic conflicts over territorial sovereignty, for example, we are more likely to imagine demos as an ideal political community than to ask what must this ideal hide, or rely on, in order to present itself as an embodiment of the ideal of political equality. In other conflicts, that question becomes unavoidable. By way of example, the ongoing socioeconomic crisis in Greece, provoked by the policy of fiscal austerity followed since 2011 by successive Greek governments. In that context, the figure of a Greek demos—the sovereign people of Greece—continued to play a radically different role than the figurations of other demoi in constitutional struggles elsewhere. Unlike in the ethno-nationalist conflicts in the Balkans, the Greek demos is to a much smaller extent haunted by its pathological other: the toxic ethnos, incarnated in the anti-immigrant filo-fascist political movement Golden Dawn. In the context of the Greek austerity crisis, demos is not just a normative ideal against which to measure the so-called democratic backsliding, but also an essential constituent in a partisan rhetoric of concealment.

To act in this role, demos doesn't need to be called by its name. What counts are the effects it produces: helping render the manifestations of the popular 'will' of the Greek sovereign decider constitutionally inconsequential, and distracting us from the forces that shape the way in which the ideal of equal concern and respect materializes itself in reality. Put formulaically: to imagine a self-governing demos of co-equal citizens in present-day Greece, is to not imagine three other figures which are far more consequential when it comes to rethinking the relationship between the dimensions and terms of institutional responsiveness and the ideal of equal concern and respect. Staying with the Greek-themed terminology of this section, we might call them:

XENOS
NOMOS
EMPORIOS
AGROS

Hiding behind demos, Xenos is the figure of a foreigner. That foreigner can neither be reduced to Schmitt's enemy, nor to Rousseau's benevolent Lawgiver, nor should it be understood as Mouffe's 'constitutive outside', an abstract ontological condition of all acts of constitution-making. As an ontic category, Xenos acts as the actually existing external constituent power, which determines the constitutional consequences of the 'will' of a self-governing demos from the outside. In some cases, this constituent power manifests itself brutally and explicitly. Such was case of the US-steered constitutional transition in Iraq. In other cases, as in the case of the financial crisis in Greece, the projection of power of the external *pouvoir constituant* is subtler. As Costas Douzinas explains,

> The loan agreements impose on Greece an immunity waiver and the exclusive jurisdiction of English law. . . . Public assets can be seized by the lenders and the government cannot protect itself under international or European law since it has accepted the exclusive application of English law. The loan and memorandum agreements imposed taxation increases and savage salary and pension cuts before they reached Parliament, which was reduced to the role of rubberstamping a fait accompli. The law implementing the agreement was adopted with a simple majority despite constitutional provisions requiring a three-fifths majority for such onerous international agreements. The complex memorandum imposing the austerity measures was passed under 'guillotine' procedures with minimal debate. This law gives carte

> blanche to ministers to issue executive decrees which can cover all aspects of economic and social policy, repeal pre-existing laws and sign further binding agreements giving away parts of national sovereignty without Parliamentary approval. . . . Another act with a single section specified that the agreements and memoranda apply from the point of their signing. . . . Attempts by Parliament to amend the odious measures agreed will lead to the non-payment of loan installments turning the troika into the ultimate lawmaker.[7]

Blindsided by the time-honored imaginary of Western constitutional theory, we ignore the constituent power not only of concrete Xenoi, but also the power of governing rationality—the global *Nomos* of neo-liberal globalization—that make external constituent power invisible at the scene we hold so dear: the scene of a demos governing itself without the interference from the outside. Within that scene, there is no place for a particular Xenos—dubbed in this chapter as *Emporios*—which keeps the neo-liberal Nomos in operation. Emporios is a trader who together with his other fellow colleagues forms disembodied, but veritable constituent subjects: 'the markets', which anticipate or react to the manifestations of the will of a particular people by demos by becoming 'confident', 'nervous', 'optimistic', 'pessimistic', or 'panicking'. Seen from this perspective, the aspirational picture of a self-legislating people—where demos forms its 'will' after a period of vigorous democratic deliberation, will appear less as a persuasive ideal, and more as distracting simulation. Within the horizon of possibility delineated by a constituent Nomos, that demos is neither a prudent Ulysses, or an awe-inspiring god-like Sovereign, but rather a slave to the fickle passions of a homunculus 'markets'.

These figures are of course not included in the imaginary of constitutional theory, and it is easy to see why: with them constantly in mind, the ideals of constitutional self-government would become less intelligible and perhaps even less attractive. To emplace them on the scene of constitutional self-government, on the other hand, would be unproductive: everyone already knows how consequential external political influence can be. Likewise, everyone already seems to know the extent to which global economic rationality restricts the political autonomy of sovereign peoples. But even though these figures seem not to add anything useful to our folk understandings of the scale and magnitude of the factors that shape the will, autonomy, and identity of 'the people', finding a place for them in the imaginary of constitutional theory is important for a reason that is intimately related with the theme of this chapter. They allow us to move beyond infinite variations of what Kenneth Burke called 'constitutive anecdotes' within which demoi self-constitute themselves within a smooth bounded space, in a hollow constitutive environment.[8]

Instead, they allow us to envision *Agros*: the terrain of constituent struggle. Depending on the criterion used, its morphology will always look different. What is important, however, is *who* shapes it: never demos alone, but always, to a greater or lesser extent, Xenos, and the logos he creates, enforces, and sustains, through a variety of transmission belts, where one of the cogs is always the affective reactions of an Emporios, feeding the collective mind of 'the markets'. Foregrounding those figures will allow us to envision the ideal of equal concern and respect in a new light: not as a general aspiration imperatively applicable to all in a blank constitutional space, but rather as a device that conceals a more granular morphology of socioeconomic injustices, indignities in space and time. With the help of those figures, the acts of democratic self-legislation through which the Greek parliament adopted austerity measures in conformity with the constitutional ideals of equal concern and respect will obtain a better chance of appearing for what they are: acts of conformity with external constituent power that led to the dramatic erosion in the standards of social protection and led to the escalation of poverty, depression, even suicide.

For the purposes of this essay, it is not necessary to explore whether or not external constituent powers ought to be held accountable for the suffering they produced, but which the vocabulary of sovereign peoplehood helped normalize. What is more important is the capacity of the figures of Xenos (Emporios), Nomos, and Agros to point to the costs of the attitude of blanket dismissiveness towards more agile and discriminating forms of institutional and para-institutional responsiveness, which are thus far occluded from the imagination of 'the peoples', their sovereign wills, and democratic self-government. Invoking the ideal of equal concern to prefigure our judgment about the limits of constitutional responsiveness, also makes us more insensitive towards the actual geographies of socioeconomic deprivation and political disempowerment.

The examples of that abound on the other side of the Atlantic as well. Consider, for example, the morphology of socioeconomic deprivation shaped by the practice of self-government in Michigan. According to a piece of legislation passed in by a legislature that otherwise conforms to the standards of democratic legitimacy, the state governor is entitled to dismiss local assemblies and appoint 'emergency managers' with the power to govern local communities in disregard of their fundamental interests.[9] Michigan's morphology of equal concern and respect allows not only for the creation of the spatial pockets of what journalists called 'financial martial law'[10] but has also proven exceptionally tolerant towards actual pockets of gross disrespect towards basic standards of human dignity. The most famous example of that is Flint, Michigan, where, in an attempt to reduce a budgetary deficit, the emergency manager opted for a less costly and less safe system of water supply, which caused a genuine humanitarian crisis. The decision to start drawing water directly from the river resulted in a spike of the fecal bacteria *E. coli* and carcinogenic trihalomethanes in potable water.[11]

Behind the unitary *vox populi,* as Elmer Schattschneider famously argued, there is a 'heavenly chorus', which, irrespective of its diversity, sings with 'an upper-class accent'.[12] In the context of the American constitutional scholarship, Schattschneider's conclusion was already anticipated in Charles Beard's analysis of the socioeconomic drivers of the republican ideology behind the adoption of the American Constitution, whose main nemesis was not Madisonian factionalism, but socioeconomic redistribution.[13] Today, that idea is far less resonant. While arguing in favor of the capacity of 'we, the people' to engage in the interpretation of the US Constitution, for example, Larry Kramer nonetheless argues that the account of American legislators as 'thoroughly unresponsive to those they represent and attentive only to private interests dangling campaign dollars before their eyes [has been] . . . exaggerated and overdrawn'.[14] Against Kramer's cautious optimism in the progressive potential of the idea of popular self-government, recent empirical research presents a picture even bleaker than the one painted by Schattschneider several decades ago. According to Martin Gilens and Benjamin Page, '[T]he preferences of the average American appear to have only a minuscule, near-zero, statistically non-significant impact upon public policy'.[15]

4. Responsiveness beyond 'the people': Culturalist, non-democratic, historic, peripheral

The verdict of Gilens and Page is damning:

> When a majority of citizens disagrees with economic elites or with organized interests, they generally lose. Moreover, because of the strong status quo bias built into the U.S. political system, even when fairly large majorities of Americans favor policy change, they generally do not get it.[16]

If they are right, increasing responsiveness towards their preferences is a task that is not only important, but also urgent. As we've already seen, however, neither liberal-democratic nor radical-democratic constituent imaginations accord dignity to minoritarian impatience, nor do they accord any legitimacy to the demands for accelerated responsiveness to their aspirations.[17] Four groups, however, come close: counter-hegemonic culturalists, democracy skeptics, republican deviationists, and postcolonial theorists. Let me discuss their approaches in turn. In the first group are those who, such as Upendra Baxi, call for 'equal dignity [of] all constitutional discourses',[18] or who, such as James Tully, call for opening the template of Western constitutionalism to 'intercultural dialogue'.[19] However, while Baxi's account of constitutionalism—as 'a set of ideological sites that provide justification [and] mystification for constitutional theory and practice'—enables us to demask the *ideological* character of liberal-democratic constitutionalism, it still doesn't equip us with the conceptual categories that would enable us to extend that critique further and provide us with a reason to be *tendentially* responsive to those whose ideals of constitutionalism diverge from the Eurocentric, liberal-democratic template. Tully's constitutionalism does that. However, against Tully's hopes for raising the profile of 'strange multiplicity' suppressed under the 'monolithic and masculine' image of liberal-democratic constitutionalism and finding the non-Western within the Western itself,[20] the socio-political project of Western constitutionalism proved remarkably immune to these challenges. In qualifying the demands coming from his multiplicity as 'strange', Tully made it easier to treat them as exceptional—and in the second step, containable and in principle absorbable. As a result, his argument left the *familiar* multiplicity of all those who don't rely on the language of cultural difference with no vocabulary in which they could express the *urgency* of their demands, except for the one already offered through the propositions of peoplehood. Finally, as they made their conceptions of constitutionalism deliberately shallow—and therefore strategically ecumenical—Baxi and Tully emptied them from the categorical apparatus which would set the stage for a conversation among different constituent imaginations—a conversation which would, at the same time, be counter-hegemonic, self-critical, and forward-looking.

The second group is populated by democracy skeptics, who are suspicious both of liberal-democratic as well as radical-democratic visions of democracy. Unlike counter-hegemonic constitutionalists who continue embracing the idea of democracy, democracy skeptics refuse its 'blackmail',[21] its 'sacrosanct place',[22] or embrace a 'post-representative system' as being better equipped to deal with social complexity in modern industrial societies.[23] Their problem is similar to the one above. What is being refused, rejected, or overcome as part of these approaches is not *democracy* (liberal and radical alike) but a system of hope-, anxiety-, desire-, and purpose-management. From the perspective of the figure of peoplehood, which acts as the arbiter, warden, and manager of popular expectations, the question is not whether to refine democracy, redefine it, move beyond it, or reinvigorate it. Rather, the question is how to reimagine the material and institutional dimensions of a constitutional order, so that it allows us to manage our hopes, purposes, anxieties, and desires differently.

The third group belongs to republican deviationists, inspired by the venerable episodes of grassroots resistance in the history of republican Rome, such as *secessio plebis*. The first *secessio* occurred in 494 BC, when disenfranchised plebeians abandoned the confines of Rome, and encamped on the adjacent Mons Sacer, vowing to remain there until their fundamental demands were met. Their purpose was not secession, the extraction of concrete material benefits, or the establishment of a new constitutional order—but rather radical constitutional *reform* that would create new institutions (*tribunate*) giving them more power and, by implication, more equality vis-à-vis ruling patricians.[24] In order to open space for such possibility today requires moving beyond the central tenet of liberal-democratic republican constitutionalism: abandoning the imagination of 'the people' as a unified political body and vesting constituent power in the plebs as the guarantee of its capacity to make 'equal law'.[25]

The limitations of this approach, however, are visible once we recall the *spatial* circumstances in which *secessio plebis* took place: plebeians did not challenge the authority of Roman constitution, neither did they violate its spatiotemporal integrity, nor did they violate any immigration regulations by stepping outside of its confines. Nor did they finally violate the patricians' legitimate interests because the labour power they denied to the patricians was theirs to withdraw. A contemporary *secessio plebis*, in contrast, would find itself incapable of demonstrating that it doesn't harm someone who is in a similar position, 'in the same boat', but doesn't fall under the category of plebs. In contrast, Sieyès' constituent power of the *nation* solved that problem, not by postulating a split between the rich and the poor, but by relying on the polit-economic description of the character of exploitation under the *Ancién Regime*, which allowed Sieyès to close the gap between the plebs and the nation and dismiss the questions such as the ones we have encountered earlier.

The final approach is exemplified in Partha Chatterjee's analysis of the way in which Western understanding of the concept of the norm (which can be understood as both 'normal' and 'desirable'), and its relationship with the conception of exception provided the intellectual rationalization and political justification of European colonialism. According to Chatterjee, the understanding of the norm as 'desirable' allowed European colonialists to translate the plurality of political experiences they encountered into the deviations from the norm. Having been identified as deviant, those locations qualified for the application of the norm's *other*: sovereign exception.[26] The 'structure of justification' prefigured by the interplay between two binaries—norm/deviation and norm/exception—enabled the European colonialists to have it both ways: on the one hand assert 'the universal claims of normative standards of Western political institutions', and on the other, exempt themselves from their application. Unlike other postcolonial theorists who have satisfied themselves to demask the intimate relationship between European colonialism and Western constituent imagination, Chatterjee's project is more radical. Instead of calling for pluralisation of the concept of constitutionalism (such as Baxi and Tully) Chatterjee calls for the redefinition of its normative standards from the periphery—'in the light of considerable accumulation of new practices that may at present be described only in the language of exceptions but which in fact contain the core of a richer, more diverse, and inclusive set of norms'.[27] But how could that be done?

5. Chatterjee and Pettit go to Flint: At the limits of constituent imagination

If liberal-democrats remain unwilling to understand themselves as in the role of the conjurers of the figures whose role is, in turn, to prefigure the dimension of the anticipatory consciousness of those on the ground, how—if at all—could various imaginative deviations discussed here ever hope to disturb the indifference of liberal democrats to minoritarian impatience and their allergy to acceleration? Instead of trying to confront this question through a linear academic argument, I propose we inhabit, for a moment an imaginary world of local grassroots resistance, and eavesdrop ourselves on one imaginary conversation. The conversation we are interested in occurs between four characters—Chatterjee, Pettit, Lefort, and Rosanvallon—and takes place on board the *Lakeshore Limited* en route from New York to Detroit, forty-eight hours before the US government declares martial law and calls the National Guard to restore the rule of law in Michigan. Like in the case of the alternate-universe Occupy movement, the positions of the participants in this conversation bear similarity to the positions of their real-life namesakes.

CHATTERJEE: Philip, if someone told you fifty years ago that one of the American governments would consider potable water a luxury item, would you believe him? Not only that: What would you say if someone told you that this government would actually be complicit in depriving some of its citizens of potable water and then continue ignoring the massive health crisis it caused? I will probably sound bitter, but I will say it: you don't need to be a cultural anthropologist to see how, in many respects, the West is indeed evolving towards the global south and not just the other way around.[28] In fact, I would even go further: at least in one respect, the American constitutional imagination should find some inspiration in the way some postcolonial states confront the demands of the downtrodden. In India, for example, when squatters insist they have a 'right to housing and livelihood', the force of their demand resonates more than you might expect: unlike in the United States, it 'hinges on the generally recognized obligation of the government to provide for the poor and underprivileged'.[29]

PETTIT: I agree that the situation in Flint is a disgrace. I don't see what this has to do with the American imaginary of popular sovereignty (if that's what you had in mind). In my mind, the question of social injustice should be treated separately from the question of the legitimacy of constitutional order. The legitimacy of the system of popular self-government depends on whether citizens have equal control and influence over their government, and not on the degree of economic inequality in the society.

CHATTERJEE: But surely you recognize that Western democracies are, 'without exception, oligarchies of property and expertise' (not that non-Western democracies are much better). Since the wealthy abuse their influence, more systematic sensitivity towards the interests of the poor on behalf of the government would only 'restor[e] the balance of fairness' between different groups in the society.[30] I don't think this logic is culturally sensitive; I don't see why the same logic would not be applicable to the United States.

PETTIT: I assume you are speaking about the restoration of 'the balance of fairness' outside of the constitutionally prescribed political process. If you are, this would amount to an arbitrary exercise of political power and would by definition violate the rule of law. This is unacceptable both from a commonsensical and from an ethical point of view. On the one hand, the state would become '[u]nable to respond to rational expectations' and would cease to exist as an 'entity with which it was possible to do business'.[31] This, in the end, you will surely agree, would hurt everybody. On the other hand, accommodating the illegal behavior of some citizens is deeply unethical. Doing so would effectively grant them the privilege to violate the law at will, destroying one of our most cherished political ideals: political and legal equality for all citizens.[32]

CHATTERJEE: Just to make one thing clear: Are you suggesting that the residents of Flint have equal control and influence over their government? I just read that some commentators called that situation 'financial dictatorship'. They don't seem to be far off.

PETTIT: I know, and that's unfortunate. However, things are a bit more complicated. One might argue that their collective right to self-government is denied, but this view would rest on an erroneous understanding of the American constitution. The constitutions of the United States and Michigan don't recognize the right to local self-government. Your objection is misplaced, as long as the residents of Flint have equal control and influence as members of the people of Michigan and of the United States.

CHATTERJEE: This always confuses me. Why should the legal fictions such as 'the people' be allowed to shortcut our reasoning about the legitimacy of constitutional orders and their particulars? Why should the residents of Flint or any other locality be forced to drink actual fecal bacteria together with the kool-aid of Western constitutionalism? Rather than being blindsided by the mirage of peoplehood, why don't we ask this: 'Is justice better served by non-arbitrary procedures that entail an equal application of the law, or by contextual and possibly arbitrary judgments that address the peculiarities of a particular case?'[33] I see no reason why we would deprive ourselves of the 'possibility of inviting the arbitrary power of government to mitigate the potentially tyrannical power of the law'.[34]

PETTIT: Ha! I knew it! I knew that you would at some point draw out the paradox-of-circularity wildcard. I know it's been very popular in constitutional theory, but it's getting lame.

CHATTERJEE: That's not what I had in mind. But now you mention it, please explain.

PETTIT: OK. There is no such 'paradox' because the 'constituting' people is causally responsible for the constitution. That causal responsibility does not require temporal precedence. Very simple: as 'constituted', 'the people' can change its constitution through regular channels, and as 'constituting' through a revolution.[35]

CHATTERJEE: So, you are saying that if they don't like the way they are being treated by the socioeconomic system locked in in the US Constitution, those dissatisfied can choose only between a rigged democratic system and a revolution? But before I forget: I think you have misunderstood the objection of circularity. The problem stems from the fact that the identity of 'the people' derives from the American Constitution, which in turn prefigures it. The distinction between 'constituting' and 'constituted' does not solve your problem because the paradox continues haunting the 'constituting' people as well. So I can restate my points in these terms as well: Why would the citizens of Flint, together with their comrades throughout Michigan, sacrifice their basic dignity at the altar of this performative contradiction?

PETTIT: So you are asking why should they respect the spatiotemporal integrity of American constitutional order if they don't like it? Well, I don't want to sound harsh, but tough luck if they don't like it![36] They should be reasonable enough to recognize that 'states [are] locked into a pattern' that would enable the external predatory states to exploit radical ruptures in the fabric of constitutional order.[37] A state-bound world is a historical and functional necessity and cannot offer you to live in 'a natural, rather than a political' condition, or in any other state you might prefer'.[38] Because of that, no state is in a position to grant you the privilege, no matter how virtuous you may be, of obeying the law on a non-coercive basis'.[39]

CHATTERJEE: I can't for the love of me see how the United States are '*locked* into a pattern'! Can you explain who are those rivals who might exploit the situation in which the will of the residents of Flint take precedence. . . . I can't understand how you can continue to insist on this black-and-white image inherited from the social contract tradition. Are you disputing that 'many of the features conventionally associated with international anarchy have moved into states and made life there precarious [and that] many of the features associated with domestic order have moved out into the international system, which has increasingly been stratified according to the standards of good governance'?[40]

PETTIT: OK, fine. So what do you suggest? I am, as much as you, irked by what you've called the 'paradoxical reality' power differentials 'in capitalist countries'.[41] Earlier, I heard you speak about the 'redefinition of citizenship' and 'differentiated citizenship'. I cannot imagine *in whose name* would such a system be entrenched in a constitution? Finally, when you speak affirmatively about 'contextual and possibly arbitrary judgments', aren't you worried where that would lead? If a state accommodates one partial interest out of turn, why should everyone else expect to be treated differently? And honestly, looking at the Bundy standoff in Oregon, I am surprised that you are being so flippant about rethinking the template of constitutionalism that rests on an image of a people as a unity of free and equal citizens.

As Chatterjee was preparing to respond, two strangers appeared out of nowhere.

LEFORT: Good afternoon, gentlemen. I look very pale, I know—I am sorry if I startled you! I apologize for interrupting your very interesting conversation. My name is Lefort, and this is my friend Rosanvallon. It was interesting to listen you speak because just the other day Pierre and I were having a very similar conversation. If you allow me . . .

PETTIT AND CHATTERJEE: By all means.

LEFORT: I agree with both of you to an extent. I agree with you, Mr. Chatterjee, about the abominable way in which contemporary liberal-democratic constitutionalism treats the question of economic equality and socioeconomic emancipation. But, I think that the vocabulary of Western constitutionalism is much more capacious than you give it credit for. 'The symbolic efficacy' of the notion of rights, their capacity to make the public sphere responsive to a myriad of social demands, is intrinsically linked with the symbolical order of popular sovereignty.[42] Regimes based on the idea of popular sovereignty, in order to not lose their claims to transcendence and 'fall into [the] triviality' of coercion, must respond to its implicit promise of justice. To make use of their symbolic efficacy, you can't challenge this order head on, only 'obliquely'![43] And if you look at it, this is indeed how it's been challenged. In the case of Flint, the grassroots have, at least initially, mobilized around the vocabulary of rights and precisely in the name of 'the people'.

CHATTERJEE: I can't but observe how poorly that is working out for them.

LEFORT: Forgive me if I get too excited, but when my friends in France used to tell me the same thing, I always asked them: '[I]s it not in the name of their rights that workers or employees challenge[d] the right of a management to deprive them of work, that they press their claims to the point of taking over the management themselves, as happened at the Lip factory, that they rebel, here and there, against the working conditions that they have to endure, that they demand new measures for their safety? Is it not in the name of their rights that peasants, like those in the Larzac, resist[ed] the expropriation which is regarded as indispensable by the state? Is it not again in the name of their rights that women claim[ed] recognition of their equality with men, that homosexuals r[ose] up against the prohibitions and repression to which they [were] subjected, that consumers band[ed] together or that city-dwellers and country people oppose[d] the devastation of the natural environment? [Were] these various rights not affirmed by virtue of an awareness of right, without objective guarantee, and equally with reference to publicly recognized principles which are partly embodied in laws and which must be mobilized in order to destroy the legal limits that restrict them? And, lastly, can one not see that under the thrust of these rights, the web of political society either tends to change, or appears more and more susceptible to change?'[44]

CHATTERJEE: I dare note that your examples are all from France, and from a while ago. Personally, I refuse to accept that our institutional imagination can choose only between Philip's republicanism and your radical democracy that fights the emancipatory struggles with the same dull instruments. Surely, there must be something more than—

ROSANVALLON: Exactly! Sorry to interrupt you. I completely agree. . . . While I agree with Claude about the symbolic efficacy of rights, this is far from being the only thing that can contribute to the projects of social emancipation, along the lines proposed by Mr. Chatterjee. But first, I think it's important to recognize that the idea of republican peoplehood implicit in Mr. Pettit's argument has already been historically superseded not only in France but in the United States as well.[45] I understand that it may be difficult to estrange ourselves from the view of 'the people' as a 'corporate body', but you need to keep in mind that image is just the result of your way of looking.

PETTIT: I am not sure what you mean.

ROSANVALLON: OK. Imagine you are examining an object—'the people'—with a 'telescope'.[46] In that case, 'the people' will appear as a (celestial) body, a 'monist unity' that speaks through periodic elections, which detect that unity's will. However, we can also gaze at 'the people' through a 'microscope'. In that case, instead of seeing 'the people' as a 'homogenous mass', we would detect its 'various cross-sections'.[47] Gazing through the microscope, our picture of 'the people' would be Kelsenian: 'the people's' 'will' would reveal itself as 'an arithmetic aggregate . . . with unanimity as an underlying ideal'.[48] Instead, what I am suggesting is to 'explore the object by tracing a series of paths through it'.[49] Instead of being a homogenous 'monolith' of the Jacobin peoplehood, a Kelsenian granular entity in a petri dish, or Claude's empty space, 'the people' is . . .

PETTIT: Some kind of a hologram?

ROSANVALLON: Something like it. In any event, the image is a composite of three scans of 'the people' from different directions that shows us not just one body but its three bodies: the electoral, the principled, and the social.[50] Your mistake, Philip—can I call you Philip?—is that you rely on an image of the first two bodies only. I call that body the 'electoral people'. It is incarnated in majorities, produced through periodic elections.[51] A closer look, however, reveals how 'unrealistic' it is to assume that general elections can manifest the will of social generality. '[T]he fragility of the logic should be obvious'.[52] In contrast to the body of the electoral 'people', 'the people's' second body is 'a form with which everyone can identify': the community of all rights-bearing citizens, independent from the vagaries of majoritarian will. Finally, its third body is 'social': unlike the first two, this one reveals 'the problematic truth of being-together', and doesn't hide its identity of a 'container filled with diverse elements and movements'.[53] As part of this, third people minorities are not the opposite of majorities but rather 'multiple and fragmented expressions of the social totality'.[54]

PETTIT: Still, it's hard for me to see how any of this differs from the conventional institutional prescriptions of the republican popular sovereignty . . .

ROSANVALLON: Oh, it does. What I am describing is a 'modern mixed regime'—beyond electoral democracy—that responds to the failed emancipatory promises of the electoral and the principled people. This regime is marked by three imperatives: it must be impartial, attentive to particularity, and reflexive. First, the historical manifestations of impartiality, such as civil service and independent judiciary, are now complemented by the institutions of 'constitutive impartiality' at the level of 'social infrastructure'. Such institutions maintain a 'realm of common existence . . . apart from the realm of partisan politics' and reflect the wish of the citizens to 'institute a democratic society'.[55] Second, the attentiveness to particularity is reflected not only in periodic elections but also in the ability of the government 'to share, to pay attention to the problems of ordinary people, and to display sensitivity to the trials and tribulations of everyday life'.[56] Attentive to different temporal registers of particular demands, the government must be able to speed up: it must 'interact more and faster, with all the risks that this new capability implies'.[57] It is intrinsic to the idea of modern popular sovereignty to be more responsive to the interest of one of its segments! It does not stop at that. Finally, the attitudinal register of the mixed regime is complemented by the institutions of 'counter-democracy'. These institutions are all around us—watchdog groups, evaluation boards, systems of veto—but we haven't got used to seeing them as evidence of the radical reshaping of the idea of 'the people' as an agent possessed by only one electoral body.[58]

PETTIT: But doesn't this capitulate to populist pressures?

ROSANVALLON: Don't get me wrong, I detest populism as much as you do. In my opinion, populism is nothing but 'an acute manifestation of contemporary political disarray and a tragic expression of our inability to overcome it',[59] and a 'compulsive and permanent stigmatization of ruling authorities, to the point where these authorities are seen as radically alien enemy powers'.[60] I don't think that's productive.

CHATTERJEE: I am sorry, but I think you are greatly exaggerating the dangers of populism. Populism is one of the forms of 'strategic politics' 'that could be used by demand-makers as well as by those who hold governmental power'[61] that can unmask the ruling oligarchy.

ROSANVALLON: I think you are wrong there, and that you are underestimating the importance of impartiality as an important social ideal. We don't need to, and should not, sacrifice it because of our attention towards particularity. Take the independence of central banks, for example. By making them independent, they are set apart from the realm of 'partisan politics', and 'their independence thus depends on delineating a realm of common existence that one believes ought to be set apart from the realm of partisan politics'.[62]

CHATTERJEE: But this is precisely my point! Rather than being seen as exemplars of constituent impartiality, they should be seen as part of the neo-liberal institutional package, in many cases actively promoted by powerful states and the international financial institutions. I would even go as far as to say that rather than reflecting the desire of citizens to establish a democratic society, they would be better seen as desensitizing them to the imminently political and socially redistributive effects of monetary policy . . .

PETTIT: I think we are moving away from our subject. I can understand how populist politics may be strategically useful in the case of Flint. I also understand why the attention to the particularities of each case ought to be part of the ethos of every civil servant. But I don't understand, what implications could this ever have for the way in which we think about constitutional design and constitutional change? Also, Pierre, you say that it is 'unrealistic' to assume that general elections can manifest the will of social generality, and that 'the fragility of the logic should be obvious'.[63] Well, it is not obvious to me at all, especially when I ask myself what this concretely means in the case of constitutional change: What other alternative would preserve the equal control and equal influence of all citizens in the process of constitution-making? Equally, when you say that there should be 'attention to particularity' and sensitivity to 'proximity', I wonder whose proximity and whose particularity? Where would we end in that case? I think that such a system would be attractive only to 'fanatics or zealots who insist on special treatment'.[64]

CHATTERJEE: I can't speak for Pierre, but I don't have a good answer to your objection. However, I cannot restrain myself from noticing that the worries about fanaticism and zealotry speak not only about objective evils but also about the mental states of those making such charges. As a colleague of mine observed in a different context: 'By projecting the panic and anxiety on native custom and ethnic particularity, the British [colonialists] attempted to contain and "objectify" their anxiety, finding a ready "native" reference for the undecidable event that afflicted them'.[65] Why would you assume that the militant activists who are seizing governmental buildings across Michigan are 'fanatics' or 'zealots'? Why can't you see these developments as a response to injustice that requires an urgent and systematic response, if necessary over and above existing constitutional norms? More importantly, what are you afraid will happen if their demands are accepted?

6. For love of the purpose: Acceleration, responsiveness, and the anxieties of peoplehood

Our imaginary ticket controller interrupted this conversation and prevented us from hearing the response of 'Pettit' to this question. Nonetheless, from what we've heard during the discussion, we have enough to form an opinion not only about the positions of our imaginary characters, but also on the answers that their real-life namesakes might give in such a situation. From what we've heard, Pettit, the republican theorist of peoplehood, would probably ignore this question altogether. Though there is nothing in his argument that could demonstrate this as a fact, Pettit's exaggerated assumption of inhospitable international environment ought to be seen as symptomatic not simply of the depth of republican commitment to political equality (which would have called for such exaggeration), but rather of the refusal to consider anxiety as a legitimate object of reflection in republican theories of peoplehood. Perhaps ironically, in making that assumption Pettit's republicanism echoes the pattern of Schmitt's visual imagination. Schmitt also needed the contrasting image of the Outside in order to make the anxiety about his 'Gestalt', 'stop'.[66] In this respect, the difference between the two is that of a degree: in Schmitt's case, the Outside is an 'enemy', in Pettit's case, a potential enemy. This brings us back to our initial question: how—if at all—do various imaginative deviations from the template of republican peoplehood respond to this republican indifference?

The answer of republican deviationists, such as Miguel Vatter, comes in the form of a reminder. Rather than attacking liberal-democratic republican anxieties, the attribution of constituent power to 'plebs' may be interpreted as serving to remind contemporary republicans that their insistence on unitary peoplehood stands in the way of achieving political and socioeconomic equality. The second answer was put forward by Chatterjee. Though he denounced the role of Western constituent imagination—republicanism included—his call to develop new normative standards in light of accumulated exceptions ignored the underlying republican anxieties altogether. As we saw from our imaginary train conversation, 'Chatterjee' (and probably Chatterjee) considered them politically irrelevant in light of the substantive injustices caused by the 'the potentially tyrannical power of the law'.[67] Finally, 'Rosanvallon' agreed with 'Chatterjee' about the need for a constitutional order to be responsive to the plight of the poor and marginalized over and above the template of Pettit's republicanism. However, he made that argument without deviating from the orbit of the republican imagination of peoplehood. Seen as an attempt to render the need for such responsiveness recognizable to the republicans of Pettit's kind, Rosanvallon's account made ample and explicit use of visual imagination. By making clear that the image of a republican 'people' depends on ways of seeing—which includes visual aids ('telescope' and 'microscope') and gazing from different vantage points—his implicit message to the republicans of Pettit's persuasion is that they have a choice in how they imagine the reconciliation of the ideals of equality and responsiveness.

That choice exists as a matter of principle. However, by practicing his visual re-imagination against a particular past space of experience (institutional development of the United States and France over the last two centuries), Rosanvallon was subtly suggesting that Pettit's republicanism doesn't have that much choice after all: the trajectory he detected in these countries' constitutional histories makes his tricephalous people the imaginative condensation of emerging reality, not an act of fantasy. As 'Rosanvallon' petitioned 'Pettit' to accept the tri-cephalous—as the truth of 'Pettit's' monocephalous—'people', he also ignored the function of a republican 'people' as an anxiety-manager: both in practice and in theory. As a result, his re-imagination simply presumed (or prescribed; it is not completely clear) that the officials, once confronted with exceptional demands, will be willing to 'interact more and faster', including '*all the risks* that this new capability implies'.[68] From a theoretical perspective, this claim might appear as an unimportant detail in Rosanvallon's overall argument. From the perspective of partisan eavesdropper, a relevant question is rather: why would they ever want to do that? From the eavesdropper's perspective, this immediately raises another question, this time directed toward the conjurer of peoplehood: on the basis of what can one expect that the tricephalous people (in case of Rosanvallon) will prove motivating enough so that the public official accelerates the pace of his responsiveness towards the demands the partisan made out of order? While Rosanvallon assumed that the historical trajectory of modern republicanism makes his relativization of majoritarian democracy 'obvious', that obviousness is not obvious at all. To invoke 'the will' of 'the people' is less a matter of naively asserting its capacity to speak for the 'social totality', and more a matter of saying-without-saying: the amount of desires we've satisfied is *good enough*.

This confronts us with a final question. Is looking beyond 'the people' and envisioning the tropes of not-yet and good-enough, itself good enough to encourage Pettit's republicans to see the alleged 'fanatics or zealots who insist on special treatment' with new eyes, as citizens demanding accelerated *responsiveness* towards their desires, and towards their own, perhaps idiosyncratic projects, which cannot be reduced to the vocabulary of peoplehood? The answer to this question is a predictable and resounding 'no'—if for nothing else, than for the fact that a similar project, in a different form, was proposed several decades ago, but never gained traction, irrespective of the high acclaim enjoyed by the book in which it was put forward. The book in question is, of course, Philippe Nonet's and Philip Selznick's seminal *Law and Society in Transition*, subtitled 'Toward Responsive Law'.[69] Though the authors preoccupied themselves neither with acceleration nor with impatience, nor with minoritarian political aspirations, their account of *responsive law* is the closest that contemporary jurisprudence got to embracing them, without recoiling into the worldview governed by what Nonet and Selznick call 'autonomous law'. The choice of the qualifier 'responsive', rather than 'open or adaptive', is deliberate: it 'suggest[s] capacity [of law] for responsible, and hence discriminate and selective adaptation'.[70] However—and this is an important point we haven't confronted thus far—'[t]o assume this posture, an institution requires the guidance of purpose. Purposes set standards for criticizing established practice, thereby opening ways to change'.[71] In discussing 'the sovereignty of purpose', Nonet and Selznick admit that 'the quest for purpose is a risky venture for legal institutions'. In contrast to collectively autonomous law, 'depende[nt] heavily on ritual and precedent to sustain identity or uphold legitimacy . . . the road to responsiveness is necessarily perilous'. Such a road, the authors aver, 'cannot be contemplated with easy optimism':

> The differences between autonomous and responsive law follow in part from contrasting assessments of that risk. Autonomous law adopts a 'low risk' perspective. It is wary of what might encougrage questioning of received authority. In calling for a more purposive and open legal order, the advocates of responsive law opt for a 'high-risk' alternative.[72]

The ideals of an 'autonomous law'—embraced both by the liberal- and radical-democratic conjurers of peoplehood, 'recoils from the unsettling effect of purposive thinking'.[73] The reason for closing this enquiry with Nonet's and Selznick's ideals is not only to situate the blind spots of contemporary constituent imagination in their wider jurisprudential setting, but to also identify the role of *purpose and purposefulness* as a thus far suppressed theme, which might be necessary to bring 'Chatterjee', 'Pettit', and 'Rosanvallon'—as the imaginary figures of postcolonial, liberal-democratic, and radical-democratic constituent imaginations—into a more productive dialogue with each other. Without the figure of purpose, the tropes of *(why)-not-yet* and *(not)-good-enough* will remain unintelligible to both liberal- and radical-democrats, even if both managed to miraculously estrange themselves from their commitments to the vocabulary of peoplehood. Without the figure of purpose, (why)-not-yet and (not)-good-enough are unable to answer a question that haunts them both in turn: *so that what?*

Nonet's and Selznick's account of responsive law is important for another reason: their unwillingness to not only speak to the anxieties of the conjurers of collectively autonomous law, but to also re-examine their own. From that perspective, the problem with their account lies less in their optimism about the capacity of responsive law to 'attenuate' both the 'prescription and symbolism' and encourage 'overcoming the parochialism of communal morality', and to contribute to 'a problem-centered and socially integrative approach to crises of public order', and an overall 'civility' of discourse.[74] Nor does the problem lie in their willingness to take 'a sober look' at the 'risks' that the template of responsive law generates: 'the spectre of a multitude of narrow-ended, self-regulating institutions, working at cross-purposes and bound to special interests'.[75] In fact, the willingness of Nonet and Selznick to own up to the 'risks' involved in their alternative is one of the virtues of their approach.

The problem, rather, lies in their unwillingness to turn the diagnosis of risk into an object of conversation. Without that, there is nothing much to be said, apart from expressing hope that responsive law can compensate for 'the erosion of the authority' of collectively autonomous law 'by more effectively tapping the resources of these social orders'.[76] While Nonet and Selznick speak of that as a 'possibility', that possibility can never be ascertained objectively, as a matter of weighing 'risks' and 'benefits' entailed in the idea of responsive law. Like all artifacts of legal consciousness, those risks and benefits are the outcomes of a constituent imagination. That imagination is not simply theoretical. It is always polemical, visual, and affective. Envisioning risks and benefits is part and parcel of a political struggle, and is always colored by the conjurer's own anxieties about fragmentation and heteronomy. And as the conjurers of responsive law and of the sovereignty of purpose, Nonet and Selznick are no exception. So from that perspective, their claim that

> in ministering to legal values, responsive law leans upon and preserves a political community that is inclusive, not the property of a few . . . the fundamental difference between repressive and responsive law is what separates 'power politics', the raw conflict and accommodation of special interests, from 'high politics', the reasoned effort to realize an ideal of polity[77]

ought to be seen not as their axiomatic ethical starting point, but rather as the symptom of their unwillingness to allow their interlocutors to inspect their own anxieties about 'the spectre of'—the choice of words is telling—'a multitude of narrow-ended, self-regulating institutions, working at cross-purposes and bound to special interests'.[78] In contrast, the central message of this chapter is that it is possible to go beyond that point. Instead of cutting off further debate about 'Why not yet?' and about 'What is good enough?' by positing 'an ideal of polity' as 'a political community that is inclusive', this chapter argued that Nonet and Selznick, together with other sympathizers of responsive law, could have asked the question that the imaginary 'Chatterjee' posed to the imaginary 'Pettit': 'What are you *afraid* will happen if their demands are accepted?' This question might be followed by the second wave of questions: where, how, when, and based on what do you anticipate the mushrooming of 'a multitude of narrow-ended, self-regulating institutions, working at cross-purposes and bound to special interests'?[79] And in Pettit's, Selznick's, and Nonet's local context: *So what* if such mushrooming undermined the precious ideal of an inclusive polity? If what it took to corrode the enduring power of the American constitutional oligarchy were the class-based institutions along the lines proposed by Vatter, why should anyone shed a tear for what proved to be the ruse, not the ideal of inclusivity? If what it took to remove African-Americans from the mercy of militarized police forces were to transform the United States into a consociational democracy, in which African-Americans become a constituent nation, enjoying both the territorial and non-territorial autonomy, together with the power-sharing institutions at the central level, why should responsiveness stop at the limit of what republican constituent imagination finds politically, emotionally, and aesthetically pleasing? Without the willingness to practice constituent imagination openly—polemically, visually, and affectively—the call to devote 'legal energies . . . to diagnosing institutional problems and redesigning institutional arrangements [and to imagine] [n]ew models of supervision, new ways of increasing the visibility of decision, new organizational units, new structures of authority' will lead to predictable results: perpetual folding back into the existing imaginative templates. Without a new style of imagination, the dignity of impatience, the legitimacy of the demands for accelerated responsiveness beyond the R/A binary, and finally, the intelligibility of impatient demands made not in the name of 'the people', but rather in the name of one of its minoritarian segments, will remain the blind spots shared by most contemporary constituent imaginations. Without a new, less quietist style of constituent imagination, the available alternatives will remain the same: act as a reasonable revolutionary, exhausted with your suffering, as advised by liberal democrats; irrupt unpredictably without apologies, as advised by radical-democrats; claim postcolonial exception as advised by counter-hegemonic constitutionalists and postcolonial theorists; claim that your class-based project conforms with the heritage of Western constitutional thought as advised by republican deviationists; or, finally, send democracy and democratic self-government to hell, as put forward as a possibility by democracy skeptics.

The contours of the template sympathetic to Nonet's and Selznick's project that I've sketched in this chapter are not intended as a superior alternative to other imaginative templates on offer. The choice among them cannot but be contextual. In any case, such choice will always be the outcome of the work of imagination, based not on the conjurer's theoretical argument, but on her own anticipatory consciousness. Irrespective of how one feels about a template capable of offering new modes of accelerating constitutional responsiveness, or about dignifying minoritarian impatience, the central point of this chapter should be seen in that light. Instead of obsessing about who, when, how, and where is 'the people', plebs, demos, ethnos, multitude, crowd, swarm, or constituent power—we, the conjurers and partisans alike—may devote part of our imaginative energies to a preliminary project. So before diagnosing problems and designing 'models of supervision, new ways of increasing the visibility of decision, new organizational units, [or] new structures of authority' we should pause to ask: once we've confronted the polemical, visual, and affective nature of conjurations of peoplehood, what prevents us desiring differently, planning deliberately, worrying consciously, and hoping for more? That question is the limit of constituent imagination. Against the general attitude implicit in the dominant approaches to the vocabulary of peoplehood, I've argued that it ought to be seen as the starting, not the ending point.

Notes

1 Ernst Cassirer, *The Myth of the State* (Yale University Press, 1949) 47.
2 Charles Taylor, *Modern Social Imaginaries* (Duke University Press, 2004) 23. For the historically bi-directional relationship between theoretical imagination and social imaginary, see Charles Taylor, *A Secular Age* (Harvard University Press, 2007) 175–76. For 'double hermeneutic', the idea that not only social reality, but ideas from social sciences shape social reality, see Anthony Giddens, *The Constitution of Society: Outline of the Theory of Structuration* (Polity Press, 1984) 284. Others may think that corrosion or refurbishment of constitutional imagination are not particularly impactful when it comes to the changes in the wider *social imaginary*. While they may admit that social imaginary 'begins with a theory', they may nonetheless hold that social imaginaries 'can never be fully explicated and made available for discussion'. Michael Warner, 'Social Imaginaries: A Conversation' (2015) 1:1 *Social Imaginaries* 195. Finally, others may believe that a theorist's practice should actually move in reverse: 'going from a people's embodied practices to their narrative representations and further into theoretical articulations'. Dilip Gaonkar, ibid., 195.
3 Stephen Holmes, *Passions and Constraint: On the Theory of Liberal Democracy* (University of Chicago Press, 1996).
4 Martin Luther King Jr., 'Letter from a Birmingham Jail' in Roger S Gottlieb (ed.), *Liberating Faith: Religious Voices for Justice, Peace, and Ecological Wisdom* (Rowman & Littlefield, 2003) 180.
5 Ibid.
6 Jesse Williams, BET Humanitarian Award acceptance speech (26 June 2016). I transcribed his remark from a video of his speech available at www.youtube.com/watch?v=jLbrhcoGzus (accessed on 20 July 2016).
7 Costas Douzinas, *Philosophy and Resistance in the Crisis: Greece and the Future of Europe* (Polity, 2013) 46.
8 Kenneth Burke, *A Grammar of Motives* (first published 1945, University of California Press, 1969) 331.
9 Local Government and School District Fiscal Accountability Act (2011) Mich. Legis. Serv. 4 (West) (codified as amended at Mich. Comp. Laws H§ 141.1501–1531 (2011)).
10 Chad Selweski, 'Michigan Senate Passes Emergency Manager Bills' *Daily Tribune* (Clinton Township, 10 March 2011), www.dailytribune.com/article/DT/20110310/NEWS/303109994.
11 Laura Gottesdiener, '"Something is Rotten in Michigan": Poisoned Water Supplies, Dissolved School Districts and a Massive Unraveling of American Democracy' (*Salon*, 15 June 2015), www.salon.com/2015/06/12/something_is_rotten_in_michigan_poisoned_water_supplied_dissolved_school_districts_and_a_massive_unraveling_of_american_democracy_partner/.
12 Elmer E. Schattschneider, *The Semisovereign People: A Realist's View of Democracy in America* (Wadsworth Publishing, 1975) 34.
13 Charles A. Beard, *An Economic Interpretation of the Constitution of the United States* (1913).
14 Larry Kramer, *The People Themselves: Popular Constitutionalism and Judicial Review* (OUP, 2004) 239.
15 Martin Gilens and Benjamin I. Page, 'Testing Theories of American Politics: Elites, Interest Groups, and Average Citizens' (2014) 12:3 *Perspectives on Politics* 564, 575.
16 Ibid., 576.
17 The partial exception to that is Bruce Ackerman, whose work I discuss elsewhere. See Bruce Ackerman, 'Higher Lawmaking' in Sanford Levinson (ed.), *Responding to Imperfection: The Theory and Practice of Constitutional Amendment* (Princeton University Press, 1996).

18 Upendra Baxi, 'Constitutionalism as a Site of State-Formative Practices' (2000) 21 *Cardozo L. Rev.* 1183, 1188. For a different way to expand the concept of constitutionalism see Larry Catá Backer, 'Theocratic Constitutionalism: An Introduction to a New Global Legal Ordering' (2008) 16:1 *Ind. J. Global Legal Studies* 101. Larry Catá Backer, 'The Structural Characteristics of Global Law for the 21st Century: Fracture, Fluidity, Permeability, and Polycentricity' (2012) 17:2 *Tilburg L. Rev.* 177.
19 James Tully, *Strange Multiplicity: Constitutionalism in an Age of Diversity* (Cambridge University Press, 1995) 207.
20 Ibid., 199.
21 David Scott, 'Norms of Self-Determination: Thinking Sovereignty Through' (2012) 4:2–3 *Middle East Law and Governance* 195, 198.
22 Adrian Little, 'Democratic Melancholy: On the Sacrosanct Place of Democracy in Radical Democratic Theory' (2010) 58:5 *Political Studies* 971, 984.
23 Danilo Zolo, *Democracy and Complexity: A Realist Approach* (Penn State University Press, 1999) ix.
24 Miguel Vatter, 'The Quarrel between Populism and Republicanism: Machiavelli and the Antinomies of Plebeian Politics' (2012) 11:3 *Contemporary Political Theory* 242, 244.
25 Ibid.
26 Partha Chatterjee, *Lineages of Political Society: Studies in Postcolonial Democracy* (Columbia University Press, 2011) 10.
27 Ibid., 22.
28 Jean Comaroff and John Comaroff, 'Theory from the South: Or, How Euro-America Is Evolving toward Africa' (2012) 22:2 *Anthropological Forum* 113.
29 Chatterjee (note 26) 15.
30 Ibid., 16.
31 Philip Pettit, *On the People's Terms: A Republican Theory and Model of Democracy* (CUP, 2012) 283 [emphasis mine].
32 Similarly, the idea of equal human dignity and political equality is not necessarily related to democracy nor, by implication, republicanism. See Adam Przeworski, *Democracy and the Limits of Self-Government* (Cambridge University Press, 2010) 71.
33 Chatterjee (note 26) 16.
34 Ibid., 17.
35 Pettit (note 31) 292.
36 Ibid., 153.
37 Ibid., 161.
38 Ibid., 163.
39 Ibid.
40 Jens Bartelson, *Sovereignty as Symbolic Form* (Routledge, 2014) 99.
41 Chatterjee (note 26) 16.
42 Pettit (note 31) 264.
43 Ibid., 265.
44 Claude Lefort, *The Political Forms of Modern Society Bureaucracy, Democracy, Totalitarianism* (MIT Press, 1986) 261–2.
45 Pierre Rosanvallon, *Democratic Legitimacy: Impartiality, Reflexivity, Proximity* (Princeton University Press, 2009) 7.
46 Ibid.
47 Ibid.
48 Ibid.
49 Ibid., 130.
50 Ibid.
51 Ibid.
52 Ibid., 123.
53 Ibid.

54 Ibid., 116.
55 Ibid., 119.
56 Ibid., 188.
57 Ibid., 215.
58 Pierre Rosanvallon, *Counter-Democracy: Politics in an Age of Distrust* (Cambridge University Press, 2008) 302.
59 Ibid., 273.
60 Ibid., 268.
61 Chatterjee (note 26) 144.
62 Rosanvallon (note 45) 114.
63 Ibid., 123.
64 Pettit (note 31) 170.
65 Homi Bhabha, *The Location of Culture* (Routledge, 1996) 46.
66 Quoted from Gopal Balakrishnan, *The Enemy: An Intellectual Portrait of Carl Schmitt* (Verso, 2000) 113.
67 Chatterjee (note 26) 17.
68 Rosanvallon (note 45) 215 [emphasis mine].
69 Philippe Nonet and Philip Selznick, *Law and Society in Transition: Toward Responsive Law* (Octagon Books, 1978).
70 Ibid., 77.
71 Ibid.
72 Ibid.
73 Ibid., 82.
74 Ibid., 86–94.
75 Ibid., 103.
76 Ibid.
77 Ibid., 117.
78 Ibid., 103.
79 Ibid., 103.

3 The multifaceted sovereign

Domestic and international actors in constitutional regime change

Andrew Arato and Gábor Attila Tóth

The concept of the constituent power emerged in the revolutions of the 17th and 18th centuries. Classical theories have implied a strong link between the constituent power and a single organ of the state in which the powers of sovereignty were concentrated. Today we are also able to speak of non-revolutionary forms of regime change and constitution-making. Democratic constitutions from Spain to South Africa can now be seen as products of many players—not only representative organs but also roundtables and popular involvement—acting through multiple procedures and stages. The plurality of agents involved raises the question whether international actors too can or should participate. Indeed, international law still insists that constitution-making is a purely domestic matter. Given the experiences of Bosnia, Iraq or most recently Hungary and Poland, however, we can no longer neglect the significant role of international monitoring institutions, advisory committees and courts.

Our claim concerns procedural legitimacy in constitutional regime changes. We argue in this chapter that learning from the lessons of post-revolutionary constitution-making by internal and external actors can greatly help in solving the problem of imperfect procedural justice. We make this case first by comparing revolution and post-revolution, and second by highlighting some of the procedural principles of constitution-making. We will then consider the legitimate role of domestic and international actors in the non-revolutionary constitution-making. We conclude that prior to the adoption of a constitution, international advisory and monitoring bodies as deliberative institutions legitimately take part in the national constitution-making procedure. After the adoption of a constitution, international courts as decision-makers may legitimately review the process of national constitution-making and constitutional norms on the basis of universal human rights and constitutional standards.

1. Types of constitutional regime change

Revolutionary forms

One of the contemporary normative meanings of the revolution goes back to Condorcet, the French philosopher and advocate of human rights and constitutionalism. He argued famously that revolution—radical, quick, progressive, often violent regime change—aims at freedom. It thus presupposes the existence of despotism.[1] In other words, it can be applied only to revolts that are aimed at replacing an illegitimate regime with a normatively right political system. Revolutionaries believe that in the age of revolution the spirit of liberty flames in the hearts of men and women. Revolutions are of course empirical phenomena. Bringing together political and legal definitions, in a broader sense we can speak of revolution when empirical legitimacy is in crisis, legality is ruptured, and there is open struggle of two or more political forces to establish a new sovereignty, in other words a new foundation for both legality and legitimacy.[2]

Classical theories on "organ" rather than state sovereignty from Sieyès to Schmitt have implied a strong link between the constituent power and the organ of the state in which the powers of sovereignty were concentrated.[3] Representative bodies stood at the heart of the classical American and French types of revolutionary constitution-making. In the path of the American Revolution, Hannah Arendt contested the link between constituent power and the sovereign representative body, but could only do so for a revolutionary society that was already constituted in the form of small republics that wished to federate.[4]

In the Arab world, but not only there, revolutions have returned in a dramatic manner. The same is true, though less obviously, for the specifically revolutionary method of constitution-making: a relatively quick, basically one-stage process dominated by constituent assemblies. This form of the "constituent power" has also returned in some settings where the process, missing the stage of liberation, differed from classical revolutions, in particular the Andean republics of Latin America. Hannah Arendt, however, considered revolutionary origins, though necessary, to be a hardly sufficient condition for the creation of fully legitimate constitutions. It is also true that she hoped to tame revolutions by postulating constitution as the necessary second stage, after liberation, of a successful revolutionary process. Yet she was quite aware in 1962 when *On Revolution* was written that such domestication was rarely successful. Thus, she was forced to operate with the dichotomy of failed (including permanent) revolutions and American exceptionalism.

Revolutions, of course, have been strongly disputed before. Plenty of empirical evidence from the last three centuries demonstrates the dangerous outcomes of revolutionary ruptures. T.G. Ash, naming the guillotine as the totem of 1789-type revolution, recalls that classical-type revolutions often culminate in terror.[5] Revolutionaries to whom a given revolution or a given type did not or cannot go far enough have also seriously criticized revolutions. Such was the oft-repeated critique by Marx of the merely political or bourgeois revolutions. Note that he did not criticize substitution of part for whole as such, but only when the part is neither truly universal in its interests nor radical in its needs. Similarly, Trotsky's critique of "the revolution betrayed" or "the unfinished revolution," typical of the revolutionary critique of revolutions, no longer criticized Leninist substitution, but only its bureaucratic deformation that in 1905 he thought inevitable, assuming the Bolshevik model. In a sense the self-critique of revolution was more radical in the French revolution, when representative democracy and later the Jacobin dictatorship were attacked in the name of direct grass-roots forms. But even these conceptions of the Enragés and the Hébertistes, like those of the radical groups of the English Revolution before them, did not challenge sovereign embodiment itself but only the instance that claimed it, whether the Legislative Assembly, the Convention or Parliament. Neither the issue of political plurality nor that of genuine legality ever came up especially as constraints of the radical groups themselves.[6]

Non-revolutionary forms

From the outset, the revolutionary paradigm faced rival conceptions and constitutional developments, notably in England, where a set of written and unwritten constitutional norms derived from judicial precedents, parliamentary statutes and constitutional customs have been substituting the American type charter constitution adopted by a constitution-making assembly.[7] Famously, the concept of revolution found its place in English constitutional tradition as a *restoration* of monarchial power in its corrected shape during the "Glorious Revolution" rather than a demand for a written constitutional foundation of government raised by the Levellers, or Cromwell's Protectorate set up by a charter called "Instrument of Government."[8]

Many new constitutions since then have been made through a variety of non-revolutionary processes. As the examples of Belgium, Switzerland and other democratic countries show, an old-fashioned but democratic constitution can be plainly replaced by a new one in a *reformatory process* of legitimate constitutional bodies.[9]

Following the Spanish and Portuguese experiences, the peaceful, negotiated regime changes in East Central Europe established a new model of *post-revolutionary* constitution-making. The historical turning point for the transformation from authoritarian regime to democracy was 1989. With the exception of only Romania, the dismantling of the communist regimes proceeded peacefully, involving at some point roundtable negotiations between delegates of the state party and those of the opposition-in-the-making. These developments are labeled "coordinated transition."[10] Moreover, the dissolution of the federal state of Czechoslovakia and the establishment of the separate Czech and Slovak Republics in 1993 is often referred to as the "Velvet Divorce," a reference to the term "Velvet Revolution" that was used internationally to describe the 1989 transformation.[11] These classifications express that the Central European single-party systems did not collapse due to a classical revolution, but through negotiations and compromises between the old regime and the democratic opposition. However, the political transition did result in revolutionary changes in the political and constitutional system and did so without a revolution as such.[12]

In what follows, we now identify the main components of the post-revolutionary alternative in democratic constitution-making, and compare it to the logic of revolution. After the experience of Spain, East-Central Europe and South Africa we are able to speak of both non-revolutionary forms of regime change and post-revolutionary forms of democratic constitution-making.[13]

First and foremost in a post-revolution, no group, no institution nor leader is in the position, as in the constructive phase of all revolutions, to claim the right to speak for the people as a whole. If such a claim is nevertheless made, the institutional structure of the post-revolution helps to defeat it without the kind of open and violent struggle over the embodiment of the sovereign characteristic of many revolutions. The central institution of post-revolution is the roundtable, but, unlike constituent assemblies of the classical type in most revolutions, it does not claim sovereignty, and frankly admits its own legitimation problems. Its form of representation is plural and accountable, rather than the absolute and unitary representation of revolutions.

Second, the initial rules of transition are negotiated, rather than imposed. These rules are generally incorporated in a kind of interim constitution. Thus, while revolution tends to produce one constitution, post-revolution produces two: an interim and a final constitution.

Third, parties or at least individuals who have participated in the old regime, are part of the negotiations, rather than the object of a new exclusion. Thus, previous friend and enemy relations are converted into those of political opponents.

Fourth, the public sphere and public discussion participate in the process autonomously and in plural forms, rather than as unitary opinion mobilized from above.

Fifth, there may be legal continuity, but if that is impossible the process is quickly brought under rules of law. In revolutions, the will of an assembly or the prerogative of the executive dominates, at least provisionally. Or, while the legality of revolution is based on the principle that the will of the revolutionary agency is law, post-revolution is legal in the more demanding sense that its provisional government itself is under the rule of law.

Sixth, whereas in revolutionary governments there is in general no separation of powers, in post-revolution a constitutional court is established that controls the acts of the provisional government, and, in South Africa at least, even the output of the constitutional assembly.

Finally, revolutionary constitution-making is relatively fast, and imposition is rarely time consuming.[14] Post-revolutionary process is slow, not only because consensus takes more time than imposition, but also because of the very character of a multi-stage process. As we found out in the externally imposed revolution in Iraq, even the acceleration of one stage, in that case the last one, on American wishes, can have disastrous consequences.[15] Conversely, the South African process took six years or more, with the last stage, the Constitutional Assembly, taking almost two years. In Iraq the last drafting stage took a mere three months. While a multi-stage process was adopted in that country, its first stage was exclusionary, due to American wishes, and the last stage even more so because of the pressure of time. Similarly, the Egyptian 2012 process lasted eight months, with the second constituent assembly deliberating for only five before a constitution was voted on in a referendum. In contrast, the Tunisian constituent assembly worked for almost two and a half years before recently enacting the new constitution. The pluralistic Colombian assembly deliberated and drafted for one year, as against the Venezuelan assembly with its immense Chavista majority, that did its job in five months. As these examples show, learning from the way time was used in the post-revolutionary paradigm can be highly significant in revolutions too, and also where quasi-revolutionary constituent assemblies are used.

Originally, this concept of post-revolutionary constitution-making implied only going beyond "organ" sovereignty in the sense of the German Staatslehre of the late 19th century and the French public law of the early 20th.[16] Yet the normative link between democratic forms of constitution-making and revolution, deeply embedded in the notion of the constituent power of the people, has survived in both political and legal theory.

The question remains whether revolutions can be banished by mere normative critique or even by the existence of other alternatives of radical transformation.

2. The power of procedural legitimacy

Many theoretical considerations presuppose that constitutions can be divided into procedural and substantive domains. Fundamental rights belong to the *substantive* field, while the rules of the authority and powers of governmental branches belong to the *procedural* area. Herbert Hart argued that a written constitution restricts the competence of the legislature by specifying the form and manner of legislation (limitations of procedure) and by excluding certain matters from the scope of its competence (limitations of substance).[17] John Rawls went further when he asserted that, ideally, "a just constitution would be a just procedure arranged to insure a just outcome."[18] Framed by Rawlsian ideas, Ronald Dworkin's theory distinguishes the constitutional clauses protecting substantive individual rights from a great many instrumental norms. The former are drafted in the language of abstract moral principle, the latter are neither particularly abstract nor written in moral language.[19]

The procedure-substance split may have implications in *constitution-making*. The linkage between process and outcome that is often contested today used to be commonplace. The classical figure of the lawgiver indicates two dimensions to such linkage: the likelihood that knowledge and impartiality produce more legitimate outcomes. It was not only the wisdom of this figure, but even more his disinterested perspective that was to guarantee the substantively excellent as well as legitimate result. In different ways, the mythical narratives of Moses, Lycurgus and Solon all ensure that the lawgiver, as Rousseau insisted, receive no office nor position in the state. Of course, the requirements guaranteeing knowledge and impartiality are and have always been difficult to adhere to.

There are two ways of replacing both procedural requirements. One of them is *imputation* from the result. The approach through imputation recommends that the relevant issue is not how a constitution was actually made, probably through acts of extra-legal violence, but whether a constitution has such a content that it could have been produced by a wise and impartial legislator, or under Rawls' veil of ignorance.

Many writers are oriented to the result rather than the process of constitution-making. The pragmatic idea that result excuses deficient process was promoted by Machiavelli in the case of Romulus, and by Madison for the Philadelphia Convention. It seemed to be confirmed by authoritarian states that imposed rule of law constitutions throughout the 19th century. Even the current Constitution of Japan was adopted under illegitimate circumstances: US army officers with law degrees drafted the text, and General MacArthur imposed it on the reluctant government of the emperor. Today, of course, imposed models are much less in fashion. Yet there are even social scientific attempts relying on a large number of cases trying to show that neither stability nor quality of constitutions can be correlated with any particular process of their making. This view, mostly directed against participatory models, opens the door to imposition and to the intellectual legitimation of deficient process. The conclusion many draw is that process does not matter as long as the result is well designed.

However, orientation to result in general, and the argument from imputation in particular, is unconvincing. The argument that a constitution is such that it could have been the act of an ideal agency carries little weight where political actors know full well that the makers were self-interested actors seeking incumbent advantages. Imputation of this type tends to work only with the passing of a significant period of time, when the legitimacy of the constitution is produced through its interpretation and enforcement. Imputation works only if one has in mind a constitution made hundreds of years before, with origins shrouded by the myth of founding fathers. Yet even the US Constitution's legitimacy was initially in a great deal of doubt, and started to emerge, as scholars have shown, only with the culmination of the process, the making of the first ten amendments, the Bill of Rights.

Claiming that process matters in constitution-making, we offer another way to replace mythical or purely hypothetical prerequisites for procedure: seeking *functional equivalents*. It seems plausible that a post-revolutionary complex is in general legitimated in terms of plurality of principles that can be interpreted in Weber's sociological or *empirical* conception of legitimacy, but can also be justified on more demanding Rawlsian *normative* level.

Empirical facts cannot rigorously prove that, of the world's hundreds of constitutions since the 18th century, those that have been produced in more legitimate ways (however that is defined) led to more stability and better outcomes than those that have been imposed by force.[20] What is more, there are many constitutions that can become legitimate in the long run, disregarding how they are made. The Japanese Constitution is a good case in point, and so are those of Norway and the Fifth Republic of France.

However, recent experience, whether in Hungary or Egypt, Colombia or Tunisia seems to tell us and future actors that regardless what they put in constitutions, *how* they go about doing so can delegitimize even largely acceptable outcomes, as well as legitimate others that may in many ways remain imperfect.

Empirically we have seen that plurality of inclusion, mutual recognition by former enemies, bargaining under consensual rules, openness to publics, legality in the sense of rule-of-law-governed process, and free and competitive elections under fair rules midway in the process all play an important role in gaining the acceptance of most political forces and mass constituencies. As a matter of prudential judgment at the very least, actors involved in constitution-making should aim to make not only the result but also the process legitimate. They should not delude themselves with the idea that in the long run their constitution may acquire legitimacy, because the long run may never come, as it did not come in Egypt's effort in 2012.

The approach of seeking functional equivalents thus continues to focus on process, and seeks to demonstrate its consequences for the result. It may involve many devices: from the nonre-electability of members of the constitution-making body, to institutionalized roles for public discussion as well as inclusive and highly pluralistic negotiating frameworks, before there are free elections. In the case of each substitute, the idea is to break the link between incumbency and outcome, to make it likely that no actor is in the position to determine their precise future advantage under the constitution to be negotiated.

This apparently eclectic group of principles can be justified normatively. The principle of the rule of law, powerful as it is, arguably does not alone suffice, nor does it allow us to distinguish post-revolution from system-preserving reform. But more normative principles are available. Pluralistic inclusion and consensual or at least compromise-based decision-making can be interpreted as empirical forms of functional equivalents of the Rawlsian veil of ignorance. With a large number of negotiating actors, and consensual rules, the likelihood is that no one can control the process in terms of foresight, especially given the absence of previous free elections, nor predict the power distribution afterwards. This idea has more recently given rise to the "insurance model" of Thomas Ginsburg.[21]

Derrida's idea of the gift makes it possible for formerly dominated groups to accept their enemies as opponents. And we can adopt Claude Lefort's idea that democracy should be defined not in terms of elections, but more fundamentally in terms of opening up the space of power and allowing no one to reoccupy it.[22] The post-revolutionary model can be linked exactly to this concept of democracy, which is not far from the famous partnership concept from Dworkin.[23]

The involvement of the public sphere throughout the process and elections midway through the process remain important, however, if the empty space is to be kept open by an inclusive, public political process and not merely by competing elites as in some versions of polyarchy and elite pluralism. This stress on the public sphere is the Arendtian and Habermasian dimensions of the justification complex.

In sum, not only the substance of a constitution, but also constitution-making procedure can be analyzed in accordance with the concepts of empirical and normative legitimacy. Post-revolutionary constitution-making can represent real forms of normatively legitimate procedures instead of speculative standards. But how can we adapt apparently diffuse normative features to claims of procedural legitimacy? The Rawlsian notion of the hypothetical consent or consent under the veil of ignorance as the basis of legitimate constitution is not a convincing argument for two reasons: first, supposed consent is no consent at all, and second, in reality people do not consent to their constitution.

The idea of procedural justice in constitution-making nevertheless still stands. The independent criteria for the just (right, fair) result of constitution-making are the substantive normative principles of constitutionalism. These substantive standards can be defined separately from the constitution-making procedure, which is to be followed. Therefore *pure procedural justice* in Rawlsian terms does not apply because the result of constitution-making, namely the written text of the constitution, is not justified solely because it is reached by following a fair procedure.

What is more, although there are independent criteria for deciding which outcome is just, that is to say, whether a constitutional text is more or less correct, there is no feasible procedure that is sure to lead to it. Rawls calls this *imperfect* procedural justice because it is possible to devise a procedure that is sure to give the desired outcome.[24] In short, since there is no scheme of constitution-making rules that guarantees just constitutional legislation, the best attainable scheme is one of imperfect procedural justice.

This argument may lead one to the conclusion that procedural norms embody instrumental values, while just outcomes (substantive norms) are intrinsic values. We argue here, however, that a constitution is a coherent legal text that embodies political morality. The principles, institutions and procedures of a constitution are designed to unite a community of free and equal persons. Since the substantive and procedural norms of the constitution both embody integrated political values, or serve such values, there is no clear borderline between procedural and substantive constitutional norms. Moral considerations may apply to procedural norms too.[25]

Our fundamental claim is thus that process matters in constitution-making. The revolutionary constitution-making process remains highly problematic from the point of view of the legitimacy of the constitution, as well as from the perspective of the legitimacy of constitution-making. The introduction of procedural norms such as inclusion, consensus, legality and public involvement of post-revolution can actually influence the process of contemporary revolutions in a positive sense, as in Tunisia (2011–2014) and Colombia (1991), but it can also lead to its crisis with uncertain (possibly: counter-revolutionary) outcomes, as in the cases of Egypt and Venezuela. Constitutionalism is not only the intended result, but is applied to the actual process of constitution-making. Such is the function, once again, of different actors and interim constitutions in post-revolutionary constitutional regime changes.

3. Domestic actors

Although revolutions will continue to take place in the future, learning from the lessons of post-revolutionary constitution-making can greatly help in solving the problem of imperfect procedural legitimacy. In the multi-stage roundtable-led paradigm that dominated the early 1990s, there was no longer a need for preexisting republics to deconstruct the sovereign embodied in a single organ. Democratic constitutions could now be seen as products of many internal and external actors, acting through multiple procedures and stages, thus over a significant length of time. Undoubtedly, even the making of the US Federal Constitution could also be retrospectively reconceptualized in similar terms.

Plurality of political players

Post-revolution, in terms of the totality of its components, is admittedly path-dependent, applying to the transition from dictatorships to a freer political form. Moreover, it presupposes a relatively equal balance of forces, or at least that things should appear so to the major contending forces in a society.

Without doubt, the negotiations during the East-Central European post-revolutionary transformation were processes led not by the common interests of the parties, but by a clash of values and interests, in which both parties, the Communists and the democratic movements, were compelled to make compromises. The demand to reach compromises can thus be seen as one of the underlying characteristics of peaceful transitions.

The roundtables did not, however, actually have a mandate for constitution-making. They had no formal authorization to make law for the old regime. Nor did they have popular authorization to make law for the new regime. János Kis argues that the roundtables understood their task to be limited to facilitating the run-up to free, competitive elections, and were determined to leave an elected assembly to give a constitution to the new regime. For their decisions to come into legal effect, those decisions must have been sent for enactment to the old legislature. And so the agreements were meant to regulate the transition from the old regime to a new one. Consequently, the roundtables were exceptional bodies having the capacity to start a coordinated process of constitutional change but leaving the completion of the process to an assembly with the democratic mandate that they were lacking.[26]

We should make no mistake about it, where the elite of an old regime is strong and secure enough, it will most likely choose a path of quasi-reform seeking so that things in reality can remain the same. Similarly, where a revolutionary elite is capable of overthrowing an old regime and occupying the space of power, it will generally try to do so. Finally, it is possible that disagreements between relatively equal sides will be so deep that no compromise seems possible, and if there is an attempt to produce a complete interim constitution, or especially a permanent one, negotiations will fail totally. Yet none of these important considerations need condemn the new model to irrelevance whenever its exacting demanding preconditions are not available. Both the norms that its protagonists rely on and some of the devices they have introduced may become relevant, even in revolutions. And even in the case of continued fundamental disagreement on some issues, constitutions can be agreed upon.

We also know the problem of disagreement from Indian history. There, elections in 1946, still under colonial rule but with the British departure on the agenda, led to the overwhelming victory of just two parties, Congress and the Muslim League, parties that were unable to agree about the nature of the state despite several rounds of negotiation.[27] These parties were subsequently unable to function within the framework of a single constituent assembly. Negotiations before elections, including many more actors who were still on the scene, could have perhaps led to a different result. So they would have more time, which could have made the parties realize the consequences of their choices, namely three, eventually four partitions, rather than only one, with disastrous consequences.

In Iraq, too, elections occurred before inclusion, but here the Americans chose a different strategy than the British in India, and tried to subsequently include the excluded, the Sunni, by co-option. When at an earlier time the Americans created a Governing Council by co-option, such a move could have worked. But after the elections the legitimacy gap between elected representatives and ones "imposed" by the Americans was huge. In the end the Shi'ite and Kurdish leaders just made a deal among themselves, and told the Sunnis they must take it or leave it. Though the constitution was narrowly ratified, a tremendous intensification of the civil war was the short-term result.

Constitution-making assemblies

The conventional problem is how to create constitutionalism constitutionally when there is none before. How to begin democracy democratically? Because authoritarian regimes typically rely on paper constitutions based on at least a fiction of the rule of law, transforming those constitutions via their own amendment rules into genuine constitutions is actually possible. Even if the constitution is authoritarian, its amendment rule may allow it to be changed and even democratized. That is part of the answer concerning democratic beginning, namely relying on existing democratic fictions.

While it is not possible to have elections determining the initial rules of elections, thus a purely electoral beginning is impossible, it is possible to empty the space of power without reoccupying it. While such a move in itself produces only a polyarchy, rather than democracy in Dahl's terms, even an incomplete democracy should have the mechanisms to produce free and fair elections before elections. That mechanism is precisely the inclusive negotiated process, supervised by the public sphere.

This constitution-making profile of the paradigmatic East-Central European post-revolutionary transformation consists of two stages. In the first stage, a roundtable agreement determines the ground rules of preparing and holding free elections. The second stage takes place when a body of freely elected representatives adopts, in the sovereign people's name, a new constitution. In this way the coordinated transition constitutes an interruption of empirical legitimacy of the authoritarian regime, but a continuity of legality.[28]

In the aftermath of the Polish Roundtable Agreement, the old constitution was amended in April 1989, and the first democratic parliament then reshaped the relations between the legislative and executive branches of the state ("Small Constitution"). The reformed constitution was finally replaced in 1997 by a completely new constitution for Poland. The old constitution of Czechoslovakia was also amended in 1989. The Charter of Fundamental Rights and Basic Freedoms was incorporated in 1991. After the dissolution of the federal state, the Czech Republic and the Slovak Republic adopted a new constitution in 1992. In Bulgaria and Romania, the second step was made in 1991. By contrast, Hungary was the only nation that did not adopt an entirely new constitution after the fall of Communism. It is true, however, that Hungary has been a constitutional democracy since 1989. Like other countries in the region, the peaceful, coordinated political transition resulted in revolutionary outcomes: democratic institutions replaced an authoritarian regime; pluralist society replaced the dominance of communist ideology.

The Arab Spring and Latin America provide significant contrasts between procedures and outcomes. In Tunisia a constitutional assembly has completed its work producing a document that most sides declared as a very acceptable "second best." Such an outcome does not emerge from nothing. The constitutional assembly, as it has been often noted, could only operate on the basis of a coalition, since no party, not even the leading Ennahda, had a majority. It is less often realized that the assembly was a product of a relatively proportional electoral rule, and it is almost never noticed that the electoral rule was itself a product of inclusive participation and negotiation in the Ben Achour commission of 2011.[29] In Colombia two decades earlier, the initiative for a constitutional assembly outside the legal rules of change came from a highly public student movement organizing an informal referendum. Nevertheless, the rules of transition, including the highly and unusually proportional electoral rule, were negotiated by President Gaviria with all the main political parties.[30] The outcome was a genuinely pluralistic assembly that stayed within its rules in spite of having been declared "sovereign" by the Supreme Court, and wound up producing a constitutionalist constitution that has functioned in an impressive manner for 20 years or more.

The contrast with Egypt and Venezuela is also impressive. Without going into detail, in the earlier and extremely well-documented case of Venezuela, in 1999, the rules of transition were established from above, by the presidency. The electoral rule hidden in a referendum, and its manipulation by the president, wound up producing a wildly disproportionate assembly that moved on to capture the plenitude of powers formally for itself but in reality for the chief executive. As a very predictable result a hyper-presidentialist constitution was produced. Venezuela has since moved from one constitutional crisis to another.

Egypt's almost classical revolution is the much more interesting case, with so far even worse results. Here, in a genuinely popular uprising, the Supreme Command of the Armed Forces, the SCAF, was able to grab governmental power relatively early. All interim rules and constitutional arrangements were declared unilaterally by the SCAF, and if there were any consultations they were on a very narrow basis that included at times the Muslim Brotherhood, but not the new grassroots activists who were the main subjects of the uprising. These activists demanded a delay of elections, and the prior formulation of a constitution that would make these genuinely free and competitive. They were disregarded. The end results were rules that helped to produce two decisive victories in very early parliamentary and presidential elections for the Muslim Brotherhood: aside from the military, the only truly organized political force. The Egyptian electoral rule was not much more disproportional than the one in Tunisia, but it appeared so, given the way it was made and the fact that it benefited just one party rather than several. Moreover, the initially imposed rules for forming a constituent assembly allowed the parliamentary majority to construct a majoritarian body. When this led to a conflict both with the activists and the courts, the latter dissolving parliament and one but not both of its constituent assemblies, the newly elected MB president declared by decree the constitutional process to be free from further judicial interference. A new constitution was enacted, and lasted for six or so months. It was then brought down by the largest popular mobilization yet, and another military intervention leading to the imposition of a series of highly repressive policies, including the enactment of a second constitution by a group chosen by the military leadership alone. Neither of the two ratificatory referenda in 2012 and 2013 were fair, since the voters only had the choice of agreement or the continuation of emergency government, first Morsi's, and then the SCAF's. In the end, the introduction of the norms of inclusion and consensus only disorganized the process, but failed to improve it.

Direct participation

Although modern constitutionalism is seen as representative government based on a limiting constitution created by a representative assembly, participatory democracy also has its roots and role in constitutionalism. Enumerating constitution-making actors may lead back to the old questions about the priority of representative versus direct democracy, and popular versus parliamentary sovereignty.

According to the democratic participatory idea popular in many parts of the world, it is the task of "the people themselves" to create their own constitutions in highly participant forms, "from below." This approach dates back to the writings of Thomas Paine and Sieyès, but was already cast into doubt by Madison in *Federalist 40*. To avoid getting lost in this jungle, it is worth recalling that the USA federal constitution-making process had an important feature of popular participation but not decision-making. Since Article VII of the constitution provided that it should enter into effect when ratified by the popularly elected conventions of at least nine states (two-thirds), the opposing parties were engaged in fruitful debates in town halls and in the press. Famously, the one-time debate upon clause by clause between the *Federalists* and *Antifederalists* may remind us that the country's electorate should be involved, convinced, and finally, in favor of the new constitutional architecture.[31]

Although the flawless sociological identification of the relevant agency, the people as the constituent power, is nearly impossible, it seems equally unjustified to escape reliance on this hypothetical construct. Thus, to avoid fateful circularity it is necessary for the conception to suffer from a *pars pro toto* logic that necessarily involves the substitution of a segment of the people for the whole. The step between a model of the constituent power, based on popular sovereignty, and what Carl Schmitt called sovereign dictatorship is, as he knew, a small one.

Beyond comprehensive normative and sociological difficulties, democratic constitution-making "from below" seems troublesome nowadays too. Financial and social crises have bolstered not only anti-elite populism but also anti-democratic sentiments. There is a global trend for populist leaders to exploit popular emotions; and it is also the case in many states that the general public is systematically manipulated by the government. Only authoritarian heads of state have the power to react to the "people's voice," and adopt new constitutional norms by gaining formal consent from manipulated citizens via unfair popular vote.

From Albania to Taiwan many democratic constitutions require public referendums to approve amendments, and constitutions were adopted as a result of a ratification by referendum. Sociological facts, however, warn that a referendum, far from lending sociological legitimacy to the new constitution, may simply reveal that the nation is deeply divided. The 1997 constitutional referendum in Poland, for example, resulted both a relatively low turnout (43%) and a marginal approval rate (53.5% voting in favor, 46.5% against). Additionally, the famous 2010–2013 case of Iceland shows how difficult it is to complete an inclusive, transparent constitution-making procedure, using new participatory methods but lacking cooperation and compromise in parliament, even in a country of hardly 300,000 inhabitants. Although various forms of pioneering assemblies were established, such as the almost randomly selected, demographically representative National Forum and the Drafting Assembly of gender-balanced, elected delegates, and a non-binding referendum was held, as well as unprecedented transparency being provided by social media and online streaming, the mission remained incomplete due to deep political disagreements and an attempt to bypass common representative organs.

In sum, on the one hand, parliament or another representative form of constitution-making assembly no longer has the absolute privilege of adopting a new constitution; yet on the other, the "people" as an entity cannot take over this task. Public involvement in the process, however, is not only a visible empirical trend but also a justifiable normative claim. As we have argued, procedural principles (inclusivity, transparency, free and fair deliberation, etc.) support the claim that sociological legitimacy may be enhanced if those people who are subjects of the same legal system have *a* say, but not the final say.

Constitutional courts

In post-revolution, constitutional courts are established that control the process in transition from authoritarianism to democracy, as well as the acts of the provisional governments. As a result of two-stage constitutional transformations, the constitutions of the new democracies contain enforceable legal provisions rather than a collection of mere good wishes. The purpose of constitutions is seen as limiting the authority of state power. From Spain to South Africa, constitutional courts—or in Poland, the Tribunal—have been considered to be the safeguards of fundamental rights and institutional guarantees of the separation of powers. Judicial protection of the constitution in all European post-revolutionary countries is closer to the centralized German model than to the diffuse US judicial review.[32] (With one exception: after the transition, Estonia—following the Scandinavian model—set up a constitutional review chamber in its Supreme Court.) The counter-majoritarian activity, indeed time-to-time zealotry, of the constitutional courts in issues of transitory justice as well as hard cases of constitutional justice is well known. The Hungarian Constitutional Court called the radical constitutional transformation respecting the procedural and substantive principles of legality "a revolution under the rule of law."[33]

The role of supreme or constitutional courts in South American and African transformations is also significant. In Colombia and Venezuela they have acted in a permissive manner, and when the Court in Venezuela finally did not, it was packed and sidelined by the presidency. In Egypt the courts attempted to restrain political imposition and force the creation of various consensual schemes, but they failed. Nevertheless, such a role for courts, which has been identified as an aspect of the "new constitutionalism" by Said Arjomand and others, is extremely unusual in a revolutionary constituent process. Whether permissive or not, the intervention of a mere constitué in the constituent implies the need to legitimate the very process of constitution-making as legal. Given that aspiration, in at least three countries, it is striking that in Venezuela and Egypt legality was repeatedly ruptured, or the rule of law was replaced by executive prerogative. In Egypt the various declarations of the SCAF and of President Morsi implied that the only law is the will of the one who embodies the sovereign. The same was true, technically, in the case of the Venezuelan Constituent Assembly that abrogated the powers of Congress, in spite of a Supreme Court decision that refused to recognize the assembly's claim of sovereignty, of the exercise of the "original constituent power."

The subversion of legality in two of the four cases does not, however, indicate the irrelevance of post-revolutionary normative criteria in contemporary revolutions. There was in fact a veritable contest (Wettkampf), as Schmitt might have noted, in Venezuela and Egypt between institutions representing legality, and those relying on will or prerogative. It was not predetermined that legality would lose, as he believed. In Colombia, where legality won, it was probably because of a combination of consensual beginning and strategic self-limitation by the Supreme Court. In Tunisia, where constitutional jurisprudence was extremely weak before the revolution, a constitutional court was first established by the Constituent Assembly in the new 2014 Constitution (articles 115–121). Legality was, however, never seriously challenged or broken during the process, and in any case given the plural assembly no one was in position to usurp the power to violate the rules of transition agreed upon. This example shows that strong participation by a court is not a necessary, but at best a desirable condition of enforcing legality in radical change. At the same time, over-reach by a court seems to lead to its defeat, with damaging consequences for both legality and its legitimating role. When that happens, as the Egyptian case showed, not only the judicial institutions but also their executive antagonist can turn out to be losers.

What is more, if the standard activity of constitutional courts constitutes "counter-majoritarian difficulty," their demands for review of constitutional amendments are more controversial. A famous case from a transitory country shows this: according to the interim constitution of South Africa, the Constitutional Court had the duty to review the output of the constitutional assembly. Although a few courts have a similar, clearly expressed constitutional authority to safeguard the integrity of the constitution from substantially unconstitutional amendments and/or unconstitutional amending procedures, several have adopted this doctrine by referring to "eternal clauses" (Germany) or the "basic structure" (India) of the existing constitution. Some post-revolutionary courts are entitled to examine amendments prior to adoption by representative assembly (Moldova, Ukraine), while others may act following it (Colombia). Taking the recent but differing examples of Georgia, Hungary, Poland and Turkey, the limits of the ultimate competence were tested when constitutions and their courts were under attack. Consequently, constitutional or other apex courts in many countries are or can be veto players in the constitution-making procedure.

4. International actors

The US constitution-making process initially involved a plurality of sovereign states that made the formation of the Federal Union not merely a domestic matter, but also an act of treaty-making under customary international law. This dimension can be neglected in the cases that inspired the post-sovereign paradigm, because within already established states there was initially no reason to dethrone state sovereignty along with the one embodied in an organ. Indeed, international law today insists that constitution-making is a purely domestic matter. That insistence, as old as Vatel, may now be in part obsolete and myopic. We can no longer neglect another group of constitution-making experiments from Namibia to East Timor, and from Bosnia to Afghanistan where there was a significant international role, and where state sovereignty itself had to be constituted in the first place under the guidance of other sovereigns. Unfortunately, in spite of the high prestige of the South African case, we cannot at all assume that the relevant international agents have learned the lessons of the post-sovereign paradigm of the 1990s.

Given the American and international role in Iraq, this case also cannot be treated as no more than an instance of domestic though pathological post-sovereign constitution-making, grafted onto what was, legally speaking, a revolution. With Iraq we can recognize that revolutions can be imposed externally, when the preconditions of a Spanish, Polish or South African type of process are absent. Nevertheless, the Iraqi process, deficient as it was, reveals that elements of the new post-revolutionary paradigm could be adopted even in the midst of revolutions. Whether this happens or not depends at the very least on the international dissemination of the new principles of constitution-making, and possibly on the role of powerful international actors that have come to understand the significance of these principles for subsequent constitutional legitimacy.[34]

International institutions and human rights norms may provide other kinds of apparatus for peaceful constitutional resolution too. After nearly 30 years of severe conflict between Roman Catholics, Protestants and British police, the *Northern Ireland Peace Agreement* (or Good Friday Agreement), reached in multi-party talks between the UK government, the Republic of Ireland and political parties of Northern Ireland, resulted in constitutional changes in the UK. Subsequently, the Republic of Ireland also modified its constitution, removing territorial claims to the whole geographical landmass of Ireland. As a novel development, the Agreement considers the ECHR to be a cornerstone of peaceful coexistence. In order to ensure the rights of people in Northern Ireland equally, regardless of their religious or political views, the Agreement states that "the British Government will complete incorporation into Northern Ireland law of the ECHR, with direct access to the courts, and remedies for breach of the ECHR, including power for the courts to overrule Assembly legislation on grounds of inconsistency."[35]

Yes, foreign states or international instances can and almost always do play a role in state formation, as in Namibia, Cambodia, East Timor, the Balkans and Afghanistan. They can also dramatically fail, as did the British Cabinet Mission Plan in India in 1946, leading to partition and autochthonous constitution-making in two territorial states in forms no one initially intended, with countless attendant disasters. But in either case we should ask Rousseau's question concerning such efforts, namely, "What can make it legitimate?" Today it is possible to refer to the Hague and Geneva conventions and the UN charter, which certainly allow peace-making by states and the international community even if they involve territorial changes, including sometimes secession, though not in general annexations. These same instruments deny, however, the right of a foreign state or even international representatives to dominate constitution-making. Even the American conquerors of Japan and Iraq tried to satisfy this principle, at least formally, though in the first case hypocritically.

Of course, for legitimacy one needs more than just a set of international norms, norms that are in reality difficult to enforce, among other things, because it is difficult to fully differentiate state and constitution-making. Yet not making that distinction contributed to the failure of the British Cabinet Mission Plan in India. The plan proposed not only a method of constitution-making, and the outlines of the territorial settlement, but also prejudged the result in a developed constitutional form that could satisfy neither the Muslim League nor Congress. As Granville Austin suggests, this was a task that no non-Indian should have attempted.

The two-stage process of the post-revolutionary paradigm can be an important help in the effort of at least partially differentiating state and constitution-making, meaning by the former the construction of the territory and sometimes the population of the state, and including in the latter the formation of a coercive organization. In the South African case, the territorial parameters of the new state, including federalism, were affirmed and entrenched as parts of the judicable constitutional principles. In Iraq, too, this happened in a weaker form, with American and international authorities participating. But here, unfortunately, the territorial principles were not fully entrenched against changes by the constitutional assembly. It was this issue that led to the later exclusion of Sunni representatives, though they had initially been included. In any case, after the American role in making the interim constitution, the final one was largely made by Iraqi actors, with US and UN pressure on very few points. Unlike in Germany in 1948, on issues concerning state structure there was no external input.[36] The differentiation between two stages in both South Africa and Iraq did allow a (partial) separation of the territorial dimension of state-making and constitution-making, but it was violated when the Iraqi Assembly radically changed the formula for region formation. In South Africa the terms of the original federal bargain were enforced by the new but certainly domestic Constitutional Court even against the constitutional assembly. The difference between these two deeply divided societies was striking, yet in neither one should we speak of an international *pouvoir constituant*, or an externally imposed final constitution, but only of an ultimately failed international role in territorial state-making in the Iraqi case.

The two distinctions, one between territorial state formation with a likely international role and constitution-making, and the other between power and legitimate authority, should be relevant also in revolutions in deeply divided societies. These distinctions could provide the key to the solution of the Ukrainian crisis. Very briefly, in Ukraine it is obviously very difficult to identify the subject of popular sovereignty, namely "the people." One can make the claim that "the people" is the grassroots movement identified as the Maidan, but one can also claim that the people are represented only through the results of that election, where parties representing the East have been victorious. The subject of democratic self-determination is moreover in doubt. Is it only the people of the whole of Ukraine, or do the people of specific regions also have the right to determine their territorial fate? In any case, there is a fundamental disagreement not only concerning the identity of the people, but the structure of the state in which its or their political capacities should be institutionalized. That disagreement can be solved in four obvious ways: imposition, civil war, secession/partition or negotiations. Obviously, negotiations are the preferable option, since imposition may lead to civil war, and possibly partition as in India and elsewhere. Moreover, partition or secession will repeat the same problems in two smaller-scale states.

International bodies as advisors

Prior to the adoption of a constitution, international advisory and monitoring bodies as deliberative institutions may legitimately take part in the constitution-making procedure.

Probably one of the most influential institutions is the Venice Commission, established at the time of the fall of the Berlin Wall to provide assistance for post-revolutionary constitutional transformations in East and Central Europe, currently counting 60 member states from Algeria to the Republic of Korea; even the Palestinian National Authority possesses a special cooperation status. Its opinions on draft legislations, most importantly on constitutional amendments and proposals of new constitutions, serve as clear guidance on the contemporary minimum standard of constitutionalism and rule of law. The customary law is that it is member states that request an opinion on their draft constitutions. In the event that a government fails to submit its draft law for examination, as it happened in the case of the 2011 Constitution of Hungary, leading institutions of the Council of Europe or certain international organizations can initiate procedure. Since the Venice Commission—and similarly, the OSCE, another relevant international institution devoted to democratization—adopts a nonbinding approach based on dialogue and discussions instead of imposing resolutions, open noncompliance is implausible and can hardly be reasoned.

As to the European Union, which developed from a narrow economic cooperation into a political and legal fusion of constitutional democracies, now characterized as a mixture of supranational and intergovernmental structures, Article 7 of the TEU aims at ensuring that all EU countries respect the common values of the EU, including the rule of law. The preventive mechanism allows the Council to give the EU country concerned a warning before a "serious breach" has actually materialized. The sanctioning mechanism allows the Council to suspend certain rights deriving from the application of the treaties to the EU country in question, including the voting rights of that country in the Council. In this case the "serious breach" must have persisted for some time. As a pre-Article 7 procedure, in 2014 the European Commission adopted a new Rule of Law Framework for addressing systematic threats in a member state. This mechanism is an "annual dialogue" between the national and supranational levels.

Not surprisingly, far-from-pro-European constitutional changes provoke extensive proceedings from supranational institutions. In the cases of Hungary and Poland, the list of contradictions is lengthy, from individual infringement procedures initiated by the European Commission and judged by the CJEU, as well as examinations of human rights violations by the ECtHR, to general assessments of the European Parliament and other political bodies. Although Hungarian national authorities have been inclined to be uncooperative on the merits, the general preventive mechanism of the EU has so far not been applied, as opposed to the case of Poland, where the European Commission has launched a dialogue on the Rule of Law Framework.[37]

After careful thought, taking advice or following recommendations from foreign scholars or international institutions is surely in the best interests of countries. *Pacta sunt servanda* may also require them to respect review procedures and comply with duties stemming from inter- or supranational norms. In this respect, the case of Rwanda, where foreigners were not allowed to participate in constitution-making processes, is unsatisfactory.[38] But our claim is stronger than that: No representative assembly and no government can plausibly refer to its people's or the country's sovereignty in order to exclude external influence, because universal or regional standards of constitutionalism and human rights are beyond the scope of popular or national sovereignty.

International courts

International courts as decision-makers may legitimately review national constitutional norms after the adoption of a constitution. A compelling phenomenon in contemporary international constitutional law is the review of state constitutions by the European Court of Human Rights. The ECtHR repeatedly points out that the European Convention on Human Rights makes no distinction as to the type of rule or measure concerned and does not exclude any part of the member states' jurisdiction from scrutiny under the Convention.[39] The political and institutional organization of the member states must respect the rights and principles enshrined in the Convention. It matters little in this context whether the provisions at issue are constitutional or merely legislative. From the moment that such provisions are the means by which the state concerned exercises its jurisdiction, they are subject to review under the Convention.[40]

The judgment of the ECtHR in the case of *Sejdić and Finci v. Bosnia and Herzegovina* serves as a leading precedent of this type. The Constitution of Bosnia and Herzegovina is an annex to the 1995 Dayton Agreement. Since it was part of a peace treaty after the Yugoslavian civil war, the constitution was drafted and adopted without the application of such procedures as could have provided democratic legitimacy. It constitutes a unique case of a constitution that was never officially published in the languages of the country concerned but was agreed and published in a foreign language, English. This is why we can call this an imposed constitution. In the preamble to the constitution, Bosniaks, Croats and Serbs are described as "constituent peoples." The ECtHR emphasized that at state level, power-sharing arrangements were introduced, making it impossible to adopt decisions against the will of the representatives of any "constituent people," including a bicameral system (with a House of Peoples composed of five Bosniaks and the same number of Croats from the Federation of Bosnia and Herzegovina and five Serbs from the Republika Srpska) as well as a collective presidency of three members, with a Bosniak and a Croat from the Federation of Bosnia and Herzegovina, and a Serb from the Republika Srpska. The applicants at the ECtHR described themselves as being of Roma and Jewish origin respectively. Since they did not declare affiliation with any of the "constituent peoples," they were ineligible to stand for election to the House of Peoples (the second chamber of the State Parliament) and the presidency (the collective Head of State). The ECtHR concluded that the constitutional provisions that render the applicants ineligible for elections to the presidency must be considered discriminatory and a breach of the ECHR.[41]

This principle was applied to the Irish constitution in the case of *A, B and C v. Ireland*.[42] The ECtHR concluded that constitutional protection of the absolute right to life of the unborn child can result in a violation of the right to life and health of a pregnant woman. Similarly, the court reviewed the constitutions of post-communist countries. In the case of *Alajos Kiss v. Hungary*,[43] the court argued that people with a mental disability belong to the constituent peoples, therefore general constitutional restriction of their voting rights is a violation of the ECHR.

Facing authoritarian constitutional regime change, recently the ECtHR tried to keep European minimum standards by repeating that even the constitutions of the member states should come into line with the Convention. In the case of *Magyar Keresztény Mennonita Egyház and Others v. Hungary*,[44] the ECtHR stated that the constitutional privileges of certain churches violate the freedom of religion and association of other religious communities who lost their legal status as a result of the constitutional changes. Similarly, in the case of *Baka v. Hungary,* the ECtHR ruled in favor of the former President of the Supreme Court, declaring that the constitutional termination of his mandate before it had expired was a violation of his freedom of speech.[45] More alarmingly, after the ECtHR concluded in the case of *Anchugov and Gladkov* that the general disenfranchisement of prisoners by the Russian Constitution is a violation of the Convention,[46] the Russian Constitutional Court claimed that the national constitution has supremacy, therefore Russian authorities may and should depart from the judgment of the ECtHR.[47]

Although the jurisdiction of the Court of Justice of the EU is obviously different from the ECtHR, it has also pointed out that supranational obligations, namely EU norms, apply to state constitutions. In the case of *European Commission v. Hungary*, the CJEU ruled that the abrupt termination of the Hungarian Data Protection Commissioner's term in office by the constitution creates an infringement of the independence of the Hungarian Data Protection Authority and is hence in breach of EU law.[48]

Again, the role of international courts in matters of domestic constitutions stems not only from the principle of international law that agreements should be kept, but also from the fact that human rights violations are outside the range of national sovereignty. As to international law and domestic constitutionalism, Kumm argues that national constitutional legitimacy depends on how the constitution is integrated into the wider legal world. States should incorporate global legitimacy conditions into their constitutional structures. They also have a duty to participate in the creation and sustainment of international legal systems.[49]

Concluding remarks

In conclusion, as we have shown, several constitutions were made during unfair procedure but in the long run have become legitimate. Moreover, there is no single scheme of constitution-making rules that is sure to lead to a legitimate constitution. As we have argued, however, even if procedural justice is imperfect, procedural legitimacy matters in constitution-making. Many examples of post-revolutionary constitution-making can reveal that the powers of sovereignty are not concentrated in a single representative organ of the state: rather, various domestic and international actors take part in constitution-making. Since universal or regional standards of constitutionalism and human rights are beyond the scope of popular or national sovereignty, international advisory and monitoring bodies as deliberative institutions, as well as international courts as decision-makers, may legitimately review national constitution-making procedures and norms.

Notes

1 "Condorcet, Influence of the American Constitution on Europe," in G. Ansart (ed.), *Writings on the United States* (Pennsylvania State University Press, 2012), 21–42.
2 See in detail, A. Arato, *Adventures of the Constituent Power* (Cambridge University Press, forthcoming).
3 C. Schmitt, *Verfassungslehre* (Duncker & Humblot, 1928), Chapters 7 and 29.
4 H. Arendt, *On Revolution* (Penguin Books, 1990).
5 T. G. Ash, "Velvet Revolution: The Prospects," *The New York Review of Books* 56 (2009): 20–23.
6 See in detail, A. Arato, *Adventures of the Constituent Power* (Cambridge University Press, forthcoming).
7 For a classical account, see A. V. Dicey, *Introduction to the Study of the Law of the Constitution*, R. E. Michener (ed.) (Liberty Fund, 1982).
8 In its original form, the term "revolution" was introduced by Copernicus to designate the recurring, cyclical movement of celestial bodies.
9 For a comparative account, see C. Klein and A. Sajó, "Constitution-Making as a Process," in M. Rosenfeld and A. Sajó (eds.), *The Oxford Handbook of Comparative Constitutional Law* (Oxford University Press, 2012), Chapter 20.
10 J. Kis, "Between Reform and Revolution: Three Hypotheses about the Nature of Regime Change," *Constellations*, I:3 (1995): 399–421.
11 But see the birth of the Czech Constitution from a critical point of view, P. Gümplova, "Democracy and the Politics in Extraordinary: The Constitutional Making in Czechoslovakia, 1992," available at www.newschool.edu/uploadedFiles/NSSR/Departments_and_Faculty/Political_Science/Recent_Placements/Gumplova-Democracy_Extraordinary.pdf?n=3438.
12 Recent cases of pre-Maidan Ukraine, Turkey, Hungary and Poland represent a different scenario, where we do not witness political transformation to, but *away from* constitutional democracy. The constitutional regimes of Janukovic, Erdogan, Orbán and Kaczyński were created for the sake of incumbent advantage only, rather than separating constitutional powers, granting human rights and embracing political competitors within an integrative constitutional framework.
13 See in detail, A. Arato, *Post Sovereign Constitutional Making: Learning and Legitimacy* (Oxford University Press, 2016).
14 See the largest, purely empirical study by Z. Elkins, T. Ginsburg and J. Melton, *The Endurance of Constitutions* (Cambridge University Press, 2009).
15 In details, see A. Arato, *Constitution Making Under Occupation* (Columbia University Press, 2009).
16 For a critical analysis of different constitutional traditions, see C. Möllers, "Pouvoir Constituant—Constitution—Constitutionalisation," in A. von Bogdandy and J. Bast (eds.), *Principles of European Constitutional Law* (Hart, 2006), 185–88.
17 H. L. A. Hart, *The Concept of Law* (Clarendon Press, 1994, second edn.), 68–69.
18 J. Rawls, *A Theory of Justice* (The Belknap Press of Harvard University Press, 1999, revised edn.), 173.
19 R. Dworkin, *Freedom's Law: The Moral Reading of the Constitution* (Oxford University Press, 2005), 1–37.

20 Thomas Ginsburg and his colleagues seem to have come to the conclusion after having examined and compared hundreds of cases that the method of constitution-making does not matter. T. Ginsburg, Z. Elkins and J. Blount, "Does the Process of Constitution-making Matter?" *Annual Review of Law and Social Science* 5 (2009).
21 T. Ginsburg, *Judicial Review in New Democracies: Constitutional Courts in Asian Cases* (Cambridge University Press, 2003).
22 C. Lefort, *Democracy and Political Theory* (Polity, 1999). See also, Arato (n. 13).
23 R. Dworkin, *Justice for Hedgehogs* (Harvard University Press, 2011), 358. See also an earlier explanation, R. Dworkin, "Introduction: The Moral Reading and the Majoritarian Premise," in *Freedom's Law*, 17.
24 J. Rawls, *A Theory of Justice* (The Belknap Press of Harvard University Press, 1999, revised edn.), 74–75.
25 From a rival perspective, see J. Elster, "Deliberation and Constitution-making," in Elster (ed.), *Deliberative Democracy* (Cambridge University Press, 1998).
26 J. Kis, "Introduction: From the 1989 Constitution to the 2011 Fundamental Law," in G. A. Tóth (ed.), *Constitution for a Disunited Nation* (Central European University Press, 2011), 1–23.
27 G. Austin, *The Indian Constitution* (Oxford University Press, 1999).
28 A. Arato, "Conventions, Assemblies and Round Tables," *Global Constitutionalism*, 1:1 (2012): 173–200. J. Kis, "Between Reform and Revolution: Three Hypotheses about the Nature of Regime Change," *Constellations*, I:3 (1995): 399–421.
29 A. Stepan, "Tunisia's Transition and the Twin Tolerations," *Journal of Democracy*, 23 (2012): 89–103.
30 R. Segura and A. M. Bejarano, "¡Ni una asamblea más sin nosotros! Exclusion, Inclusion, and the Politics of Constitution-Making in the Andes," *Constellations*, 11:2 (2004): 219–21, 228–29.
31 H. Arendt, *On Revolution*, 153–54.
32 From a critical point of view, see W. Sadurski, *Rights before Courts: A Study of Constitutional Courts in Postcommunist States of Central and Eastern Europe* (Springer, 2005). See also, H. Schwartz, *The Struggle for Constitutional Justice in Post-Communist Europe* (University of Chicago Press, 2000); and L. Garlicki, "Democracy and International Influences," in G. Nolte (ed.), *European and U.S. Constitutionalism* (Cambridge University Press, 2005), 263–79. For reconsidering the regional developments between the collapse of communism and the enlargement of the European Union from the point of view of the rule of law and constitutionalism, see A. Czarnota, M. Krygier and W. Sadurski (eds.), *Rethinking the Rule of Law after Communism* (Central European University Press, 2005).
33 Decision 11/1992 (III. 5.) ABh.
34 See in detail, A. Arato, *Constitution Making Under Occupation* (Columbia University Press, 2009).
35 *Northern Ireland Peace Agreement*, Section 6, Paragraph 2.
36 Z. al Ali, *The Struggle for Iraq's Future: How Corruption, Incompetence and Sectarianism have Undermined Democracy* (Yale University Press, 2014).
37 European Commission, MEMO 16/2017. http://europa.eu/rapid/press-release_MEMO-16-2017_en.htm.
38 P. J. Ankut, *The Rule of Constitution-Building Processes in Democratization: Case Study Rwanda* (International Idea Institute, 2005).
39 Under Article 27 of the Vienna Convention on the Law of Treaties, a state may not invoke the provisions of its internal law as a justification for its failure to comply with a treaty.
40 *United Communist Party of Turkey and Others v. Turkey*, 19392/92, Judgment of 30 January 1998, § 29.
41 *Sejdić and Finci v. Bosnia and Herzegovina*, 27996/06, 34836/06, Judgment of 22 December 2009.

42 *A, B and C v. Ireland*, 25579/05, Judgment of 16 December 2010.
43 *Alajos Kiss v. Hungary*, 38832/06, Judgment of 20 May 2010.
44 *Magyar Keresztény Mennonita Egyház and Others v. Hungary*, 70945/11 et al., Judgment of 8 April 2014.
45 *Baka v. Hungary*, 20261/12, Judgment of 23 June 2016.
46 *Anchugov and Gladkov v. Russia*, 11157/04, 15162/05, Judgment of 4 July 2013.
47 Constitutional Court of the Russian Federation, No. 12-П/2016, Judgment of 19 April 2016.
48 *European Commission v. Hungary*, C-288/12, Judgment of 8 April 2014.
49 M. Kumm, "Constitutionalism and the Cosmopolitan State," *Indiana Journal of Global Legal Studies*, 20:2 (2013).

Part II

Constitutional reforms in 'established' democracies

4 Participatory constitution-making and the renovation of the UK constitution[1]

Silvia Suteu

Introduction

This chapter looks at citizen assembly-style constitutional conventions as a path towards revitalising representative democratic institutions, with specific reference to the case of the United Kingdom. Understood generically as a 'representative body collected together to discuss constitutional change',[2] constitutional conventions have received increased scholarly and practical attention. Part of a more general participatory trend in constitution-making, constitutional conventions offer promises of greater legitimacy and longevity of the constitutional agreement they produce, as well as democratic renewal. If a 'new model of democracy' is indeed emerging as some have argued, one which requires more from its citizens,[3] then constitutional conventions are an embodiment of this innovation.

Cheryl Saunders has argued that 'there is now, effectively, universal acceptance that the authority for a Constitution must derive, in one way or another, from the people of the state concerned'.[4] She has argued that we may broadly identify a trend 'towards openness, inclusivity and the active involvement of the people of a state at all stages of the process through participation, rather than mere consultation.'[5] Others have echoed this view,[6] even going so far as to identify a right to participate in democratic governance, which extends to constitution-making, in international law.[7] Examples of this trend have included the rise in recourse to constitutional referendums – referendums that bring to the voting public questions of constitutional significance.[8] Scotland and Catalonia are two of the most recent and visible examples of what has been called Europe entering the 'age of referendums',[9] while the UK Brexit referendum is perhaps the most unpredictable. When it comes to experiments with deliberative mini-publics, understood as 'forums, usually organised by policy-makers, where citizens representing different viewpoints are gathered together to deliberate on a particular issue in small-N groups',[10] British Columbia, The Netherlands and Ontario are prominent first examples. British Columbia in particular was a groundbreaking experiment with a citizen assembly, sparking a 'demonstration effect' in the other two[11] and, subsequently, in Iceland and Ireland.[12] These earlier examples were all aimed at effecting electoral reform and not far-reaching constitutional change. Nevertheless, they also shared a commitment to participatory and deliberative democracy aimed at 'inject[ing] some popular legitimacy into policymaking'.[13]

Participatory mechanisms of constitutional change have also been linked to the crisis of democracy generally, and of representative democracy in particular. In an age where citizens feel detached from regular politics, participatory and deliberative forms of engagement may yet resurrect their interest. Perhaps it is not unrelated that these mechanisms have been called for in the aftermath of economic crisis (as in Iceland and Ireland) or of 'once in a generation' decisions (as in Scotland). The advantages promised by participatory and deliberative institutions – creativity, openness and consensus-based (rather than adversarial) politics among them – are that much more attractive when confronted with constitutional failure and stale institutions.

Similar arguments have been made in the UK context. Calls for a UK constitutional convention gained momentum in the aftermath of the 2014 Scottish independence referendum, when they appeared closer than ever to gaining political traction. The 2016 Brexit referendum vote, however, sent shockwaves through British society, including its political establishment. On the one hand, Brexit seemed not to change much: the same questions remained as to how to reform the UK constitution so as to make it reflect political reality and respond adequately to 21st century challenges. In other words, Brexit may move the country in an unexpected direction when it comes to European Union (EU) membership, but it has not fundamentally changed the need for wholesale constitutional revision that a constitutional convention might prompt. On the other hand, of course, the Brexit vote has changed everything. It has become priority number one, pushing every other large-scale policy reform plan to the side – for example, plans to revisit the status of the European Convention on Human Rights in the UK and replace the Human Rights Act of 1998, the statute incorporating the Convention into UK law, with a so-called 'British Bill of Rights'.[14] Not only that, but the Brexit fallout – also catalysed by debates around the *Miller* Supreme Court case[15] – brought into stark relief virtually all the unresolved tensions at the heart of the UK constitution. These included the weakness of executive control mechanisms and of the parliamentary scrutiny process, the devolution (un)settlements, the uncertain status of EU and international law, and problems of fit of the doctrine of parliamentary sovereignty to modern-day British constitutional realities.

As will be seen, these and other issues have all, at one point or another, been considered ripe for deliberation by a constitutional convention. And, while Brexit has certainly put a question mark as to the wisdom of resorting to the people on matters of constitutional significance, not to mention on whether resources should be allocated for another potentially divisive experiment with citizen engagement, calls for a convention have not fully abated. Such a convention remains on the agenda of its supporters not only in spite of Brexit but precisely because of it, being seen as a potential solution to the political stalemate dogging the UK constitution and rendered so visible in the EU membership referendum aftermath.

A careful analysis of what employing such a mechanism to achieve constitutional reform in Britain would entail is thus essential. This chapter proceeds by, first, outlining the types of proposals hitherto on the table. It then explores three potentially controversial areas which require delineation before such a convention can be set up: ensuring its legitimacy, explored here from the point of view of its capacity to represent the relevant political community; entrusting it with a clear substantive mandate; and avoiding the alienation of political institutions. While these three aspects are here labelled as 'challenges', my aim is not to negate the potential benefits of constitutional conventions. Nor am I putting forth a defence of representative democracy in the face of participatory challenges. Instead, I wish to raise key questions which need to be asked before a participatory instrument is set up in the UK. In doing so, I apply a comparative lens to arguments in favour of a UK constitutional convention, which helps illustrate that much more thought needs to be given before taking such a step.

Calls for a UK constitutional convention

At the same time as the British constitution has been said to be in crisis,[16] calls for one or more constitutional convention(s) in the UK have grown louder. Such calls are not new,[17] but they have been reinvigorated in recent years. The issue was discussed in a March 2013 Report of the Political and Constitutional Reform Committee of the UK Parliament titled *Do We Need a Constitutional Convention for the UK?*[18] The report recommended that the government consider establishing a constitutional convention with a clear remit, popular participation, involvement of politicians and a timetable of one to two years. However, its recommendations were not unanimous and the resolution of the English Question[19] featured as the priority, preceding any such wider convention. Models considered were the Philadelphia Convention, the Scottish Constitutional Convention, Iceland and British Columbia. In 2014, the Committee again considered a constitutional convention as one of the institutional options available to draft 'a new Magna Carta',[20] and by 2015 more confidently declared that 'perhaps the "constitutional moment", which in quieter times some believed was a prerequisite for change, is now close at hand.'[21] Talk of a constitutional convention was prominent in the run-up to the Scottish referendum, with the Scottish Government pledging one tasked with the aim of drafting a constitution for an independent Scotland. Both the November 2013 White Paper[22] and the June 2014 draft Scottish Independence Bill[23] detailed these plans, with models invoked therein being British Columbia, the Netherlands, Ontario, Iceland and Ireland.

In fact, the Scottish referendum created a veritable participatory momentum, with all but one of the major political parties coming out in favour of holding a constitutional convention. The Green Party called for a 'People's Constitutional Convention' to 'map out a new settlement for the rest of the United Kingdom', stating, 'If it is possible to negotiate Scottish Independence in less than two years it need not take decades to agree a new settlement for the rest of the United Kingdom'.[24] Ed Miliband at the Labour conference in September 2014 also stated:

> If the problem is Westminster we can't have a quick fix, a stitch up in Westminster. We've got to mobilise and harness the energy of people all across the country. That's why only a constitutional convention will do. And giving voice to everyone in Britain is also about who we are.[25]

Nick Clegg welcomed 'Labour's decision to embrace the longstanding Liberal Democrat call for a constitutional convention', but indicated the need to seize the moment, set it up with a clear mandate which would include House of Lords reform, and have citizens at its heart.[26] Even Nigel Farage called for a convention 'to be rapidly established to put in place a plan for a Federal UK'.[27] All parties maintained these stances in their manifestos for the 2015 general election.[28] The All-Party Parliamentary Group for Reform, Decentralisation and Devolution in the UK had in fact called on parties to adopt a common platform on this issue, believing that 'a constitutional convention is an accepted method of securing broad agreement (and is tried and tested, in differing forms, in the Scottish and Welsh contexts as well as internationally)'.[29]

Notably missing among these were Conservative voices. This is perhaps less surprising when considering that the government's response to the Political and Constitutional Reform Committee's report on the matter had been to reject the timeliness of setting up a constitutional convention due to competing economic priorities and the lack of public appetite.[30] David Cameron's post-referendum speech mentioned the need for 'wider civic engagement' but made no direct reference to a convention; he instead brought up the need to deal with the 'English votes for English laws' as central to any constitutional reform.[31] The same concern was at the core of the December 2014 policy paper addressing devolution in England.[32] The latter also briefly touched on the prospect of a constitutional convention, emphasising the need for decisions on its terms of reference and scope; its composition; timescales; and how it would interact with parallel changes taking place, notably devolution in Scotland.[33] But whereas the Liberal Democrats reiterated their desire that such a body 'should be legislated on at the earliest possible opportunity so its work can start as soon as possible',[34] the Conservative stance remained noncommittal.[35]

The political landscape after the 2015 general election, in which Conservatives won a majority of votes, did not seem welcoming of a constitutional convention. Nevertheless, in June 2015 a private member's bill was put forth in the House of Lords again calling for such a convention and an identical bill was later also tabled in the House of Commons.[36] Neither bill was successful. The same political divide remained between those supporting such an initiative and those maintaining their scepticism. This division likely accounts for the seeming lack of enthusiasm for the two parliamentary bills. The latter's slow moving through Parliament may also, however, be on account of the lack of clarity behind the initiatives themselves. As Section III discusses, there are complex questions which a constitutional convention for the entire UK raises, and parliamentary debates in the two Houses have reflected the confusion and uncertainty attached to whether and how to pursue constitutional renovation via such a participatory mechanism.[37]

Post-Brexit vote, a constitutional convention has understandably not been foremost on politicians' minds. Nevertheless, previous supporters have retained their enthusiasm for such a mechanism and perceive Brexit as a catalyst for greater constitutional reform. Former Labour Prime Minister Gordon Brown, for example, found there to be 'an overwhelming case for a UK-wide people's constitutional convention'.[38] His stance, which echoed his interest in a people's convention dating back to his time in office,[39] was not so much about extolling the virtues of a constitutional convention and explaining how it might actually work. Instead, Brown's imagining of the convention is inextricably linked to certain outcomes: resolving the devolution question, repatriating powers from Brussels to the regions instead of to London, placing bottom-up economic power in the hands of regional authorities, and reforming the House of Lords into a Senate of Nations and Regions – in short, 'setting a roadmap towards a more federal constitution that empowers all of the nations and regions'.[40] Calls in the Labour Party (especially from Scottish Labour) for a 'people's convention' to be established by summer 2017 to consider federalisation built on similar considerations and aimed to provide an alternative to Scottish independence.[41] Given their long-standing commitment to similar aims, the Liberal Democrats may end up endorsing such a course of action; the Scottish Lib Dems have, in fact, already made it clear they remain committed to federalism, also as a way to stave off 'the siren sounds of nationalism and independence'.[42] Of course, in the absence of support from the ruling Conservative Party, these initiatives may not have far-reaching impact, at least in the near future.

Nevertheless, a participatory momentum has also been growing in civil society and academic circles and was particularly strong around the time of the Scottish independence referendum. Certain civil society organisations have also publicly backed establishing a constitutional convention after the Scottish independence referendum.[43] The most prominent of these are the Electoral Reform Society and Unlock Democracy. Both have endorsed the establishment of a constitutional convention as a way to achieve an inclusive debate on holistic rather than piecemeal reform of the UK constitution, and as a means to ensure public confidence in the results.[44] They subsequently joined forces with academics and ran two pilot citizen assemblies, in Sheffield and Southampton, as a testing ground for deliberative approaches to constitutional reform.[45] These drew on previous such experiments, notably the Canadian citizen assemblies, Iceland, Ireland and also the Scottish Convention.

Academic discussions have revolved around whether a constitutional convention is opportune, the various types of conventions one could opt for, the best model to emulate and the issues it should be entrusted with.[46] Scholarly opinion is split on whether a constitutional convention would be the best way to achieve the constitutional reform most agree is needed. Some have pointed to 'the accumulation of unresolved constitutional problems' as creating a strong case for a convention with popular participation and tasked with considering the constitution as a whole.[47] Others, however, have preferred alternative bodies similarly tasked, assuming public apathy and governmental resource shortage.[48] Even those taking the constitutional convention option seriously point to past failures in pan-UK constitutional renovation as cause for pessimism.[49] Experiments such as the above-mentioned pilot citizens assemblies, as well as the LSE-run *Crowdsourcing the UK Constitution* project,[50] confirmed their initiators' confidence in the value of asking the input of ordinary citizens. Lessons from all of these will surely be useful in the event that a UK constitutional convention is established. Whether these initiatives have also helped persuade any of those sceptical of the value of popular participation in constitution-making, however, is less clear.

What emerges, thus, is a mixed picture. While few would dispute the need for serious thought on Britain's constitution in light of recent changes, the process by which this is to be achieved has been more controversial. Even the aims attached to this process have varied. They have included: seizing the Scottish referendum moment, with a desire to channel popular energy into concrete change (an aim tempered now by the Brexit experience); fixing the perceived inadequacy of current mechanisms to achieve such change; correlating the type of mechanism to the scale and holistic nature of the constitutional overhaul; as well as the desire for genuine democratic innovation and a willingness to experiment in order to achieve it. However, there is a real risk of instrumentalisation, with the convention instrument being manipulated by political parties wishing to see their own agendas reflected in its mandate and outcomes. Moreover, occasionally arguments for a UK constitutional convention have been combined with those for a written constitution for the country, which unhelpfully mixes two very different avenues of constitutional debate.

Constitutional conventions have been discussed as one possible mechanism for effectuating the needed change, with their advocates believing such a convention to be the only way to achieve both comprehensive constitutional change and democratic legitimacy. The normative assumption behind such arguments has been that direct citizen engagement in constitutional revision processes can supplement or even replace traditional political institutions and thereby invigorate democracy. Involving the people in constitution-drafting, the argument would go, actualises the hitherto mythical 'people' and turns self-government into an empirical reality. In what follows, I scrutinise this assumption with reference to the UK context in comparative perspective. My aim will not be to debate whether a constitutional convention is adequate for UK constitutional reform today or not. Rather, I am interested in the UK case as a potential testing ground for participatory democracy and in the distinct challenges it poses to the promise of constitutional conventions more specifically.

Challenges to the promise of constitutional conventions

The legitimacy challenge

Fundamental constitutional change needs to be, or at least to be perceived as, legitimate if it is to take root. This is even truer in the UK considering the scale and scope of the reforms said to be needed in order to give coherence to the

British constitution. Several authors have discussed the prospect of a UK constitutional convention as needing to 'command . . . such legitimacy that it would be able to create a new "rule of recognition" supplanting notions of parliamentary "sovereignty"'.[51] The notion that '[f]or the outcome to be legitimate so must be the process'[52] is widespread in constitution-making scholarship today. To quote Saunders again,

> Process can underpin the legitimacy of a Constitution, increase public knowledge of it, instil a sense of public ownership and create an expectation that the Constitution will be observed, in spirit as well as form. A constitution-making process may assist to set the tone for ordinary politics, including the peaceful transfer of power in accordance with constitutional rules.[53]

In other words, there is an educational element involved in having a constitution-making process perceived as legitimate, as it can serve as model for subsequent political interactions. There is also a link to public ownership and increased vigilance: an informed public will know when the constitution has been transgressed and demand accountability.[54]

I have suggested elsewhere five principles of participatory constitution-making good practice, on the basis of lessons drawn comparatively (mainly from Iceland and Ireland).[55] These five principles were: (1) inclusiveness, aimed at ensuring the process is representative and responsive at all stages; (2) clarity of process, achieved via advance notice of the steps of the process and its outcome; (3) the involvement of all relevant actors, so as to avoid alienation and to ensure public and political ownership of the process (I discuss this in greater detail in part 3 below); (4) equality as parity of esteem, referring to responsive and transparent decision-making procedures; and (5) consensus-based decision-making, aimed at avoiding the mere aggregation of preferences and at facilitating true deliberation.[56] These types of considerations would be equally relevant to a UK constitutional convention, which would, like its predecessors, also face complex decisions over inclusiveness, clarity of mandate, allocated resources, working methods and over how to define its success. Of these, I will focus on inclusiveness in this section and on mandate in the following section. My choice relates to the centrality of these two questions for the legitimacy of any participatory body set up to effect constitutional change, but also to their elusiveness in the literature on a British constitutional convention. Moreover, while other aspects such as budgets, time-frames or terms of reference may be resolved at the stroke of a governmental pen, the inclusiveness and mandate questions pose fundamental problems that require more careful theoretical consideration.

When discussing the need for a UK constitutional convention to be inclusive, the question immediately arises: what is the relevant political community that this convention would be tasked with representing? Those writing on this topic, whether academics or politicians, have given rather different answers and have discussed a convention for the UK as a whole, Scotland only, the rest of the UK minus Scotland, or even England alone. These disagreements are not inconsequential: path dependence theory tells us that subsequent decisions will be constrained by initial ones. Thus, whether an English pre-convention is to be established, as the current government has at various times suggested, is a decision whose outcome could influence the parameters of a wider convention, if the latter would still be held at all.

Moreover, we must remember that a UK constitutional convention would be concerned with constitutional change, including in the form of further devolution of powers from the centre to a unit, in the context of a multi-level, plurinational, asymmetrical system.[57] Thus, whatever lessons are sought from comparative work need to be measured against and adapted to the UK's distinct context. As noted above, the comparators most often invoked were always small countries, or sub-units of a federal state, and most have relatively homogenous populations. Thus, achieving inclusiveness may have been difficult but manageable in places like Iceland or Ireland, but would certainly prove even more complex in the UK. The latter would at the very least add another, territorial, layer to considerations of representativeness. As of yet, there are no adequate comparators for the accommodation of such territorial diversity in the composition of a citizen assembly-style constitutional convention. While there is some evidence that participatory mechanisms can be scaled up in federal systems,[58] there remain many unanswered questions as to their suitability to one constitutional context or another. Given that the most recurrent theme in criticism of the Smith Commission process has had to do with precisely achieving a coherent reform of the territorial constitution, this is not an issue to be cast aside lightly.

Even were the issue of the relevant political community to be resolved, the inclusiveness requirement would still need to be addressed at the level of individual convention member selection. Proponents of a UK constitutional convention have tended to agree that it would comprise representatives of civil society, political actors and individual members of the public, whether directly elected or randomly selected. Again, comparisons here have tended to focus on Ireland in particular, which included citizens as well as politicians in equal proportion (civil society organisations, though invited to submit proposals, were not directly represented in the convention itself), selected quasi-randomly, i.e., adjusted for gender, geography and age. While that model could be emulated in the British case, it bears noting that it was itself contested in the Irish context. Civil society organisations in particular lamented their exclusion from actual deliberations.[59] The fear related to statistical notions of representativeness is that, in its attempt to mirror society at large, it fails to ensure that minority voices are also included. In a constitution-making context, where majoritarian usurpation could have dire consequences, silencing minorities via non-inclusion in the body drafting the constitution might bear a heavy price.

A separate point concerns timing. It may seem a trivial observation, but a UK constitutional convention would come in the aftermath of (and possibly spurred by) the Scottish independence referendum, with its high turnout, closer than anticipated result and distorted meaning of the 'No' vote (to mean more devolution rather than closure). It would also come in the aftermath of the unexpected Brexit result of a second, highly divisive referendum whose effects the country is still grappling with. Some have suggested that what has occurred after the Scottish experience has been a 'chain reaction . . . which has transformed the seemingly straightforward 'yes/no' of the Scottish referendum into something more complex and unpredictable that spills over across the UK's internal boundaries'.[60] Interpreting a relatively narrow 'No' vote to Scottish independence is difficult and potentially speculative, but it is not meaningless. It is true that 'the constitutional debate looks completely different once the threat of independence drops out of the equation',[61] but it is not the same as it would have been without that referendum. There is work suggesting that even constitutional amendments which fail at the ratification stage may, by providing evidence of growing national consensus, amount to de facto constitutional change.[62] Even more so given that, following the Brexit vote, whether independence is truly off the table is no longer a given. Following the disparate result in Scotland, which together with Northern Ireland voted in favour of remaining in the EU, the case for a second independence referendum was suddenly strengthened.[63]

In short, expectations differ because our constitutional imagination has been enriched. What this means for the inclusiveness requirement of a UK constitutional convention is that what would have seemed legitimate before these two referendums may now no longer suffice. Who sits at the table is determined by who wields influence, and both the Scottish and Brexit referendums may have tilted the scale in this regard irreversibly. The need for all devolved units to be represented and the strong bargaining power of a majority Conservative Government seemingly still bent on enforcing a centralising agenda are not easily reconcilable. The chances of finding a compromise between these competing forces will have a bearing on any decision to set up a constitutional convention and on who that body would be tasked with representing.

The mandate challenge

No less controversial may prove to be the question of what mandate a UK constitutional convention would have. The scope of its remit would need to be clearly set out before the convention started its work so as to ensure that the process was seen as legitimate and the 'rules of the game' were known to all. Such clarity would also help prevent abuse or the later delegitimising of the convention's work. Similar calls have been made with reference to the increased use of referendums in the UK, whose 'lack of regulation has opened up the potential for [their] manipulation'.[64] Others have echoed this need for codification irrespective of the type of process or set of procedures resorted to for constitutional change.[65] Indeed, we may be witnessing the realisation of a perceptive observation made almost two decades ago, namely that it may be 'that in the future, constitutional amendment will become a more controlled process, with greater constraints on the government being exercised not only by Parliament and the courts, but also by the people'.[66] The need for a clear mandate for a constitutional convention would be part of that increased control, but also a logical requirement: an unclear process would be unlikely to achieve clarification of the UK constitution.

More contentious would be to set out the content of a UK convention's mandate. As already noted, one of the criticisms levied against the Smith Commission process was that its limited remit meant it could not adequately address the need for a coherent territorial constitution.[67] There was a sense, after the Scottish referendum, that a more profound (re)thinking of the substantive content of the UK constitution was needed and that Smith was not an adequate process to achieve it.[68] (Such fundamental rethinking of the UK constitution had been demanded for some time, with authors warning that the centrifugal dynamics of devolution required a 'sustained attempt to review and renew the purposes of union'.[69]) If it is to avoid such criticism, therefore, a constitutional convention would have to have a mandate that was not only clear and manageable, but also sufficiently ambitious so as to provide the answers the Smith Commission could not and to warrant the investment in its work.

Options for the scope of the convention's mandate include for it to produce a written constitution or merely to make recommendations on discrete issues. The latter may result in the same type of piecemeal constitutional reform which advocates of a constitutional convention have deplored in the past. Nevertheless, it is precisely what the Irish constitutional convention, the model most often invoked in the UK context, was entrusted to do. In Ireland, the convention was called on to make recommendations on seven issues, to which it added two more based on public input. In fact, the Irish process's relative success, and avoidance of any blockages, has been attributed by some to precisely this sequencing of its work.[70] Most of the other instances of constitutional conventions invoked as models (British Columbia, the Netherlands and Ontario) similarly dealt with isolated issues of electoral reform. The sole exception was Iceland, whose convention had a full constitutional project to deliver. This list shows some promise for far reaching reform being possible via constitutional convention, but there is still no direct model for the type of territorial reallocation of powers the UK would seek.

A last observation here refers to the lack of unanimity with regard to the need for a written constitution in the UK.[71] While the fervour of writings on a constitutional convention for the UK would seem to indicate agreement on this issue, there are still prominent voices which hold such a development to not be essential.[72] Such disagreements raise the broader question of the type of document the constitutional convention would be tasked to prepare. I have been writing on the assumption that it would be a substantive identification and reimagining of core constitutional tenets and not a purely technical exercise in codifying existing rules. As others have noted, such a technical endeavour would be better suited for professionals; a 'written constitution proper' would instead 'be more intensive and complex than a non-legal Code or Consolidation Bill, as it would symbolically become *the* Constitution in the state, providing the basic law and primary source of authority in the United Kingdom'.[73]

The exceptionality challenge

Finally, one must remember that the high costs of popular constitution-making, including in terms of political will and citizen interest, will unavoidably render constitutional conventions exceptional. The majority of constitutional reforms are bound to come about via more traditional channels. This is especially true of the UK, where almost all major constitutional change 'needs to be formulated and presented to Parliament by the government of the day'.[74] Thus, focusing solely on popular involvement in times of crisis may be shortsighted and ultimately detrimental. If democracy is a work in progress, it is still representative democracy that we are working towards improving, including via boosts of participatory activity. The question then becomes how best to balance, or integrate, the two types of processes – the participatory and the representative democratic – in such a way as to have them reinforce each other's strengths. How to do this in the British context where, as Dawn Oliver has observed, democracy 'is a slippery term, and one about which UK politicians are rather coy',[75] may prove even more challenging.

Paradoxically, the UK had experience with both a highly participatory event, the Scottish independence referendum, and a more conventionally political one, the Smith Commission, within the same year. While the former was lauded as ultimately a good example of a participatory process,[76] the latter was received with much unease. The procedurally problematic aspects of the Smith Commission were in fact commented upon soon after it was set up.[77] They included the fact that the Smith process was distinctly elite-driven, having been initiated by political elites but also because, outside of a month-long period during which it gathered proposals from citizens and civil society, it was only open to political parties. Unsurprisingly, the parties' submissions to the Commission largely reflected previously expressed positions.[78] However, the Commission's broader outreach efforts were not insignificant: despite the tight timeline, it received 407 submissions from civic institutions, organisations and groups, and 18,381 from members of the public.[79] And, while its final report has been criticized for failing – due to the Commission's limited remit rather than anything else – to consider the wider and longer term impact of its proposals for the Union as a whole,[80] the Smith process itself was more in line with UK constitutional practice than the independence referendum had been.

A similar if not starker point may be made about the Brexit vote. While the EU referendum campaign was criticised by some for being uninformed at best and maliciously dishonest at worst, its participatory credentials were never truly in question. As Tierney has argued, the regulation of the 2016 referendum process, the high turnout, and absence of major voting irregularities make its outcome 'a narrow but clear constitutional decision of the highest significance'.[81] There is a certain degree of irony, however, in what followed the Brexit vote. The government, under the new leadership of Theresa May, set about turning Brexit into a reality by invoking the executive's prerogative powers to conduct foreign affairs as the basis for notifying the EU of the country's withdrawal. As stated above, the *Miller* Supreme Court decision put a brake on proceeding in that manner, as it required parliamentary involvement in the process. Nevertheless, the Government has pushed on, proposing the so-called 'Great Repeal Bill' which, in a few short paragraphs, would give a parliamentary rubber-stamp to the executive initiating withdrawal negotiations.[82] This course of action is again more in line with old habits in UK constitutional reform, notably the executive exercising tight control over Parliament in order to push through its agenda, than with any participatory ethos.

To this descriptive point – that British constitutional tradition favours piecemeal reform through political channels rather than revolutionary change through participatory processes – I wish to add two more, which build on comparative insights. One is that it is not at all clear that all constitutional crises are best resolved via recourse to the people. Jon Elster, for instance, has advocated for constitution-making processes to contain both elements of secrecy and of publicity due to their disparate strengths and drawbacks: 'With total secrecy partisan interests and logrolling come to the forefront, whereas full publicity encourages grandstanding and rhetorical overbidding.'[83] To uncritically advocate for popular involvement in constitutional change is thus to take for granted that anything imbued with the participatory aura will be better and more legitimate than politically negotiated products. Concerns over popular expertise and interest are relevant here, alongside the shortcomings of publicity when seeking delicate compromise.

With regard to the assumed lack of the public's expertise, sceptics would do well to consider the British Columbia, Ontario and Netherlands citizen assemblies tasked with the complex and technical matter of electoral reform. In spite of this technical nature of their mandate, those involved succeeded not only in understanding the various options available to them, but also in deliberating upon the best alternative for their polity. However, these assemblies only worked in the context of ample time allocated for learning and deliberation (for example, a full year for the learning phase in British Columbia, and another year for its deliberative work). All three of their proposals eventually failed due to a lack of popular interest, the two Canadian ones via popular referendums, which did not meet the necessary thresholds, and the Dutch due to political changes which deprived the assembly of its support.[84]

In the context of the UK, we may well wonder whether the kind of complicated financial and monetary policy arrangements which came under the remit of the Smith Commission were ever really going to be decided otherwise than via political negotiations. Even commentators critical of Smith have contrasted the further devolution debates to the buoyant independence referendum ones, calling the former 'deadly dull',[85] 'a long trudge through closed committees and impenetrable reports',[86] and something to at best '[muddle] through'.[87] This is not to say public input and oversight was not desirable in the process, but that the minutiae of negotiation were likely never truly going to escape elite hands. The same point may be made about Brexit negotiations: the intricate political, legal and economic bargains to be struck may not be easily opened up to popular involvement, even while public oversight (such as by Parliament) may yet be sought.

Of course, this only addresses the problem of technical constitutional change and its public palatability. Most advocates of a constitutional convention for the UK link it to a need to (re)consider fundamental values and principles of the British constitution, the scale of which only a broad public debate can achieve. My answer to this is to caution against alienating political elites, which bears a heavy price in any process of constitutional change. Here, again, comparative insights may suggest tempering our participatory optimism.

Iceland's experiment with a constitutional convention in the aftermath of the country's economic collapse in 2008 may serve as a warning tale. Despite the clamour with which the draft constitution produced by the convention was received, and notwithstanding a successful referendum which approved it, the text never came into force. The Parliament failed to discuss the bill a third and necessary time in 2013 and the new constitution dropped from amidst priorities in the general election that same year. A new procedure to amend the existing constitution by 2017 was instead proposed and thus the so-called 'first crowdsourced constitution' in the world 'ultimately fell at the final hurdle'.[88] Iceland's failure to adopt the popularly produced constitutional draft had a lot to do with the late involvement of political elites, which as a consequence felt alienated from the process.[89]

Indeed, Ireland's positive experience with the 2012–2014 constitutional convention has been partly attributed to maintaining political actors engaged with the constitutional convention's work.[90] In fact, the process itself was initiated by the Irish executive, which also clearly indicated its response to the outcome of deliberations. This, together with its seeming success, may help explain the support which the Irish model has seemed to elicit in the UK.[91] Nevertheless, that very success of the Irish constitutional convention has more recently come to be questioned.[92] It was not a lack of interest from citizens, nor poor quality work that have doomed the Irish convention to futility, these critics have argued; instead, it was the ability of the government to only partially acquit itself of its obligation to respond to the convention's reports and its choice to put only the most frivolous matters to referendum votes.[93] Thus, the Irish constitutional convention 'brand' has been said to be in jeopardy due to the government's attempts to sideline the reform process.[94]

This brief comparative excursion yields contradictory results: involving politicians in the deliberations of a constitutional convention seems both to help increase its effectiveness and to not guarantee eventual success. Nevertheless, the limited comparative evidence that does exist suggests the exclusion of political elites is more prone to doom the work of a popular constitutional convention to irrelevance than keeping them invested in, and thus protective of, the constitutional change process. I admit that this may be a strategic consideration more so than a principled one, though not entirely. Given that it is political representatives who will then have to implement and work with new constitutional tools, there is value in attempting to have participatory democracy enhance rather than supplant or alienate representative institutions. And to the fear of elite control – of political actors exploiting their role for narrow political advantage[95] – the Irish constitutional convention's success in avoiding this suggests hope.[96]

Although reverting to an elite-driven process in the aftermath of the Scottish referendum was decried as 'disappointing'[97] and called 'deeply ironic' given that the impetus for it was the referendum itself,[98] the political process is in fact the typical arena for effecting constitutional change, at least in the UK. Recent experiments with popular mechanisms such as constitutional conventions are exceptional. Their success rate, partial at best, has had much to do with the degree to which political actors were engaged in the process alongside the citizenry. Thus, while a trend towards more direct democracy may be afoot, including in the UK, it would be a mistake to embrace the participatory promise at the expense of, rather than alongside, representative institutions.

Conclusion

The choice of mechanism to decide on and enact constitutional change is nowhere an easy one. The recent participatory turn in constitution-making scholarship, including advocacy of mechanisms such as constitutional conventions which involve the citizens directly in deliberations included, has much persuasive force. Indeed, who could resist the promise of better decisions taken in a more legitimate manner and resulting in a long-lasting constitutional settlement?

As I have tried to show in this chapter, however, the evidence on the potential of such mechanisms to trigger constitutional reform is still incomplete. The precursor citizen assemblies in British Columbia, the Netherlands and Ontario were not only very different from the type of convention discussed in the UK, but also – for all the resources expended and success as micro-deliberation experiments – failed to incite broader support for reforms to the electoral systems in question. The two most prominent examples of constitutional conventions discussed in the UK context, that of Iceland and Ireland, have both recently seen U-turns in terms of perceptions of their achievements. Iceland's 'crowdsourced constitution' was ultimately not adopted. And while the Irish convention received early praise, its track record since completing its work has been mixed.[99] Two referendums have been held, one endorsing the convention's recommendation and the other vetoing it; more worryingly, though, the government's response to the convention's reports has been less swift and occasionally obfuscating.

Given these mixed results elsewhere, policymakers and academics in the UK who support setting up such an instrument must do so with caution. They must at the very least be ready to answer the three challenges raised in this chapter. Any UK constitutional convention would need to have, from the outset: legitimacy in the form of inclusiveness, both at the level of individual members and of the territorial unit(s) represented; a clear mandate, likely to go beyond the merely technical codification of existing constitutional rules and into substantive rethinking of the constitution; and a link to the political process to ensure that representative institutions are not alienated but supported, and are thus likely to endorse its work. Perhaps antecedent questions to all these are how to define the success of such a convention and whether embarking on such a resource-intensive process is the best way to achieve what many agree is the much-needed renovation of the UK constitution.

While this chapter raised more questions than it provided answers, the comparative lessons invoked throughout are a first step in finding the best solution for the UK context. What is clear is that the choice of constitutional change instrument should not be made casually, for in the words of Edward McWhinney, 'What looks like a simple, technical machinery choice may in fact predetermine or influence the final substantive recommendations as to the content and direction of a new, or "renewed," constitutional system.'[100] Given the significance of the constitutional moment the UK may find itself in, this cautionary note is here even more pertinent.

Notes

1 This is a revised and updated version of an article that first appeared in (2015) 4 CJICL 405.
2 Political and Constitutional Reform Committee, *Do We Need a Constitutional Convention for the UK?* (HC 2012–13, 371) 9.
3 David M Farrell, Eoin O'Malley, and Jane Suiter, 'Deliberative Democracy in Action Irish-Style: The 2011 *We the Citizens* Pilot Citizens' Assembly' (2013) 28 Irish Pol Studies 99, 100, citing Russell J Dalton, *The Good Citizen: How a Younger Generation Is Reshaping American Politics* (2nd ed., Congressional QP 2009) 1.
4 Cheryl Saunders, 'Constitution Making in the 21st Century', 4 (2012) International Review of Law 2–3.
5 Ibid., 9.
6 See Vivien Hart, 'Constitution-Making and the Transformation of Conflict' (2001) 26 Peace & Change 153; Claude Klein and András Sajó, 'Constitution-Making: Process and Substance', in Michel Rosenfeld and András Sajó, *The Oxford Handbook of Comparative Constitutional Law* (OUP, 2012) 435–36.
7 Vivien Hart, 'Democratic Constitution Making' (United States Institute of Peace Special Report 107, July 2003) 1 <www.usip.org/sites/default/files/resources/sr107.pdf> accessed 15 April 2016.
8 Stephen Tierney, *Constitutional Referendums: The Theory and Practice of Republican Deliberation* (OUP, 2012).
9 Stephen Tierney, 'Europe Is Entering the "Age of the Referendum", but There Is Nothing to Fear for European Democracy if Referendums Are Properly Regulated' (*Democratic Audit*, 22 October 2014) <www.democraticaudit.com/?p=8777> accessed 15 April 2016.
10 Kimmo Grönlund, André Bächtiger and Maija Setälä, 'Introduction', in Kimmo Grönlund, André Bächtiger and Maija Setälä (eds.), *Deliberative Mini-Publics: Involving Citizens in the Democratic Process* (ECPR Press, 2014) 1.
11 Patrick Fournier and others, *When Citizens Decide: Lessons from Citizen Assemblies on Electoral Reform* (OUP, 2011) 28.
12 For more on the experience of British Columbia, see Mark E Warren and Hilary Pearse, *Designing Deliberative Democracy: The British Columbia Citizens' Assembly* (CUP, 2008).
13 Fournier and others (n 11) 18.
14 Heather Stewart, 'Ministers Put British Bill of Rights Plan on Hold until after Brexit' (*The Guardian*, 29 December 2016) <www.theguardian.com/law/2016/dec/29/ministers-put-british-bill-of-rights-plan-on-hold-until-after-brexit> accessed 8 March 2017.

15 *Miller and Dos Santos v Secretary of State for Exiting the European Union* [2017] UKSC 5. The case concerned the question whether the UK Government could invoke Article 50 of the Treaty on the European Union to notify the EU of the UK's withdrawal based on royal prerogative powers or whether it needed to consult Parliament before doing so. The UK Supreme Court ruled 8–3 that Parliament needed to have a say.
16 Vernon Bogdanor, *The Crisis of the Constitution: The General Election and the Future of the United Kingdom* (*The Constitution Society*, February 2015) www.consoc.org.uk/wp-content/uploads/2015/02/COSJ2947_The-Crisis-of-the-Constitution_WEB_FINAL.pdf> accessed 15 April 2016.
17 For a discussion of debates predating the Scottish referendum, see Owain Roberts, 'Towards a UK Constitutional Convention?' (2012) National Assembly for Wales Commission Paper No 12/023, 4–5 <www.assembly.wales/Research%20Documents/Towards%20a%20UK%20Constitutional%20Convention%20-%20Research%20paper-21052012-234096/12-023-English.pdf> accessed 15 April 2016.
18 Political and Constitutional Reform Committee (n 2).
19 The report defined it as 'the issue that the people of England, outside of London, are governed by Westminster, with little authority to propose local solutions that benefit their own communities'. Political and Constitutional Reform Committee (n 4) para 68.
20 Political and Constitutional Reform Committee, *A New Magna Carta* (HC 2014–15, 463).
21 Political and Constitutional Reform Committee, *Consultation on A New Magna Carta* (HC 2014–15, 599).
22 Government of Scotland, 'Scotland's Future: Your Guide to an Independent Scotland' (26 November 2013) 22 <www.gov.scot/resource/0043/00439021.pdf> accessed 15 April 2016.
23 Government of Scotland, 'The Scottish Independence Bill: A Consultation on an Interim Constitution for Scotland' (June 2014) 61 <www.gov.scot/resource/0045/00452762.pdf> accessed 15 April 2016.
24 Green Party, 'Democracy for Everyone: The UK after the Scottish Referendum' (September 2014) <www.greenparty.org.uk/assets/files/democracy_for_everyone.pdf> accessed 15 April 2016.
25 Ed Miliband, 'Speech to the Labour Conference: Full Text' (*New Statesman*, 23 September 2014) <www.newstatesman.com/politics/2014/09/ed-miliband-s-speech-labour-conference-full-text> accessed 15 April 2016.
26 Nick Clegg, 'This Opportunity Cannot be Hijacked' (Liberal Democrats, 22 September 2014) <www.libdems.org.uk/nick_clegg_this_opportunity_cannot_be_hijacked> accessed 15 April 2016.
27 Nigel Farage, 'A Voice for England' (United Kingdom Independence Party, 19 September 2014) <www.ukip.org/nigel_farage_a_voice_for_england> accessed 15 April 2016.
28 See 'Policy Guide: Where the Parties Stand' (BBC News, April 2015) <www.bbc.co.uk/news/election/2015/manifesto-guide> accessed 15 April 2016.
29 Jeremy Purvis and Andrew Blick, 'A Parliament for Reform 2015–2020: Legacy Paper of the All-Party Parliamentary Group for Reform, Decentralisation and Devolution in the United Kingdom' (March 2015) <www.local.gov.uk/sites/default/files/documents/parliament-reform-2015-20-b9a.pdf> accessed 15 April 2016.
30 Deputy Prime Minister, 'Government Response to the House of Commons Political and Constitutional Reform Committee Fourth Report of Session 2012–13: Do We Need a Constitutional Convention for the UK?' (November 2013) paras 1.3, 2.1, 3.18, 4.1 <www.gov.uk/government/uploads/system/uploads/attachment_data/file/264086/8749.pdf> accessed 15 April 2016.
31 See 'In Full: David Cameron Statement on the UK's Future' (*BBC News*, 19 September 2014) <www.bbc.co.uk/news/uk-politics-29271765> accessed 15 April 2016.

32 First Secretary of State and Leader of the House of Commons, 'Implications of Devolution for England' (December 2014) <www.gov.uk/government/uploads/system/uploads/attachment_data/file/387598/implications_of_devolution_for_england_accessible.pdf> accessed 15 April 2016.
33 Ibid., 21.
34 Ibid., 32.
35 Ibid., 27.
36 Constitutional Convention Bill (HL Bill 10) 2015–16 and Constitutional Convention (No. 2) Bill (Bill 61) 2015–16.
37 See Constitutional Convention Bill [HL] Committee: 1st Sitting (Minutes of Proceedings): House of Lords 11 December, 2015.
38 The Office of Gordon and Sarah Brown, 'Gordon Brown Proposes UK People's Constitutional Convention' (3 November 2016) <http://gordonandsarahbrown.com/2016/11/gordon-brown-proposes-uk-peoples-constitutional-convention/> accessed 8 March 2017.
39 See Alex Barker, 'Brown Flags Constitutional Convention' (*Financial Times*, 21 May 2009) <www.ft.com/content/41183a02-459a-11de-b6c8-00144feabdc0> accessed 8 March 2017.
40 Brown (n 38).
41 Severin Carrell, 'Labour Expected to Consider Possibility of Federal UK' (*The Guardian*, 24 February 2017) <www.theguardian.com/uk-news/2017/feb/24/labour-constitutional-reforms-federal-uk-scotland> accessed 8 March 2017.
42 Scottish Liberal Democrats, 'Scot Lib Dems Launch Federalism Drive' (5 March 2017) <www.scotlibdems.org.uk/scot_lib_dems_launch_federalism_drive> accessed 8 March 2017.
43 For a list of civil society initiatives predating the Scottish referendum, see *A New Magna Carta?* (n 20) 376.
44 See Unlock Democracy, 'Guide to a Constitutional Convention', October 2014, and Electoral Society, 'The Next Four Years for Reform: Our 2020 Strategy', 7 September 2016 <www.electoral-reform.org.uk/the-next-four-years-for-reform-our-2020-strategy/> accessed 29 July 2017.
45 See the website of the two pilot assemblies, http://citizensassembly.co.uk/ accessed 15 April 2016.
46 See, among others, Alan Renwick, 'After the Referendum Options: For a Constitutional Convention' (*The Constitution Society*, May 2014) <www.consoc.org.uk/wp-content/uploads/2014/05/J1847_Constitution_ Society_Report_Cover_WEB.pdf> accessed 15 April 2016; Cormac Mac Amhlaigh, 'For a Constitutional Convention for the United Kingdom' (*UK Constitutional Law Blog*, 22 September 2014) <https://ukconstitutionallaw.org/2014/09/22/cormac-mac-amhlaigh-for-a-constitutional-convention-for-the-united-kingdom/> accessed 15 April 2016; Alan Renwick, 'How to Design a Constitutional Convention for the UK' (*Our Kingdom*, 22 September 2014) <www.opendemocracy.net/ourkingdom/alan-renwick/how-to-design-constitutional-convention-for-uk> accessed 15 April 2016; Robert Hazell, 'You Want a Constitutional Convention? This Is What You Need to Think through First' (*The Constitution Unit Blog*, 8 October 2014) <http://constitution-unit.com/2014/10/08/you-want-a-constitutional-convention-this-is-what-you-need-to-think-through-first/> accessed 15 April 2016; David M Farrell, 'The Irish Constitutional Convention Offers a Potential Route-Map for Renewing UK Democracy' (*Democratic Audit*, 15 October 2014) <www.democraticaudit.com/?p=8625> accessed 10 July 2015; Clodagh Harris, 'The UK has Much to Learn from the Irish Constitutional Convention' (*LSE British Politics and Policy*, 17 November 2014) <http://blogs.lse.ac.uk/constitutionuk/2014/11/17/the-uk-has-much-to-learn-from-the-irish-constitutional-convention/> accessed 15 April 2016. More recently, see statement by academics of Constitution Society and Constitution Unit, 'What a Constitutional Convention Needs to Succeed' (*UCL Constitution Unit Blog*, 30 April 2015)

<www.ucl.ac.uk/constitution-unit/news/what_a_constitutional_convention_needs_to_succeed_apr15> accessed 15 April 2016.

47 Bogdanor (n 16) 36–37.

48 See Robert Blackburn, 'Enacting a Written Constitution for the United Kingdom' (2015) 36 Statute L Rev 1, 21.

49 See Adam Evans, 'Back to the Future? Warnings from History for a Future UK Constitutional Convention' (2015) 86 Pol Q 24.

50 See ConstitutionUK, LSE Institute of Public Affairs <http://blogs.lse.ac.uk/constitutionuk/> accessed 15 April 2016.

51 Andrew Blick, 'Entrenchment and the United Kingdom Constitution' (*The Constitution Society*, 16 December 2014) 6 <http://consoc.org.uk/publications/entrenchment-and-the-united-kingdom-constitution-new-discussion-paper/> accessed 15 April 2016. See also Bogdanor (n 14), 39.

52 Richard Simeon, 'Constitutional Design and Change in Federal Systems: Issues and Questions' (2009) 39 Publius 241, 251.

53 Saunders (n 4) 3.

54 See Jennifer Widner, 'Constitution-Writing in Post-Conflict Settings: An Overview' (2008) 49 William & Mary L Rev 1513, 1519.

55 See Silvia Suteu, 'Constitutional Conventions in the Digital Era: Lessons from Iceland and Ireland' (2015) 38 Boston College Intl & Comp L Rev 251.

56 Ibid., 275–76.

57 Also noting the added difficulties of the UK's multinational nature for a constitutional convention is Evans (n 49) 29.

58 See Thamy Pogrebinschi, 'The Squared Circle of Participatory Democracy: Scaling Up Deliberation to the National Level' (2013) 7 Critical Policy Studies 219.

59 See Irish Council for Civil Liberties, 'Developing a Model for Best Practice for Public Participation in Constitutional Reform' (7 June 2012) <www.iccl.ie/attachments/download/260/ICCL_%20Best%20Practice%20for%20Constitutional%20Reform%2020%20June%202012%20FINAL.pdf> accessed 15 April 2016.

60 Charlie Jeffrey, 'Constitutional Change – Without End?' (2015) 86 Pol Q 275.

61 Scott Hames, 'No Face Paint beyond this Point: Pro-Independence Politics after No' (*Scottish Constitutional Futures Forum Blog*, 29 September 2014) <www.scottishconstitutionalfutures.org/OpinionandAnalysis/ViewBlogPost/tabid/1767/articleType/ArticleView/articleId/4330/Scott-Hames-No-Face-Paint-Beyond-This-Point-Pro-Independence-Politics-After-No.aspx> accessed 15 April 2016.

62 See Rosalind Dixon's discussion of the failed 1972 Equal Rights Amendment to the US Constitution in Rosalind Dixon, 'Amending Constitutional Identity' (2012) 33 Cardozo L Rev 1847.

63 As of the time of writing, the First Minister of Scotland, Nicola Sturgeon, remained non-committal about a second independence referendum. Nevertheless, she has indicated that were a second referendum to be held, it would take place between when a final Brexit deal is negotiated and actual withdrawal. See 'Sturgeon: Autumn 2018 "Common Sense" for Indyref2' (*BBC News*, 9 March 2017) <www.bbc.co.uk/news/uk-scotland-scotland-politics-39213767> accessed 9 March 2017.

64 Peter Leyland, 'Referendums, Popular Sovereignty, and the Territorial Constitution', in Richard Rawlings, Peter Leyland and Alison Young (eds.), *Sovereignty and the Law: Domestic, European and International Perspectives* (OUP, 2013) 163.

65 Robert Blackburn, 'Constitutional Amendment in the United Kingdom', in Xenophon Contiades (ed.), *Engineering Constitutional Change: A Comparative Perspective on Europe, Canada and the USA* (Routledge, 2013) 380.

66 Peter Oliver and Adam Tomkins, 'Constitutional Change in the United Kingdom', in Mads Andenas (ed.), *The Creation and Amendment of Constitutional Norms* (BIICL, 2000) 357.

67 Select Committee on the Constitution, *Proposals for the Devolution of Further Powers to Scotland* (HL 2014–15, 145) para 23.
68 See Christine Bell, 'Separation or Sharing? The Critical Choice for the Union (and Smith)' (*Scottish Constitutional Futures Forum Blog*, 4 November 2014) <www.scottishconstitutionalfutures.org/OpinionandAnalysis/ViewBlogPost/tabid/1767/articleType/ArticleView/articleId/4568/Christine-Bell-Separation-or-Sharing-The-Critical-Choice-for-the-Union-and-Smith.aspx> accessed 15 April 2016.
69 Charlie Jeffrey, 'Devolution in the United Kingdom: Problems of a Piecemeal Approach to Constitutional Change' (2009) 39 Publius 289.
70 See 'Constitutional Reform in Ireland: Legal Memorandum' (Public International Law and Policy Group, 17 February 2014) 27 <www.mreza-mira.net/wp-content/uploads/Constitutional-Reform-in-Ireland-Feb-2014.pdf> accessed 15 April 2016.
71 See Blackburn (n 48), *A New Magna Carta?* (n 20).
72 James Melton, Christine Stuart and Daniel Helen, 'To Codify or Not to Codify? Lessons from Consolidating the United Kingdom's Constitutional Statutes' (*Constitution Unit*, March 2015) <www.ucl.ac.uk/constitution-unit/publications/tabs/unit-publications/162.pdf> accessed 15 April 2016.
73 Blackburn, 'Enacting a Written Constitution for the United Kingdom' (n 48) 20 (emphasis in original).
74 Blackburn, 'Constitutional Amendment in the United Kingdom' (n 65) 369.
75 Dawn Oliver, 'The United Kingdom', in Dawn Oliver and Carlo Fusaro (eds.), *How Constitutions Change: A Comparative Study* (Hart Publishing, 2011) 353.
76 Stephen Tierney, '"And the Winner is… the Referendum": Scottish Independence and the Deliberative Participation of Citizens' (*I-CONnect Blog*, 26 September 2014) <www.iconnectblog.com/2014/09/and-the-winner-is-the-referendum-scottish-independence-and-the-deliberative-participation-of-citizens/> accessed 15 April 2016. See also Stephen Tierney, 'Reclaiming Politics: Popular Democracy in Britain after the Scottish Referendum' (2015) 86 Pol Q 226.
77 See Stephen Tierney, 'Solomon Grundy does Constitutional Change: The Smith Commission Timetable to Transform the Scottish Parliament' (*UK Constitutional Law Association Blog*, 31 October 2014) <https://ukconstitutionallaw.org/2014/10/31/stephen-tierney-solomon-grundy-does-constitutional-change-the-smith-commission-timetable-to-transform-the-scottish-parliament/> accessed 15 April 2016. See also Tom Mullen, 'Further Devolution: Evaluating the Parties' Proposals' (*Scottish Constitutional Futures Forum Blog*, 30 October 2014) <www.scottishconstitutionalfutures.org/OpinionandAnalysis/ViewBlogPost/tabid/1767/articleType/ArticleView/articleId/4518/Tom-Mullen-Further-Devolution-Evaluating-the-Parties-Proposals.aspx> accessed 10 July 2015, which raises questions about the appropriateness of the Smith Commission process, its outcome and aftermath.
78 See political party proposals, Smith Commission website, <http://webarchive.nationalarchives.gov.uk/20151202171105/http://www.smith-commission.scot/resources/political-party-proposals/> accessed 15 April 2016.
79 The Smith Commission, 'Report of the Smith Commission for Further Devolution of Powers to the Scottish Parliament' (27 November 2014) para 11 <www.smith-commission.scot/smith-commission-report/> accessed 15 April 2016.
80 House of Lords, Select Committee on the Constitution, 'The Union and Devolution' (25 May 2016) <www.publications.parliament.uk/pa/ld201516/ldselect/ldconst/149/149.pdf> accessed 8 March 2017.
81 Stephen Tierney, 'Was the Brexit Referendum Democratic?' (*UK Constitutional Law Blog*, 25 July 2016) <https://ukconstitutionallaw.org/2016/07/25/stephen-tierney-was-the-brexit-referendum-democratic/> accessed 8 March 2017.
82 European Union (Notification of Withdrawal) Bill 2016–17.

83 Jon Elster, 'Ways of Constitution-Making' in Axel Hadenius (ed.), *Democracy's Victory and Crisis* (CUP, 1997) 138. See also discussion in Fernando Mendez and Jonathan Wheatley, 'The Constitution-Making Process: An Analytical Framework' in Jonathan Wheatley and Fernando Mendez (eds.), *Patterns of Constitutional Design* (Ashgate 2013) 12–13.

84 On the causes of their failure, see Fournier and others (n 11) 126–44.

85 Hames (n 61).

86 Ibid.

87 Aileen McHarg, 'What Does the Union Need to Do to Survive?' (*Scottish Constitutional Futures Forum Blog*, 25 September 2014) <www.scottishconsti tutionalfutures.org/OpinionandAnalysis/ViewBlogPost/tabid/1767/articleType/ArticleView/articleId/4325/Aileen-McHarg-What-Does-the-Union-Need-to-Do-to-Survive.aspx> accessed 15 April 2016.

88 Hélène Landemore, 'Iceland's "Crowd-sourced" Constitution May Have Stalled, but the Experience Offers Lessons for Constitutional Reform in Other States' (*LSE EUROPP Blog*, 24 July 2014) <http://blogs.lse.ac.uk/europpblog/2014/07/24/icelands-crowd-sourced-constitution-may-have-stalled-but-the-experience-offers-lessons-for-constitutional-reform-in-other-states/> accessed 15 April 2016.

89 Baldvin T Bergsson and Paul Blokker, 'The Constitutional Experiment in Iceland', in Ellen Bos and Kálmán Pócza (eds.), *Verfassunggebung in konsolidierten Demokratien: Neubeginn oder Verfall eines Systems?* (Nomos, 2014) 171.

90 See David M Farrell, 'The Irish Constitutional Convention: A Bold Step or a Damp Squib?' in John O'Dowd and Giuseppe Franco Ferrari (eds.), *Comparative Reflections on 75 Years of the Irish Constitution* (Clarus Press, 2013) 198.

91 See sources listed above at n 38.

92 Fintan O'Toole, 'How Hopes Raised by the Constitutional Convention were Dashed' (*The Irish Times*, 3 March 2015) <www.irishtimes.com/opinion/fintan-o-toole-how-hopes-raised-by-the-constitutionalconvention- were-dashed-1.2123435> accessed 15 April 2016.

93 Ibid.

94 David M Farrell, 'Constitutional Convention "Brand" is in Jeopardy' (*The Irish Times*, 17 March 2015) <www.irishtimes.com/opinion/david-farrell-constitutional-convention-brand-is-in-jeopardy-1.2142826> accessed 15 April 2016.

95 Tierney, *Constitutional Referendums* (n 8) 23.

96 Jane Suiter, David M Farrell, Eoin O'Malley and Clodagh Harris, 'It's Good to Talk: Citizen-Politician Deliberations in Ireland's Constitutional Convention of 2012–14' (ECPR General Conference, Glasgow, 3–6 September 2014).

97 McHarg (n 87).

98 Tierney, 'Solomon Grundy Does Constitutional Change' (n 77).

99 For an analysis tempering enthusiasm for the success of the Irish constitutional convention, see Eoin Carolan, 'Ireland's Constitutional Convention: Behind the Hype about Citizen-Led Constitutional Change' (2015) 13 I-CON 733.

100 Edward McWhinney, *Constitution-Making: Principles, Process, Practice* (U Toronto P, 1981) 27.

5 Constitutional paradigms

The Italian 1948 Constitution between conservation and reform

Paul Blokker

The recent attempt at a 'Grande Riforma' of the Italian Constitution, rejected in a referendum held on 4 December 2016, is the latest addition to a string of reform attempts in Italy, in particular since the early 1990s.[1] The objective of the chapter is to engage with the Italian 'season of constitutional reform' (1990–), by focusing on Italian constitutional politics as well as shifting constitutional discourses, analyzing particularly the period 2005–16. The reform season shows a more or less permanent political attention to the theme of constitutional reform, and the regular set-up of political reform projects: two bicameral commissions in 1993 and 1997 respectively, comprehensive reforms followed by constitutional referenda in 2001, 2006, and 2016 (with different outcomes). The aim in this chapter is to contribute to a political sociology of constitutional politics and reform,[2] paying systematic attention to constitutional conflict, a variety of constitutional subjects and interpreters, shifting understandings of constitutionalism, and emphasizing the relative openness of the constitutional imaginary to interpretation.

The chapter is a contribution to the analysis of prevalent constitutional subjectivities and variegating views of the purposes of constitutions in democratic societies in Europe.[3] In addition, the objective is to explore, by means of the case-study of Italian constitutional reform, the changing nature of European constitutionalism, away from the constitution as an anti-totalitarian stronghold in the form of an entrenched higher law (in some cases), and evermore towards an instrument of technocratic constitutional engineering as well as an increasingly instrumental approach to the constitution. This tendency, which is not confined to the Italian case, seems, at least in part, in contradiction with the post-WWII trend towards what some have called 'new constitutionalism',[4] indicating a form of constitutionalism grounded in higher laws, entrenched rights, judicial review and independent constitutional courts, and, finally, an understanding of constitutional democracy as both a mode of protecting society from authoritarian and totalitarian tendencies and of safeguarding key democratic principles and rights.[5]

The chapter further reflects upon what seems to be a consistent phenomenon in the Italian reform season, which is constitutional resistance from below. The increasing propensity of, in particular, political forces to engage with constitutional reform has been contrasted with the emergence of a consistent resistance to such change emerging from civil society. Indeed, the most recent attempt to reform, as well as the reform attempt in 2005, were successfully resisted by means of popular mobilization that translated into rejections of reform in popular referenda.

In general terms, in Italy, one significant and evident change in political and social attitudes towards the 1948 Constitution in the season of reform (and in many ways already since the 1970s) is a move away from a form of *constitutional veneration*,[6] that is, generally, a relatively uncritical and respective attitude towards the original document and its crafting (as expressed in expressions such as 'la più bella costituzione del mondo' and a certain worship of the Founding Fathers of the Italian *costituente* or constituent assembly), towards a form of *constitutional engineering* or *instrumentalism*. The latter generally entails a critical if not negative view of the 1948 Constitution, and the perception that the Constitution keeps in place a form of government ('forma di governo') that inhibits efficient and modern governance.[7] The phenomenon of constitutional engineering seems not unrelated to one of 'populist constitutionalism',[8] a term that has emerged increasingly in scholarly debates recently, and that in the Italian case points to a critical attitude towards extensive checks and balances, extensive parliamentary debate of legislation, as well as a desire to create a direct relation between the political leader and the people.

The trend towards constitutional engineering and instrumentalism, in which there is more proclivity to use constitutional means for governance purposes, is not unrelated to the emergence of a distinctive, allegedly novel set of ideas on (majoritarian) democracy. The latter includes the aforementioned populist view, which in some cases translates into the populist constitutional idea that the relation between political governance/the political leader and the people ought to be a direct one, unhindered by extensive constitutional constraints. In populism, important dimensions are anti-elitism and a promise of bringing politics closer to the people.[9] As Cas Mudde has argued, populism 'opposes any institutions or procedures that impede the direct and full expression of the people's voice'.[10] Indeed, '[p]opulism deems that nothing supersedes the general will of the people, and consequently, no one should interfere with it'. 'For populism everything is political', '[t]he idea that certain things are non-political, in the sense that they are outside of the scope of majority rule, is alien to populism'.[11] The specific view of constitutional democracy is one in which the modern, mediated view of politics – of popular sovereignty through representation, political pluralism, and the insulation of political and legal power from wider society – is replaced by one in which popular sovereignty is expressed through a leader who directly represents the People-As-One, and in which political and legal power are at the 'service' of the people. This also means that the leader is absorbing constitution-making or constituent power.[12] In the Italian context, the populist view has often been linked to a plebiscitarian idea of democracy.[13]

The objective of this chapter is to explore some of the most prominent constitutional attitudes, discourses, and critiques as expressed by relevant political parties as well as civil society movements in the Italian 'season of constitutional reform' that started in the early 1990s. I will, first, discuss the constitutional claims and discourses of the centre-right part of the Italian political spectrum, which includes the relatively new parties that emerged in the 1990s, not least Umberto Bossi's *Lega Nord* and Silvio Berlusconi's *Forza Italia*, as well as transformed older parties, such as the post-fascist *Alleanza Nazionale*. Subsequently, I will discuss the views of the centre-left, in particular a formation of various centre-left forces currently gathered in the *Partito Democratico* (previously gathered in the *Unione* and *Ulivo* coalitions). Both the centre-right and centre-left can be understood as the main driving forces behind constitutional reform and as promoters of constitutional engineering. In the latter part of the chapter, I will discuss oppositional forces and views in terms of what I will label *constitutional resistance*,[14] focusing on the recent attempt at reform. Resistance to the recent reform attempt is partially related to the political opposition in Parliament (including the novel, populist force the *Movimento Cinque Stelle*), but also to significant forces in society, such as the association *Libertà e Giustizia* and the more marginal and less visible (radical left-wing) movement for 'common goods' (*beni comuni*).[15]

Constitutional instrumentalism

In the Italian context, a significant change in the perception of the role and status of the 1948 Constitution emerged, in a particularly visible way, in the early 1990s, a period of radical political change in the Italian political system as well as in larger society. The emergence of a historically novel, instrumentalist view of the constitution emerged on both the right and left sides of the political spectrum. In this, the political right has played a particularly prominent role in the transitional period in general, and in the endorsement of a novel understanding of constitutionalism, in particular.

The centre-right

The centre-right parties – consisting largely of new (and transformed) political formations emerging in the aftermath of *Tangentopoli*,[16] in particular *Forza Italia*, the *Lega Nord*, and *Alleanza Nazionale* – were part of various constitutional reform attempts in the form of *Bicamerali* or bicameral parliamentary commissions in the 1990s. After the failed second *D'Alema Bicamerale* in the late 1990s, and the unilateral imposition of constitutional reform by the centre-left (regarding the status of the regions) in 2001, the centre-right moved towards an independent constitutional agenda, which culminated in a project of constitutional reform of 2005. A key argument of the centre-right was that, in 2001, the centre-left had used an 'illegitimate majority to change the Constitution'.[17]

The constitutional narrative of the centre-right contains a number of core argumentative figures, which could be contributed to a constitutional-populist approach.[18] As argued by the Italian scholar Michele Prospero,

> An inclination to emphasize the image of a leader as supreme embodiment of an uncontrolled power has diffused in the Italy of the 1990s, in the aftermath of traumatic events which have undermined the historical subjects of mediation (parties and the parliament). The last fifteen years of the Italian republic are in reality to a large extent years of triumphing populism and of the erosion of spaces of representation.[19]

Below, I will explore some of the key justificatory arguments in the discourse of constitutional change of the centre-right. A first element in the centre-right discourse is a comprehensive critique of the 1948 Constitution and the claim that the 'First Republic' is responsible for the *ingovernabilità* that allegedly defined the post-1948 period. The 1948 Constitution is in this criticized for its institutionalization of a party-dominated, pluralistic, and fragmented system, in contrast to a desirable executive-driven or presidential system. A key justification for the comprehensive reforms of the second part of the Italian Constitution provided by the centre-right in the 2000s was the designation of the 1948 Constitution as obsolete and in dire need of modernization. For instance, in the parliamentary debate in November 2005, in which an extensive reform package of the centre-right was adopted, Senator Lauro of *Forza Italia* stated that the reform will contribute to a move away from a 'defeated Italy, divided by hate, poverty, in ragged clothes' towards a 'modern Italy, strong, respected, rich, and finally more free'.[20] Indeed, Lauro was content to 'contribute to the modification of the Constitution in order to bring it into alignment with the necessities and culture of our times'. Even though the 2005 reform failed to be adopted, as it was rejected in a popular referendum in 2006, the justification for reform in the form of a need for adaptation remained a priority in the centre-right. In the recent, extensive constitutional reforms of the centre-left and centre-right coalition of Matteo Renzi, the centre-right continued to allude to the need to modernize the constitution. As parliamentarian Elena Centemero argued, 'today we live in a historical period tied to the consequences of globalization'. 'In this context, we have tried to give an answer.'[21]

A second, strongly related, element is the endorsement of a more efficient, and promptly operating, government. The idea of efficient government is based on a distinctive view of democracy, emphasizing the need for a powerful leader, in political terms understood as a prime minister who is directly chosen by the citizens and who has key decision-making prerogatives. In the debate on the 2005 reforms, Senator Schifani (*Forza Italia*) put this idea as follows:

> I believe that with today's vote Italy will not lose, but all those Italians will win, [those] who honestly believe in, and want the amelioration, and speeding up of, decisional processes of the institutions; who want that laws are made more quickly, who want the governments and *Premier* voted for by the people [and] are not substituted by other majorities and other men; who want in substance a modernized system Italy and want the reduction of the costs of politics.[22]

The perceived need for a more efficient and simplified form of government has remained a priority in the 2013–16 reforms. A key element in these reforms is the reform of the biparliamentary system from one of 'bicameralismo perfetto' into a 'monocameralismo partecipato', which means in reality a reinforced *Camera*, and a reformed *Senato*, which only shares few powers with the *Camera*, and is now given a largely territorial function. The justification for this reform is the alleged continuity with the idea of the control or guarantee function of the Senate (in a number of key areas), whereas at the same time government is simplified and sped up. The head of the Commission for Constitutional Reform Sisto (*Forza Italia*) put it as follows:

> [A] constitutional reform of superior efficiency and in perfect harmony and in historical continuity with that which was the will of the founding fathers: the attempt to give efficiency without even for a second forgetting the extraordinary force of parliamentary democracy, it appears to me to constitute the *mantra* of that which we have tried to achieve.[23]

The objective of the reforms is clear according to MP Elena Centemero: 'to make the country governable, renovating the legislative capacity of Parliament and simplifying the institutional system, but equally [to strengthen] territorial representation in the Senate'.[24] In terms of governance structures, Italy is worse off than other countries, according to the MP Dorina Bianchi (*Area Popolare*):

> When the sovereign debt and real economic crisis exploded, Italy found itself in a condition of heightened fragility with regard to other countries, also of the same EU and, as a result of the accumulation of problems that remained unresolved during the years, amongst which, in particular, that of the lacking modernization of our institutional system, not anymore capable of expressing, in the long run, a stable political direction and [suffering from a lack of being] rooted in the consensus of the social body.[25]

A third justification for the (2005) constitutional reform, particularly articulated by the *Lega Nord*, was the direct inclusion of the citizenry in decision-making, including the constitutional reform process. Hence, the introduction of the principle that all constitutional reforms have to be put to a popular referendum,[26] not only in the case of the lack of a two-thirds majority in parliament, as stated in the revision rule of article 138. According to Senator Pirovano (*Lega Nord*), the constitutional reform of 2005 would lead to 'the increase in the powers of the people'[27] and the 'force of the reform comes from the people [themselves]'.[28] Senator Nania (*Alleanza Nazionale*) equally underlined the fact that 'in the future every constitutional amendment will need to be subjected to an affirmative *referendum* independently from the parliamentary majority that adopted it'.[29] Also, according to Senator D'Onofrio (*Unione Democristiana e di Centro*), the reform 'increases popular sovereignty because for the future it foresees that in all instances the people will participate in the process of constitutional reform', while the reform 'allows the Italians to choose the Prime Minister and the government programme'.[30] D'Onofrio elaborated the impact of the reform on popular sovereignty:

> The question is: Will this grand reform increase or diminish the sovereignty of the people? Does a grand reform increase or reduce popular sovereignty? ... We increase popular sovereignty with regard to two fundamental aspects.... [T]he Constitution currently in vigour foresees that when a constitutional reform is approved by a two-third majority in Parliament, the people is left by-stander, it cannot be called upon to discuss [the reform]; the people remains external.
>
> We have changed this fundamental norm of the Constitution; from our examination onwards, any constitutional reform can be put to popular vote. We are not dealing with a concession here, but with a fundamental point: popular sovereignty can be exercised, if this reform will be approved – as I hope – even by means of popular *referendum,* also on constitutional issues.
>
> The second increment, Mr. President, honoured Ministers, regards the formation of the Government. Until today the Italians cannot vote for a parliamentary majority and a President of the Council, or Prime Minister. They vote for parliamentarians, who, after the elections, can decide what to do. The popular vote, for the first time with this constitutional reform, will allow the Italians to vote for parliamentarians, for the head of government and for the programme.[31]

It is striking that in the 2013–16 reforms much less mention is made of the importance of direct citizen participation.[32] In this case, an original proposal to modify article 138, including an obligatory, confirmatory referendum, was abandoned and not included in the final text of the constitutional reform. In procedural terms, only relatively late in the reform process (summer 2013), an attempt to include citizens is made, in the form of public consultation. The minister of reforms, Gaetano Quagliariello, justified the need for such public inclusion as follows (in the final report regarding a public consultation on constitutional reform):

> The constitutional Charter represents the frame of the order, codifies the public lexicon of a community, fixes the fundamental rules of the game of civil cohabitation. It belongs to everyone. Its revision represents therefore a very complex and delicate matter, and much in need of the widest inclusion. Hence two initiatives activated by the government [...]: on the one hand, the Commission for constitutional reforms, which has gathered the most authoritative scholars and experts that Italian constitutionalism provides for; on the other, an initiative which takes the reform outside of the institutions and attempts to engage the citizens.[33]

It is illuminating that the minister refers to the citizens as 'non-authorized personnel' ('non addetti ai lavori'), also as the consultation was confined to a multiple-choice questionnaire, with the objective to inform parliamentarians on citizens' opinions, but without any binding nature and with little direct possibility for citizens to actively engage in the reform process and propose distinctive reforms.[34]

A fourth key element in the centre-right's justification for comprehensive constitutional reform is related to devolution and the decentralization of the Italian state, particularly promoted by the originally secessionist party, the *Lega Nord*. In 2005, the 2001 reform of the centre-left was portrayed as having caused damages to the political system and uncertainties with regard to the relation between the central state and the regions. Indeed, 'The centre-left . . . has put upside down the principle [of a central state which guards the national interest]: it is not anymore [the case that] the State . . . has all and the Regions have little [power], but the Regions have all and the State [only] some'.[35] The main critique of the 2001 reforms were, first, that it had been a reform by a limited, partisan majority, without a wide consensus, and, second, that it introduced chaos in the state-region relationship. Thus, Senator Nania (*Alleanza Nazionale*) argued: 'preferable is a reform that explicitly says what belongs to the State and what to the Regions, as it is desirable in a warm, authentic, participatory democracy, which feels the citizens' breath'.[36]

The reforms of 2013–16 equally attempted to revisit the state-regional nexus. But this time, the reform (which by many has been understood as involving a recentralizing streak) was not supported by the *Lega Nord*. Indeed, the *Lega Nord* denounced the reform as introducing a constitutional change in which 'local autonomies in reality are devalued, are destroyed, are killed *in nuce*'. The *Lega Nord* does support the change from bicameralism into monocameralism, but at the same time has doubts regarding the usefulness of the new Senate as a territorial institution of which 'one does not understand easily which functions it will have'.[37]

The centre-left

I will now turn to the discourse on, and justifications for, constitutional reform as expressed by the centre-left. While political parties from the centre-left have traditionally been the inheritors of the original constitutional pact and as such for much of the post-war period defenders of the 1948 Constitution, in particular from the mid-2000s onwards, the constitutional views of the centre-left increasingly overlap with those of the centre-right.[38] This is so, even if the 2005 reform of the centre-right was strongly contested by exponents of the centre-left. In all, the centre-left has increasingly shown considerable agreement with an important part of the key tenets of constitutional reform as articulated by the centre-right (as outlined above). As argued by Michele Prospero, the 'newist' emphasis – which pushes for continuous large reforms – can be found on both sides of the political left and right. What is more, distinctive features of constitutional reform proposals – such as the need for strong leadership, 'lean' governance, and an unmediated relation between politics and the citizens, stem from the political right, but are now equally shared by a good part of the left: 'the right has lost the referendum [on the 2005 constitutional reform], but its constitutional ideas seem anything but defeated'.[39]

A first, basic idea that is widely shared already since the 1990s is that the 1948 Constitution cannot anymore be understood as up-to-date with regard to the governing institutions as well as with regard to definitions of contemporary democracy. Indeed, a representative of the centre-left in the Commission for Constitutional Affairs, Emanuele Fiano, stated:

> The decades succeeding the constituent assembly [of 1948], our decades, the decades of our generations, [lasting] until today, have demonstrated the need for an adaptation of the mechanism of institutional functioning, of its revision in the view of an ever increasing efficiency of democracy, [a democracy] which asks to be efficient, as a democracy incapable of providing adequate replies in a relevant and fast time frame belies a relevant part of its objectives.[40]

Indeed, as Fiano further argued, 'democracies cease to function when procedures are not anymore respected and when institutions appear ungovernable. In this case, the general sense of malaise and delusion vis-à-vis democracy increases'.[41]

> [Democracy's] values are still the right ones, but in a world that is changing at a speed that is so much faster than that of politics and to which our societies need to adapt continuously in order to keep up, democracy seems slow, bureaucratic, and weak.
>
> If we really believe, as I believe and we believe, in democracy, as a whole of rules which guarantee the liberty of all citizens, it is time to ameliorate it, to render it faster and stronger. It is time for reforms.[42]

Despite the need for reform, the centre-left equally wants to hold onto a direct link with the Constituent Assembly and the founding fathers of the 1948 Constitution. In the debate on the 2013–16 reforms, various parliamentarians proposed a justification for the reform project that argues that the reforms actually fortify the original design of 1948, in particular the parliamentary system, rather than significantly modifying it. The argument is that the constitution is 'living material' and needs to be adapted to changing times,[43] but also that the reforms only touch the second, organizational part of the constitution, not the first part on fundamental principles. If the first part were to be reformed, this would touch on the very 'spirit of the Constitution'.[44]

Second, in a related way, the key justification for comprehensive constitutional reform is the observation that the obsolete nature of the 1948 Constitution is a result of its non-correspondence to apparent exigencies of governance that have emerged in a globalized, and more directly relevant, Europeanized situation. The functioning of the parliament is described as too laborious and time-consuming. The significant reform of the Senate – into a *Senato delle Autonomie* – will correct for the alleged overlap in functions of the first and second chambers. The 2013–16 reforms prioritize in this a restyling of the parliamentary institutions that emphasizes the *output* function of parliamentary institutions, that is, efficient governance and adoption of legislation, and tends to depict the *input* function, that is, inclusive deliberation, as potentially compromising the output legitimacy of parliament. The minister for Constitutional Reforms and Relations with the Parliament Maria Elena Boschi confirmed this view by designating the reform as a process

> that brings us in line with the dynamics, with a simplification not only of the legislative procedure but also of the diverse institutional levels, of the organization of our Republic in territorial terms, analogous to trajectories that also other European countries are following.[45]

One example of this is the introduction of 'participated unicameralism' in which only a limited part of the legislative process will involve the Senate, reducing its original control functions. Further examples are the proposition of a 'data certa' or fixed end date for parliamentary discussion of legislative proposals as well as the recentralization of the state, the suppression of the provinces as a layer of governance, and the introduction of the notion of 'supremacy', giving the central state final saying power over regional matters. The regional reform is intended to diminish constitutional conflict over competencies between state and regional institutions, and favours the 'national interest', but it includes the risk of undermining a form of semi-federal institutional differentiation. In addition, the reforms are defended by reference to sociological legitimacy:

> The legislative proposal that is examined in the Parliament today does not do anything else than finalize that process of modernization of the institutions which we have been discussing for decades, welcoming solutions that are widely shared, not only by public opinion, but also by the majority of the academic world and, I allow myself to say, by the political history of the Italian left of the decades.[46]

Third, regional reform, originally a key element in the centre-right constitutional agenda, is equally central in the centre-left reform propositions. The first important reform attempt came in the wake of the bicameral commission D'Alema, in 2001. In the context of the constitutional reforms of 2005, the centre-left admitted to the incomplete nature of the 2001 reforms and called for a continuation of the 'federal reform' in its 'autonomistic' and 'pluralistic' direction. The main objective was to 'include the territorial autonomies into the definition of the national political direction', in order to 'institute a Senate which is to be the chamber of effective representation of the regions and the autonomies'.[47]

The regional reform project was continued in the 2013–16 reforms, in which the territorial nature of the new Senate is reproposed, but in which there is also an important drive for recentralization. As identified above, one justification for recentralizing the Italian state, and reducing the exclusive competences of regions, is the idea of institutional modernization and the acceleration of governance. A related justification is the idea that to '[r]ewrite the institutional architecture of our country also signifies the transcendence of some forms of slowness that have been there in the past', also related to slowness with an 'economic character' and to the 'development of our country'.[48] This, according to minister Boschi, justifies the 'return of the exclusive competences regarding the promotion and safeguarding of competition, the protection and security of labour, and the active policies regarding labour, to the State'.[49]

Fourth, the centre-left generally identifies itself as a promoter of democratic reform and increased participation. In the 2006 programme of the *Unione* (the predecessor of the *Partito Democratico*), the argument is to 'amplify and enrich occasions for participation, also by means of revitalizing the abrogative referendum'.[50] What is striking in this regard is that there is no endorsement of the extension of participation to civil society in terms of the constitutional reforms themselves. Particularly in the 2013–16 reforms, it becomes clear that the centre-left prioritizes technocratic objectives of lean governance, rather than the extension of possibilities of civic engagement. In this, the centre-left appears to be by and large convinced of the idea of representative democracy as the main democratic form enshrined in the constitution. As expressed by Member of Parliament Rosy Bindi in the context of the reform of the bicameral system, the objective is to 'strengthen parliamentary democracy, not to weaken it'.[51] The emphasis in the constitutional reforms is on accelerating the decision-making process, not on the extension and proliferation of moments of participation and deliberation. This becomes particularly clear in debates on a possible extension of instruments of direct democracy in the Italian Constitution, as promoted in particular by the *Movimento Cinque Stelle*. In the Commission on Constitutional Affairs of the lower house or *Camera*, a proposal by the opposition to abolish the quorum in the case of referenda, with the intent to facilitate and strengthen direct democracy, was rejected by the *Partito Democratico* and judged 'excessive',[52] while proposals for the strengthening and expansion of various referendum instruments in the constitutional framework, amending article 75 (such as constitutional, agenda, and legislative initiatives), were equally rejected.

Regarding a persistent critique on the reduction of the Senate to an indirectly elected forum as weakening representative democracy, the centre-left argued that

> [t]he indirect election of the Senate is not detrimental to the principle of popular sovereignty, as of article 1 of the Constitution. This is so not only because of the [fact that] indirect election is one of the possible manifestations of the democratic principle – one only needs to think of the President of the Republic – but also because the same article 1 foresees that sovereignty is to be exercised by the people in the forms and limits as provided by the fundamental Charter. The legislative proposal under examination, therefore, affects the forms in which, and the limits within which, popular sovereignty is expressed, without however damaging the democratic principle.[53]

Equally, there is a shared view regarding the constitutional reform process as largely an elite and expert matter. In an interview, one senator, Franco Russo, of the *Partito Democratico*, by and large rejected the idea of more active involvement of citizens, and rather emphasized the need for well-informed experts in the constitutional reform process.

> A populist deviation that helps us imagine that all of us are capable. . . . If I have to write a book on neuroscience I will not sort 66 citizens [as in the Irish Constitutional Convention], as when I have to guarantee that a surgery room

> functions well, I will not sort citizens. There is a level of technicality with regard to a collectively identified necessity, which we approach however at the foundation, that is, that of increased velocity, of a leaner, more efficient State, but I would say also one that is more balanced in its powers [. . .]. [Constitutional reform] should not even include all parliamentarians. Parliamentarians, but supported by experts of the sector, who are constitutionalists [. . .].
>
> (Interview with MP from PD, 12-02-14)

Within the ranks of the *Partito Democratico* itself, doubts have been expressed about this justification. Rosy Bindi, for instance, remarked that '[t]he speed of decisions cannot, ever, deny the principle of the centrality of Parliament in the choices that the constituents have made and that we want to renovate'. 'One cannot go into the direction of surreptitious forms, that weaken Parliament and which always provide fertile ground for degenerative thrusts of an authoritarian, demagogic, and populist type that we clearly cannot afford ourselves in this moment.'[54]

Constitutional resistance

A recurrent pattern in the Italian season of constitutional reform is significant and continuous resistance from, in particular, non-parliamentary, civil society organizations as well as novel political formations. One way of understanding 'constitutional resistance' in the Italian context is related to the idea of a right to resistance or rebellion against domination, in this case more specifically against the undoing of the constitutional principles, values, and rights enshrined in the 1948 Constitution.[55] The emphasis here would be on an 'action intended to change in order to conserve'.[56] As one observer puts it: 'If [the State] deviates, as happens, it acts in an illegitimate way, to which one needs to resist, but [the State] does not have predatory finalities'.[57]

But resistance can also relate to a more imaginative, creative, and transformatory approach to the constitutional order, invoking an alternative constitutional world. Both attitudes – a conservative and a transformative one – are clearly present in the Italian constitutional debate.[58] The first major stance in constitutional resistance, often referred to as a *conservative* (i.e., preservationist) or *reformist stance*, endorses the preservation of (the spirit of) the 1948 Constitution and its implementation, even if it is not necessarily averse to 'constitutional maintenance'. The conservative stance predominantly promotes the protection of the representative, parliamentary system. Key proponents here include the *Comitati Dossetti, Libertà e Giustizia*, and the (related) *Comitati per il No*, but also the *Movimento Cinque Stelle* (M5S) in some of its claims. A second important stance could be labelled an *innovative stance* in that it departs from a critique of (important parts of) the 1948 Constitution as such and seeks a new constituent moment. The innovative stance emphasizes a participatory view of constitutional reform. Key proponents can be found on the radical left, particularly in the variegated movement for the *beni comuni* or 'the Commons', but also within the M5S. Both the conservative and innovative attitudes are prominently present in the Italian public debate, and often form conflicting views within specific movements themselves.

In the context of the reform season, we can speak of a *pattern* of constitutional resistance, often engaging not only civil society proper, but equally important parts of the academic and cultural community, in resistance to the various majoritarian reform projects. Significant examples of this are the so-called *Comitati Dossetti*, after Don Giuseppe Dossetti, a Catholic father and one of the protagonists of the original Constituent Assembly, which formed throughout Italy from 1994 onwards. These grassroots committees strongly opposed the idea of constitutional reform and defended the fundamental values as expressed by the 1948 Constitution. They mobilized against the D'Alema Bicameral Commission in 1997 and again against the Berlusconi reform in 2005. Dossetti expressed himself against the inflationary tendencies of simplified constitutional reform towards what, in his view, ought to be considered as a rigid constitution or a higher law. The understanding of comprehensive constitutional reform as a panacea to the political crisis was a 'substitutive mythology' and distracted from serious reflection on structural political reform,[59] and a strong insistence on direct democracy through referenda created the danger of another myth, that of unmediated popular sovereignty at the expense of parliamentary debate.

Resistance reemerged in the context of the latest reform wave, which started in 2013. The Renzi reform was heavily, and ultimately successfully, opposed by various forces: political parties within parliament (significant opposition was present even within Renzi's own *Partito Democratico*), various (constitutional) experts, journalists, and other public figures, and organized groups in civil society. Some oppositional political parties rejected the reforms from the start, such as the *Lega Nord*, while others initially supported the reforms and only much later reversed position (in particular *Forza Italia*).[60] In civil society, some groups, as mentioned above, continued a long-standing mobilization and opposition to constitutional reform.

In the recent reform project, a significant part of the political claims of the opposition regarded the majoritarian approach to democratic politics (in contrast to pluralism), the lack of involvement of citizens and civil society in the reform process, and the impoverished standing of citizens (and the parliament) in the democratic-institutional landscape created by the reforms. The critique depicted the Renzi reform as a governmental imposition of a majoritarian, partisan view of constitutional change, even if the reform was embedded in a (fragile) reform coalition of centre-left and (some of the) centre-right parties. The thrust of the critique was that a large, inter-party consensus was absent, given that the main opposition parties were radically opposed (the M5S and the *Lega Nord*), while important exponents of civil society and the scholarly community were ignored in the reform process.[61]

A form of constitutional resistance as constitutional conservation is the campaign pursued by a high profile nonprofit organization called *Libertà e Giustizia* (*LeG*), which was formed in 2002, and whose president currently is Nadia Urbinati, a well-known political theorist. *LeG* endorses public knowledge of the 1948 Constitution and emphasizes a priority for the implementation of existing constitutional norms, rather than recourse to constitutional engineering. The latter is particularly denounced when pursued by, what *LeG* understands as, democratically problematic (non-elected) governments that have governed Italy since the downfall of Silvio Berlusconi in 2011 and the promotion of 'plebiscitarian democracy'.[62] Gustavo Zagrebelsky, former president of the Italian Constitutional Court and prominent member of *LeG*, argued that 'we defend the Constitution as something of everyone and we oppose all those that consider it theirs, acting without mandate'.

> When we say that the Constitution is everyone's and not of a few, we want to say this: that the change of the Constitution of which is spoken currently is promoted by a part, for their own objectives, and is not neutral, with respect to democracy.[63]

In *LeG*'s public appeal 'For a Constitutional Season. No empty words but acts of contrition', a clear defence of the 1948 Constitution is provided and a form of 'constitutional resistance' is offered against attempts to override the constitution:

> Where to find support in order to exit from the mess, in order to provoke courage, enthusiasm, in a moment of political depression as the one we are going through at the moment? Where to find the ideal of a just society, for which it is right to put aside egoisms and particularist privileges, that makes it possible for us to distinguish a society in which we ourselves, our children, and the children of our children may live in freedom and justice? It is surprising that one does not think that this ideal, this supportive element is already there, and it is the CONSTITUTION. And it is surprising that the referendum of June 2006, in which almost 16 million citizens have expressed themselves in favour of its principles, has been reduced to a parenthesis. Equally surprising is the fact that no significance is given to – perhaps because one does not notice it – the enthusiasm that every discourse on the Constitution meets, in particular amongst young people, on its historical significance and its contemporary political and civic value. Isn't here a big force that awaits to be interpellated to change society? It is not paradoxical that one looks back in order to look forward. The difficulties in which we find ourselves do not stem from the Constitution, but from the ignorance, the maltreatment, the abuse, sometimes the violence that have been inflicted upon it.[64]

A further point of critique of the ongoing reform process since 2013 is the observation that the procedures for constitutional change are not being observed and that the comprehensiveness of reforms calls for wide public consultation and input. As argued by Stefano Rodotà, a well-known constitutional lawyer and representative of *LeG*, the reforms would require a comprehensive social consensus:

> For some years now a perverse relation has been institutionalized between economic emergency, political impotence and constitutional changes. With a violent acceleration, and without a real public debate, in 2012 a change of article 81 of the Constitution has been adopted, which foresees a balanced budget. At the time, parliamentarians were asked, in vain, to not approve that

> reform with a majority of two thirds, so as to allow for the eventual promotion of a referendum on such a profound reform. The reason was clear. The inclusion of citizens is much talked about and it is forgotten that that majority had been foreseen when the electoral law was still proportional, in this way providing guarantees in Parliament, which have been strongly reduced with the transition to a majoritarian system. Today, the same request is made to the senators which are to vote on the second reading of the modification of article 138. Will there be a group amongst them that will have the institutional sensibility to welcome this invitation, entrusting also the citizens with the judgment to suspend a procedure of guarantee that others, in the future, might use invoking some other urgency or emergency? It is not sufficient, in fact, to have a referendum at the end of the trajectory of the final reform, [when] the correctness regarding the way in which that trajectory started, remains in doubt.[65]

One particularly outspoken adversary of the 2013–16 reforms is the *Movimento Cinque Stelle*, a political, populist movement around the comedian Beppe Grillo, which obtained a significant electoral result in the 2013 general elections, and became the main opposition force. The position of constitutional resistance as both constitutional conservation and constitutional creation can be identified in the arguments used by the *Movimento Cinque Stelle,* which are – at least in part – not dissimilar to the ones used by *LeG.* The position of M5S combines constitutional conservation – a 'cult of the Constitution' – with innovation.[66] The arguments used by the M5S were – at least in part – not dissimilar to the ones used by *LeG.*[67] M5S was a particularly outspoken adversary of the 2013–16 reforms.[68] Key justifications for both the protection or conservation of the 1948 Constitution and for a different type of constitutional reforms are, according to the movement, first, the idea that the 1948 Constitution is unjustly blamed for the malfunctioning of politics; second, the view that comprehensive constitutional reform is necessary but can only be pursued by means of an inclusive, consensualist approach (in contrast to a majoritarian approach); and, third, the idea that comprehensive constitutional change necessarily needs to include the voice of citizens and civil society, in particular because of the malfunctioning of representative democracy and the 'partitocrazia'.

The evaluation of the 1948 Constitution by the *Movimento Cinque Stelle* is in stark contrast to that of the reformist political forces.

> I believe that the current legislative proposal draws its inspiration from a macroscopic, basic mistake: the mistake that the crisis of the institutions stems from the dispositions of the constitutional Charter and not instead from the incapacity of politics to reform itself. The inefficiency of the institutions, in other words, is attributed – as a result of this mistake – to the body of laws that guarantees its democratic structure, and not to the failures of the contemporary anti-democratic system of parties. The *ratio* that inspires this proposal is therefore that the Constitution is the cause of

> the decadence of the governing classes. [But] the exact opposite is true: it is the progressive decline of politics that has promoted the attempt to override the Constitution.
>
> (Interview with MP of M5S, 1-8-2013)

The view is not one of strict originalism and conservatism regarding the 1948 Constitution, but rather that the reform process needs different objectives and ought to involve the majority as well as the political opposition.

> Paradoxically they argue that we do not want to enter into dialogue, when we retain that from an ideal point of view the decisions of the country need to be shared, have to search for a consensus amongst the larger part of the active political [and] civil forces in society. Particularly the citizens, no? And we clash however paradoxically with regard to that which comes from outside . . . with a system that points at decisionism, that is, the majority needs to decide. . . . There is almost the perception that the rules wanted by the Constitution, for the discussion, the [various] passages, are something that is too much, that irritates, ok?
>
> (Interview with MP of M5S, 1-8-2013)

The *Movimento Cinque Stelle*, often labelled as populist, criticizes (Italian) representative democracy for being based on a 'partitocrazia', in which parties compete for power and resources, while ignoring the common good or the needs of ordinary citizens. The Movimento contrasts a corrupted representative model with forms of direct democracy. The 1948 Constitution in this regard is understood as part of the problem, in that it has institutionalized a certain distrust of the people.

> The Italian Constitution was born also from the experience of fascism, and therefore . . . is a constitution which has seen popular participation . . . with a certain diffidence, much power has been given to the parties and little to the people, something which was understandable at the time. . . . As a result of that Constitution, the way it has been conceived, we could say that legislative political as well as economic power has been concentrated in the parties. States have become partitocracies. In Italy, the phenomenon is perhaps much more evident than elsewhere . . . and therefore . . . the system of 'partitocrazia' is evermore in crisis, which, rather than opening up and modifying in order to let citizens enter into the governance of the public good . . . they close themselves in and increasingly centralize power. . . . There is in my opinion a push into the direction of technocracy, centralism, in the direction of pushing towards more power for the government rather than for parliament . . .
>
> (Interview with MP of M5S, 1-8-2013)

In this, the *Movimento Cinque Stelle* is one of the few political forces in Italy that explicitly calls for citizen participation in constitutional reform. The movement proposes to:

> Remove the material limits imposed on the traditional abrogative referendum; we have introduced obligatory forms of referendum for the ratification of international treaties, of evident political interest and susceptible to directly affect the lives of all citizens. Still from this perspective of direct citizen participation in the fundamental choices of politics, [we propose] the introduction of a criteria of homogeneity regarding constitutional referenda: we do not want citizens to be put in front of the choice 'take it or leave it', as would happen with the confirmative referendum in your reform. To the contrary, we want citizens to be called with the right awareness and responsibility, point by point.[69]

A third form of constitutional resistance – more radically innovatory, but at the same time also conservative – is represented by the (radical) left-wing movement for the 'commons' or 'beni comuni'. The idea of 'the commons' potentially strikes at the core of the Italian Constitution, in that it concerns the access and usage of public goods, which are deemed fundamental for human existence (such as water, education, knowledge, culture, the internet) as well as the actual possibility of enjoying rights. The argument by the Commons movement is that there is a 'constitutional asymmetry' in liberal constitutionalism that favours private and state property over other, collective and horizontal approaches towards goods of social importance.[70] The Italian movement for the Commons pursues a creative constitutional project in that it refers to constitutional law as a means to safeguard the commons (as in a 'right of commons'), but also redefines constitutions as dynamic and emancipatory instruments, open to participation, and amenable to the recuperation of politics from narrow definitions of economic governance.

First, according to the Commons movement, the existing 1948 Constitution is largely unable to respond to the crisis of liberal, representative, and capitalist democracy that set in in the 1970s. The 1948 Constitution is in general portrayed as an obstacle.

> When we say that the Constitution of 1948 is bloodless and non-recoverable, they treat us as enemies of the state. You are reciting a *De Profundis* not only of that Charter but also of democracy, they say. Is this really true? Couldn't it be that exactly by repeating those defences (by now only ideological) that the little of democracy that is left in Italy is consumed as well?[71]

According to one prominent exponent of the Commons movement, the original emancipatory thrust of the Italian Constitution and public law has been interrupted by the reforms of the last two decades:

> A combination of normative interventions has radically interrupted that process of evolution and transformation of liberal and post-liberal public law that, from 1948 onwards, even if in alternating phases, was moving towards the effective actualization of constitutional principles, liberating itself from that combination of political and legal absolutism which in various phases

> of the middle ages had characterized the origins and development of public law. [. . .] From the 1990s onwards, a process of crisis and transformation of public law is underway, which has progressively undermined classical categories and subjects and which, above all, has hit the sphere of organization and that of power, beyond the dimension of substantive equality and solidarity.[72]

For the Commons movement, the inadequate nature of the Italian Constitution has to do with its neoliberal or economic-liberal nature, and the reproduction of a public/private distinction. This distinction has informed the classical market-state dichotomy with regard to economic governance, in which particular goods can only be understood as either privately or publicly owned and administered. For the Commons movement, the property logic tends, however, towards the exclusion of some (or sometimes many) in terms of access and usage of distinctive goods,[73] particularly so in times of the widespread privatization of public goods. The Commons movement endorses a third dimension, which emphasizes the equal access of all to specific 'primary goods', such as water, culture, education, or knowledge, beyond the logic of property and market rationale, and prioritizing the essence of such primary goods for the possibility of full participation of all citizens in society.

Second, the critique on liberal constitutionalism is its disregard for a different rationality, that of the commons or *res communis omnium*, which largely escapes the public-private property dichotomy, and points to the importance of access to and usability of specific common goods, rather than the title of ownership.[74] The alternative constitutional world proposed by the Commons movement suggests using the existing Italian Constitution for the purpose of the realization of common goods and their collective governance. The argument is that the commons are of great importance for socioeconomic and territorial cohesion as well as for the actual satisfaction of fundamental rights.[75] A constitutional language that includes the commons therefore relates to the commons or common goods in distinct local contexts and the articulation of the specific needs of distinct communities. Stefano Rodotà, a constitutional lawyer who has been spearheading the legal promotion of the commons, indeed invokes the term of a 'constitutionalism of needs'.[76] The Commons movement's view of the constitution proposes a different view of the individual as well as of the governance of society:

> In the universe of the commons, the primary position is for the individual with his needs, as in the Constitution, in which the focal point is the recognition of the value of the person, in his dignity and free development. It is not by coincidence that the personalist principle is considered the principle. It is a person, the one of the Constitution, open to others and in solidarity: the individual is understood as singular but also as part of social formations and the recognition of the inviolability of his rights relates to the request for the fulfilment of duties of solidarity (art. 2).[77]

Third, for the Commons movement, the current constitutional order tends to be inadequate in terms of its promotion of popular sovereignty and representation.[78] For Rodotà, national sovereignty obfuscates the 'communities' that inhabit states, but also transcends these communities, by giving the exclusive right to dispose over national 'own' resources to the State.[79] In more specific democratic terms, the notion of popular sovereignty is seen as ignoring the diversity of communities and people that are part of a larger political community. As Lucarelli argues,

> There is a need to force oneself to imagine, and therefore to contribute to construct, a public debate that fulfills its function in the presence of instances that tend to and intend to get rid of the hypocritical application of the principle of popular sovereignty.[80]

The critique of popular sovereignty consists in its negligence of substantial inequalities and significant diversity, and therefore its fictional character. Popular sovereignty as the basis of representative democracy is not able to protect the diversity that is at the basis of every society and to counter the dominating logic of powerful and privileged minorities over powerless majorities. The opposite of popular sovereignty would then be a notion of participatory democracy in which 'all citizens are really able to participate on the basis of effective, reciprocal equality, and, therefore, with full and conscious self-determination to the formation of the governing popular will'.[81] Ugo Mattei, a radical exponent of the Commons movement, puts things more drastically:

> In this phase, [Italian society is] divided between those who believe we live in a democracy and those who do not believe that anymore. I believe that . . . there is nothing democratic in our system. Nothing. That is, our system is in substance an authoritarian structuration with strong post-fascist traits, with a concentration of power in the hands of economic and political technocracies of various kinds, of an elite, which in substance uses the democratic rhetoric, which is a total show. I do not believe in Italian democracy.
>
> (Interview with Ugo Mattei, 28-11-2013)

Mattei believes that the current political and constitutional order lacks in political subjectivity, and hence, one cannot speak of democratic constitutionalism in the Italian context.

> For me, democratic constitutionalism exists when there is a public political subjectivity. The consumer is not a political subject: the consumer of today has been massacred; that is, for the largest part by far, persons have been fooled by the idea of universal suffrage, they are convinced to be citizens, [but] instead they are consumers, they do not have any type of political agency and are simply part of the show, aren't they? They are biological tissue, living meat, consumers of which the needs are to be satisfied in an animal sense, I am not sure how to put it to you, [but] there is no political subjectivization. When the latter is lacking, there cannot be democratic constitutionalism.
>
> (Interview with Ugo Mattei, 28-11-2013)

Concluding remarks

The 1948 Constitution appears to be losing its hold on Italian (political and civil) society. The period of 1990 until 2016 has seen a widespread adherence to constitutional engineering amongst political elites and a general political attitude of constitutional instrumentalism. The latter approaches the constitution less as a foundational document enshrining the ultimate principles of the political community, and more as a vehicle for particular political projects. In this, the sociological legitimacy of the Italian constitutional order has been weakened. Sociological legitimacy can be understood as the idea that if a constitutional framework is to integrate a larger polity and is to make such a polity meaningful to its participants, important linkages between formal institutions and wider society need to exist. In the current 'season of constitutional engineering', the effective linkages between society and political institutions have come increasingly under strain, even if the constitutional projects of both centre-left and -right claim to have means to overcome this.

The mainstream political forces that have emerged out of the political earthquake of the early 1990s prove to be the main proponents of constitutional reform, promoting the objectives of strong leadership, lean governance, and a restructuring of the relations between the political centre and the regions. The 'grande riforma' combines a populist with a technocratic thrust. The first comes through in the insistence on strong leadership and a direct relation with the citizens or people and in general emphasizes plebiscitarian rather than substantive democratic engagement by the citizenry. The second, technocratic, approach comes through in the emphasis on the technical nature of the reforms and the prominent role of experts. There is an attempt to portray constitutional reform as a mere project of scientific rationalization, and, in this, of depoliticization.[82] Governance is not about public choices and collective autonomy, but rather about the scientific management of already known objectives. Also, in the latter case, the role of society in the reforms is understood as (at most) a supportive one, rather than an active, inclusive one.

Various exponents of civil society engaged successfully in constitutional resistance against the political-constitutional reform project, as has occurred again in the recent constitutional referendum at the end of 2016. The populist tendency is denounced as authoritarian and the constitutional-instrumentalist thrust is criticized for its erosion of the original principles and values of the 1948 constitutional pact. Constitutional resistance is highly variegated, and includes both more conservative and revolutionary components, but a general thrust is towards more substantive societal and civic engagement with the constitutional reforms. The latest reform attempt of the Renzi government faced this resistance once again and lost.

Notes

1 Constitutional reform was part of the political agenda in Italy already since the mid-1970s, first proposed by Giuliano Amato (currently a constitutional court judge) and later also by PM Bettino Craxi. The first bicameral Commission for Constitutional

Reform was the Commissione Bozzi, which operated from 1982–85. This commission had the mandate to study constitutional reform. Only in the 1990s, actual political projects of constitutional revision were engaged in. Cf. Alessandro Pizzorusso, *La Costituzione. I valori da conservare, le regole da cambiare* (Einaudi, 1996): 22–23; Nadia Urbinati and David Ragazzoni, *La vera Seconda Repubblica. L'ideologia e la macchina* (Raffaello Cortina Editore, 2016).

2 See for political-sociological approaches: P. Blokker (2012), 'Constitutions and Democracy in Post-National Times: A Political-Sociological Approach', in *Irish Journal of Sociology* 20.2: 68–90; M. El-Ghobashy (2008), 'Constitutionalist Contention in Contemporary Egypt', in *American Behavioral Scientist* 51, no. 11: 1590–610; H. Klug (2017), 'Towards a Sociology of Constitutional Transformation: Understanding South Africa's Post-Apartheid Constitutional Order', in P. Blokker and C. Thornhill (eds.), *Sociological Constitutionalism* (Cambridge University Press, 2017).

3 Research on which this chapter is based is part of a comparative research project 'Constitutional Politics in Post-Westphalian Europe' (CoPolis), funded with a Unità di Ricerca 2011 grant, Provincia Autonoma di Trento, held at the Department of Sociology, University of Trento.

4 A. Stone Sweet, 'Constitutions and Judicial Power', in D. Caramani (ed.), *Comparative Politics* (Oxford University Press, 2008): 217–39; Ran Hirschl (2004), 'The Political Origins of the New Constitutionalism', in *Indiana Journal of Global Legal Studies* 11.1: 71–108; see also Paul Blokker, *New Democracies in Crisis?: A Comparative Constitutional Study of the Czech Republic, Hungary, Poland, Romania and Slovakia* (Routledge, 2013).

5 Ronald Dworkin (1995), 'Constitutionalism and Democracy', in *European Journal of Philosophy* 3.1: 2–11.

6 Sanford Levinson, *Constitutional Faith* (Princeton University Press, 2011).

7 A condemnation of the existing constitutional order, as *inter alia* indicated by the notion of 'partitocrazia', cf. Pizzorusso (n 1) 24, fn 47.

8 See P. Blokker, 'Populist Constitutionalism', in C. De la Torre (ed.), *Routledge International Handbook of Global Populism* (Routledge, forthcoming). For the Italian case, see M. Prospero, *La costituzione tra populismo e leaderismo* (FrancoAngeli, 2007).

9 Cas Mudde (2013), 'Are Populists Friends or Foes of Constitutionalism?', Policy Brief, The Social and Political Foundations of Constitutions, Oxford University. Cf. L. Thio, 'Constitutionalism in Illiberal Polities', in M. Rosenfeld and A. Sajo (eds.), *The Oxford Handbook of Comparative Constitutional Law* (Oxford University Press, 2012): 133–52.

10 Mudde (n 9) 3.

11 Mudde (n 9) 4.

12 Cf. Andrew Arato (2013), 'Political Theology and Populism', in *Social Research* 80.1.

13 The critique of the tendency to institutionalize a plebiscitarian model is indicated by the notion of a 'deriva autoritaria' or authoritarian turn (e.g., in relation to the most recent reform project of the government of Matteo Renzi).

14 Ermanno Vitale, *Difendersi dal potere. Per una resistenza costituzionale* (Laterza, 2010).

15 While the resistance to the Renzi reform was extensive, it should be acknowledged that important scholars, such as Carlo Fusaro, Stefano Ceccanti, and Roberto Bin have campaigned in favour. The same can be said for important societal actors, such as the primary Italian business association Confindustria.

16 'Bribe city', the major and extensive corruption crisis that emerged in Italy in the early 1990s, which has generally been understood as a significant rupture in the history of the post-war First Republic.

17 Schifani, Resoconto sommario e stenografico, 900, mercoledì 16 novembre, Senato della Repubblica (2005): 39.

18 Cf. Prospero (n 8) 84–85.

19 Prospero (n 8) 13.

20 Resoconto sommario e stenografico, 900, mercoledì 16 novembre, Senato della Repubblica (2005): 5.
21 Resoconto stenografico, 350, seduta di martedì 16 dicembre, Camera dei deputati (2014): 92.
22 Resoconto sommario e stenografico, 900, mercoledì 16 novembre, Senato della Repubblica (2005): 35.
23 Resoconto stenografico, 350, seduta di martedì 16 dicembre, Camera dei deputati (2014): 71.
24 Resoconto stenografico, 350, seduta di martedì 16 dicembre, Camera dei deputati (2014): 91.
25 Resoconto stenografico, 350, seduta di martedì 16 dicembre, Camera dei deputati (2014): 43.
26 The constitutional reform proposed to abolish the third part of article 138, which stipulates the modalities of constitutional revision. The third part says: 'A referendum shall not be held if the law has been approved in the second voting by each of the Houses by a majority of two-thirds of the members. [Non si fa luogo a referendum se la legge è stata approvata nella seconda votazione da ciascuna delle Camere a maggioranza di due terzi dei suoi componenti]'.
27 Resoconto sommario e stenografico, 900, mercoledì 16 novembre, Senato della Repubblica (2005): 17.
28 Resoconto sommario e stenografico, 900, mercoledì 16 novembre, Senato della Repubblica (2005): 18.
29 Resoconto sommario e stenografico, 900, mercoledì 16 novembre, Senato della Repubblica (2005): xi.
30 Resoconto sommario e stenografico, 900, mercoledì 16 novembre, Senato della Repubblica (2005): x.
31 Resoconto sommario e stenografico, 900, mercoledì 16 novembre, Senato della Repubblica (2005): 18–19.
32 I explore the marginal role of experimentation with civic participation in the Italian process of constitutional reform in: P. Blokker (2017), 'The Grande Riforma of the Italian Constitution: Majoritarian versus Participatory Democracy?', in *Contemporary Italian Politics* 9.2: 124–41.
33 Rapporto Finale, *Consultazione Pubblica sulle Riforme Costituzionali* (Roma: Dipartimento per le Riforme Istituzionali, 2013): 3.
34 For a concise analysis of the consultative process, with comparative dimension, see Blokker (n 32). For the relation of civic participation and constitutional reform in general, see Xenophon Contiades and Alkmene Fotiadou (eds.), *Participatory Constitutional Change: The People as Amenders of the Constitution* (Routledge, 2016).
35 Resoconto sommario e stenografico, 900, mercoledì 16 novembre, Senato della Repubblica (2005): 28.
36 Resoconto sommario e stenografico, 900, mercoledì 16 novembre, Senato della Repubblica (2005): 29.
37 Resoconto stenografico, 352, seduta di giovedì 18 dicembre, Camera dei deputati (2014): 47.
38 Urbinati and Ragazzoni (n 1).
39 Prospero (n 8) 28.
40 Resoconto stenografico, 350, seduta di martedì 16 dicembre, Camera dei deputati (2014): 74.
41 Resoconto stenografico, 350, seduta di martedì 16 dicembre, Camera dei deputati (2014): 75.
42 Resoconto stenografico, 350, seduta di martedì 16 dicembre, Camera dei deputati (2014): 76.
43 Fiano, Resoconto stenografico, 350, seduta di martedì 16 dicembre, Camera dei deputati (2014): 75–76.

44 Bindi, Resoconto stenografico, 351, seduta di mercoledì 17 dicembre, Camera dei deputati (2014): 17.
45 Resoconto stenografico, 351, seduta di mercoledì 17 dicembre, Camera dei deputati (2014): 7.
46 Fiano, Resoconto stenografico, 352, seduta di giovedì 18 dicembre, Camera dei deputati (2014): 77.
47 Unione, 'Per il bene dell'Italia', Programma di Governo 2006–2011 (2006): 14.
48 Boschi, Resoconto stenografico, 352, seduta di giovedì 18 dicembre, Camera dei deputati (2014): 7.
49 Boschi, Resoconto stenografico, 352, seduta di giovedì 18 dicembre, Camera dei deputati (2014): 9.
50 Unione (n 47) 11.
51 Bindi, Resoconto stenografico, 351, seduta di mercoledì 17 dicembre, Camera dei deputati (2014): 17.
52 Camera dei Deputati, Commissione degli Affari Costituzionali, della Presidenza del Consiglio e Interni, 351, 5 dicembre (2014): 5.
53 Ferrari, Resoconto stenografico, 352, seduta di giovedì 18 dicembre, Camera dei deputati (2014): 48.
54 Bindi, Resoconto stenografico, 351, seduta di mercoledì 17 dicembre, Camera dei deputati (2014): 18.
55 Vitale (n 14) viii–ix.
56 Vitale (n 14) x. Resistance stems from the Latin verb *sto, stare*, 'to stay', indicating a static dimension (cf. Paul Blokker and Andrea Brighenti (2011), 'Politics Between Justification and Defiance', in *European Journal of Social Theory*) 14.3).
57 Alessandra Algostino (2014), 'La Costituzione e i "beni comuni". Una tutela assolutamente necessaria', in *Patria Indipendente*: 29–31, 30.
58 These two forms are derived from an extensive study of constitutional resistance, on the basis of the analysis of documents, (media) statements, as well as of interviews the author held with main representatives, as part of a comparative research project. The argument is not that these are the only or even always the most important dimensions of resistance, but rather that they are an intrinsic and continuous part of constitutional resistance over time.
59 Giuseppe Dossetti (2005), 'I valori della Costituzione'. Napoli: Istituto Italiano per gli Studi Filosofici, available at: http://eprints.bice.rm.cnr.it/3252/1/Trentennale_5.pdf: 46 (accessed on 10 July 2016).
60 Carlo Fusaro (2016), 'Le ragioni della riforma costituzionale. Una guida': 36, available at: www.carlofusaro.it/materiali/Guida%20ragionata%2015052016.pdf (accessed on 18 January 2017).
61 The reform saw a continuous polemic between PM Renzi and Reform Minister Boschi, on the one hand, and part of the scholarly, constitutional expert community, on the other (pejoratively referred to as 'professoroni'), Marco Plutino, 'Equilibri e squilibri costituzionale tra la tentata revisione costituzionale del 2005 e il d.d.l. costituzionale "Boschi"', in Vincenzo Baldini (ed.), *La Costituzione e la sua revisione* (Pisa University Press, 2015): 117–72, 149–50. One of the constitutionalists, Gaetano Azzariti, spoke in an interview of a 'strategy of delegitimization of all critical reflection' (cf. Plutino 2015: 150). Equally, from the side of trade unions (e.g., CGIL), critical comments regarding the reforms were raised as well as concern related to a lack of societal participation in the reforms.
62 *LeG*, March 2014, 'Verso la svolta autoritaria', available at: www.libertaegiustizia.it/2014/03/27/verso-la-svolta-autoritaria/ (accessed on 11 July 2016).
63 Gustavo Zagrebelsky (2013), 'La Costituzione non è cosa vostra', *Micro Mega online*, available at: http://temi.repubblica.it/micromega-online/la-costituzione-non-e-cosa-vostra/: 8 (accessed on 11 July 2016).

64 Gustavo Zagrebelsky, 'Per Una Stagione Costituzionale', 12-11-2012, available at: www.libertaegiustizia.it/2012/11/12/per-una-stagione-costituzionale/ (accessed on 11 July 2016).
65 Stefano Rodotà, 'Riforma costituzionale, voce ai cittadini', *la Repubblica*, 23-10-2013.
66 Some observers evaluate this as contradictory, see Antonio Floridia and Rinaldo Vignati (2014), 'Deliberativa, diretta o partecipativa? Le sfide del Movimento 5 stelle alla democrazia rappresentativa', *Quaderni di sociologia* 65: 51–74.
67 Cf. Floridia and Vignati (n 66): 63. Such affinity between the two entities did not, however, lead M5S to adhere to national public manifestations of *LeG* and various other organizations, such as in Rome on 12 October 2013. Loris Caruso (2015), 'Il Movimento 5 Stelle e la fine della politica', *Rassegna Italiana di Sociologia* 56(2): 315–40, 323–24.
68 This became very 'visible' in September 2013, when 12 MPs of the Movement occupied the roof of the Italian parliament, in order to defend the constitution.
69 Toninelli, MP of M5S, Resoconto stenografico, 350, seduta di martedì 16 dicembre, Camera dei deputati (2014): 80.
70 Ugo Mattei, *Beni Comuni. Un Manifesto* (Laterza, 2012).
71 Uninomade, 'Insistiamo: la critica della costituzione è necessaria', 1-1-2013, available at: www.uninomade.org/la-critica-della-costituzione-e-necessaria/ (accessed on 11 July 2016).
72 Alberto Lucarelli, *Costituzione e beni comuni* (Diogene Edizioni, 2013a): 12, 14.
73 Cf. Stefano Rodotà, *Il diritto di avere diritti* (Laterza, 2012): 106–7.
74 Alberto Lucarelli, *La democrazia dei beni comuni* (Laterza, 2013b): 60–61.
75 Lucarelli (n 74) 61.
76 Rodotà (n 73) 94.
77 Algostino (n 57) 31.
78 Cf. Rodotà (n 73); Lucarelli (n 74).
79 Rodotà (n 73) 124–25.
80 Lucarelli (n 74) 56; emphasis in original.
81 Lucarelli (n 74) 56.
82 Cf. Paul Blokker (2014), 'The European Crisis and a Political Critique of Capitalism', in *European Journal of Social Theory* 17.3: 258–74.

6 Ireland's evolving constitution

Jane Suiter, David M. Farrell, and Clodagh Harris

Introduction

Ireland's 2016 election, its second since the onset of the Great Recession, sent shockwaves through the political system.[1] In common with many other European countries, particularly those requiring a bailout, Ireland has experienced a dramatic fragmentation of the party system, increased difficulties in forming governments, and a rise in support for populist parties and independent candidates.[2] In tandem with the strains on the party system and process of government formation (which saw the current government elected after 70 days of negotiations – an unprecedented delay by Irish standards), the Constitution, Bunreacht na hÉireann, is being found increasingly wanting as it approaches its 80th birthday in 2017. Demands for changes to it and efforts to do so have been coming with increasing regularity, with little sign of this dissipating.

Unlike other newer EU states, where the direction of constitutional change has tended to be by means of appeals of a homogenous ethno-national majority, often to the detriment of minorities,[3] in Ireland the direction of travel has, at least in the past decade, been towards pluralism and liberalism, in part, perhaps reflecting its starting point – that of a Constitution written in the much more conservative era of the mid-1930s. Given that the Constitution can only be changed by referendum, Ireland is in the top tier of European countries in terms of the numbers of referendums held in the postwar years. The large number of the reforms that have occurred to date can be grouped into three main types: European Union (EU) Treaty-related, institutional change, and social change/ modernisation issues. This will be the focus of the first part of the chapter, which sets the scene in terms of how constitutional reform occurs in Ireland, and its increasing regularity over the past 25 years.

The remainder of the chapter examines recent, and ongoing, efforts at constitutional reform. Our starting point for this is the 2011 election of the Fine Gael/ Labour coalition – elected in the depths of Ireland's economic crisis – whose programme for government promised a 'democratic revolution' that included a spate of constitutional reform measures. There are two parts to this that are of particular interest: one focused on process and the other on content. In the first instance – and the theme of the second part of this chapter – is the unusual experiment in citizen-oriented discussion about constitutional reform that took shape in the Irish Constitutional Convention of 2012–14. We argue that the Convention was a bid by the government parties to not only include the citizens to a greater extent than heretofore in referendum decision-making but also to allow some potentially divisive decision-making to be outsourced. The third section of the chapter deals with the content of the constitutional reforms that were attempted throughout the period of the last government (2011–15), most of which were passed successfully. We conclude with a discussion of how the range and variety of constitutional reform show no sign of abating: more referendums are promised, and the practice of including citizens within a deliberative framework, the Irish Citizen Assembly, similar to the Irish Constitutional Convention is being repeated by the new government elected in spring 2016.

Constitutional context and key actors

Because of the rigid nature of the Irish Constitution, the sole route to constitutional revision is via referendums. The referendum must pass by a simple majority of those voting (there is no minimum turnout threshold) and should it succeed it must then be signed into law by the president. This means that the word of the people is binding; but the people have little direct say in determining the topics for referendum. Given the strongly centralised system of government in Ireland, with a powerful executive and weak parliament,[4] in practice this means that constitutional change in Ireland is controlled by the governing parties and specifically by the Taoiseach (prime minister).[5] However, this has not proved to be a bar to constitutional change, and since the Constitution was approved in 1937 there have been some 29 amendments to it, although 2 of these were completed within the first three years of its enactment and did not require referendums. In recent years, the pace of constitutional revision has quickened with eight referendums resulting in 5 amendments being approved since 2010 and 14 amendments since the turn of the century. This trajectory is perhaps not surprising as it reflects a state that is seeking to modernise with the changing times.

Irish referendums cover a broad range of themes, which we categorise as EU Treaty-related, institutional change, and social change/modernisation issues.[6] Under this categorisation there have been 9 EU Treaty-related referendums (2 of these repeat referendums), 18 institutional votes, and 13 on social change/ modernisation issues. Each of these tends to involve different sets of actors campaigning on opposing sides.

By their nature EU Treaty referendums are made necessary by changes to EU Treaties. According to the standard view of Irish constitutional theory, all EU Treaty reforms are required to pass into Irish law through the aperture formed by Article 29.4 of the Constitution;[7] as a result, any Treaty reform that would require a change to this Article must be put to a referendum of the people. To date, Article 29.4 has been amended on no less than seven separate occasions in the evolving process of European integration. The most recent

EU-related referendum was held on 31 May 2012 to ratify the Fiscal Stability Treaty (discussed in greater detail below). The extent of the process of change is testified to by the fact that what we may call the 'European clauses' in the Irish Constitution have now expanded to over eight separate subsections (now numbered Article 29.4.3° to Article 29.4.10°). The ease of passage of these referendums has diminished over time – as shown most starkly by the Nice and Lisbon Treaty referendums that each required two attempts to succeed.[8] The reasons for those difficult outcomes were quite complex.

In contrast to the EU-related referendums, those focused on institutional change are endogenous to the Irish political system. In general, they tend to take the form of constitutional updating or revision rather than as issues of major reform, dealing with technical aspects in the running of the state including proposed changes to the electoral system, the courts, franchise, and so on. They are often what LeDuc would categorise as low salience referendums.[9] Prominent actors in these instances commonly include the politico-legal elite with the legal community in particular tending to be on the side of constitutional preservation and hence the status quo. A recent example of this was the referendum in 2011 to remove a constitutional block on parliamentary (Oireachtas) committee inquiries, which saw a powerful 'No' campaign mounted by former attorneys general.

Social change referendums tend to be of higher salience, speaking to more deeply held beliefs of the populace. Plebiscites here have included issues such as divorce, abortion, death penalty, and marriage equality. Prominent among the actors here tend to be church and conservative religious groups generally being on the side of the status quo and constitutional preservation. In the 2015 marriage equality referendum (discussed below) the notably high level of engagement by civil society groups on the liberal side of the divide was a particular feature.[10]

Examining Figure 6.1 we can see the changes underway since the 1970s with a growing number of EU Treaty referendums necessitated through EU membership and consequent Treaty revision. The most notable development has been the increasing focus on institutional change referendums in the past

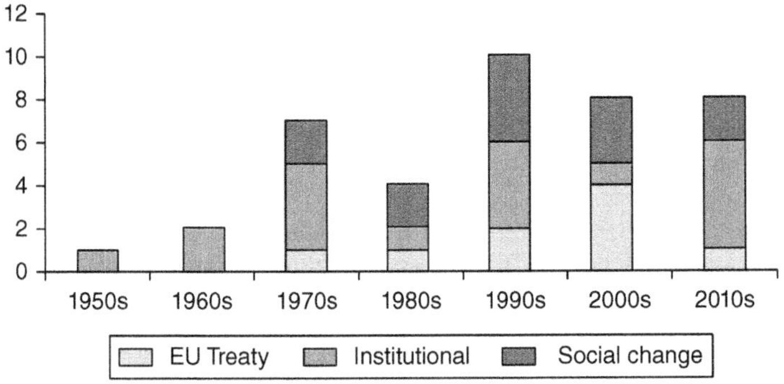

Figure 6.1 Type of constitutional referendum: Ireland

Source: Authors

number of years. In part, this reflects a general move to modernise and reform political institutions;[11] more recently perhaps it reflects a sense that institutional weaknesses were at least in part responsible for the failings leading to the 2008 financial crisis.[12]

The international Great Recession hit Ireland particularly hard: inside the Euro area, Ireland was among the countries most affected due to its high dependence on international short-term funding.[13] The crisis prompted a reassessment of relations between the government and citizens,[14] with many questioning whether the existing political system was fit for purpose. There were some who argued that using a deliberative approach to reform the Constitution would be valuable as it would directly involve citizens in discussions of constitutional reform thereby enhancing democratic legitimacy and potentially reconfiguring democratic practice. It was this discussion that fed into the decision to establish the Irish Constitutional Convention, which we discuss next.

As we have noted, the pace of constitutional change has accelerated in the last few decades. While unavoidable EU Treaty reforms account for some of this, the bulk of the referendums have focused either on institutional or social change. These have tended to follow the usual route of referendums on relatively minor and technical issues, much of this revealing little evidence of joined-up thinking. We examine these in our third section below.

The 2012–14 Constitutional Convention

In their 2011 general election manifestos, the parties that went on to form the coalition government (Fine Gael and Labour) promised some form of citizen-oriented process of constitutional review. This was to culminate in the Irish Constitutional Convention (ICC), a constitutional review body whose members consisted of 66 citizens selected at random by an opinion poll company and 33 members of parliament, with an independent chair comprising the 100th member.[15] The ICC was given a brief to report within 12 months on eight matters: review of the Dáil (parliament) electoral system; reducing the presidential term to five years (from its current seven); provision for marriage equality; amending the clause on women in the home; measures to encourage greater participation of women in politics and public life; removing blasphemy from the Constitution; reduction of the voting age; and votes for emigrants (and Northern Ireland residents) in presidential elections. Space was given for the ICC to consider other possible areas of amendment, once their work on these items was complete, in the event the ICC members considered two other areas: parliamentary reform, and whether to insert a clause into the Constitution recognising economic, social, and cultural rights.

The modus operandi of the ICC was 'deliberation', with the members distributed into roundtable groups of eight with a trained facilitator guiding the discussions. Expert briefing documents were provided in advance of each meeting; the experts addressed the members and stayed on hand to answer questions and clarify points of detail. Having initially been given a 12-month deadline, the

ICC was to operate for 14 months, meeting on average about once a month (with the exception of the summer period). The 10 topics it discussed (the 8 originally allotted to it and the 2 additional topics it took on itself) resulted in no less than 41 separate recommendations, 23 of which (such as, for example, recommendations to establish an electoral commission, or to change parliamentary procedures by way of parliamentary rule changes) would not require constitutional reform to implement.[16]

The Convention's recommendations were non-binding: it was an advisory rather than a declaratory body. On establishing the ICC the government committed to responding to its reports in a timely fashion by way of parliamentary debate. In the event, while it did respond to all reports, the responses were late, generally rushed through at the end of a parliamentary session (such as just before the parliament was about to go into recess) and in poorly attended debates. Of the ICC's 41 recommendations, 18 would require constitutional reform, and of these just 2 were taken forward to a vote of the people in May 2015 (we discuss these below); the remainder, together with the bulk of the recommendations that wouldn't require referendum, were kicked into the long grass (though at the time of writing, a portion of these – notably measures to reform the Irish parliament – are in the process of being implemented by the subsequent government elected in 2016).

The work and outcomes of the ICC are explored in more detail elsewhere,[17] but two points of particular relevance to this chapter are worth drawing out. First, there was the unusual dimension of involving a random selection of ordinary citizens in the process. Nothing like this had ever been tried before in Ireland. Irish policy makers were influenced by the citizens' assemblies on electoral reform in the Canadian provinces of British Columbia (2004) and Ontario (2007) and the Dutch citizens' forum (*BurgerForum*) of 2006.[18] In all these cases the citizen members were selected at random rather than running for election and deliberation was the modus operandi: what distinguished the Irish case from the others was the decision to include members of parliament in the membership and the broader range of topics it covered. The Irish Constitutional Convention and the Canadian and Dutch citizens' assemblies represent a new type of constitutional convention that is not covered by existing typologies:[19] this new type is a constitutional convention as a 'mini-public'.[20] It is clear from observations of the operation of the ICC by outsiders and by analysis carried out by the members themselves that the ICC operated well as a process,[21] so that even if there may be doubts over the success of the ICC in terms of outcomes (because of the government's unwillingness to implement many of its recommendations), it certainly can be judged successful as a process of deliberation.

And it may yet produce more outcomes. In its 2016 election manifesto Fine Gael, the outgoing leading coalition partner, which returned with the highest vote share, pledged to hold a referendum on Article 41.2.1 of Bunreacht na Éireann regarding a 'woman's life within the home' as well as one on the question of amending Article 40.6.1(i) of the Constitution to remove the offence of blasphemy. Both of these were recommendations by the Constitutional Convention.

Fine Gael has also promised to hold a referendum to give the Office of the Ceann Comhairle (the speaker of the parliament) and parliamentary committees constitutional standing, two other recommendations by the Constitutional Convention. In addition, the minority government, newly elected in 2016, established a new citizens' assembly (this time not including politicians) to consider a number of issues including, in particular, the hot topic of abortion.

A second point of interest that we draw from the experience of the ICC is the fact that the bulk of its recommendations (23 out of 41) would not have required referendums to enact; these were changes that could have been implemented without the need to change the Constitution. This speaks to a wider debate over the informal norms and rules that lie outside of a country's formal constitutional document.

2011–15: A patchwork of referendums

A third feature of interest about the Irish case is how the work of the ICC operated in conjunction with a series of other constitutional reform initiatives by the government, which revealed little attention to a joined-up strategy of large-scale constitutional reform. In the manifestos they issued prior to the 2011 general election all the major parties focused to a greater or lesser extent on constitutional reform.[22] The Fine Gael and Labour coalition government elected in 2011 took an amalgam of the proposals and inserted them into its 2011 Programme for Government. This was to result in the largest number of referendums of any Irish government in the history of the state.

Table 6.1 sets out the details on the referendums held between 2011–15 using the three-category framework set out at the start of the chapter. In total, over the course of the government's term from 2011–16: five referendums targeted at institutional reform were held with two passing; there were two referendums focused on social change, both of which passed; and there was one EU-related referendum that passed. The table shows that there were two referendums that were not indicated in the Programme for Government, one on the Fiscal Treaty necessitated by an important EU Treaty Reform held in the midst of the EU crisis resulting from the international Great Recession, and the other on a new Appeal Court whose creation was necessitated by long overruns and waiting times at the Supreme Court; both of these passed. Just two of the referendums held during this period – on marriage equality and presidential candidate age – were preceded by discussions at the Irish Constitutional Convention.

The bulk of the referendums were focused on institutional changes. The coalition parties promised a radical package of constitutional reform, which was broken down into a number of sub-components: parliamentary reform issues, other specific priority amendments, and broader constitutional review. As regards parliamentary reform, the coalition promised three specific referendums: to abolish the Seanad (Ireland's upper house of parliament); a constitutional amendment to enable parliamentary committees to carry out full investigations; and an introduction of protections to the right of citizens to communicate in

Table 6.1 Irish constitutional reform referendums, 2011–15

Referendum topic	*In the 2011 Programme for Government*	*Discussed by the Constitutional Convention*	*Date of referendum*	*Yes vote (%)*
EU Treaty				
Fiscal Treaty	No	No	31 May 2012	60.3
Social change/Modernisation				
Children's rights	Yes	No	10 Nov 2012	58
Marriage equality	Yes	Yes	22 May 2015	62.1
Institutional reform				
Judges' salaries	Yes	No	27 Oct 2011	79.7
Oireachtas inquiries	Yes	No	27 Oct 2011	46.7
Seanad abolition	Yes	No	4 Oct 2013	48.3
Appeal court	No	No	4 Oct 2013	55.2
Age of presidential candidates	No	Yes	22 May 2015	26.9

confidence with public representatives. As we shall see, it took action on the first two of these, losing the referendum vote on both occasions; the third issue was inexplicably dropped.

The government also promised to give priority to two specific constitutional amendments: a referendum to allow the State to cut the salaries of judges as part of a general pay cut across the public sector; and constitutional reforms to ensure that children's rights are strengthened. Both of these changes were passed by a majority of the people. And there were also the referendum proposals recommended by the Constitutional Convention.

In the remainder of this section, we briefly review each referendum examining to what extent it emanated from a post-crisis narrative, what the justification for it was, and how it fared. We start with the EU Treaty-related referendum that occurred soon after the government's election: this was undoubtedly a consequence of the wider European economic crisis. The 30th amendment to the Constitution in 2012 was to permit Ireland to ratify the 2012 European Fiscal Compact Treaty on Stability, Coordination, and Governance in the Economic and Monetary Union. It was approved by a clear majority of 60.3% to 39.7%, on a turnout of 50%. The referendum debate was dominated by a single question: how can Ireland, which was due to leave an EU/IMF bailout programme the following year, fund itself if it could not then borrow on sovereign debt markets and was thus required to apply for a second bailout? The 'Yes' campaign, led by the government parties and supported by Fianna Fáil, the leading opposition party, argued that only countries that ratified the Fiscal Treaty could access the European Stability Mechanism, the Euro zone's permanent €500 billion ($618 billion) bailout fund. Sinn Fein and some smaller left-wing parties that led the 'No' campaign struggled to produce an answer to convince a sceptical electorate in sombre mood.[23] Unlike the two previous EU-related referendums necessitated by changes to EU Treaty law, this one passed first time; the size of the government satisfaction effect (helped by the fact that it was still seen as a relatively new administration) was particularly large in this vote on the Fiscal Treaty.

Turning next to the referendums on social change and modernisation, the subsequent referendum on children's rights was specifically on the right and duty of the state to take child protection measures. The proposed amendment derived from a series of recommendations from crisis driven reports and commissions on the failure of both the church and the state to protect Irish children. There was broad consensus on the need for the amendments and all political parties were in favour. As a result, there were few voices against the amendment which may have diminished media coverage due to strict rules about balance in broadcasting following a Supreme Court ruling, known as the Coughlan judgment stemming from the 1995 divorce referendum, which means that television and radio broadcasters must give equal treatment to all sides when covering any election or referendum.[24] Such opposition as there was argued that the amendment would imply a transfer of sovereignty from parents to State, and/or from State to transnational groupings such as the European Union or the United Nations.

Perhaps in part to counter this, the Department for Children and Youth Affairs issued an information booklet during the campaign, as well as engaging in website and radio, television and print advertising, ostensibly to promote voter information and turnout. In general, such material would be produced solely by the Referendum Commission, which is legally obliged to produce a balanced argumentation and information. This action by the Department for Children precipitated court proceedings on the grounds that these actions were unconstitutional. The argument was made that the website contained an emotional message with the use of photos of children, children's handwriting, and the letter 'o' in 'Vote' containing a smiley face, therefore encouraging a vote in favour of the constitutional amendment. Two days before referendum polling day, the Supreme Court ruled against the government in the case of *McCrystal v Minister for Children and Youth Affairs & Ors* finding that public funds had been inappropriately used to produce publicity materials that were biased in favour of a 'Yes' vote in the referendum. The Judge distinguished the circumstances from the *McKenna (No 2)* case in 1995 where the Dáil had voted for funds to be provided with the explicit purpose of a campaign encouraging a 'Yes' vote. The Judge's view was that great care had been taken to comply with the principles of *McKenna (No 2)*, and therefore he found that the campaign had not tended towards any particular outcome. But he warned that if there are such actions by government departments in future referendums, similar court proceedings will be inevitable. He recommended an expansion of the Referendum Commission and an increased budget, whereby it would have sole responsibility for informing the electorate. In the event, the amendment was approved in a vote on 10 November 2012, by 58% of voters on a turnout of 33.5%.[25]

The next referendum on social change and modernisation was on marriage equality and was, by a long stretch, the most high profile. This referendum originated in a long campaign by the LGBT community. The smaller coalition party, the Labour Party, had included a promise of a referendum on the issues in its election manifesto in 2011. However, the more senior partner, the Christian Democratic Fine Gael, had a more lukewarm position on the matter and a decision was taken to refer the matter to the Constitutional Convention. In its report on 2 July 2013, the convention recommended that the Constitution be amended to introduce marriage equality. This is the first time in Irish history that a referendum was called as a result of a process of deliberation involving ordinary citizens; indeed, it is also one of the first times in the world that a deliberative process has resulted in a referendum[26] and certainly the first to have succeeded[27] when on 22 May 2015 it was passed by a large majority of Irish voters and the definition of marriage in the Constitution was broadened to introduce marriage equality.

The remaining referendums in this period were all within our institutional change category: the plebiscites on judges' salaries; Oireachtas inquiries; Seanad abolition; whether to establish an appeal court; and the rather bizarre question – resulting from a minor recommendation of the Constitutional Convention – over the age of presidential candidates. Turning first to the amendment on judges' pay, the 1937 Constitution had contained a prohibition on reducing the pay of a judge during their term of office. The purpose was to protect judicial independence by preventing the government from reducing the pay of judges in order to dissuade judges from exercising judicial review in a manner not deemed appropriate by the government. At the heart of the austerity policies enacted in the midst of the economic turmoil was the passing of the Financial Emergency Measures in the Public Interest Act 2009 (placing a levy on pension contributions made by public sector workers) and the Financial Emergency Measures in the Public Interest (No. 2) Act 2009 (which allowed for a reduction in public sector pay). The government was advised that these measures could not apply to judges, thus resulting in the referendum on the 29th amendment allowing for pay cuts for judges on 27 October 2011. This was passed by over a million votes with 79.8% voting in favour and 20.2% against.

The next referendum was also one promised in the Programme for Government and was to allow the Houses of the Oireachtas to conduct public inquiries. The background followed an earlier case where a man suffering from bipolar affective disorder had barricaded himself into his residence with a shotgun in a dispute over plans to move to a new house. In the subsequent stand-off with the police force, the Garda (Irish police) Emergency Response Unit (ERU), he was shot dead. His family claimed the Garda had mishandled the situation and that a planned Garda internal inquiry would be inadequate. As a result, an Oireachtas Joint Committee on Justice, Equality, Defence, and Women's Rights established a sub-committee on the incident (which had occurred in the village of Abbeylara). The sub-committee claimed the right to compel ERU members to give evidence, under the Committees of the Houses of the Oireachtas (Compellability, Privileges, and Immunities of Witnesses) Act, 1997. The Garda sought judicial review arguing that the sub-committee would be acting *ultra vires* in compelling them to attend prior to the issuing of their report. The Supreme Court concurred by six votes to one. The government's proposal, therefore, was for a constitutional amendment which would allow Oireachtas committees to make findings of wrongdoing but not impose sanctions. However, amid concerns over the perceived overreaching of public representatives and general confusion as to what the referendum was about,[28] the referendum was defeated in October 2011 by a narrow margin of 53.3% against and 46.7% for.

The next proposed amendment to the Constitution was on the abolition of the upper house or Seanad. The subject of upper house reform has been ongoing for many years, focussing on whether it was better to reform or abolish it. The larger coalition party Fine Gael had promised its abolition as a central plank of its 2011 political reform programme despite its leader having earlier argued it would be better to reform rather than abolish it. However, a directly elected upper house, especially if elected at a different date than the lower house and given more substantial legislative powers, could emerge as a powerful constitutional player, significantly reducing the government's room for manoeuvre. Newspaper opinion polls during the course of the referendum suggested that the proposal was seen as a bid to centralise power in the lower house and government rather than as a political reform. The proposal was rejected by the electorate in a referendum on 4 October 2013 by 51.7% voting against to 48.3% in favour.

The proposed 33rd amendment to the Constitution was to establish a new Court of Appeal. The Constitution provided for the establishment of two courts: the Supreme Court and the High Court. Other courts may be established by statute but may not question the constitutionality of legislation. While the Supreme Court has the final authority to interpret the Constitution, many cases it hears are not constitutional in nature, resulting in judicial logjams of several years. The purpose of the Court of Appeal is to sit between the High and Supreme Courts, taking over the existing appellate jurisdiction of the Supreme Court, the intention being to reduce the workload of the Supreme Court and allow it to concentrate on a smaller number of more important cases. The bill was put to a referendum on 4 October 2013, at which 65.1% voted in favour, on a turnout of 39.15%.

In the final technical referendum of the period, on the same day as the marriage equality referendum, voters were also asked if they wanted to reduce the minimum age for presidential candidates from 35 to 21. This referendum, which also emanated from a proposal at the Constitutional Convention, was sidelined due to the focus on the marriage equality referendum. It attracted virtually no coverage and it was evident on polling day that most voters were blissfully unaware of this second referendum. The proposal was defeated 73.1% to 26.9% – the worst outcome of any referendum in the history of the state.

Conclusion

In conclusion, the pace of constitutional revisionism in Ireland has quickened, perhaps unsurprisingly for a relatively detailed document that was first enacted almost 80 years ago. One way to estimate likely future change is to examine the number of referendums promised in the 2016 general election manifesto of the largest party, Fine Gael[29] – the party that, by dint of a complex deal with the main party of opposition and a number of independent TDs, was re-elected into government (albeit a rather precarious minority one) in May 2016. The vast bulk of the proposed referendums were included as recommendations from the 2012–14 Constitutional Convention. Those which would be categorised as technical include strengthening Committees' powers; a referendum to give the Office of the Ceann Comhairle constitutional standing; a referendum on Article 41.2.1 regarding a 'woman's life within the home'; and a referendum on the question of amending Article 40.6.1(i) of the Constitution to remove the offence of blasphemy. The one proposed technical amendment that did not follow an ICC recommendation is a referendum on Ireland's participation in the Universal Patent Court.

The Programme for Partnership Government agreed between Fine Gael and some independents with the tacit support of the largest opposition party, Fianna Fáil, included a commitment to a Citizens' Assembly to make recommendations to the Dáil on further constitutional changes, including on the 8th amendment, on fixed term parliaments, and on the manner in which referendums are held (e.g., should 'super referendum days', whereby a significant number of referendums take place on the same day, be held). In the event in October 2016, an Assembly was set up, chaired by a Supreme Court judge who was asked to consider not only the repeal of the 8th amendment but also fixed-term parliaments, how referendums are held and how best to deal with the country's ageing population.

Reflecting on the main justifications for constitutional change in the above discussion it becomes clear that while economic and political crisis formed the immediate backdrop for most of the recent constitutional changes, the underlying narrative pointed more towards the anachronistic/obsolete nature of the Constitution, at least in terms of modernity and pluralistic values. On the other hand, mooted changes in the technical area, while often preceded with a discussion of political reform, were not always perceived in this vein by the electorate. And where it did not believe the party bona fides it was liable to vote against the reform. While the Constitutional Convention resulted in only two referendums with a mixed record of being passed, both the long list of proposed referendums which emanated from it as well as the government's predilection for putting further controversial measures towards a reincarnation point to its perceived usefulness in at least diffusing more controversial political decisions.

Notes

1 David Farrell and Jane Suiter, 'The Election in Context', in Michael Gallagher and Michael Marsh (eds.), *How Ireland Voted 2016* (Houndmills, Basingstoke: Palgrave Macmillan, 2016); Michael Marsh, David Farrell, and Gail McElroy (eds.), *A Conservative Revolution? Electoral Change in Twenty-First Century Ireland* (Oxford: Oxford University Press, 2017).

2 Enrique Hernández and Hanspeter Kriesi, 'The Electoral Consequences of the Financial and Economic Crisis in Europe', *European Journal of Political Research* (published online, 2015; accessed on April 28 2016); Toril Aalberg et al. (eds.), *Populist Political Communication in Europe. A Cross-National Analysis of 24 European Countries* (New York: Routledge, 2017).

3 Gabor Halmai, 'Illiberal Democracy and Beyond in Hungary' Verfassungsblog (2014), available at: www.verfassungsblog.de/en/illiberal-democracy-beyond-hungary-2/#.VMDQ2-ZdrMs.
4 Something that may be about to change as a result of the uncertain electoral outcome in 2016, the election of a minority government reliant on the support of the second largest party in parliament, and the introduction of significant parliamentary reform. See Farrell and Suiter, 'The Election in Context'.
5 Aside from constitutional referendums, the Constitution also provides for a referendum on an ordinary bill – known as the ordinary referendum – but this is complicated to implement and to date there have been none.
6 We differ from Sinnott's earlier categorisation, which distinguished between regime (amalgamating EU with other institutional reform votes), religious-moral (which tended to downplay other social-related votes), and other referendums. Richard Sinnott (2002), 'Cleavages, Parties and Referendums: Relationships between Representative and Direct Democracy in the Republic of Ireland', *European Journal of Political Research* 41: 811–26. It is also worth noting that some of the social change referendums in the 1980s and 1990s were towards more restrictive social policy on abortion, for example.
7 Barrett Gavin, *The Oireachtas and the European Union: The Evolving Role of a National Parliament in European Affairs* (Dublin: Houses of the Oireachtas, 2013).
8 Laffan Brigid (2016), 'European Economic Governance: Fillip or Foil in the Shadow of Crisis'. Paper prepared for the UACES Annual Conference, London, 5–7 September 2016. www.uaces.org/documents/papers/1601/laffan.pdf.
9 Lawrence LeDuc (2002), 'Opinion Change and Voting Behaviour in Referendums', *European Journal of Political Research* 41(6): 711–32. For further discussion see Jane Suiter and Theresa Reidy (2013), 'It's the Campaign Learning Stupid: An Examination of a Volatile Irish Referendum Parliamentary Affairs', first published online 14 July 2013 doi: 10.1093/pa/gst014.
10 Johan A. Elkink, David M. Farrell, Theresa Reidy, and Jane Suiter (2016), 'Understanding the 2015 Marriage Referendum in Ireland: Constitutional Convention, Campaign, and Conservative Ireland', *Irish Political Studies*. http://dx.doi.org/10.1080/07907184.2016.1197209.
11 For example, Bruce Cain, Russell Dalton, and Susan Scarrow (eds.), *Democracy Transformed?: Expanding Political Opportunities in Advanced Industrial Democracies* (Oxford: Oxford University Press, 2003).
12 David Farrell, 'Political Reform in a Time of Crisis', in Bill Roche, Philip O'Connell, and Andy Prothero (eds.), *Austerity's Poster Child: Ireland in the Great Recession and Recovery* (Oxford: Oxford University Press, 2017).
13 Philip Lane and Gian Maria Milesi-Ferretti (2012), 'External Adjustment and the Global Crisis', *Journal of International Economics* 88(2): 252–65.
14 David Farrell, Eoin O'Malley, and Jane Suiter, 'The 2011 We the Citizens Pilot Citizens' Assembly', in David Farrell, Eoin O'Malley, and Jane Suiter (eds.), *Citizens' Voices: Experiments in Democratic Renewal and Reform* (Galway: Irish Centre for Social Gerontology, 2012).
15 Jane Suiter, David M. Farrell, and Clodagh Harris, 'The Irish Constitutional Convention: A Case of "High Legitimacy"', in Mins Reuchamps and Jane Suiter (eds.), *Constitutional Deliberative Democracy in Europe* (Colchester: ECPR Press, 2016).
16 For more details, see http://politicalreform.ie/2016/01/23/final-report-card-on-the-governments-reactions-to-the-irish-constitutional-convention/
17 Jane Suiter, David M. Farrell, and Clodagh Harris, 'The Irish Constitutional Convention: A Case of "High Legitimacy"', in Mins Reuchamps and Jane Suiter (eds.), *Constitutional Deliberative Democracy in Europe* (Colchester: ECPR Press, 2016).
18 Patrick Fournier, Henk van der Kolk, Kenneth Carty, Andre Blais, and Jonathan Rose, *When Citizens Decide: Lessons from Citizen Assemblies on Electoral Reform* (Oxford: Oxford University Press, 2011).

19 On these, see Jonathan Wheatley and Fernando Mendez (eds.), *Patterns of Constitutional Design: The Role of Citizens and Elites in Constitution-Making* (London: Ashgate, 2007).

20 David Farrell (2014), 'The 2013 Irish Constitutional Convention: A Bold Step or a Damp Squib?, in John O'Dowd and Giuseppe Ferrari (eds.), *Comparative Reflections on 75 Years of the Irish Constitution* (Dublin: Clarus Press, 2014).

21 Jane Suiter, David M. Farrell, and Eoin O'Malley (2014), 'When do Deliberative Citizens Change their Opinions? Evidence from the Irish Citizens' Assembly', *International Political Science Review* 37(2), first published on 11 September 2014, doi: 10.1177/0192512114544068.

22 Jane Suiter and David Farrell, 'The Parties' Manifestos', in Michael Gallagher and Michael Marsh (eds.), *How Ireland Voted 2011* (London: Palgrave, 2011), 29–46.

23 See (*The Economist* 2012 <www.economist.com/blogs/newsbook/2012/06/ire-lands-referendum-fiscal-compact0 > accessed 25 March 2016. More generally, see Michael Marsh (2015), 'Voting on Europe, Again and Again: Stability and Change in the Irish Experience with EU Referendums', *Electoral Studies* 38(2): 170–82.

24 Theresa Reidy and Jane Suiter (2015), 'Do Rules Matter? Categorising the Regulation of Referendum Campaigns', *Electoral Studies* 38: 159–69.

25 However, its enactment was then delayed by a High Court case challenging the government's conduct of the referendum. The High Court rejected the challenge, which led to an appeal to the Supreme Court, which on 24 April 2015 found in favour of the government.

26 David Farrell (2014), '"Stripped Down" or Reconfigured Democracy', *West European Politics* 37(2): 439–55; Patrick Fournier, Henk van der Kolk, R. K. Carty, Andre Blais, and Jonathan Rose, *When Citizens Decide: Lessons from Citizen Assemblies on Electoral Reform* (Oxford: Oxford University Press, 2011).

27 Johan A. Elkink, David M. Farrell, Theresa Reidy, and Jane Suiter, 'Understanding the 2015 Marriage Referendum in Ireland: Constitutional Convention, Campaign, and Conservative Ireland', *Irish Political Studies* http://dx.doi.org/10.1080/07907184.2016.1197209.

28 Jane Suiter and Theresa Reidy (2013), 'It's the Campaign Learning Stupid: An Examination of a Volatile Irish Referendum', *Parliamentary Affairs*, first published online 14 July 2013, doi: 10.1093/pa/gst014.

29 'Programme for Government 2016', http://cdn.thejournal.ie/media/2016/05/programme_for_partnership_government.pdf, accessed 11 May 2016.

7 The constitution as a political tool in Iceland

From the periphery to the center of the political debate

Baldvin Thor Bergsson

With the election of Donald Trump as the president of the United States, Brexit in the UK, and the growing support for populist parties throughout Europe, the debate about the disgruntled and alienated has intensified. The demand for structural changes to societies takes different forms but they seem to have a common theme – namely that power and wealth have to be distributed in a fairer way. The economic crisis in 2008 gave birth to groups such as the Occupy movement, and several others, focusing on democratic reform all over the world.

When the Icelandic financial system collapsed in 2008 the economic crisis was followed by an even deeper political crisis. Protests in front of Althingi (the Icelandic parliament) escalated and in January 2009 Prime Minister Geir H. Haarde resigned and called for elections. With growing skepticism towards politicians and political institutions, the need to reconnect with the public was obvious. The most drastic decision was to set up a Constitutional Council, made up of 'ordinary citizens', tasked with the revision of the Icelandic Constitution. While the process was hailed as unprecedented and inclusive, it was contested on all stages by both opponents of the government formed after the general elections in 2009 and those skeptical of constitutional changes. Despite a referendum on the constitutional draft that showed support amongst the public, and an anticipated majority in Althingi, the process came to a dramatic halt in 2013. It is unlikely that the 1944 Constitution will undergo a major revision in the coming years, although some changes are probable.

The year 2016 was turbulent in Icelandic politics. The Panama Papers revealed ties between three ministers and off-shore companies and, following one of the largest protests in Iceland's history, the Prime Minister resigned in April. General elections, scheduled for May 2017, were moved forward to September 2016 and received unprecedented attention in the international media due to the expected success of the Pirate Party. The Icelandic Constitution was continuously discussed before the elections with the Pirate Party, making it the central theme of its campaign. Furthermore, a new president was elected in June after a twenty-year reign by the former president Ólafur Ragnar Grímsson. During the presidential elections, all candidates had to answer questions on the constitutional role of the president and give their view on the draft constitution from the Constitutional Council.

How did the constitution become a central theme in Icelandic political debate? This chapter will focus on the struggle between the social movement arguing for a revision of the constitution and the more traditional elites who, for different reasons, opposed it. While constitution-making has often followed major political upheaval or revolutions,[1] it is rarer that such a process follows an economic crisis. Elster mentions the French Constitution from 1789 as an example of constitution-making following an economic crisis,[2] but most would agree that a mixture of political, societal, and economic issues are usually involved. The failure of the political institutions in Iceland to deal with the aftermath of the crisis was surely a major factor. The process has been described as 'an attempt to write a participatory social contract',[3] and phrases such as 'a crowd-sourced constitution' have floated in both academic circles (ibid.) and the media.[4] It is fair to describe the procedure as an innovative democratic experience, but the question remains whether it suited the political reality and enjoyed the active support of the public?

By looking at the process leading up to the draft of a new constitution we can see how every-day politics and a volatile and sometimes nonrational debate can muddle good intentions. The Icelandic lesson also reminds us how a group that for some reason is thought to be responsible for an economic crisis is likely to fight back at every given opportunity.

The chapter first discusses the constitutional revision process that started in 2010, analysing, among others, the early protests and formation of social movements around constitutional change, the revision process itself and the set-up of the Constitutional Council, and the subsequent developments in the revision process that led to its stalling. In the second part, recent developments of the ongoing 'constitutional saga' are discussed, including the role of the Panama Papers and the October 2016 elections. In conclusion, it is argued that important elements that explain the deadlock of the constitutional revision process are the alienation between the Constitutional Council and politicians as well as the diminishing enthusiasm amongst citizens. The empirical data used in this chapter primarily come from two sources. The first is a set of semi-structured qualitative interviews with several people involved in the process in Iceland. The second is the Icelandic National Election Study (ICENES), which gives an indication of the public's view on constitutional change.

The Icelandic constitutional revision

Social movements are often advocates of democratic or indeed constitutional changes, although their success may be limited.[5] Therefore, it is hardly surprising that a demand for a new political system in Iceland after the crisis in 2008 grew into a full-fledged movement. Its origin can be traced to several individuals and groups, which helps explain the fragmentation that later occurred.

Snow and Soule use five key elements to conceptualise a social movement. '[T]hey are challengers to or defenders of existing structures or systems of authority; second, they are collective rather than individual enterprises; third, they act, in varying degrees, outside existing institutional or organisational arrangements;

fourth, they operate with some degree of organisation; and fifth, they typically do so with some degree of continuity'.[6] Using this definition, it is clear that a social movement was born in Iceland. It erupted in the protests outside Althingi when the movement first called for new elections and argued that the political system was corrupt. While individual effort certainly played its part during the initial stages, it is evident that the government did not respond until the masses in front of Althingi had grown considerably, and in fact only after the protests had become more violent. Citizens' meetings provided a forum for the 'ordinary citizen' to voice their concerns, and several organisations, such as the *Constitutional Society* and *Alda: Association for Sustainability and Democracy*, campaigned for a new constitution. Both organisations have continued their work, hosting a debate on the different roles of constitutions in October 2016 just before the general elections. In 2014, the *Organisation for a New Constitution* joined forces with the *Constitutional Society* to create a single front campaigning for a new constitution. Katrin Oddsdóttir, a former member of the Constitutional Council, is the current (February 2017) chairperson. Thus, a durable movement has been created with participants that have been directly involved in the constitutional process.

The first official mention of the need to write a new constitution after the crisis in 2008 came from Prof. Njörður P. Njarðvík, an author and a well-known social critic, first in a television interview on January 11, 2009, and three days later in a newspaper article.[7] The article received attention during the protests that same month and after the government had resigned and called for elections, smaller groups began meeting and discussing the possibility of a new constitution (Geir Guðmundsson, interview with the author, 11-11-2013).

Geir Guðmundsson, chairman of the *Constitutional Society*, mentions that ideas about radical changes to the constitution have been in circulation for decades. He dates his own interest back to the Alliance of Social Democrats that won four seats in Althingi in 1983, and its chairman Vilmundur Gylfason who spoke extensively about a corrupt political system, nepotism, and the failure of the media to report on those issues. It was during that time that Geir became interested in the constitution and confident that it maintained a political system that served its own interests instead of the public's (Geir Guðmundsson, interview with the author, 11-11-2013).

Jóhanna Sigurðardóttir (Prime Minister 2009–2013, parliamentarian 1978–2013) has repeatedly submitted proposals to Althingi regarding the constitution. In 1994, she submitted a proposal regarding a constitutional assembly that should revise the constitution. A similar proposal was submitted three years later but neither made it to a final vote. Furthermore, she has on at least seven occasions proposed an amendment which would enable the public to call for a referendum on issues by collecting signatures.[8] Before the elections to Althingi in 2009, all parties declared that a constitutional revision was needed and most of them stated that the public should be involved. The Progressive Party posted a campaign video on Youtube[9] where it was clearly stated that a new constitution should be written by a constitutional assembly made up from elected representatives of the public. The Independence Party remained skeptical about a constitutional council, and before the elections in 2009 its parliamentarians stated their opposition regarding the idea of a council that could refer its proposals directly to a referendum.[10] After the elections in April 2009, the center-left government of the Social-Democrats and the Left-Green Movement promised a revision of the constitution and elections to a constitutional council.[11]

With this in mind, it is clear that the idea of a constitutional council enjoyed widespread support in Althingi and amongst the public in the spring of 2009. However, the conceptualisation of the movement fighting for a new constitution has to take into account its relationship with the government of the time. After all, the establishment of the Constitutional Council was a political decision and the process enjoyed majority support in Althingi, at least during the initial stages. Some members of the Constitutional Council expressed skepticism towards the political establishment and insisted that Althingi should not make any material changes to the draft.[12] Ólafsson has claimed that the somewhat confrontational rhetoric alienated the political class and caused them to question the intent of the Constitutional Council.[13] The view was that the political class had failed and that members of the Constitutional Council were direct representatives of the public expressing only its will. This cleft between perceived comrades proved difficult to bridge and certainly did not help the process. Let us now turn to the events leading up to the draft from the Constitutional Council.

Public participation as a response to the crisis

When the three largest Icelandic banks fell in September and October 2008, the initial reaction was that of total shock. The Prime Minister, Geir Haarde, addressed the nation on live television on October 6 finishing his talk with the words, 'May God bless Iceland'. While intended to raise the spirits of the public, this soon became a popular phrase of those criticising the government and the political establishment. The first protests were held in front of the Central Bank on October 10. They were organised by two individuals and promoted on Facebook. Some two hundred individuals showed up and one of them was Hörður Torfason, a singer and human rights activist.[14] The following day, he organised the first protests in front of Althingi in the name of a new group called 'the voices of the people', which would be repeated weekly until January 31, 2009. While the protesters were few at first, they grew rapidly and numbered several thousands during the later stages. They demanded the resignation of the government and new elections, and the resignations of the directors of the Central Bank and the Financial Supervisory Authority. A new constitution was not a central demand of the organisers, but the need for a revision of the entire political system was often mentioned. Several 'citizens' meetings' were also held in the fall of 2008. During one of those meetings, the foreign minister and leader of the Social Democrats, Ingibjörg Sólrún Gísladóttir, said that she doubted that those in attendance could speak in the name of the nation, invoking loud protests from the audience. The claim to represent the 'voice and will' of the public has since been popular in the constitutional debate.

In June 2010, Althingi passed Act No. 90/2010 establishing a consultative Constitutional Assembly. A committee of seven members was elected to prepare a 'National Gathering' where approximately one thousand people would be selected by means of random sampling. The Gathering should

> endeavor to call for the principal viewpoints and points of emphasis of the public concerning the organisation of the country's government and its constitution; the committee shall process the information collected at the National Gathering and deliver to the Constitutional Assembly when it convenes.[15]

The National Gathering was influenced by a similar meeting in November 2009, which was organised by several grassroots movements called 'The Anthill'. Twelve hundred were randomly selected by The Anthill and additional three hundred representatives of institutions and organisations were specially invited. The meeting sought to discover the 'value' of the nation divided into nine preselected themes: education, family, welfare, economy, environment, sustainability, opportunities, equality, and public administration. The deliberative nature of the meeting was unique in Iceland and, although the results were quite abstract, they did offer a form of decision-making-from-below.[16]

The National Gathering produced eight different themes reflecting what the participants wished would form the basis of a new constitution. Again, the results could be described as abstract and general, although several common ideas could be identified between the two meetings. The organisers used 'word-clouds' to describe the results, with words such as equality, democracy, honesty, respect, human rights, justice, and liberty representing the values the participants wanted the new constitution to be built on.[17] A more detailed description of the values followed and was later presented to the Constitutional Council. The process has been criticised by academics who claim that limited time and the vague wording of results cannot form the base of a new constitution. More in-depth discussion was needed to determine the 'will of the nation'.[18] Vilhjálmur Árnason, a professor of philosophy, argued that Iceland was a perfect setting for 'citizens' meetings' where democratic deliberation is used to answer complicated questions.[19] In his view, the National Gathering did not seem to provide such a debate and appeared based on a method more suitable for businesses reflecting on clear-cut issues, than for debating complicated moral questions. He concludes that the setup and the way in which some members of the Constitutional Council interpreted, and later claimed to represent only the will of the public as expressed during the meeting, drove the debate towards confrontation and created a hindrance for further democratic discussion, for example in the Althingi.[20]

Elections for the Constitutional Council were held on November 27, 2010. Everyone could stand for election except the president, ministers, and members of Althingi. A total of 522 candidates stood for office, which created several logistical problems leading up to the elections.[21] For the first time in Iceland's history a proportional STV system was used and voters had to choose and rank up to 25 names in the voting booth. A new voting system and difficulties in choosing between so many individuals surely influenced the turnout, with only 36 per cent of the electorate casting its votes. Compared to normal elections this must be considered a very low turnout. Because of the special nature of the elections a new computer system was used to scan and count the ballots, meaning that special paper had to be used and the ballots could not be folded before being placed in the ballot box. Furthermore, each ballot had a special barcode and serial number. After the elections three individuals complained to the Supreme Court, arguing that election laws had been broken. The Supreme Court ruled that the elections had been flawed, partly because of markings on the ballots which theoretically could be used to discover who had cast the vote, and because the ballots could not be folded. The Supreme Court annulled the elections, creating a legitimacy problem for what would later become the Constitutional Council.

Althingi debated how it would proceed after the ruling and decided to appoint the 25 who had been elected to a Constitutional Council, with all but 1 accepting a position. In total, 30 parliamentarians voted yes, 21 voted no, and 7 abstained. Many of those who voted no stated that the proposal was a direct violation of the ruling of the Supreme Court, and some, such as the chairman of the Progressive Party's parliamentary group, declared that due to the flawed process they would not respect the proposals from the Constitutional Council.[22] A rift had thus formed between the parties in Althingi, but furthermore between some parliamentarians and the Constitutional Council that had yet to convene.

The Constitutional Council

The Constitutional Council gathered on April 6, 2011. The preparatory committee submitted a 700-page report, using the results from the National Gathering to make suggestions to the Council. A final draft of a new constitution was presented to the Speaker of Althingi on July 29, giving the Council just under four months to complete its work. Three American constitutional scholars who reviewed the draft were highly supportive of its participatory features. Their conclusion was that

> Iceland's constitution-making process has been tremendously innovative and participatory. Though squarely grounded in Iceland's constitutional tradition as embodied in the 1944 Constitution, the proposed draft reflects significant input from the public and would mark an important symbolic break with the past. It would also be at the cutting edge of ensuring public participation in ongoing governance, a feature that we argue has contributed to constitutional endurance in other countries.[23]

The draft included articles that would fundamentally alter the civic-participatory nature of Icelandic politics. For example, 10 per cent of the electorate would be able to demand a referendum on laws passed by Althingi (Art. 65), 2 per cent could present an issue to Althingi, and 10 per cent could present a bill to Althingi (Art. 66).[24] The draft also included an article on natural resources, stating that those that were not private property should be the property of the nation and that no one could acquire them for permanent use. Included were marine stocks, water rights, and rights to geothermal energy and mining (Art. 34). The draft also introduced a new election system, a changed role for both the president and Althingi, and an updated chapter on human rights.

The Council allowed the public unprecedented access to its work on all stages through open meetings, its website, and social media. Members of the Council have also said that they received numerous emails and phone calls from the public during the work (interviews with the author in 2014). Written comments numbered 3,600, and 370 suggestions were sent to the Council's website.[25] An analysis of the comments reveals that they came from a total of 218 individuals and organisations, 13 per cent came from women, 77 per cent from men, and 10 per cent from organisations. A further analysis of 40 random commenters showed that few young people sent in suggestions and most comments were from men aged 40–65.[26]

While the phrase 'crowd sourced constitution' has been used to describe the draft, it seems that it is an overstatement. Prof. Eiríkur Bergmann Einarsson, a member of the Council, claims that they 'welcomed this focus and even played on it and used it to its advantage in domestic politics'. He adds that it was 'never a realistic description of the drafting', partially because of limited time meaning that Council members were unable to 'plough through all the extensive input'.[27] While the phrase itself seems overstated, the public was certainly allowed to send in suggestions and comments. That, however, is no different from the legislative process in Althingi, where everyone can send in comments to parliamentary committees. The difference lies rather in the website's design with its easiness to send in comments and the use of social media.

The Council welcomed comments and suggestions from the public but it also published on its website 24 'expert opinions' it had specifically asked for.[28] It seems that the only group that was not welcomed during the Council's work were politicians. Prof. Þorvaldur Gylfason, a member of the Council, wrote in a newspaper article that Althingi should not intervene in the Council's work because 'it should not be a judge in its own cause'.[29] When the Council handed the draft to Althingi, all delegates agreed that the population should be given a chance to vote on the new constitution before Althingi's final vote on it. Some have interpreted this as meaning that Althingi should not discuss it materially until after the public's vote. Pawel Bartoszek, a Council member, disagrees, and writes that different opinions existed within the Council and that it was up to Althingi to decide on the timing of a referendum.[30]

Parliamentarians were unsure how to continue the work. In February 2012, it was decided to recall the Council for four days in March to answer questions that Althingi's Constitutional and Supervisory Committee would refer to it. The former chairman of the Constitutional Council, Salvör Norðdal, criticised Althingi for the procedure and did not attend due to prior engagements. She claimed in a letter to the committee that the notice was too short, the purpose unclear, and four days would not suffice to discuss possibly complicated issues. At this point no material discussion on the draft had taken place in Althingi.

Interpreting referendums

In May 2012, Althingi decided to hold an advisory referendum on the draft from the Constitutional Council, in October that same year (see for the results, Table 7.1).[31] Six questions were posed to the electorate:

1. Do you wish the Constitutional Council's proposals to form the basis of a new draft Constitution?
2. In the new Constitution, do you want natural resources that are not privately owned to be declared national property?
3. Would you like to see provisions in the new Constitution on an established (national) church in Iceland?
4. Would you like to see a provision in the new Constitution authorising the election of particular individuals to the Althingi more than is the case at present?
5. Would you like to see a provision in the new Constitution giving equal weight to votes cast in all parts of the country?
6. Would you like to see a provision in the new Constitution stating that a certain proportion of the electorate is able to demand that issues be put to a referendum?

The questions were criticised for being vague and the opposition of both the Independence Party and the Progressive Party was obvious. The leader of the Independence Party encouraged the party's members to turn up and vote no to the first question. A turnout of 48.3 per cent was a significant improvement from the elections to the Constitutional Assembly but markedly less than in the two Icesave referendums in March 2010 and April 2011.[32] Remarkably, between the general elections in 2009 and 2016, the Icelandic electorate cast its vote eleven times in three referendums, elections to the Constitutional Assembly, two local elections, two presidential elections, and three general elections.

Björg Thorarensen, a law professor at the University of Iceland and an expert in constitutional matters, has written that advisory referendums could be used to seek the nation's opinion on 'clearly defined issues'. If the questions were unclear

Table 7.1 The results of the 2012 referendum

	Yes / % of votes cast	*No / % of votes cast*	*Total / % of the electorate*
Question 1	73,509 / 67%	36,302 / 33%	109,811 / 46.3%
Question 2	84,760 / 83%	17,470 / 17%	102,230 / 43.2%
Question 3	58,455 / 57%	43,914 / 43%	102,369 / 43.2%
Question 4	78,451 / 78%	21,660 / 22%	100,111 / 42.3%
Question 5	66,653 / 66%	33,590 / 34%	100,243 / 42.3%
Question 6	72,633 / 73%	26,440 / 27%	99,073 / 41.8%

Source: www.kosning.is/thjodaratkvaedagreidslur2012/english/nr/7993.

or open for interpretation, political groups would be able to put forward competing interpretations of the results and make claims about citizens who did not vote.[33] This is indeed what happened in Iceland.

The political response to the referendum was predictably divided among party-political lines. The two government parties, the Social Democrats and the Left-Green Movement, declared the results as an important step towards a new constitution. The Movement, which grew out of the protests in 2008–2009 and claimed to represent ordinary citizens outside of traditional politics, supported the Council throughout and was delighted with the results. The Independence Party and the Progressive Party were skeptical. The leader of the Independence Party pointed out that 70 per cent of voters had either stayed at home or voted against, thus interpreting the will of those that had not participated. The chairman of the Progressive Party's parliamentary group said that the referendum clearly showed that parts of the constitution needed to be revised but added that it was unlikely that Althingi had sufficient time to discuss those changes due to general elections coming up six months later.[34]

The question remained whether Althingi should or could make material changes to the draft. The Icelandic Constitution can only be changed if two different majorities in Althingi vote for the changes with general elections being held in between. The Prime Minister, Jóhanna Sigurðardóttir, stated in a television interview the morning after the referendum that Althingi had limited permission to make material changes to the draft. She added that Althingi could have a finalised version of the draft ready within two weeks. The government had asked a group of legal experts to review the draft to make sure there were no internal inconsistencies and to clarify words and concepts. While most people saw the need for such a revision, many believed it should be purely technical, and that no material changes could be proposed by the legal experts. Hafsteinn Þór Hauksson was one of the legal experts asked to review the draft. He says that the group made over 80 suggestions, but furthermore they also handed in a letter stating that several other changes should be considered which the group thought lay outside its official assignment (interview with the author, February 2014). One of the suggestions was that the draft would be sent to the Venice Commission for a review, which was subsequently done. The Venice Commission released its opinion in March 2013. It commended

> [t]he authorities' firm willingness to provide Iceland, following the recent economic and financial crisis, with sound, modern, and democratic legal and institutional foundations for the Icelandic people to build a more just society and more adequately benefit from the common heritage.

Increased transparency and the special attention to the active involvement of citizens in the process was also commended. However, it criticised the proposed institutional system as being too complex, especially regarding the division of power between Althingi, the government, and the president. And while they welcomed in principle new ways of peoples' intervention through referendums, the commission warned that they seemed too complicated. Too many provisions were 'formulated in too vague and broad terms', which might 'lead to serious difficulties of interpretation and application'.

> Overall, there are reasons for the Venice Commission to see the risk of political blockage and instability, which may seriously undermine the country's good governance. Similar considerations have been raised by the proposed electoral system, which would also need more careful consideration.[35]

The most vocal member of the Constitutional Council was Þorvaldur Gylfason, a professor of economics at the University of Iceland. He has repeatedly stated that the Council projected the will of the nation, represented by the findings of the National Gathering and continuous dialogue during the Council's work, and later approved through a referendum.[36] In February 2014, he stated that the failure to adopt a new constitution was a betrayal of Althingi, and of academic elites that had hindered the process due to their insistence that they should write the constitution instead of non-experts (interview with the author, February 2014). This criticism of the academic community has been repeated by other members of the Constitutional Council as well as several supporters of the process outside of traditional institutions of power. Much of the criticism from academics revolved around the same issues the Venice Commission had mentioned. Several academics, most of whom were legal scholars or political scientists, criticised parts of the draft in a series of conferences at the University of Iceland. The university was criticised for the lack of supportive voices amongst the speakers, especially by members of the Constitutional Council.[37] Þorvaldur Gylfason wrote that it seemed that some academics viewed the Council as intruders in a private party and asked where they had been when the Council was working. Time for criticism had simply passed since the nation had already voted.[38]

Discussions in Althingi had been concentrated on procedural issues and the question how Althingi should continue with the work. With time running out a new bill based on the draft from the Council was submitted to Althingi on November 16, 2012. It went through two discussions but never made it to a final vote. On March 6, 2013, the newly elected chairmen of both the Social Democrats and the Left-Green Movement, along with the chairman of the newly formed party, Bright Future, presented an amendment to the constitution that effectively postponed discussions on the draft from the Constitutional Council until after the elections. According to the amendment the Icelandic Constitution can be changed up until April 30, 2017, in the following way: If two-thirds of parliamentarians agree on changes, they will be put to a referendum. The changes have to be confirmed by a majority of votes, and that majority must constitute at least 40 per cent of the electorate. The chairman of the Social Democrats said in a speech that more time was needed for Althingi to carefully discuss the new constitution and to build a consensus surrounding it.[39] It was clear that the majority feared a filibuster from the Independence Party and Progressive Party. As expected, neither party admitted that a filibuster was taking place, but it was evident from the proceedings in Althingi.[40] The amendment passed with 25 votes, 2 were against, 21 abstained, and 15 were absent. The Prime Minister, Jóhanna Sigurðardóttir, who for decades had promoted the idea of a constitutional assembly, abstained. After the general elections, the new Althingi passed the amendment for the second time with 42 voting yes, 15 voting no, and 2 abstaining.

While it seems obvious that the draft from the Constitutional Council produced substantial criticism from both academics and politicians, it had also received support from the public through a referendum. Therefore, one would think that it became an important issue during the campaign leading up to the elections. As we will see, the constitution was not high on the voters' agenda, and the parties that focused on it during the campaign did not receive much support.

2013 general elections

The general elections in 2013 proved to be historical in many ways. The total collapse of the two government parties was unprecedented in Iceland's history, the fragmentation of the electorate was evident through the number of parties running, and more people than ever voted for parties that did not cross the 5 per cent threshold needed to gain seats. A total of eleven parties ran for election when the average number is around seven. The rift between the groups campaigning for a new constitution resulted in a new party being created. The Movement joined forces with other small parties and organisations and created a new list called Dawn. While some members of the Constitutional Council joined Dawn, others created a new party called the Democracy Watch, led by Þorvaldur Gylfason. Another Council member founded a third party, called The Party of the Households. Many found it odd that the three parties did not join forces since they shared many of the same values and campaigned on similar grounds. Personal issues seem to have played a role and on some issues, such as the indexation of mortgages, which is an important issue in Iceland, the parties did not agree.

An opinion poll showed that the constitution was not high on the list of voters' priorities. When asked to name the three most important campaign issues, only 15.8 per cent mentioned the constitution, while the most important issue was households' debts.[41] No party campaigned on the grounds of rejecting the new constitution or stopping the bill in Althingi, and all agreed that some changes were needed.

The Social Democrats lost almost 17 per cent of the total vote and eleven parliamentarians, and the Left-Green Movement lost almost 11 per cent and seven parliamentarians. Total support for the two parties fell from 51.5 per cent down to 23.8 per cent, in an unprecedented collapse of voter support. Two new parties crossed the 5 per cent barrier, Bright Future and the Icelandic Pirate Party. Dawn received 3.1 per cent, the Democracy Watch, 2.5 per cent, and The Party of the Households, 3 per cent. Had the three parties joined forces, or even just the first two, they would probably have gained seats in Althingi. Almost 12 per cent of the electorate voted for parties that did not gain any seats and a quarter of the electorate voted for parties other than the traditional four.[42]

The clear winner was the Progressive Party with 24.4 per cent, a gain of 9.6 per cent from 2009. The Independence Party remained the largest party with 26.7 per cent, which is still its second worst result in a general election, the worst being in 2009. The two parties later formed a government with the 38-year-old leader of the Progressive Party, Sigmundur Davíð Gunnlaugsson, becoming the youngest Prime Minister since independence in 1944.

Voters' attitude towards constitutional change[43]

The Icelandic National Election Study (ICENES) is an ongoing study from 1983 directed by Dr. Ólafur Þ. Harðarson, professor of political science at the University of Iceland. ICENES is part of the Nordic Electoral Democracy (NED), a Nordic collaborative program on democracy and elections, Comparative Studies of Electoral Systems (CSES), and True European Voter (TEV), which are international collaborative programs on election studies. The 2013 study shows that although the public is willing to change parts of the constitution, and that interest is not considered an important election issue (see Table 7.2). When participants were asked whether they had voted in the referendum on the constitution in October 2012, 1,025, or 71 per cent of those that answered the question, had voted, while 419, or 29 per cent, had not. Considering that the turnout in the referendum was 48.3 per cent, people who participated are over-represented in the survey.

In total, 54.6 per cent answer that it is somewhat or very important to change the constitution, while 35.7 per cent said it was not very or not at all important. This view has routinely been confirmed in polls on specific constitutional issues, such as whether to include an article about natural resources. The ICENES survey asked whether the public should be able to demand a referendum on specific issues, and 80 per cent of those that answered (N = 1,102) said they somewhat or strongly favoured the idea, but only 14.8 per cent (N = 203) somewhat or strongly opposed the idea.

When asked to name the most important political issue Iceland was facing only 1 per cent (N = 13) mentioned the constitution. And when asked what they had considered the most important issue in the general elections only 1.4 per cent (N = 18) said the constitution. The number was slightly higher when people were asked to name the second most important issue, yet only 2 per cent (N = 24) said the constitution. This is, of course, not very surprising. The economy and

Table 7.2 Do you consider it important to change the current constitution?

Not at all important	162 / 10.9%
Not very important	367 / 24.8%
Somewhat important	522 / 35.4%
Very important	284 / 19.2%
Does not answer	29 / 1.9%
Does not know	110 / 7.4%
Total	1474 / 100%

the economic situation of households was by far the most important issue in the minds of voters, with almost half mentioning it as either the most or second most important issue. Labour issues, the EU, health care, and the tax system all rated higher than the constitution.

A continuous constitutional saga

The Icelandic Constitution could – until the temporary amendment was passed in 2013 – only be changed by two different majorities in Althingi, with elections being held in between. Theoretically, this means that the electorate can have their say on constitutional affairs by voting for parties that support their views. This has, however, never been a political actuality in Iceland. From 1944 the constitution has been changed a total of seven times and usually through a prolonged discussion and consensus in Althingi. A new parliament has never rejected changes to the constitution passed by a prior session. The 2013 elections show us that even when the constitution has become a highly contested and politicised issue, it still does not manifest itself in voter behaviour.

Perhaps the explanation is simply that the political parties had avoided the discussion by passing the temporary amendment instead of the new bill as a whole. It is highly likely that the Independence Party would have campaigned against the bill and probably the Progressive Party as well. That might have resulted in voters casting their votes based directly on their opinion of the new constitution.

The Panama Papers, the Pirate Party, and the return to the right

In November 2013, the Prime Minister appointed a new seven-member constitutional committee to continue the work. The committee was made up of six current or former politicians and three legal scholars, and so it seemed that the 'professionals' had retaken control of the process. It should be noted that several other committees have been appointed since 1944 to review the constitution, but none have succeeded in writing a new one. The committee prioritised four subjects in its work: natural resources, environmental protection, referendums, and the partial transfer of sovereignty to international institutions. In June 2014, the committee published a provisional report inviting the public to comment on the work. Although several comments were received, most of them were a reminder of the referendum in 2012.[44] In February 2016, the committee introduced three different amendments, having failed to agree on an amendment on the partial transfer of sovereignty.[45] The decision to submit three amendments was intentional since one amendment would have forced the public to vote on a take-it-or-leave-it package.

The three amendments were as follows: Article 79 concerned the protection and accessibility of nature, giving the public a constitutional right to access information on any developments that might affect the environment. Article 80 stated that Iceland's natural resources belonged to the Icelandic people and that nobody could obtain ownership or permanent utilisation of them. Furthermore, it stated that an appropriate fee should be charged by the authorities for the utilisation of natural resources. Article 81 stated that 15 per cent of the public could force a referendum on laws or resolutions adopted by Althingi. However, the budget, supplementary budgets, acts on matters concerning taxation, and acts adopted to fulfil obligations under international law would not be put to a referendum according to the proposal. To reject an act or a resolution, according to the article, a majority in a referendum but no less than a quarter of the population would have to vote against it.

The proposals did not receive a great deal of attention when submitted by the committee. The reason was probably that they had to be officially submitted to Althingi, which then would have to debate on the issue. Before that could happen, the Panama Papers leak sent a shockwave through Icelandic society.

On April 3, 2016, over 100 media organisations in around 80 countries published stories based on the Panama Papers. The origin was one of the biggest leaks of documents in history, some 11.5 million documents detailing financial and attorney-client information on over two hundred thousand offshore entities. The names of three Icelandic ministers were in the papers, including the Prime Minister's and the Finance Minister's. The following day over twenty thousand Icelanders protested in front of Althingi calling for the resignation of the government and general elections. On April 5, the Prime Minister met with the Icelandic president giving an unorthodox statement afterwards on the content of their talks.[46] Later that day the Prime Minister stepped aside with the Progressive Party's vice chairman taking over as Prime Minister. According to Article 24 of the constitution the president can dissolve Althingi. However, Article 13 states that the president entrusts his authority to ministers. The role and power of the president has been a contested issue in Icelandic politics. The power to dissolve Althingi has generally been considered to be de facto combined in the positions of the president and Prime Minister, meaning that both would have to agree. But during those days in April, it became clear that the wording in the constitution allowed for different interpretations. Thus, the constitution was high on the political agenda and one of the major themes in the political debate during those turbulent times.

Later that summer the constitution was yet again a central part of political discussions before the presidential elections in June. Every candidate had to answer questions about his view of the role of the president in the political system and his view on the draft from the Constitutional Council. After 20 years, President Ólafur Ragnar Grímsson had decided to step down. He was the first president to invoke Article 26 by rejecting to sign a bill passed by Althingi, thereby forcing a referendum. President Grímsson has in many ways changed the role of the president leaving some scholars to describe the system as a semi-presidential government.[47] The new president, Guðni Th. Jóhannesson, is a professor of history and an expert on his predecessors. During the campaign, he seemed to suggest that the presidency under Grímsson had become too politicised and that he would return to a more ceremonial role.

On August 25, 2016, the Prime Minister, Sigurður Ingi Jóhannsson, submitted a bill to Althingi containing the three amendments proposed by the constitutional committee. Interestingly enough, the bill was not a formal proposal by the government, but a parliamentarian bill which usually is much less likely to go through. After a single debate, the bill was sent to a committee but did not make it back to Althingi before the elections.

New general elections were called for on October 29, 2016, six months before schedule. The Pirate Party had enjoyed miraculous support in the polls with 36.1 per cent in a Gallup poll on March 31, just before the release of the Panama Papers. From then until the elections in October there was an almost continuous decline. There are several possible explanations but that analysis lies outside the scope of this chapter. It should, however, be said that the party campaigned on few but very distinct issues, one of them being the adaption of the Constitutional Council's constitution. The Icelandic National Broadcasting Service (RUV) requested a poll on voters' preferences before the elections. In total, 36.4 per cent answered that they thought it was very or somewhat important to discuss the revision of the constitution before the elections. When asked to rank issues, the revision of the constitution came eighth with 5.4 per cent saying it was the most important issue and a further 4.1 per cent that it was the second most important issue. Whatever the reason, the Pirate Party received 14.5 per cent of the vote and 10 out of 63 parliamentarians. While the party grew from the 2013 elections, the result was met with disappointment from within, especially when compared to the polls. The Pirates are seen as an outsider party campaigning for structural changes through a new constitution. It is clear that they have gathered much of the dissent vote but that has not allowed them to gain a foothold in government.

New government

After the elections, a prolonged discussion took place between the political parties on the formation of a new government. On January 11, 2017, a new coalition government under the leadership of the Independence Party was formed. Made up from three parties, it enjoys a single seat majority in parliament, making it extremely fragile in a complex political environment. Besides the Independence Party, Bright Future and the Reform Party joined the coalition. The Reform Party is a liberal, EU-enthusiastic party, which during the campaign promised several structural changes in the fishing and agricultural industries. The new government mentions the constitution in its manifesto. It states that:

> A review of the Icelandic constitution will be undertaken on the basis of the wide-ranging work that has taken place in recent years. The government will invite all parliamentary parties to nominate a representative for a parliamentary review committee which will collaborate with the most skilled specialists in the field of constitutional law in order to reach the best possible agreement on a proposal for amendments, which will be put forward no later than 2019. It is an important goal that all amendment proposals should be thoroughly publicised and discussed before they are submitted to the Althingi and they should be given thorough treatment in parliament, in open

> meetings as appropriate. Consideration will be given to a review of constituency boundaries in the light of the experience gained from the most recent changes made. In parallel with this, electoral legislation will be reviewed with a view to simplifying it and increasing equality in the weighting of votes.[48]

Conclusions

Why did the process that began with such high hopes falter and eventually stop? Björg Thorarensen, a professor of law at the University of Iceland, offers four possible explanations. Firstly, she questions whether it is possible to shift the task of constitution-making from a political forum to a consultive body. Defining it as a non-political process had been doomed to failure from the beginning since it could never replace the legitimate process provided for in the constitution. Secondly, she feels the need to distinguish between the involvement of people on the one hand, and the technical aspects of writing a constitution on the other. Too many inconsistencies had been found in the text. Thirdly, the hesitation in Althingi and the dragged-out process limited the time available for discussions. Almost a year was spent on deciding to have an advisory referendum, leaving only four months to discuss the bill. Finally, the goal to achieve a consensus was ambitious from the beginning, but became almost impossible after the ruling from the Supreme Court. From then on, the process became political with two opposition parties fighting it at every turn.[49]

While I agree with points three and four, the first two are open for debate. It is true that the constitution dictates that politicians make the changes and that they are only bound by their conviction. It is also to be expected that a group of individuals with limited experience in writing bills will run into problems and inconsistencies. But while these are descriptions of what happened, they are not a necessary truth. Politicians can clearly decide that their conviction is to follow the public's will as represented in an advisory referendum. It may not be legally binding, but many would argue that it could be morally binding. Furthermore, the writing of a legislative text is a logistical problem easily circumvented by professional assistance. That a group of legal scholars found it necessary to make several changes to the text from the Constitutional Council does not in itself invalidate its work or the process.

I would, however, offer two further explanations regarding the process that might explain it. A leading politician from the Social Democrats has said that the confrontational rhetoric of some Council members came as a shock. They felt that they were being unfairly attacked by a group that they had not only established but supported throughout (interview with the author). This begs the question how social movements should communicate with political elites. By placing themselves on the side of the public and against politicians who lack the public's trust might seem a good idea. The danger is that it alienates possible partners. After the financial crisis, the public's trust towards political institutions was at an all-time low, with merely 10 per cent saying they trusted Althingi. A new constitution written with the involvement of the public was indeed seen as an attempt to regain that trust. And while voter volatility has increased, voters still work within the traditional boundaries set by the political system. The Constitutional Council misinterpreted the public's enthusiasm, alienated potential political partners, and made it easy for the center-right parties to paint it as a tool for a leftist political agenda.

The second explanation is the enthusiasm of the public and its participation in the process. Throughout, the public had access to the Council's work and with the referendum they had a chance to speak their minds. The ICENES survey also shows a willingness to change parts of the constitution. At the same time, it is not seen as an election issue, as other issues are simply more important in the minds of voters. If the public's will is reflected through elections, it is at least clear that its desire to obtain a new constitution based on the Council's draft was not so great so as to transform itself into votes. A small group has been extremely interested in the constitutional process from the beginning and the social movement campaigning for change has been vocal and in many ways successful. In a post-crisis or even a post-revolutionary scenario the voices campaigning for change are often the loudest. The silent majority might still win in the end.

Enthusiasm can fade quickly. In Iceland, the public prioritised financial issues such as debt relief and housing over changes to the constitution. The belligerent rhetoric of parts of the Council's members did not help due to the following politicisation of the draft submitted. Although the Pirate Party is still arguing for the draft, it seems unlikely that it will become the next Icelandic Constitution. Although most would agree that certain changes are needed – and indeed expected – the draft's supporters have not succeeded in convincing a majority of the public, academic elites, or politicians that is should be adopted. Iceland's financial success in the last couple of years has not helped their case.

Can the Icelandic constitutional experiment be described as a success? If measured in changes adopted, then no – absolutely not. However, if measured in terms of continuous discussion on the role of the constitution, it might be seen as a success. At least, it has shown that the constitution is far from forgotten or somehow unimportant in Icelandic society.

Notes

1 Paul Blokker, 2012, 'Dilemmas of Democratisation from Legal Revolutions to Democratic Constitutionalism?', in *Nordic Journal of International Law* 81(4), pp. 437–470; Jon Elster, 'Deliberation and Constitution Making', in *Deliberative Democracy*, ed. Jon Elster (Cambridge: Cambridge University Press, 1993).

2 Elster (n1) 371.

3 Susan Burgess and Christine (Cricket) Keating, 2013, 'Occupy the Social Contract! Participatory Democracy and Iceland's Crowd-Sourced Constitution', in *New Political Science* 35(3), pp. 417–431, 421.

4 *The Guardian* 09.06.2011 and *The New York Times* 24.10.2012 are just two examples of several articles using that phrase. As will be discussed the draft was never a crowd-sourced constitution.

5 Jack M. Balkin, 2005, 'How Social Movements Change (or Fail to Change) the Constitution: The Case of the New Departure', in *Faculty Scholarship Series*.

Paper 235. Available at: http://digitalcommons.law.yale.edu/fss_papers/235 (last accessed 11.03.2014).

6 David A. Snow and Sarah A. Soule, *A Primer on Social Movements* (New York and London: W. W. Norton & Company, 2010): 6.

7 Njörður P. Njarðvík, 2009. Nýtt Lýðveldi, Fréttablaðið 14.01. www.visir.is/nytt-lydveldi/article/2009133864879. While it is possible that others mentioned a new constitution before, Njarðvík's statement is generally agreed to be the first of notice.

8 A list of proposals regarding the constitution can be found in Gunnar Helgi Kristinsson, 2007, 'Ágrip af þróun stjórnarskrárinnar', in: *Endurskoðun stjórnarskrárinnar. Áfangaskýrsla nefndar um endurskoðun stjórnarskrár lýðveldisins Íslands, febrúar 2007.* Þskj. 1293–1709. Mál: 61-87.

9 www.youtube.com/watch?v=uf66Nkqiu3A.

10 Morgunblaðið 2009.

11 Samstarfsyfirlýsing ríkisstjórnar Samfylkingarinnar og Vinstrihreyfingarinnar – græns framboðs. 2009. www.stjornarrad.is/media/Skjol/rikisstjorn_8mai09.pdf (last accessed 07.03.2014).

12 See for example Þorvaldur Gylfason 14.12.2012.

13 Jón Ólafsson, 2011. 'An Experiment in Iceland: Crowdsourcing a Constitution?', a paper introduced at the conference Epistemic Democracy in Practice at Yale University, October 2011, available at: www.yale.edu/polisci/conferences/epistemic_democracy/jOlafsson.pdf (last accessed 11.03.2014).

14 Stefán Gunnar Sveinsson, *Búsáhaldabyltingin: sjálfsprottin eða skipulögð?* (Reykjavík: Almenna bókafélagið, 2013).

15 Act No. 90/2010.

16 Baldvin Thor Bergsson and Paul Blokker, 'The Constitutional Experiment in Iceland', in *Verfassungsgebung in konsolidierten Demokratien: Neubeginn oder Verfall eines Systems?* (Baden-Baden: Nomos Verlag, 2014).

17 The main conclusions can be found here: www.thjodfundur2010.is/frettir/lesa/item32858/.

18 Gunnar Helgi Kristinsson, 2012, 'Ráðskast með stjórnarskrá' (Manipulating the Constitution), in: *Icelandic Review of Politics and Administration* 8(2), pp. 565–570.

19 Vilhjálmur Árnason, 2013, 'Valdið fært til fólksins? Veikleikar og verkefni íslensk lýðræðis í aðdraganda og eftirmála hrunsins' (Power Brought to the People? Weaknesses of and Challenges to Icelandic Democracy Before and After The Crash), in *Skírnir* 187(spring), pp. 11–54.

20 Árnason (n17) 30–31.

21 One of the most bizarre demands was that the Icelandic National Radio would introduce every single candidate, since it had a legal obligation to inform the public prior to elections. The Radio decided to give each candidate a couple of minutes to answer pre-determined questions. With 522 candidates, the National Radio broadcasted over 50 hours of interviews between November 22–26.

22 Gunnar Bragi Sveinsson made the statement during the vote in Althingi. www.althingi.is/altext/139/03/r24111821.sgml (last accessed 07.03.2014).

23 Zacharia Elkins, Tom Ginsburg, and James Melton, 2012, 'A Review of Iceland's Draft Constitution', available at: https://webspace.utexas.edu/elkinszs/web/CCP%20Iceland%20Report.pdf (last accessed 11.03.2014), 11.

24 The draft can be found here: www.stjornlagarad.is/other_files/stjornlagarad/Frumvarp-enska.pdf. While the draft opens new ways of civic-participation it still added a caveat in Article 67: 'Issues presented before a referendum at the demand or initiative of voters according to Articles 65 and 66 shall concern the public interest. On their basis, a vote may not be demanded on fiscal budgets, supplementary fiscal budgets, laws enacted to enforce international obligations as well as laws concerning tax issues or the right to citizenship. Care shall be taken that a bill at the initiative of the voters shall be in accordance with the Constitution.'

25 Stjórnlagaráð 2011.
26 Ragnhildur Helgadóttir, 2014, 'Facebook-demokratiet': Et islandsk eksperiment', paper presented at the Grunnlovssymposiet ved det Juridiske Fakultet i Bergen 20.02. 2014, available at: www.academia.edu/6263582/_Facebook-demokratiet_-_et_islandsk_eksperiment (last accessed 11.03.2014).
27 Eiríkur Bergmann Einarsson, *Iceland and the International Financial Crisis: Boom, Bust & Recovery* (Basingstoke and New York: Palgrave Macmillan, 2014): 179.
28 Fourteen opinions came from legal scholars, eight from ministries, one from a political scientist, and one from the secretary of Althingi's Budget Committee.
29 Þorvaldur Gylfason, 2011, 'Þjóðaratkvæði um frumvarp Stjórnlagaráðs' (A Referendum on the Draft from the Constitutional Council), in DV, 28.10.2011, available at: https://notendur.hi.is//~gylfason/referendum%202011.html (last accessed 11.03.2014).
30 Pawel Bartoszek, 2012, 'Fyrirfram vitað eftir á' (Preknown Afterwards). Personal blog. Available at: http://pawel.is/2012/02/22/fyrirfram-vitad-eftir-a/ (last accessed 04.03.2014).
31 An advisory referendum is a problematic term but the Icelandic Constitution only allows for binding referendum on two occasions: when the president refuses to sign a bill, or when changes are made to the State Church. It further complicates the matter that according to the constitution members of Althingi are bound solely by their conviction and not by instructions from their constituents (Art. 48). It has, therefore, been discussed whether they are bound, legally or morally, to follow the results from an advisory referendum.
32 The Icesave dispute was a diplomatic dispute between Iceland on the one hand and the UK and the Netherlands on the other. It centered on whether the Icelandic state should guarantee at least for the repayment of the Icelandic minimum deposit guarantees on savings lost in the Icesave branches in the two countries when the privately owned Landsbanky went bankrupt on October 7, 2008.
33 Björg Thorarensen, 2012, 'Þjóðin er stjórnarskrárgjafi – ekki ráðgjafi' (The Nation Should Adopt the Constitution – Not Write It), in *Fréttablaðið*, 31. October, available at: www.visir.is/thjodin-er-stjornarskrargjafi---ekki-radgjafi/article/2012710319973 (last accessed 11.03.2014).
34 Skúli Hansen, 2012, 'Deila um niðurstöðurnar' (Arguing about the Results), in Morgunblaðið, 22. October, available at: www.mbl.is/frettir/innlent/2012/10/22/deila_um_nidurstodurnar/ (last accessed 11.03.2014).
35 Venice Commission, 2013, *Opinion on the Draft New Constitution of Iceland*, adopted by the Venice Commission at its 94th Plenary Session (Venice, March 8–9, 2013), available at: www.althingi.is/pdf/venice.coe.pdf (last accessed 11.03.2014), 30–31.
36 Þorvaldur Gylfason, 2012, 'Vor í lofti og varla komin jól' (Spring is in the Air and It's not even Christmas), personal blog, available at: www.dv.is/blogg/thorvaldur-gylfason/2012/12/14/vor-i-lofti-og-varla-komin-jol/ (last accessed 11.03.2014).
37 This criticism was repeated in several interviews the author has conducted with members of the Constitutional Council.
38 Þorvaldur Gylfason, 2013, 'Fræðasamfélagið og frumvarpið' (The Academic Community and the Constitutional Draft), in DV, 11. January, available at: https://notendur.hi.is//~gylfason/academic.html (last accessed 10.03.2014).
39 Árni Páll Árnason during a speech in Althingi, transcript available at: www.althingi.is/altext/raeda/141/rad20130306T173940.html (last accessed 10.03.2014).
40 It should be added that leaked text messages from the leader of the Progressive Party's parliamentary group to his fellow members suggest that a filibuster was taking place. The messages have been reported by the Icelandic media.
41 The Poll was made by the Social Science Research Institute of the University of Iceland. The results were reported by the Icelandic Television (RUV), available at: www.ruv.is/frett/skuldamal-heimilanna-mikilvaegust (last accessed 10.03.2014).

42 The traditional four are the Independence Party, the Social Democrats, the Progressive Party, and the Left-Green Movement. A fifth party has usually entered Althingi and added together the five parties have received over 95 per cent of the vote. During the 2013 elections the number dropped to 80 per cent.

43 The data in this part come from the Icelandic National Election Study (ICENES). The author wishes to thank the directors of the study: dr. Ólafur Þ. Harðarson, dr Hulda Þórisdóttir, and Eva Heiða Önnudóttir, for their support and access to the data.

44 A formal statement by the committee July 1, 2016: www.forsaetisraduneyti.is/media/stjornarskra/scan_11072016.pdf.

45 An English version of the proposals: www.forsaetisraduneyti.is/media/stjornarskra/proposed-amendments-constitution.pdf.

46 No official minutes exist and the president and Prime Minister disagree on what took place in that private meeting.

47 Svanur Kristjánsson, 2002, 'Stofnun lýðveldis – nýsköpun lýðræðis', in *Skírnir*, 176(1): 7–45.

48 www.government.is/government/coalition-platform/.

49 Björg Thorarensen, 2014, 'Why the Making of a Crowd-Sourced Constitution in Iceland Failed'. Website article, available at: http://constitutional-change.com/why-the-making-of-a-crowd-sourced-constitution-in-iceland-failed/ (last accessed 11.03.2014).

Part III

Constitution-making, constitutional reform, and deadlock in 'new' democracies

8 Constitutional revision in Romania

Post-accession pluralism in action

Bogdan Iancu[1]

1. Introduction: The dynamics of constitutional revision by stealth

In the summer of 2012, a parliamentary attempt to impeach the sitting President, Traian Băsescu, abruptly brought a local Romanian constitutional crisis to the center of wider European political and doctrinal debates. In essence, over the winter of 2011, a period of street protests (anti-presidential but also anti-political) generated a climate of dissatisfaction and turmoil, fostering defections from the governing coalition and thus also enabling a motion of censure against the government in power, a centre-right coalition close to the President. The motion brought a new Prime Minister to power, as leader of a coalition hostile to the President. This alliance, the Social Liberal Union (USL), a peculiar bed-fellowship of National Liberals and Social Democrats, won, within a few months, a landslide two-thirds majority in parliamentary elections. Once in power, the new majority quickly proceeded to take its revenge on Băsescu, at the time a controversial and abrasive head of state nearing the end of his second term. In this process, the Referendum Law 3/2000 was amended, to eliminate a turnout requirement and make the impeachment of the President, which must be confirmed by popular referendum, easier. The competence of the Constitutional Court was curtailed by amending its organic law, in order to remove from the Court's competence the power to review parliamentary decisions, such as those set in motion to remove and replace the Speakers of the Houses of Parliament. The Ombudsman was also sacked by the Parliament, ostensibly with the argument that the incumbent had surpassed his constitutional attributions but more likely in order to stave off challenges to the Constitutional Court of crucial government decrees, by appointing a new, more amenable official (the constitutionality of emergency ordinances, enactments with the force of law passed by the Government on a plea of necessity, can only be challenged directly by the Ombudsman). All these actions, albeit instrumental and in point of principle unsavory, were formally legal. Moreover, whereas the number of instrumental decisions was unprecedented, instrumentalism as such is a mainstay of constitutional politics in the country. This gaudy drama took up most of the summer. At the end of a string of partly contradictory decisions of the Constitutional Court the referendum was invalidated for lack of quorum and the lame duck President remained in office for the remainder of his term.

The conclusion of the conflict was partly influenced by external demands, undertaken in the name of the rule of law. In response to the Romanian crisis, the European Commission integrated a ten-point list of constitutional requests in its July 2012 Cooperation and Verification Report and proceeded to entrench the monitoring of constitutional developments in the mechanism.[2] The Vice-President of the Commission, Justice Commissioner Viviane Reding, analogized the situations in Romania and Hungary, and floated the idea of a post-accession, new mechanism, analogous to the Copenhagen criteria.[3] Furthermore, the Justice Commissioner exemplified her plan to solve the "Copenhagen dilemma" (i.e., the non-democratic derailment of a Member State after the accession) by reference to the Cooperation and Verification Mechanism for Romania and Bulgaria. The proposal of squaring the circle between soft power and the "nuclear option" (thus Reding) of Article 7 TEU by way of a "post-Accession Copenhagen" has resulted, meanwhile, in a soft-law monitoring procedure, pegged unto Art. 7.[4] This way, the Romanian crisis contributed indirectly to the fledgling European constitutionalism. In part due to such wider implications, the foreign political science and comparative law literature has converged on the description of the 2012 Romanian events as deviations from a norm, i.e., serious breaches of the rule of law and constitutional standards, in analogy to the Hungarian slide towards "illiberal democracy" and – more recently – to the Polish Constitutional Crisis.[5] In all these cases, as the arguments run, we encounter backsliding after the accession. The Union should therefore have the proper means to bring its recalcitrant members into conformity with common constitutional standards.

In what concerns Romanian developments, although foreign critics were correct in minute principle (in an ideal world, actions such as those described above are abnormal, both sociologically and normatively), labeling one side as lawless and one set of actions as a "coup d'état" painted in black and white, with a broad brush, on a grey Romanian canvass. Otherwise put, elated terms heaved from the conceptual arsenal of Western constitutionalism were implicitly and perhaps unwittingly put in the service of one camp in a dirty local power struggle in which neither side had pulled too many punches over the years. The rule of law as such is a lofty ideal but its invocation, particularly in unsettled legal systems, is often driven by mundane ideological interests and political contingencies. Article 10 of the Referendum Law 3/2000, to give a relevant example, has been amended to the point of satiety over the years, to reduce or eliminate turnout whenever the parliamentary coalition wanted to suspend the President, in periods of cohabitation, or to reintroduce a quorum validity requirement and heighten the majority needed to confirm an impeachment, when the "President's party" ruled. The Constitutional Court itself has revised its jurisprudence once every few years, with remarkable pliability, so that according to a decision rendered in 2007, in the course of a prior attempt to impeach Băsescu, no validity quorum for impeachment referenda was constitutionally required. In 2012 the Parliament was under a constitutional obligation to refrain from eliminating a 50% turnout requirement, whereas in 2013 30% participation and 25% validity requirements applicable to national referenda were perfectly constitutional, provided, however, that the application of these rules would be stayed for one year after the entry into force of the amendments to the Referendum Law.[6] The practical cumulative effect of these decisions has been that the turnout condition has varied from one valid hypothetical vote (no quorum requirement) to 9,146,232 citizens (quorum needed) whereas the majority requirement swung from 9,146,232 (absolute majority needed to confirm the impeachment) to a current hypothetical minimum of 12.5% of Romanian citizens registered on the permanent electoral lists for the election of the President.[7]

Seen against the backdrop of post-communist constitutional evolutions, the crisis and its political environment are revealing of deep structural problems of Romanian constitutionalism. Such shortcomings have their origins both in punctual normative choices and in deeper, underlying contextual determinations.

In what remains of my chapter, I will address the subject matter of the volume, constitutional revision as an indicator of constitutional acceleration, by showing how the option for rigid amendment rules and various limitations at the foundational moment of Romanian constitutionalism in 1991 have generated as a long-term perverse effect powerful but less tractable patterns of informal constitutional change. Although the Romanian Constitution presents at first sight an image of normative stability, its functioning has been subjected, over the last decade, to a process of intense constitutional revision by stealth.

In this respect, the 2012 crisis is indicative of relevant informal changes in the operation of the Romanian constitutional system. Majoritarian democracy has partly receded and given way to a new form of constitutional pluralism by virtue of which traditional politics is complemented with and partly supplanted by patterns and mechanisms of apolitical decision-making. In the new configuration, politically neutral institutions and institutional networks play a prominent role.

2. The avatars of post-communist constitution-making

Unlike other Eastern Bloc countries, the transition in Romania was not negotiated, a historical peculiarity that stifled procedural and substantive debate and compromise during the transitional period. After the violent overthrow of Ceaușescu, the elections in May 1990 gave one of the contenders, the National Salvation Front, a two-thirds majority. The NSF resulted from the provisional government, a coalition of reformist communist elites, now revamped as revolutionaries, and a few co-opted former dissidents and public intellectuals. The candidate – and President – of the NSF, Ion Iliescu, an "enlightened" *nomenklatura* member sidelined by Ceaușescu, was simultaneously elected by virtual plebiscite to the Presidency, in the first ballot, with 85% of the expressed popular vote. Under the circumstances, the majority did not need to consult the fragile opposition parties, with the result that drafting the new constitution was for the most part a streamlined process, with little genuine debate or social involvement; in Ackermanian jargon, there was no "constitutional moment". Return to tradition may have provided solid mooring to a model but attempts by the "historic parties" (Liberals and Christian-Democrats) in the opposition to strengthen references to the pre-communist democratic experiences of the country (the constitutions of 1866 and 1923) were downplayed in order to place a tacit gag rule on underlying arguments about a possible return to constitutional monarchy.

The constitution of 1991 is marked in its essential features by irresolution (or aimlessness), generated by the lack of a genuine constitutional moment, the avoidance of the pre-communist democratic tradition – inchoate and short-lived though it may have been – and the lack of experience of the post-communist majority and its experts with the arcane notions and practices of constitutionalism. The Constitutional Committee did undertake study trips and consulted in Bucharest and abroad with foreign practitioners and academics (for instance, with the then newfangled Venice Commission), but such consultations were fraught with the general limitations of foreign aid.[8] The epistemological benefits of conversations are usually a function of the length, depth, and openness of discussions and relative capacities and interests of conversationalists.

This is not to downplay the work of the Committee, which is easy to ridicule in retrospect, with the benefit of hindsight and a protracted transition. The reasons for undertaking a research trip to Spain are, for instance, presented as follows in the report published by its chair, Senator and law professor Antonie Iorgovan:

> [I]n our opinion, the Spanish Constitution was the most successful in Europe and relatively recent, dating back in 1978. About the Constitution of Spain, it is said that its mother is the French Constitution (1958) and its grandmother the German (1949).[9]

And yet, in fairness, behind the flamboyant rhetoric, the subsequent reasons adduced by Iorgovan were credible: Spain could be relevant to a transitional jurisdiction, other things being equal, due to the common authoritarian past. In more propitious circumstances, exposure to comparative constitutional law may have been of use to the Romanian Constitution makers. In the general context of the early 1990s, cursory foreign inputs could not be assimilated in a sophisticated local debate but rather provided additional "Western" legitimacy and some fragmentary "Ikea model" information[10] to the drafting process.[11]

The end result, assembled together from various fears,[12] a healthy dose of inexperience, and a measure of political irresolution as to the grand design, is a kaleidoscope of antinomies and tensions. The entrenchment of openness to international law (human rights provisions in the Universal Declaration of Human Rights and ratified human rights conventions prevail as a rule over domestic guarantees of fundamental rights, according to Art. 20) cohabitates uneasily with a strong statement of identity as homogeneity in Art. 3 (4), forbidding the "displacement or colonization of foreign populations" on Romanian territory.[13] The political system is semi-presidential but the effective attributions of the President are stipulated in a vague enough form to invite both abuse and deadlock, the Parliament is bicameral but the two houses still function in an almost duplicative manner, the list of rights in title two of the document combines rather haphazardly classical defensive rights (free speech, individual freedom), with aspirational provisions and declarations of state policy imperatives (e.g., protection of the youth, right to a clean environment, right to a decent living standard). Judicial review by a Constitutional Court was established in a form which uses some of the features of the weak, essentially political French model of the *Conseil Constitutionnel* (institutional make-up, structure of appointments) but gives the Court concrete review attributions, as a reluctant halfway nod to German design. Some institutions were borrowed for purely decorative or reputational purposes from what the founders deemed at the time to have constituted Western best practices. The Ombudsman, for instance ("Advocate of the People"), included at the proposal of a liberal MP, was not established until 1997, when the Parliament passed its organic law.

Paradoxically, in a constitution characterized by a significant degree of indecision and ludic experimentation ("bricolage"[14]) with foreign and domestic norms and institutions, the amendment provisions are highly determinate and demanding. Unlike the constitutions of other post-communist countries of the region, which can be changed by supermajorities in Parliament,[15] the Romanian "original constituent power" sought to entrench the limitations of transition (indecisions and inexperience) in perpetuity.[16] An amendment may be initiated by the President at the proposal of the Government, by one fourth of the deputies or senators or by 500,000 citizens, provided that at least 20,000 signatures each are collected in at least half of the counties or the municipality of Bucharest (Art. 150). The bill must be adopted in identical versions by qualified, two-thirds majorities of all members in both Houses. In the event of a divergence between the draft bills adopted by the Senate and the Chamber of Deputies, a conference committee is convened and, should mediation fail, the bill can only by adopted by a supermajority of three-fourths in the Committee of the Whole (joint session of Parliament). Should the bill be adopted, a mandatory confirmatory referendum is held within thirty days (Art. 151).

The "eternity clause", Art. 152 (limits of revision), shields the provisions concerning the nature of the state (defined as national, independent, unitary, indivisible), the republican form of government, territorial integrity, the independence of justice, political pluralism, and the official language from revision, provides that no amendment may "[result] in the suppression of the citizens' fundamental rights and freedoms, or of the safeguards thereof" and that no revision bill may be passed in wartime or during a state of siege or emergency. According to Art. 146(a) in the constitution and Arts. 19–23 of Law No. 47/1992 regarding the organization and functioning of the Constitutional Court, the Constitutional Court pronounces *ex officio* on the constitutionality of initiatives to amend the constitution, within ten days, upon receipt of the draft bill accompanied by the opinion of the Legislative Council, before the initiative is laid before Parliament, and on revision laws within five days of their adoption. A finding of unconstitutionality must be supported by a two-thirds majority of the Court, i.e., at least six justices (Art. 21(1), Law 47/1992). Given the substantive limits of revision in Art. 152, the Constitutional Court reviews draft bills (initiatives) and law both "extrinsically" (which in Romanian doctrinal jargon means procedure-wise) and "intrinsically" (i.e., in terms of substance).

The constitution was extensively amended once, in preparation for EU and NATO accession. The directly and explicitly NATO and EU-related changes are in fact marginal in the scope of Law 429/2003 for the revision of the constitution: Title VI was interspersed between the titles on the Constitutional Court and Constitutional Amendment, consisting of two articles, 148 and 149, on EU integration and accession to the North Atlantic Treaty, respectively; Art. 16 was amended to grant resident EU citizens the right to vote in local public administration elections, under the conditions set forth by organic legislation; Art. 38 was included (the right of Romanian citizens to vote and stand for election in European parliamentary elections); the provision on the right to property (Art. 44 (2)) was amended to make the acquisition of land by foreign citizens and stateless persons possible "under the terms resulting from Romania's accession to the European Union and other international treaties Romania is a party to, on a mutual basis, under the terms stipulated by an organic law, as well as a result of lawful inheritance"; and the provision on the financial system (Art. 136, C. 1991), (Art. 137 (2), C. 2003) was amended to permit the future adoption of the Euro. Most of the amendments (79 in total) dealt with ostensibly domestic institutional changes. For instance, the legislative process was overhauled, in an attempt to expedite it and delineate in a clearer manner the powers of the two houses and the mandate of the President was extended from four to five years (this amendment consequently disentangled presidential and parliamentary elections, so that terms are now staggered).

The functioning of the political system, as defined by the relationship between the political branches, was not essentially changed in 2003. Nonetheless, the 2003 amendments did produce an important transformation whose effects could only be observed after the accession, namely, the countermajoritarian elements of the constitution were significantly strengthened. First, the Constitutional Court was rendered fully autonomous from political control, save by way of appointments. The power of the Parliament to overturn a finding of unconstitutionality by readopting a law or standing order with a reinforced two-thirds majority in each house (Art. 145 (1), C. 1991) was abrogated, the effect of an unconstitutionality decision was clarified[17] and an important new power was added to the Court's competence, namely, that of "resolving legal conflicts of a constitutional nature between public authorities, at the request of the President of Romania, one of the Presidents of the two Chambers, the Prime Minister, or of the President of the Superior Council of the Magistracy" (Art. 146 (e), C. 2003).[18] An amendment also made it possible to extend the jurisdiction of the Court, adding new powers by way of legislative amendments to the organic law on the functioning and organization of the Court (Art. 146 (l)).

This set of changes had the paradoxical effect of endowing a French-style *Conseil* with German-style *Bundesverfassungsgericht* attributions. An increase of the juridical element of constitutional review (new powers and effect of decisions) was not matched by a corresponding alteration of the Court's essential make up (way of appointment, length of the terms), creating a contradictory institution: former MPs are routinely appointed as justices to an organ that now has significant court-like review competence.

Second, the entire judiciary was rendered autonomous from social or political control, in order to give effect to the European Commission's request for judicial independence. The initial version of the constitution provided for a Superior Council of the Magistracy, whose members were to be selected by the Parliament, in joint session, for four-year terms of office. The body was entrusted with nominating judges and prosecutors for appointment by the President and with disciplinary attributions (the SCM served as a disciplinary first instance court for judges) (Arts. 132–133, C. 1991). The 2003 revision effectively substituted for the initial institution a version of the Judicial Council "Euro-Model" promoted by the Commission.[19] The SCM is now overwhelmingly composed of judges and prosecutors (nine and five, respectively) elected by their peers; its attributions cover the full gamut of decisions concerning the career of judicial and prosecutorial "magistrates" (training, selection, promotion, and disciplinary actions). The three members *ex officio* (Minister of Justice, Prosecutor General, President of the High Court) cannot vote when the two sections – on public prosecutors and judges – serve as disciplinary courts, whereas the two politically appointed "civil society representatives" can only take part in plenary sessions. To be sure, this degree of autonomy is not necessarily a corollary of judicial independence as understood in constitutional traditions, not even an imitation of powerful judicial councils elsewhere; the Italian council, which served as a prototypical model for the international best practice promoted by the Commission in Romania and other CEE jurisdictions, does not enjoy this degree of insulation from majoritarian control. Given its virtual insulation, the Romanian Council can be described as a form of "judicial supremacy".[20] The amendments to the SCM-related chapter of the constitution also produced unintended consequences, due to the failure or neglect to substantively change the previous two articles, on prosecutors. A paragraph was added to Art. 131 but the constitutional definition of the "Public Ministry" preserves the initial executive connotations of the institution: "Public prosecutors shall carry out their activity in accordance with the principle of legality, impartiality *and hierarchical control, under the authority of the Minister of Justice*" (Art. 132 (1), C. 2003) [emphasis added]. As a result, two contradictions were created in the functioning of the judiciary branch as a whole. First, whereas the Romanian judicial system operates on the assumption, characteristic of Latin legal systems (seasoned with recent experiences and memories of the communist *Procuratură*), that judges and prosecutors are "magistrates" and that the statuses of judges and prosecutors are to a certain degree analogous, the two categories, in the logic of the original constitution, were not fully equated. Once the SCM, as a corporatist body of both judges and prosecutors, was charged with guaranteeing "the independence of justice" and rendered fully autonomous from the political branches, an irreconcilable confusion and tension ensued with respect to the status of prosecutors (executive, judicial, quasi-) and the proper degree of authority that ought to be exercised by the Executive through the Minister of Justice.[21] A second contradiction is idiosyncratic. The reason why the Commission insisted on this particular institutional configuration is directly related to anticorruption imperatives. Romania and Bulgaria have been subjected to pre- and post-accession monitoring along anticorruption benchmarks. In Romania, the main enforcement mechanism in the area of high- and medium-level corruption is the National Anticorruption

Directorate, formally a division of the General Prosecutor's Office but in reality fully autonomous (the terms of office and procedures for the appointment of the General Prosecutor and Chief Prosecutor of the NAD are symmetrical, the former having no effective authority over the latter). This atomized structure fits somewhat uneasily with the notion of a Public Ministry and the constitutional requirement of prosecutorial hierarchy ("hierarchical control"). The political and social will to pass these amendments could only be mustered in 2003 due to the high political stakes. The amendments were presented to the public as an EU accession-related imperative, an objective which met with quasi-unanimous approval, cutting across the entire political and social spectrum. Ironically, the same reason prevented substantial debates during the revision process, up to the point where it was difficult to even meet the quorum requirement in the confirmatory referendum, since most Romanians saw the revision as "technical" in nature. [22] They wanted to "return to Europe" but, insufficiently informed and regarding the amendments as externally imposed, a kind of constitutional *acquis* communautaire, saw no reason to go to the poll and vote in the referendum. Once they could be convinced to cast their ballots, approval of the amendments was a formality, as the revision process itself had been. Thus, the year 2003 represented another failed constitutional moment, but from a pragmatic point of view the revision law could at least be adopted in Parliament and approved in a valid referendum. In the absence of an ideal (or at least an incentive) comparable in magnitude to the EU accession,[23] this level of political and civic mobilization, needed for a successful revision process, could no longer be mustered.

Two significant attempts were recently made to revise the constitution.[24] Both were partisan in the sense of pursuing ordinary politics by other means, although in either case the two contending institutions, President and Parliament, sought to dress their designs in a neutral constitution-making garb.

The first initiative played the card of expertise. A committee of public law scholars was summoned to Bucharest and tasked with undertaking, under the institutional patronage of the presidential administration, an independent analysis of the Romanian constitutional system.[25] The commission issued a report and President Băsescu cherry-picked some recommendations from the report's conclusions, recommendations which were subsequently drafted as a bill, introduced by the President and sponsored by the Democratic-Liberal Party. Although the presidential commission attempted to frame its analysis in objective terms, providing various solutions to each problem and stating carefully all the assumptions backing each possible solution and the implications and ripple effects of discrete changes, an undertone of partisanship could at times be sensed. For instance, more emphasis was placed in the synthetic report on recommending "clarifications" of checks and balances deadlocks whose effect, if they had been adopted, would have been to strengthen the Presidency to the detriment of the Government and Parliament.[26] Procedure-wise, the works of the commission were also somewhat overshadowed by relatively numerous defections, as a specialist invited to join declined from the beginning, stating that the commission's conclusions were anyhow foregone, given its sponsor (i.e., anti-parliamentary), another member withdrew without making any statements, and two more subsequently resigned, accusing irreconcilable differences with the general tenor of the debates and pressures to conform, respectively. Losses were cut with short ceremony, by co-opting substitutes, while debates continued unabated in the makeshift commission. Accusations of authoritarian and anti-parliamentary tendencies have gained credence in the general context.[27] One of the specialists initially summoned to the presidential commission, a human right professor at the University of Bucharest, later commented as follows on the bill proposal sponsored by the Presidency:

> There is a risk of lurching towards authoritarianism in a semi-presidential regime with a unicameral Parliament. The head of state can control and manipulate easier one Chamber. . . . And then, we have the mandatory referendum, that is, the circumventing of Parliament and the countervailing transformation of the referendum into a plebiscite. . . . Antonescu[28] too had a plebiscite. . . . It will be said that each of these instruments can be found in democratic systems. Yes, but not all [in the same Constitution].[29]

The timeline of the undertaking was also somewhat strained. An attempt to impeach Băsescu failed in 2007. In the early summer of 2008, the constitutional commission was created. Its final conclusions, the Report of the Commission, were publicly presented at the Cotroceni Presidential Palace in January 2009. Later that year, Băsescu used his prerogative to initiate a consultative referendum in order to consult the citizenry as to whether the Parliament should be reduced in structure to a unicameral form, and in numbers to a maximum of 300 MPs. The consultative referendum was held simultaneously with the presidential elections and the issue was framed by the initiator as constituting a stepping-stone in the process of combatting the venality, corruption, and waste of party politics. In the general context of the crisis, the citizens expectedly voted yes to both questions on the referendum ballot card (unicameral parliament and reduction of the number of MPs to 300). A total of 77.78% voted yes to a unicameral parliament, 88.84% to no more than 300 MPs.[30] In the end, the proposal initiated by the President in 2011 faded away for lack of parliamentary support and was definitively rejected by the Chamber of Deputies in 2013.[31]

At about the same time, the Parliament initiated another, countervailing, amendment proposal, with the intention of reducing the powers of the Presidency and tilting the balance towards a strongly "parliamentarized" form of semi-presidentialism. The initiative came out in the trail of the failed 2012 impeachment. If the Presidency sought to boost the legitimacy of a politically connoted power grab by recourse to a commission of experts, the Parliament's own legitimacy bootstrapping effort relied on a veneer of procedural openness. In the months of April and May 2013, an informal body ("the Constitutional Forum") directed by a political science professor with the National University for Political Studies and Public Administration, Cristian Pârvulescu, was entrusted by Parliament with the organization of an Icelandic-style process of broad consultations, structured along three dimensions or "axes". Meetings and workshops were held in various cities, within the territorial axis, i.e., consulting with local administration and communities, the academic axis served as a sounding board for concerns and proposals advanced by public law and political science academics, and a thematic axis sought to analyze discrete, topical issues regarding the constitution in various forums (for instance, economics professors, researchers, and members of trade associations debated on the economic constitution in a workshop held at the National Bank). A brief meeting with a Venice Commission delegation was also held at the Senate. In the end, a report was compiled, comprising a synthesis of the positions, with the stated intention of offering the Constitutional Committee in Parliament a draft set of ideas and concrete proposals on which political debates could rely.[32] The concept as such was not necessarily erroneous, but the very short deadline imposed by the Parliament induced a general impression of adhockery and artificiality. There was, moreover, no guarantee that the hundreds of hastily systematized proposals coming from citizens, experts, NGOs, the Venice Commission delegation, etc., would play any role in the debates of the Joint Constitutional Committee of the House of Deputies and the Senate, which worked effectively for less than a month, until the end of the parliamentary session. An Academic Advisory Group was also summoned, with the stated purpose of gathering expertise on specific requests made by the Constitutional Committee; after a few email messages, spanning over a few weeks, Parliament simply discontinued, without explanation, any further recourse to the specialists and proceeded to draft the revision bill on its own. In the absence of either a substantial consultation process or the political will to back a clear template, many contradictory, and at times extravagant, proposals from members were placed on the agenda, such as introducing a preamble in the following form:

> By the present Social Contract, hereinafter called a Constitution, the Romanian people, in application of the principle '*respect of the citizen towards the man and of the man towards the citizen*', proclaims intangible and unalienable human rights as the foundation of the Romanian state [emphasis added].[33]

The final draft bill was plagued by these shortcomings. Accompanied by an unusually acid Legislative Council opinion,[34] the bill was in the end rent asunder by the Constitutional Court opinion. The Court declared no less than 26 amendment proposals inadmissible (in breach of the limits of revision set forth by Art. 152) and recommended countless alterations on account of poor drafting (unclear wording, contradictions, redundancies).[35] Ultimately, due to diminished political support following the disaggregation of the coalition in power, the proposal was tacitly abandoned.

3. The elements of informal change

The fact that, after 2003, no formal modifications have been made to the letter of the constitution does not mean that it has remained unchanged. Important processes have transformed the functioning of the fundamental law significantly. Although in practice the two phenomena are not isolated, they can be analytically distinguished as, on the one hand, informal amendment by Constitutional Court adjudication and, on the other, quasi-constitutional discourses whose operation significantly influences the context in which the constitutional system functions.

The most apparent informal changes have resulted from adjudication by the constitutional Court.[36] The Court, initially timid in exercising review, has recently become, as a result of both the significant extension of its powers and as a function of an unstable political system, an increasingly activist umpire of the political process. Admittedly, interpretation of the constitution is hard to distinguish *de plano* from informal change and the political/legal in-between-ness of European-style review by constitutional tribunals is acknowledged as a matter of constitutional design.[37] Nonetheless, the extreme fluctuation of the Romanian Court's recent case law and the difficulty of deriving particular solutions from methodology (text, purpose, or context) have rendered the Court vulnerable to criticism and legitimate suspicions of its playing at politics by quasi-judicial means. The conflicting interpretations in 2007, 2012, and 2013 of the Referendum Law have already been mentioned, but many similar inconsistencies could be cited. In terms of separation of powers, for instance, the exclusive right of the President to take part in European Council meetings was established by the Court in June 2012 by judicial *fiat*, with the argument that the foreign affairs prerogatives of the "head of state" prevail over the constitutional attributions of the Prime Minister (the phrase "head of state" cannot be found in the constitution). According to the June 2012 decision, the Prime Minister could take part in these meetings in the President's stead, on the basis of an express mandate (a Presidential decree) issued by the latter.[38] This somewhat "Solomonic judgment" had at least the benefit of clarifying an important matter neglected in the course of the 2003 revision. A year later, the Court muddled its own precedent, arguing that the delegation by the President to the Prime Minister of the former's power to represent the country in the Council could not be purely arbitrary but had to rest on "objective reasons", the exact nature of which remained unstated:

> The political decision to delegate or not the competence to represent the country at European Council meetings must take into account these objective criteria, with a view to reaching consensus between the two authorities . . . and must rest upon the constitutional principle of loyal cooperation.[39]

Sometimes, the Court's solutions to particular deadlocks are so pithily reasoned that they have become running diatribes, both among constitutional scholars and in the media. According to a notorious decision concerning the prerogatives of President in case of a Cabinet reshuffle the former must not endorse and automatically appoint whomever the Prime Minister nominates but may reject a nominee "only once, providing reasons".[40]

The discourses of anti-corruption and judicial independence operate as quasi-constitutional processes that significantly affect the functioning of the constitutional system. In November 2015, after a disastrous fire in a Bucharest nightclub ("Colectiv") claimed the lives of dozens of patrons and caused the serious injury of over 100, massive street protests in the capital city resulted in the resignation of the Social Democratic Cabinet led by Victor Ponta (a controversial Prime Minister, whose mandate had already been mired in a protracted plagiarism scandal) and its replacement with a technocratic government, under a former European Commissioner, Dacian Cioloş.[41] The overthrow of the Ponta Cabinet and its replacement with an apolitical cabinet staffed with "experts" are emblematic of the power of anticorruption discourses to change the operation of Romanian politics, all the more since neither the fire as such nor the subsequent substandard medical treatment of the victims could be directly linked with corrupt acts. The entire tragedy and its effects may just as well have been attributed to gross negligence, incompetence, inefficiency, or lack of resources in the health care system, respectively. Nonetheless, especially since the accession, deficiencies are routinely translated into the language of integrity.

In what concerns the functioning of the judicial system, anti-corruption, and independence as systemic autonomy are mutually reinforcing desiderata and discourses.[42] As already mentioned, one of the most important formal changes to the fundamental law in 2003 was the transformation of the SCM from a politically appointed judicial council into an umbrella institution encompassing the entire judicial system. Until recently, one rare element of consistency in the jurisprudence of the Constitutional Court has been, in fact, its extension of this new constitutional orthodoxy, as all attempts to change the composition of the Council by appointing more "lay members" (political appointees, as civil society representatives) have been deflected by the Court as incompatible with the limits of revision.[43] A 2013 decision of the Constitutional Court rendered nugatory a procedure by the operation of which qualified two-thirds majorities of judges or prosecutors in each general assembly of judges and prosecutors corresponding to the jurisdictional tier represented by a council member, voting in at least half of the courts or prosecutor's offices represented, could have recalled a Council member before the end of his or her six-year term. The rule was abrogated as a result of the unconstitutionality decision. The holding voided the rule on the basis of its unconstitutional vagueness, in breach of the principle of legality, but the *obiter* analysis of the Court would make a reinstatement of the recall sanctioning procedure in a different but nonetheless effective form difficult to imagine.[44] The conjoined effect of the constitutional amendments, the relevant constitutional jurisprudence, and 2005 amendments to the SCM organic law, weakening the role of the Council Plenary formation to the benefit of the two sections,[45] have resulted in a corporatist structure that is autonomous not only from the political or social system as such but also from the system it represents and to a certain extent – a paradox if ever there was one – even within itself (i.e., autonomy of the two sections from the Plenum; autonomy of the Council as a whole and of each of its elected members from their judicial or prosecutorial "constituencies").[46]

The European Commission Cooperation and Verification country reports went further, recommending that public (political or press) criticism directed at judges and the High Council be curbed in order to protect both the institution and affected individuals: "The situation suggests the need for a review of existing rules, to ensure that freedom of the press is accompanied by a *proper protection of institutions* and of individuals' fundamental rights as well as to provide for effective redress" [emphasis added].[47] More recent reports suggested that the SCM be consulted in future constitutional amendment processes affecting "judicial independence"[48] and advocated for the creation of a fund or mechanism to protect judges and prosecutors, by offering them "financial or legal aid", when redress in court is sought for damages to judicial reputation or image by libelous or slanderous press statements.[49]

The main reason for the insistence on this particular understanding of judicial autonomy is that the independence of the National Anticorruption Directorate and of the courts of law, in particular but not only that of the High Court of Cassation and Justice, are imperative for the successful prosecution of high- and medium-level corruption crimes. As the argument runs, since such prosecutions target the political class, it is necessary that the legal process be fully insulated from undue pressures. One of the less auspicious consequences of this new paradigm is, however, that the functioning of an increasingly larger part of the public discourse, focused on high-level corruption cases, and of the judicial system as a whole, is opaque to the citizenry. The intricacies of criminal procedure are difficult to follow even for highly trained criminal law specialists: across hundreds of pages of postponement rulings, first instance and appeals judgments, pre-trial detention requests by anticorruption prosecutors and court rulings on particular requests, intricate statistics on the effectiveness of anti-corruption campaigns, and statistics on differential acquittal rates between regular criminal court cases and high corruption cases, etc. The inevitable result has been to simplify sophisticated normative issues and to reduce cognitive burdens to Manichean clichés of anticorruption judicial heroes and corrupt political villains (or, more recently, as the public sphere has developed an anti-anticorruption discourse, the opposite).

The Constitutional Court itself has been drawn into the vortex of this efficiency-driven instrumental logic, whenever its judgments touch on the competence of the anticorruption division of the General Prosecutor's office. A recent decision imposing a restrictive interpretation of the crime of "abuse of power", on the basis of the principle *nulla poena sine lege certa*, was subjected to harsh criticism, as implicitly favoring corruption.[50] Likewise, a recent decision declaring unconstitutional a provision in the Criminal Procedure Code which enabled the participation of the Romanian Intelligence Service in pretrial criminal investigations was interpreted in a part of the press as insensitive to or as an attack on the effectiveness of the national campaign against corruption. The decision was, strictly speaking, an interpretation of Art. 142 (1) in the Criminal Procedure Code, according to which "[t]he prosecutor shall enforce an electronic surveillance measure or may order that this be enforced by the criminal investigation body or trained personnel working in the police, or *by other specialized state bodies*" [emphasis added].[51] In view of the important values at stake (secrecy of correspondence and privacy) and the intrusion of wiretapping in the exercise of these rights, the reasoning behind the holding was simply that the phrase "other specialized state bodies" was in breach of the principles of the rule of law (Art. 1 (3)) and the general requirement of legality (Art. 1 (5)) and thus, void for vagueness. The normative interpretation of the Court appeared in the public sphere, however, distorted by the instrumental logic of efficiency in the fight against corruption.

4. Conclusion: Post-accession pluralism in action

Hardly any constitution-making ready-made formulas or recipes withstand the tests of experience and time. Fads about the relevance of inclusive and transparent processes are for instance belied both by the examples of history (witness the extreme secrecy in Philadelphia debates, compared with the extreme openness of the French *Constituante*) and the recent failure of the Icelandic experiment. By the same token, some significantly expert-driven processes are doomed to failure, whereas others, in different circumstances, foster enduring constitutional patriotism (as revealed by the disastrous experience of Weimar and the celebrated success of the Bonn Republic). The same observation goes for the relevance and impact of foreign influences and models: in what concerns the latter, some institutions have traditionally been successfully transplanted (constitutional courts in post-totalitarian systems), whereas some successful models are notoriously impervious to adequate migration (think of US presidentialism in Latin America). It appears that comparative constitutional law and political science scholarship can mainly bring to the table of foundational decision-making about fundamental law an aggregate of cautionary tales related to extreme case scenarios ("paradoxes" and "dilemmas") selected from historical experiences[52] and sobering statistical data about the actual duration of putatively eternal constitutions.[53]

The optimal calibration of rules on amendment is, for related reasons, equally hard to fathom. To wit, an assessment by Sunstein and Holmes, made at the beginning of the '90s, praised the Hungarian and Polish constitutional procedures allowing for more flexible amendments, explicitly favoring them over the Bulgarian and Romanian rigid constitutions. As their argument went, in societies "where the future is so open and the options so basic and large",[54] it was wiser to leave as many issues as possible at the discretionary choice of the Parliament and thus of the ordinary political process. Yet, in light of recent backsliding in both Hungary and Poland, one may legitimately wonder if relative stability (and by implication a degree of rigidity in amendment rules) would not be, in the end, the better part of constitutional valor.

The Romanian case study is exemplary of a number of (partly idiosyncratic) contextual and normative determinations, which coalesced in the consolidation of a constitutional system whose endurance is inversely proportional with its capacity to integrate the polity and to a certain extent even with its ability to determine normative predictability and stability.[55] The lack of a clear decision and some missteps in the configuration of the political system at the beginning of the '90s have created an unstable form of semi-presidentialism, which has generated, ever since, protracted inter-branch conflicts and attempts to change the fundamental law in favor of either institution. Such initiatives have been thwarted so far by the rigidity of the amendment provisions. The empowering of the Constitutional Court (apparently a result of purely endogenous choices) and the constitutional entrenchment of judicial autonomy (externally induced, at the behest of the EU Commission), in 2003, led to the rise of additional power centers in the constitutional framework. These processes, significantly accelerated by the post-accession quasi-constitutional discourse of good governance as anti-corruption, have created a form of pluralism or heterarchy without a normative common denominator and therefore without the possibility of constitutional cohesion. In this way, Romania has plunged abruptly into a world of post-modern fragmentation, with a fashionable element of inter- and trans-national dialogical constitutionalism, without having ever experienced modernity as such, namely, integration by constitution.

Notes

1 Research for this chapter was supported by and undertaken in the framework of the research project PN-II-ID-PCE-2011-3-0115, "Governance/Government – The Constitutional Semantics of Autonomy". I thank the participants in the conference Constitutional Challenges within the EU and Beyond (March 14, 2014), Central European University, Budapest, and in a workshop on The Break-Up of Nations: The Constitutional Dimensions, Using Ukraine as a Case Study (Wolfson College, Oxford, November 27–28, 2014) for comments on arguments pertinent to that of this chapter.
2 The post-accession Mechanism for Cooperation and Verification for Romania and Bulgaria was established on the basis of the Act of Accession and was initially scheduled to lapse after three years, in 2010, but has been in the meantime maintained and extended, apparently *sine die*. Initially, the Mechanism contained only references to the specific, ostensibly technical benchmarks. These are establishing an autonomous anti-corruption agency with attributions regarding the disclosure and sanctioning of conflicts of interest, incompatibilities, and asset declarations (unjustified wealth, respectively), the implementation of anticorruption policies with respect to high- and mid-level corruption and in local administration, judiciary reforms, and the adoption of new codes (civil and criminal law, civil and criminal procedure).
3 http://europa.eu/rapid/press-release_SPEECH-13-348_de.htm.
4 Dimitry Kochenov and Laurent Pech, "Monitoring and Enforcement of the Rule of Law in the EU: Rhetoric and Reality", *European Constitutional Law Review*, Vol. 11 (2015) pp. 512–540.
5 See, for instance, Jan-Werner Müller, "Defending Democracy within the EU", *Journal of Democracy*, Vol. 24, No. 2 (2013) pp. 138–149; and contributions in Armin von Bogdandy and Pál Sonnevend (eds.), *Constitutional Crisis in the European Constitutional Area-Theory, Law, and Politics in Hungary and Romania* (Oxford and Portland: C.H. Beck-Hart-Nomos, 2015). I deal with the crisis at length in my chapter in Bogdandy-Sonnevend and with the political implications and constitutional repercussions of crisis-related interventions by the EU Commission and the Venice Commission in "Serenity in Overcoming Crises: A Parochial Gloss on the Transnational Shift in Constitutional Vocabularies", *Studia Politica*, Vol. XIII, No. 1 (2013) pp. 9–23; and "Romania under EU Influence: Note on the Constitutive Limits of External Constitutional Interventions", *PolSci-Romanian Journal of Political Science*, Vol. 12, No. 2 (2012) pp. 53–76.
6 D.C.C. No. 471/14.11.2013 (M. Of. No. 754/04.12.2013).
7 See analysis in Bianca Selejan-Guţan, "The Illusion of the Romanian Constitution?", blog post of December 7, 2012, (www.iconnectblog.com/2012/12/the-illusion-of-the-romanian-constitution/) and the comparative table and associated text in same, *The Constitution of Romania: A Contextual Analysis* (Oxford and Portland: Hart, 2016) p. 123, showing how different constitutional interpretations led to the same result ("President returns to office") in the face of significant factual disparities: the turnout was 44.45% in 2007, out of which 74.48% voted against dismissal (referendum was validated by the Court), whereas the 2012 referendum was invalidated

(46.24% participation, out of which 87.52% voted for dismissal). Also see commentary in Bogdan Dima, *Conflictul dintre palate: Raporturile de putere dintre Parlament, Guvern și Președinte în România postcomunistă* (București: Hamangiu, 2014) pp. 253–254: "Constitutional Court Decisions 727/2012 and 731/2012 did nothing else but erect [additional] bulwarks against parliamentary majorities in their exercise of the impeachment procedure, accentuating *de facto* the semi-presidential character of our system of government and aggrandizing the decisional independence of the President within the Romanian constitutional framework."

8 Stephen Holmes, "Can Foreign Aid Promote the Rule of Law?", in 8 *E. Eur. Const. Rev.* 68 (1999).

9 The works of the Constitutional Drafting Committee (which adopted draft theses) and the Constituent Assembly (i.e., the Parliament working as a constituent) were published by the President of the Constitutional Drafting Committee, Senator and law professor Antonie Iorgovan, dubbed "the Father of the Constitution", under the title *The Constitution-Making Odyssey 1990–1991: Deeds and Documents, People and Characters; Chronicle and Explanation, Unraveling and Meditation* (*Odiseea elaborării Constituției, fapte și documente, oameni și caractere; -cronică și explicații, dezvăluiri și meditații*) (Editura Uniunii Vatra Românească, Târgu Mureș, 1998) (cited paragraph at p. 66).

10 Günter Frankenberg, *Autorität und Integration. Zur Grammatik von Recht und Verfassung* (Suhrkamp: Frankfurt a.M., 2003), pp.124–132.

11 But cf. Cristina E. Parau, "Explaining Judiciary Governance in Central and Eastern Europe: External Incentives, Transnational Elites and Parliament Inaction", 67 *Europe-Asia Studies* 409 (2015), according to whom transnational influence was significant even in the initial drafting process, for instance in the rejection of including members of Parliament in the High Council of the Judiciary (Superior Council of the Magistracy). Although the author is accurate in her analysis of the 2003 amendment process, foreign influence in 1990–1991 was marginal and cosmetic at best. The judicial council established by the initial version of the constitution resembles much more its local predecessor, the Superior Council of the Magistracy created by a judicial organization law in 1909, than international best practices circulated in the early 1990s (after the adoption of the Romanian Constitution) by the Council of Europe, on the basis of the Italian-French model of judicial organization.

12 Perhaps the strongest fear underlying the constitution is that of ethnic conflict and territorial fragmentation. The elections of May 1990 were preceded by violent interethnic conflicts between ethnic Hungarians and Romanians in the Transsylvanian city of Târgu Mureș. Unlike the Bulgarian Constitution, which prohibits ethnically based parties, the Romanian Constitution does not comprise an analogous provision (both countries have sizable ethnic minorities) but insists on the national, independent, unitary, and indivisible character of the state (Art. 1 (1) The Romanian State and 152 (1) Limits of Revision).

13 This is one of relatively few provisions borrowed from pre-WWII Romanian constitutions (the Articles 3 in the Constitutions of 1866 and 1923, respectively). The norm was ignored until very recently, when some politicians pointed to it as an argument against refugee quotas allocated to Member States at the level of the EU.

14 Mark Tushnet, "The Possibilities of Comparative Constitutional Law" *Yale LJ*, Vol. 108, No. 6 (1999) pp. 1225–1310.

15 For instance, the Hungarian Constitution of 1949 was amended with a two-thirds majority (this rule was preserved by the current constitution, Art. S). The Polish Constitution can be amended by a two-thirds majority in the Sejm and an absolute majority in the Senate, provided there is a quorum (a confirmatory referendum may be required by one-fifth of the deputies, the President or the Senate, and the President of the Republic (Art. 235)).

16 See Stephen Holmes and Cass R. Sunstein, "The Politics of Constitutional Revision in Eastern Europe", in Sanford Levinson (ed.), *Responding to Imperfection: The Theory and Practice of Constitutional Amendment* (Princeton, NJ: Princeton University Press, 1995), pp. 275–306, arguing that, given all the shortcomings of post-communist transitions, a flexible, parliamentary revision process was the optimal solution for CEE jurisdictions: "A stringent amendment procedure, patented in the West, whereby constitutional provisions are cemented in the system, implies deference towards the decisions of the framers. Because such deference cannot be conjured magically out of East European air, given who the framers are and the purposes they visibly pursue, a lax constitutional amendment formula, one that will not saddle successors with the schemes and follies of their predecessors is unusually desirable" (at p. 284).

17 Art. 147 (1), C. 2003: "The provisions of the laws and ordinances in force, as well as those of the regulations, which are found to be unconstitutional, shall cease their legal effects within 45 days of the publication of the decision of the Constitutional Court if, in the meantime, the Parliament or the Government, as the case may be, cannot bring into line the unconstitutional provisions with the provisions of the Constitution. For this limited length of time the provisions found to be unconstitutional shall be suspended de jure".

18 Other changes concern the power of the Ombudsman to raise directly before the Court an "exception of unconstitutionality" concerning provisions of laws or ordinances in effect and the power of the Court to adjudicate on the constitutionality of treaties, upon notification by a Speaker, 25 Senators or 50 Deputies (Art. 146 (e), C. 2003; this power has not been exercised yet).

19 On the evolution of the judicial council international "best practice", see Nuno Garoupa and Tom Ginsburg, "Guarding the Guardians: Judicial Councils and Judicial Independence", *American Journal of Comparative Law* 57 (2009) pp. 103–134. On EU developments, see Anja Seibert-Fohr, "Judicial Independence in European Union Accessions: The Emergence of a European Basic Principle", 52 *German Y.B. Int'l L.* 405 (2009). And (for a more critical perspective) David Kosař and Michal Bobek, "Global Solutions, Local Problems: A Critical Study in Judicial Council in Central and Eastern Europe", *German Law Journal*, Vol. 15, No. 7 (2007) pp. 1257–1292 and David Kosař, *Perils of Judicial Self-Government in Transitional Societies* (NY: Cambridge University Press, 2016).

20 Cristina Parau, "The Drive for Judicial Supremacy", in Anja Seibert-Fohr, *Judicial Independence in Transition* (Heidelberg, Berlin: Springer Verlag, 2012) pp. 619–665, arguing that the adoption of "judicial supremacy" is a result of democracy-averse processes, by virtue of which "pan-European elites have consciously or unconsciously acted through accession conditionality to empower themselves over the peoples of the accession countries" (at p. 665). See also (same author), "Romania's Transnational Constitution – A Tradition of Elite Learning and Self-Empowerment" in D.J. Galligan and M. Versteeg (eds.), *Social and Political Foundations of Constitutions* (New York: Cambridge University Press, 2013) pp. 497–531, for a similar argument, covering the entire span of Romanian constitution-making.

21 The Public Ministry as an institution dates back to the first constitutional acts, the Organic Regulations introduced at the behest of the Russian administration of the two principalities that later joined to form the modern Romanian state. However, although judicial power was mentioned in the constitution of 1866 (Art. 104), and the constitution of 1923 included in the section on judicial power the guarantee of judicial independence as immovability of judges "under the terms and conditions provided by law" (Art. 104), neither of the two pre-communist liberal constitutions contained provisions on the constitutional status of the Public Ministry. The institution was only mentioned in the constitution of 1923, in a provision on ministerial responsibility (Art. 97). See V.M. Ciobanu, "Articolul 131. Rolul Ministerului Public", in

I. Muraru and E.S. Tănăsescu (Coord.), *Constituția României-Comentariu pe Articole* (The Romanian Constitution Annotated), (București: Editura C.H. Beck, 2008) pp. 1251–1256; and B. Dima and E.S. Tănăsescu, "Puterea judecătorească" (The Judicial Power), *Revista de Drept Public*, No. 1 (2013) pp. 121–128.

22 In the end, the ballot was extended by Emergency Governmental Ordinance to two days, over the weekend, so that the turnout condition could be met and the revision law approved.

23 Mihaela Serban, "Rule of Law Indicators as a Technology of Power in Romania", in S. E. Merry, K. E. Davis, and B. Kingsbury (eds.), *The Quiet Power of Indicators: Measuring Governance, Corruption, and Rule of Law* (NY: Cambridge University Press, 2015), pp. 199–221; at 205: "Once the country passed the initial bump of the first post-communist years and established the skeleton of a democratic, market-based, rule of law-based state, it became obsessed with the EU accession (1995–2007). Elites as well as ordinary citizens considered this the key test of the transition and a symbol of belonging to Europe and the West, and consequently all efforts were singularly directed toward acceding to EU demands."

24 A third, the first citizen initiative, was cleared by the Constitutional Court as this chapter was written. This initiative, supported by 3,000,000 votes, aims to entrench the definition of marriage as union between a man and a woman in the fundamental law, and was recently submitted to the Parliament for adoption. An exception of unconstitutionality is also pending on the Court docket, concerning the compatibility with the Constitution of a Civil Code provision which forbids the recognition of same-sex marriages concluded in another Member State of the EU. This entire matter is tangential to the current argument.

25 The Report of the Presidential Commission for the Analysis of the Romania Political and Constitutional System, available at: http://old.presidency.ro/static/rapoarte/Raport_CPARPCR.pdf.

26 For instance, the final report recommends either abrogating the impeachment procedure or giving the President a countervailing instrument (dissolution of the Parliament at will) or amending the impeachment article, so that, following the Austrian model, the Parliament would be automatically dissolved should the referendum be invalidated or the referendum results favorable to the suspended President.

27 www.juridice.ro/38439/raportul-comisiei-prezidentiale-de-analiza-a-regimului-politic-si-constitutional-din-romania-update-reactii.html.

28 Marshall Ion Antonescu was the pro-Axis dictator ("Leader of the State") of Romania between September 1940 until the anti-Axis, pro-Allied coup of August 23, 1944, first in an alliance with the fascist Iron Guard, during the ephemeral National Legionary State (September 1940–January 1941, officially disestablished in February) and then (until 1944) as de facto military dictator, under the formal authority of a figurehead King Michael I.

29 www.juridice.ro/38439/raportul-comisiei-prezidentiale-de-analiza-a-regimului-politic-si-constitutional-din-romania-update-reactii.html.

30 www.bec2009p.ro/rezultateRPU.html.

31 www.cdep.ro/pls/proiecte/upl_pck2015.proiect?cam=2&idp=12163.

32 The online platform of the Forum is no longer active but the final report can be accessed online at the link www.variantacojocaru.ro/ConstitutiaPoporului/Raport_FC.28.05.13.pdf.

33 Joint Commission of the Chamber and Senate for adopting the Draft Bill to Amend the Constitution, summary of proposed amendments, session of May 28, 2013 (on file with the author).

34 www.senat.ro/legis/PDF%5C2014%5C14L233LG.pdf. The Legislative Council is subordinate to the Parliament and its opinions are customarily deferential. The 33-page report rebuked the legislature, among others, for poor drafting, including inconsistently used terminology, burdening the fundamental law with unnecessary detail and an erroneous qualification of the Presidency as non-executive office.

35 D.C.C. No. 80/16.02.2014 regarding the legislative amendment proposal, M. Of. No. 246/07.04.2014.
36 Bianca Selejan-Guţan, "Informal Constitutional Changes in Romania", in *Romanian Journal of Comparative Law*, No. 1 (2015) pp. 35–53. Professor Guţan analyzes informal changes as a function of Constitutional Court adjudication.
37 Dieter Grimm, "Constitutions, Constitutional Courts and Constitutional Interpretation at the Interface of Law and Politics", in B. Iancu (ed.), *The Law/Politics Distinction in Contemporary Adjudication* (Utrecht: Eleven Publishing, 2009) pp. 21–34.
38 D.C.C. 683/2012 (M. Of. No. 479/12.07.2012).
39 D.C.C. 449/2013 (M. Of. No. 784/14.12.2013).
40 D.C.C. 98/7.02.2008, M. Of. No. 140/20.02.2008. A decision rendered in the previous year had stated that the rejection had to be grounded in the President's interpretation of whether the nominee fulfilled the legal requirement for a ministerial position (D.C.C. 356/5.04.2007, M. Of. No. 322/14.05.2007).
41 Bianca Selejan-Gutan, "A New Revolution? The Recent Governmental Crisis in Romania", *Int'l J. Const. L.* Blog, Nov. 25, 2015, at: www.iconnectblog.com/2015/11/a-new-revolution-the-recent-governmental-crisis-in-romania/.
42 I discuss this issue more extensively in B. Iancu, "Standards of 'Good Governance' and Peripheral Constitutionalism: The Case of Post-Accession Romania", in Giancarlo Corsi and Alberto Febbrajo (eds.), *Sociology of Constitutions: A Paradoxical Perspective* (London: Routledge, 2016) pp. 180–197 and "Romania: The Vagaries of International Grafts to Unsettled Constitutions", in Anneli Albi (ed.), *National Constitutions in European and Global Governance: Democracy, Rights, the Rule of Law* (forthcoming with T.M.C. Asser in 2017).
43 The initiative promoted by the Presidency aimed at the increase in the number of lay members from two (current) to six, and the decrease in the number of corporately elected judges from nine to five. The initiative of the Parliament was to increase the number of the civil society members from two to a meager four. Both proposed provisions were held unconstitutional, with the initial argument that a disparity (political appointees prevailing in the sections over elected magistrates) and the more recent argument that any increase in the number of politically appointed Council members (if it would not be matched by a countervailing increase in the number of elected judges and/or prosecutors) would be per se unconstitutional (D.C.C. 799/17.06.2011, M. Of. No. 440/23.06.2011, D.C.C. No. 80/16.02.2014, M. Of. No. 246/07.04.2014).
44 D.C.C. 1996/4.04.2013, M. Of. No. 231/22.04.2013. The reasoning assailed not simply the vague character of the impugned recall rule but also the insufficient provision of fair trial guarantees available to the Council member against whom the recall procedure is triggered. Needless to say, a recall procedure is not judicial in nature and attaching trial-like requirements to it would render any new recall rule toothless.
45 See V.M. Ciobanu, "Articolul 134. Atribuţii", in I. Muraru and E.S. Tănăsescu (Coord.) *Constituţia României-Comentariu pe Articole* (The Romanian Constitution Annotated). (Bucureşti: Editura C.H. Beck, 2008) pp. 1266–1271, at pp. 1270–1271.
46 A civil society representative (Georgiana Iorgulescu) resigned in 2012, accusing occult cabals (*jocuri de culise*) and the bypassing of the Plenum by unilateral SCM leadership action. "Georgiana Iorgulescu, Civil Society Representative, Has Resigned from SCM", Hotnews.ro article by Alina Neagu (August 23, 2012), available at www.hotnews.ro/stiri-esential-13081356-georgiana-iorgulescu-reprezentant-societatii-civile-demisionat-din-csm-ceea-intamplat-ultimele-saptamani-umplut-paharul-nu-pot-iau-parte-tot-felul-jocuri-culise.htm. "I cannot take part in cabals (*jocuri de culise*), deferrals, decisions taken without consulting the Plenum and decisions taken unilaterally by the leadership."

A second civil society member, Bucharest law professor Elena Simina Tănăsescu, refrained from public statement but published critical opinions about the functioning of the SCM, at the end of her mandate, accusing "an absolute independence of the judicial system from the rest of the Romanian state structure, including citizens" (Dima and Tănăsescu, *supra* note 21, at p. 123, also see E.S. Tănăsescu "Reforma Consiliului Superior al Magistraturii între analogia dreptului şi nimicuri etice" (The Reform of the Superior Council of Magistracy between Legal Analogy and Ethical Trifles), *Pandectele Române* 2 (2011) pp. 19–28.

47 COM (2013) 47 final, p. 4.

48 COM (2014) 37 final, p. 3.

49 Report from the Commission to the European Parliament and the Council on Progress in Romania under the Co-operation and Verification Mechanism of January 27, 2016, COM (2016), pp. 3–4 and 16.

50 D.C.C. 405/15.06.2016, M. Of. 517/08.07.2016. The crime of abuse of power is defined by Art. 297 (1) in the Criminal Code as "the act of a public servant, who, in the discharge of his official attributions, fails to act or acts faultily (*îndeplineşte în mod defectuos*) and in doing so causes damage or injury to the rights or legitimate interests of a natural or legal person is punished by imprisonment for not more than 7 nor less than 2 years and the forfeiture of the right to hold public office". The phrase "acts faultily" was restrictively interpreted by the Constitutional Court to mean "acts illegally", i.e., in breach of a legislative rule, as provided by parliamentary enactment or governmental ordinance. Unless otherwise indicated, all translations are mine.

51 D.C.C. 51/16.02.2016, M. Of. 190/14.03.2016, available in English on the CC website, www.ccr.ro/en/jurisprudenta-decizii-de-admitere.

52 Jon Elster, "Forces and Mechanisms in the Constitution-Making Process", Vol. 45, No. 2 *Duke Law Journal* (1995) pp. 364–396.

53 Zachary Elkins, Tom Ginsburg, and James Melton, *The Endurance of National Constitutions* (NY: Cambridge University Press, 2009).

54 Holmes and Sustein, *supra* note 16, p. 306.

55 Cf. Dieter Grimm, "Integration by Constitution", Vol. 3 No. 2–3 *Int. J. Constitutional Law* (May 2005) pp. 193–208.

9 Changing constitutional identity via amendment

Kriszta Kovács[1]

Introduction

Constitutional theory differentiates between the total replacement of a constitution by new constitutional structures, and the amendment of a constitution. There are cases, however, when constitutional amendments introduce new constitutional identities. The best-known examples of such identity changes are the Thirteenth and Fourteenth Amendments to the US constitution abolishing slavery and ensuring equal protection.

The present chapter reveals the conceptual elements of and the empirical tension between constitution-making and constitution-amending authority. It argues that while the former creates a brand new constitutional framework based upon certain basic principles, the latter can only modify the constitutional rules within the boundaries of those basic principles. The concept of identity is used to describe the difference between the two powers, and the concept of legitimacy may help to evaluate whether amendments that change the constitutional identity weaken or strengthen constitutionalism. A pertinent current example is Hungary, where transitions to regime (and thereby identity) changes took the form of constitutional amendments first in 1989 and again in 2011.

Constitution and constitutionalism

Since the Age of Enlightenment, we have been differentiating between constitutions and constitutionalism. Today all countries of the world have some kind of constitution. In democratic states constitutions are seen as higher regulatory laws of the given lands. In other states they serve not as normative standards but only as maps of power, or remain solely paper constitutions.[2] This chapter applies the concept of a normative constitution which complies with the requirements of constitutionalism.

Following John Locke, under the idea of constitutionalism I understand a limited representative government which is subordinated to the constitution by not being able to change it unilaterally. The authority and legitimacy of the government depends on its observing these limitations.[3] Locke suggested replacing the system 'when, by the miscarriages of those in authority, it is forfeited; upon the forfeiture of their rulers, or at the determination of the time set, it reverts to the society, and the people have a right to act as supreme, and continue the legislative in themselves or place it in a new form, or new hands, as they think good'.[4]

The duration and stability of a normative constitution is an important virtue. But it does not mean that constitutions should remain intact forever.[5] Sometimes necessary changes should take place in the given legal order as a result of some combination of (1) profound changes in the social, economic environment; (2) changes in the value system of the society; (3) unwanted or unexpected institutional effects; or (4) 'the cumulative effect of decisions made by the legislature, executive, and judiciary'.[6] In addition, extensive changes in the operation of the political system need to be reflected in the constitution. All these make it necessary that a constitution should be alterable through stipulated legal process. This is why the Americans went beyond Locke by institutionalizing the power to change the constitution, including not only replacing the whole constitution but also formally amending it.[7]

Most contemporary constitutions provide special procedures for amendment[8] to allow constitutional learning, a necessary process open to reflective self-correction.[9] These amendment rules are designed to defend the constitution's dignity as higher law.[10]

Total replacement versus amendment

As Walter F. Murphy points out, 'The word amend, which comes from the Latin *emendere*, means to correct or improve; amend does not mean "to deconstitute and reconstitute"'.[11] However, since the term 'constitutional amendment' is widely accepted as including every kind of constitutional change, I use the term in this broader sense, but I refer only to those changes enacted following the amendment rules of the constitution.

Four techniques of constitutional change exist in European countries[12] to preserve the basic principles of the existing constitution.[13] There are constitutions that apply *material* limits to the total replacement by incorporating a so-called '*eternity clause*'. Some of these declare certain *principles* to be unamendable.[14] Under Article 79(3) of the German Grundgesetz human dignity and the separation of powers are immutable. The constitution of Moldova stipulates that 'no revision shall be performed if it implies the infringement of fundamental rights and freedoms of citizens or their guarantees', Article 142(2). In both France and Italy it is forbidden to abolish the republican form of government.[15]

Other constitutions state that certain *provisions* (for instance the provision on constitutional amendment) may not be altered. The Portuguese, the Romanian and the Turkish constitutions prohibit certain amendments applying this technique.[16]

Instead of material limits, some European constitutions apply *procedural* limits to the constitutional revision. For example, the Spanish constitution contains *two different procedures*: the total replacement and the amendment. It introduces an aggregated procedure for a total replacement by requiring a qualified parliamentarian majority, the dissolution of Parliament, the renewed qualified parliamentarian majority and a referendum (Article 168). In Austria and Poland, popular approval by referendum is required for a replacement.

Many countries of the continent, however, apply *only one procedure* for constitutional amendments with no provisions excluded from possible modification. In these states, Parliament is the only institution involved in constitutional change. A fairly widespread model requires a certain qualified majority (most often two-thirds, like in the case of Luxembourg or Slovakia) in Parliament to adopt an amendment.

Last but not least there are states which seemingly *do not apply* either a material or a procedural limit to constitutional revision. The United Kingdom is a prime example of a country where all legal provisions regardless of the content can be changed by a simple parliamentarian majority. However, constitutional scholars convincingly argue that some pieces of legislation, like the European Communities Act 1972, the Human Rights Act 1998 and the devolution legislation might constitute entrenching rules.[17]

The case of Hungary

Although at first sight it seems that Hungary belongs to the category where the constitution contains only one procedure for every constitutional change and does not distinguish between amendment and replacement, the reality is more complex than this. For centuries, the political and constitutional system of Hungary was shaped by the so-called 'historical' or 'millennial' constitution, which consisted of customs and a series of cardinal laws.[18] The country's first codified constitution was adopted in 1949 after the Communist seizure of power. It was a total replacement of the former feudalistic historical constitution, since it was strongly influenced by the 1936 Soviet constitution. This constitution contained only one procedure for its amendment – that is the two-thirds majority rule.

The two-thirds rule was applied during the transition to democracy to enact the 1989 constitutional revision. Again in 2011 the parliamentary majority, using the amendment rule, adopted the new constitution called the Fundamental Law. It seems, therefore, that Hungarian constitutional texts do not differentiate explicitly between replacement and amendment. Since the country's first codified constitution of 1949, all constitutional changes have followed the only procedure for amending the constitution, that is the two-thirds majority rule.[19]

The reason why the case is more complex than it first seems is that for a specific period of time the 1989 constitutional revision had a special rule regarding total constitutional revision; thereby the constitutional text made a distinction between constitution-making power and constitution-amending power. Under Article 2(2) all powers including that of constitution-making were vested in the people. But it was Parliament which had the task to enact the constitution. The method was stipulated by Article 24(5),[20] which required a four-fifths majority of the votes of the Members of Parliament for the adoption of the detailed rules on the preparation of the new constitution.[21] Act XLIV of 1995 enacted this provision and the Act itself entered into force three days after its promulgation and was to remain in force during the parliamentary term 1994–1998. However, in 2010 the governing majority representatives argued that in 1995 Article 24(5) was adopted as a temporary provision, and that it was not Act XLIV of 1995 itself but rather Article 24(5) which was repealed *ex lege* when Parliament adjourned on 16 March 1998. A legal debate occurred in Parliament on the legal force of the four-fifths provision. Finally, an MP of the governing majority claimed that legal certainty required that Article 24(5) should not remain part of the constitution, so the four-fifths rule was revised to allow constitutional changes to be made more easily. In 2010 the parliamentary majority repealed the four-fifths rule by using the two-thirds amendment rule.[22] The legality and legitimacy of this constitutional amendment was disputed, since the constitutional text did not specify whether a two-thirds vote or a four-fifths vote was required in order to remove the given provision.[23] A year later the ruling coalition, using its two-thirds majority, unilaterally adopted a new constitution called the Fundamental Law.

The Fundamental Law refers to itself as a completely new constitution.[24] Nevertheless, in a formal sense it can only be seen as a constitutional amendment.[25] It was adopted by two-thirds majority of the vote of Members of Parliament, that is, according to the formal procedural requirement of constitutional amendment set by the previous constitution.[26] Thereby the validity of the Fundamental Law is closely connected to the validity of the 1989 constitutional revision.[27] According to this, the constitution as a whole could not be changed by a two-thirds majority, so we can consider the Fundamental Law only as an amendment in order to recognize it as a valid legal text.[28]

Constitution amendments are usually real amendments. They modify the provisions of the constitution to comply with its basic principles. In other times, however, constitutional amendments may be replacements, since they launch new constitutional structures. In Hungary both the 1989 and the 2011 constitutional revisions altered substantially the basic principles of the former constitution. In 1989, Parliament amended the 1949 constitution so as to make it suitable for governing a liberal democratic society. The 2011 Fundamental Law was adopted to overturn liberal democracy.

Different concepts of the constitution

Considering the above empirical facts it does not seem helpful to follow Zachary Elkins, Tom Ginsburg and James Melton, who call 'a constitutional change an amendment when the actors claim to follow the amending procedure of the existing procedure of the existing constitution and a replacement when they undertake revision without claiming to follow such procedure'.[29] This definition seems to be based upon the distinction applied by Hans Kelsen between constitution in a material and a formal sense. According to Kelsen and his legal positivist followers, the constitution is the basic norm in the material sense, while in the formal sense it 'is a certain solemn document, a set of legal norms that may be changed only under the observation of special prescriptions, the purpose of which is to render the change of these norms more difficult'.[30] The aim of the special amendment rules is to ensure the stability of the material constitution. This view, however, remains formalistic in the sense that it does not have an answer to the problem when the constitutional amendment does not remain in the framework of the material constitution, but leads to another political regime.

Given its opposition to this 'formal' constitutional concept, Carl Schmitt's critique of the Weimar constitution deserves some consideration.[31] Schmitt endorsed a positive concept of the constitution and made a clear distinction between the constitution-making power of the people and the authority of legislations to undertake constitutional amendments. This paper does not deal with the Schmittian concept of the constituent power, but focuses only on the latter, the constitution-making power, which according to Schmitt is by no means omnipotent: it resides in the framework of the constitution and does not include the power to establish a new constitution.[32]

In accordance with this view, many codified constitutions stipulate that the constitution-making power belongs to the people. In contrast to this, the constitution-amending power is limited by the constitution itself, and usually belongs to the legislation requiring a special procedure with qualified conditions. From a procedural point of view, the validity of such a constitutional amendment depends on whether it was adopted in accordance with the provisions regulating the amendment procedure. Looking at the substance, amendment could only modify the constitutional rules within the boundaries of the existing constitution's basic principles. John Rawls raises the question whether an amendment to repeal the First Amendment must be accepted by the US Supreme Court as a valid amendment. He suggests that '[t]he Court could say, then, that an amendment to repeal the First Amendment and replace it with its opposite fundamentally contradicts the constitutional tradition of the oldest democratic regime in the world. It is therefore invalid'.[33] This is exactly what the basic structure doctrine nowadays represents.

The basic structure doctrine was first elaborated by the Supreme Court of India in the case of Kesavananda Bharati v. State of Kerala, AIR 1973 SC 1461. In that case the Supreme Court of India decided that Parliament is not legally authorized to make any amendment to the constitution that would remove or destroy any of the basic structure of that constitution. Chief Justice Sikri explained that the concept of basic structure included the supremacy of the constitution, the republican form of the government, secularism, the principle of separation of powers and federalism. Other justices identified other lists of basic features. However, the majority agreed that 'there are implied limitations on the power of Parliament that the expression "amendment of this Constitution" has consequently a limited meaning in our Constitution' (para 308). Furthermore, the judges held that 'the power of amendment is plenary'; it would 'include within itself the power to add, alter or repeal the various articles' (para 1599, vii). However, the power of amendment does not include 'the power to alter the basic structure or framework of the Constitution' (para 1599, vii) so as to change its identity.

The basic structure concept of the Supreme Court of India was followed by many courts[34] and today is becoming a globally recognized doctrine[35] requiring that the constitutional amendment power should remain within the given constitutional framework and respect its foundational underlying principles. The question arises how these underlying principles can be determined. When identifying the very core of the constitution, the concept of identity may be of help.

Constitutional identity

The concept of constitutional identity was first developed by German scholars Carl Schmitt and Carl Bilfinger. They used it to justify implicit limits on amending the 1919 Weimar constitution.[36] Later the concept was reintroduced: the Federal Constitutional Court, when examining constitutional amendments connected to EU or international obligations, linked the concept of identity to the values protected by the constitution's eternal clause.[37]

I offer here a related understanding that views constitutions as containing specific sets of core values and principles and as such can be identified and distinguished. I do not espouse the view of the identitarian or communitarian approach, which sees constitutions as reflections of national identity or the identity of the people. And I am not dealing with the recent political claims to identity.[38] To some extent I follow what Jose Luis Martí calls 'constitutional identity'. As he puts it:

> The notion of constitutional identity normally refers to something essential or even constitutive, something permanent or stable – if not directly immutable – in a constitution, which somehow relates to the essence of a particular political community. This 'constitutional essence' is supposed to be the core of the constitution.[39]

In other words, the constitutional essentials are sets of norms (including the underlying principles and the system of constitutional organs) providing information on the fundamental structure of the given state, that, when touched by constitutional change, would result in a modified constitutional identity.

Martí argues that the whole set of constitutional values, principles and rules should be identified in order to receive information on the constitutional identity.[40] According to Constance Grewe, the constitutional text, and the amendment procedures, could be used as sources from which we are able to determine a given state's constitutional identity.[41] However, the constitutional text itself has only limited potential for giving information on the constitutional identity. The words of the constitution need to be interpreted, and socially embedded institutions, by interpreting and applying these words, could actually foster the constitutional identity. Some empirical demonstration that the text is mainly consistent with constitutional experience is thus required.[42]

Hungarian identity changes

Since 1949 new constitutional identities in Hungary have been created via constitutional amendments. The country's first codified constitution of 1949 was a nominal one, which served only as a map of political power and did not recognize the existence of human rights.

In the course of the democratic transition in 1989, Parliament amended the 1949 constitution 'with a view to promote a peaceful political transition to a rule of law State implementing a multi-party system, parliamentary democracy, and a social market economy' – as the preamble declared. This commitment to the rule of law, parliamentary democracy and the social market economy was constitutive of the constitutional regime between 1989 and 2010.

The specific content of these foundational principles was determined over time first and foremost by the Constitutional Court through practice and interpretation. In the Court's understanding, the rule of law did not encompass the ideal of substantive justice, but it was not a mere declaration either, it had a fundamental value. Legal certainty and procedural guarantees such as protection against retroactive laws emerged as important features of the rule of law (Decision 11/1992).

Deliberately rejecting both the presidential system and Westminster parliamentarianism, the 1989 constitutional revision followed the model of consensual parliamentary democracy. It was consensual in the sense that the model required that, at least in constitutional matters, governing parties involve not only their coalition partner, but also the opposition. Parliamentary democracy prevailed in that representative democracy had priority over direct democracy and the direct exercise of power was an exceptional form of exercising of the people's sovereign rights (Decision 2/1993).

The third pillar of this model was the socially aware market economy. The founding fathers of the democratic transition recognized that political freedoms and the survival of market economy institutions are inseparable from each other. Hence, the 1989 constitutional revision contained several market economy guarantees: it declared a market economy and ensured the protection of private property. And although the constitution ensured a great number of social rights, due to the narrow interpretation of these rights their constitutional presence has not interfered with the free market reform.[43]

These underlying principles and the basic structure of the state remained untouched until 2010. In that year the Hungarian Republic collapsed. Failures of the incumbent government and social tensions undermined the legitimacy of the democratic regime. A deep financial, political and moral crisis made fundamental change appealing.[44] When the governing coalition of the Fidesz party and the Christian Democratic People's Party gained a constitutional majority in Parliament, it therefore opened the way for a profound change of direction. As the first step towards a brand new regime, the ruling coalition adopted a 'Proclamation on Statement of National Co-operation':

> [A]fter 46 years of occupation, and 20 confused years of transition, Hungary has regained the right and power of self-determination. . . . In spring 2010, the Hungarian nation gathered its strength once again, and brought about a successful revolution in the polling booth. Parliament declares that it recognizes and will respect this constitutional revolution. . . . Parliament declares that in April's elections a new social contract was born. . . . The pillars of our common future will be work, home, family, health and order.[45]

According to the proclamation, the identity expressed by the 1989 constitutional revision failed to comply with the Hungarian national identity, which made it necessary to replace the existing constitution with a completely new one. Those in power argued that the period of post-communist transformation should draw to a close, and for this reason Hungary needed a new constitution which was able to provide a 'foundation for the spiritual and intellectual renewal of Hungary'.[46]

Consequently, in 2011 the Fundamental Law was enacted. The foundational principles of the first two decades of liberal democracy have changed substantially.[47] The Fundamental Law put 'society's sense of justice' above the rule of law. Contrary to the previous rule of law interpretation, Article U of the Fundamental Law asserts that society's sense of justice shall be ensured by making possible the retroactive prosecution of politically motivated crimes committed and not prosecuted during the communist regime. The holders of power are able to elevate any decision to the status of law quickly and without hindrance because they have removed all checks on their power to make law, until recently, up to and including constitutional amendments.[48] Law has become instrumentalized, to be brought into line with decisions of the government rather than constraining in advance how officials operate.[49]

Instead of a consensual parliamentary democracy, the basic feature of the new regime is parliamentary supremacy. The system is based on the principle of fusion of power, which minimizes the power of checks on governmental power, first and foremost the Constitutional Court. The governing majority reserves the right to have the final and supreme authority not only on policy matters but also on the constitutional structure. However, contrary to the Westminster model, the Hungarian Parliament is not bound by unwritten laws, rational consideration solidified into constitutional tradition and jurisdiction practiced in the spirit of common laws.

Last but not least, the Fundamental Law lacks market economy guarantees. It does not take fundamental (including property) rights seriously and it makes it possible to waive protection of fundamental rights, citing the financial problems of the state. Under Article 37(4), a private owner may only claim protection against state intervention if the national economic indicators are relatively favorable. State interests enjoy priority over individuals' property rights.

Consequently, in Hungary both the 1989 and the 2011 constitutional amendments reshaped substantially the previously existing constitutional framework.[50] The underlying principles and textual guarantees have altered in a significant way; thereby both have launched a new identity.

Constitutional courts as guardians of constitutional identity

Any constitutional amendment which did not satisfy the prerequisites enshrined in the constitution by making certain amendments more difficult or impossible would lead to an amendment which would appear to be constitutional law only by its form, but it would be unconstitutional as with respect to the procedure, or as to the material content of its provisions. In most democratic states constitutional courts are the institutions which are empowered to review the constitutionality of such amendments. The substantive judicial review of constitutional amendments is therefore an existing strategy to allow reconsidering the constitutional change in question. The courts have the potential to serve in these cases as correctional mechanisms.

Some courts are constitutionally authorized to review the constitutionality of constitutional amendments.[51] In most cases, however, constitutions are silent about this problem. They do not explicitly empower constitutional courts to review amendments. Different courts interpret this silence in a different way. There are some who argue that due to the lack of express constitutional provisions to the contrary, courts can review constitutional amendments. Using this, they determine competence for substantive judicial review of themselves.[52] They recognize their power to review the constitutional amendment that has been made in accordance with the formal requirements of the constitution, but that deviates from its basic structure. Under the basic structure of the constitution, the courts usually have competence over the core elements of the constitution, such as the fundamental underlying principles, the form of government and the framework of the state.

Hungarian judicial review

Although the 1989 constitutional revision expressly recognized judicial review of legislative acts that violated the constitution, and established the Hungarian Constitutional Court to perform this task, it did not explicitly render the power to review amendments to the constitution. For a long time, the Court did not recognize its power to determine that an amendment to the constitution was unconstitutional. The Court was in the view that it might not annul certain provisions of constitutional amendments, because 'if a provision became a part of the Constitution as supported by the vote of two-thirds of the members of Parliament, it is *per definitionem* impossible to establish its unconstitutionality'.[53] However, the Court recognized its authority to determine the constitutionality of an amendment to the constitution from a procedural point of view. That is, whether the mechanism by which the amendment was enacted in Parliament was authorized to do so. In addition, a decision made it clear that an Act of Parliament, on the entering into force of a constitutional amendment, could be subject of judicial review (Decision 1260/B/1997).

After the general election of 2010, a wide range of constitutional amendments were adopted. One such amendment curtailed the Constitutional Court's competence.[54] Several petitions reached the Court, asking for the annulment of this constitutional amendment. The question thus arose as to whether the Court can perform substantive judicial review of the amendment; and if so, what can be the scope of this review?

In 2011 the Court denied itself the competence to perform a review of the substance of the amendment. A key question of the decision was whether there were superior standards which could have invalidating primacy over constitutional provisions. The Court held that invalidating primacy might only be attributed to those standards that had been explicitly determined by the constitution maker in the constitutional text as superior to other constitutional norms. At that time, such standards had not been found by the Court for the purposes of review (Decision 61/2011).[55]

In 2012 the Court again faced the problem of examining a constitutional amendment. First, it took into account the new political situation regarding the amendment of the constitution. The then constitution had been amended ten times in the year 2011, which resulted in developing a new practice of constitutional amendments that jeopardized the stability and the endurance of the constitution. In a short period of time, numerous provisions, which otherwise fell outside the regulatory scope of the constitution, had been incorporated into it, and the frequent amendments had made it difficult to follow and identify the constitution's normative text in force. Second, the Court undertook an investigation into the constitutional validity of the amendment in terms of the procedure that led to its adoption. Moreover, this was the decision in which the Court indicated a possible competence to review constitutional amendments from the perspective of substantive constitutionality. It seemed to have cautiously suggested an inner hierarchy within the Fundamental Law, and even found a hierarchy stemming from the *ius cogens* part of international law, thereby recognizing de facto the existence of an implied eternity clause that protects the basic structure of the constitution (Decision 45/2012, 28, 40–41).

If it is easy to amend the constitution, the stakes of Constitutional Court decisions are lowered, for an unfavorable judicial decision can be overridden. That is exactly what happened with the just-mentioned decision.[56] The Fourth Amendment to the Fundamental Law confirmed the case-law of the Constitutional Court in the domain of procedural review, while negating further developments in the above-mentioned decision. The Fourth Amendment authorized the Court to examine a priori whether the formal requirements for constitutional amendments had been fulfilled, but the judicial review might not extend to the content of the constitutional amendment, or its relation to the rest of the Fundamental Law.[57] The Fourth Amendment thereby revoked the authority of the Court to review constitutional amendments on their merits. To the extent that a constitutional amendment revokes judicial review, it may encounter the claim that this amendment is itself unconstitutional.[58]

In 2013, the Court took the case initiated by the Ombudsman to deal with the issue of unconstitutional constitutional amendment. It observed that the Fourth Amendment to the Fundamental Law restricted the criteria of review previously defined by the Court itself. The Court seemed to have accepted this development by saying that it lacked the competence to compare the amendment – with regard to its content – to other provisions of the Fundamental Law and to the Constitutional Court precedents. The Decision suggested, however, that the Court could analyze the new provisions incorporated by the Fourth Amendment, once its details are outlined in further Acts to ensure that they 'make up a system with international and European Union commitments free of any inconsistencies'

(Decision 12/2013). Thereby the Court apparently accepted that there are restrictions on the authority to amend the constitution, but it did not apply those principles to examine the substance of the Fourth Amendment. Had the Constitutional Court reviewed the constitutional amendment, it would have had a standard for evaluation.

The standard of evaluation

Changing the constitutional identity by applying the constitutional amendment rule may result in weakening or strengthening constitutionalism. As Ulrich Preuss put it, the amending power 'is necessary to preserve the flexibility and sustainability of the constitutional order, but it can destroy it by amending the constitution in an anti-constitutional tenor'.[59] Therefore, constitutional courts should not apply the basic structure doctrine in a formal sense. A constitutional court's mission is not to protect an antidemocratic and anti-constitutional basic structure but to protect constitutionalism. What could be the standards for this?

Lech Garlicki and Zofia A. Garlicki argue that international law, in particular international human rights law, could serve as a standard of constitutional review.[60] Rosalind Dixon and David Landau recommend that courts 'should intervene only when they are quite confident that a given constitutional amendment, either alone or in conjunction with other changes, poses a substantial threat to core democratic values' and that courts should 'adopt a practice of grounding their decisions applying the doctrine with a transnational anchor'.[61] It is indeed appropriate that courts should take into account international law and transnational constitutional law. However, international law does not deal with domestic institutional structures and it certainly may change for the worse. As far as transnational constitutional law is concerned, there is a danger that courts might be influenced by the less democratic and less constitutional institutions and principles found in the case law of other systems. I would therefore argue that we should try to find a normative standard of evaluation.

The concept of legitimacy may be of help when evaluating the constitutionality of a constitutional identity change. The sociological sense of legitimacy based upon the works of Max Weber emphasizes that a significant part of the population should deem the power – in this case the constitutional amending power – to be justified. Here the procedural features of the process of constitution amending are relevant, and the focus is mainly on the manner in which the constitutional change has been made.[62] Therefore, the questions are three: whether the public was informed about the proposed change, whether the process was inclusive enough and whether the amendment remained within the scope of the legislators' mandate. The legitimacy of the amendment in this sense depends on the fairness of democratic decision-making.[63]

In most cases the prerequisite of gaining social legitimacy is that the new constitutional identity adopted by an amendment should not lack legitimacy in a normative sense. The legitimacy of a constitutional change depends not only on the process but also on the substantive quality of the outcome. Legitimacy in a normative (moral) sense can be attributed to constitutional amendments on the basis of their content. There are substantive constraints by which different constitutional arrangements can be judged. The relevant questions are whether the constitutional change is more consistent with the concept of the dignity of people than its predecessor and whether the amendment provides more by way of positive liberty or genuine self-government (government by the people as a whole, acting as partners).[64]

Certainly, interpretations of what the concepts of human dignity and self-government mean may differ significantly between different background conceptions. Rival theoretical conceptions – whether deontological, consequentialist, teleological or else – provide rival answers to the question of exactly what kind of regulation the concept of dignity and self-government require. Taking into account the existence of different conceptions, constitutions do not set out explicitly a particular conception. Although constitutional texts occasionally contain some guidelines for the judicial interpretation, they typically do not determine any authoritative way of interpretation, thereby letting the respective court interpret its own role in ensuring fundamental rights protection with coherence.

It is the responsibility of the Court to accept a plausible background conception. It is possible to choose between better and worse background conceptions or even to endorse the pluralism of readings, but the conception should be in harmony with the wording of the constitution. Once the Court opted for a specific reading, this reading may serve as a background theory. And although there may be significant alterations over the years, within this relatively solid framework the conception can still be applied for evaluating the constitutionality of a constitutional identity change.[65]

Applying the standard in the Hungarian case

The legitimacy of the 1989 and 2011 identity-changing amendments has never been tested before the Constitutional Court. Constitutional scholars, however, have written at length on this issue. Many argued that in the case of the 1989 constitutional revision, some kind of legitimacy deficit can be detected. On the symbolic level some have challenged the legitimacy of the 1989 constitutional revision by claiming that it was basically only an amendment to the 'Stalinist constitution' originating in 1949.[66] Moreover, the 1989 constitutional revision declared itself an interim constitution. Considering the legitimacy in the normative sense, mainly the structural problems of the 1989 constitutional revision were identified: the extremely powerful Constitutional Court, the easy amendment two-thirds rule, together with the disproportionate electoral framework which benefitted the largest parties.[67]

These structural problems played a leading role in the process, which led to the adoption of the 2011 Fundamental Law and its further amendments. Nevertheless, the process and the outcome of the 2011 constitutional revision did not result in a corrected constitutional system; on the contrary, the

2011 Fundamental Law lacks both sociological and normative legitimacy. The adoption of the Fundamental Law and its further amendments lacked transparency, there was insufficient dialogue with the opposition and civil society, and those in power failed to institute substantial professional and open public debate, not to mention the hastiness of the procedure.[68]

However, not only the manner in which the new constitutional identity was launched, but also its substance failed to gain legitimacy. The 2011 constitutional change is less consistent with the dignity of people[69] and provides less by way of positive liberty than its predecessor, by abandoning the idea of a secular state, by connecting fundamental rights to responsibilities and obligations, and by introducing limitations on personal liberty (only a man and a woman can marry, life imprisonment without parole, protection of fetal life from the moment of conception, free speech restrictions).[70] The amendment fails to fulfill the requirement of genuine self-government (government by the people as a whole acting as partners) by rewriting the category of the 'We the people',[71] and by restricting constitutional checks.[72]

Applying the concept of legitimacy in the Hungarian case, it can be argued that although with the 1989 constitutional revision some kind of legitimacy deficit can be detected, the Fundamental Law, adopted by using the amendment rules, lacks both normative and sociological legitimacy.

Conclusion

From a theoretical point of view the constitution-making power is ideally in a position to change the identity of a constitution. Empirical facts illustrate, however, that a constitutional amendment that has been made in accordance with the procedural requirements of the constitution can deviate from the constitution's basic principles, thereby changing its identity. Changing constitutional identity via constitutional amendments may result in weakening or strengthening constitutionalism. Unamendable constitutional provisions may help to preserve the constitutional constitution, but one should take into account the limited ability of unamendability. Without the self-restraint of power-holders, even eternal clauses remain fragile, and are not able to operate as a real limitation upon the constitution-amending power. When a party or a party coalition has the necessary majority at its disposal and is in a position to satisfy the requirement of qualified alterability, the stability of a constitutional constitution can only be secured by the Constitutional Court applying the basic structure doctrine.

In many democratic countries, constitutional courts are in a position to preserve the constitutional constitutions that are worthy of defense. Accepting the basic structure doctrine and applying the concept of identity and legitimacy in the constitutional adjudication may act as a limit upon the constitutional-amending power, and thereby as a valuable tool of securing the stability of a constitutional constitution. Constitutional amendments changing the identity of the constitution can last only if in the long run they succeed in gaining social and normative legitimacy.

The current Hungarian example illustrates that identity change is especially easy if the constitutional amendment process is relatively flexible and the Constitutional Court is not authorized to review a constitutional amendment that has been made in accordance with the formal requirements of the constitution, but which deviates from its basic principles. And since the Constitutional Court did not create itself the authority for substantive judicial review, and did not accept the basic structure doctrine, it was not in the position to review either the 1989 or the 2011 constitutional revision. Both affected the essential character of the previous constitution, but while the former established a liberal democratic regime, the latter broke down the existing constitutional regime and replaced it with an illiberal one. And although there exists a legitimacy deficit in the cases of both the 1989 and the 2011 revisions, it is the latter which completely lacks social and normative legitimacy.

Notes

1 Associate Professor, UNESCO Chair on Human Rights and Peace, ELTE University, Budapest.
2 Eric Barendt, *An Introduction to Constitutional Law* (Clarendon 1998) 6. Karl Loewenstein called this type of constitution a semantic camouflage, Karl Loewenstein, 'The Value of Constitutions in Our Revolutionary Age' in A. Zurcher (ed), *Constitutions and Constitutional Trends since World War II* (NY 1951) 204. Giovanni Sartori referred to a facade constitution, Giovanni Sartori, *Democratic Theory* (Wayne State 1962) 861.
3 Wil Waluchow, 'Constitutionalism' in Edward N. Zalta (ed), *The Stanford Encyclopedia of Philosophy* (Spring 2014 Edition) http://plato.stanford.eedu/archives/spr2014/entries/constitutionalism/.
4 John Locke, *Two Treaties on Government* (Cambridge 1988) 213.
5 See for instance the debate between James Madison and Thomas Jefferson. Madison had almost sacralized the constitution (The Federalist, No. 49), while Jefferson held that every generation has the right to a new constitution.
6 Donald S. Lutz, *Principles of Constitutional Design* (Cambridge 2008) 153–154.
7 Donald S. Lutz, 'Toward a Theory of Constitutional Amendment' in Sanford Levinson (ed), *Responding to Imperfection. The Theory and Practice of Constitutional Amendment* (Princeton 1995) 238–239. This chapter does not deal with the question whether constitution-amending power should be regarded as a constituent, a constituted or a *sui generis* power.
8 Francesco Giovannoni, 'Amendment Rules in Constitutions' (2003) 115 *Public Choice* 37.
9 Andrew Arato, *Post Sovereign Constitution Making* (Oxford 2016) 78.
10 Günter Frankenberg, 'Comparing Constitutions. Toward a Layered Narrative' (2006) 4 *I.CON* 439, 457.
11 Walter F. Murphy, 'Merlin's Memory. The Past and Future Imperfect of the Once and Future Polity' in Sanford Levinson (ed), *Responding to Imperfection. The Theory and Practice of Constitutional Amendment* (Princeton 1995) 163, 177.
12 More on this see the Report of the European Commission for Democracy through Law on the Constitutional Amendment, CDL-AD2010(001), and Constance Grewe, 'Methods of Identification of National Constitutional Identity' in Alejandro Saiz Arnaiz and Carina Alcoberro Llivina (eds), *National Constitutional Identity and European Integration* (Intersentia 2013) 37–49.
13 Richard Albert offers a three-tiered classification of the foundations, frameworks and specifications of formal amendment rules, which help identify and understand formal

amendment design possibilities. Richard Albert, 'The Structure of Constitutional Amendment Rules' (2014) 49 *Wake Forest Law Review* 913.

14 I use this term in the Dworkinian sense. Ronald Dworkin, 'The Model of Rules' (1967–1968) 35 *U. Chi. L. Rev.* 14.

15 Article 89 of the French constitution, Article 139 of the Italian constitution.

16 Article 288 of the Portuguese constitution, Article 148 of the Romanian constitution, Article 4 of the Turkish constitution.

17 See Nick Barber, 'Why Entrench?' (2016) 14 *I.CON* 330. Scot M. Peterson grounds entrenchment historically: 'Constitutional Entrenchment in England and the UK' (2014) https://ukconstitutionallaw.org/2014/03/25/scot-peterson-constitutional-entrenchment-in-england-and-the-uk/.

18 János Bak and Anna Gara-Bak, 'The Myth of the "Millennial Constitution" in Hungary' (1981) 15 *East European Quarterly* 307.

19 Article 24(3) of the 1949 constitution required a two-third vote for changing the constitution. The first sentence of Article 24(3) of the 1989 constitution stipulated that 'a majority of two-thirds of the votes of the Members of Parliament is required to amend the Constitution'. Article S(2) of the Fundamental Law has retained this rule.

20 It was adopted by the second democratic Parliament, when the two governing parties had more than a two-thirds majority (72 per cent) of the parliamentary seats.

21 In 1995–1996 a serious attempt to draft a completely new constitution following this procedure was failed, therefore no constitution was adopted according to the four-fifths rule.

22 Constitutional amendment of 5 July 2010.

23 Gábor Attila Tóth, 'Hungary' in Besselink, E and others (eds), *Constitutional Law of the EU Member States* (Kluwer 2014) 785. In the opinion of Arato, this repeal of the implicit self-entrenchment constitutional provision by a two-thirds majority was unconstitutional. Arato (n8) 206.

24 The last sentence of the Fundamental Law reads: 'We, the Members of Parliament elected on 25 April 2010, being aware of our responsibility before God and man, and availing ourselves of our power to adopt a constitution, have thereby determined the first unified Fundamental Law of Hungary as above'.

25 But see Scheppele, who argues that Hungary is currently operating under a government which has claimed by its new constitution an unconstitutional constituent power. Kim Lane Scheppele, 'On the Unconstitutionality of Constitutional Change. An Essay in Honor of László Sólyom' in Zoltán Csehi, Balázs Schanda and Pál Sonnevend (eds), *Viva Vox Iuris Civilis* (Szent István Társulat 2012) 310.

26 See point 2 of the Closing Provisions, under which Parliament adopted the Fundamental Law according to Articles 19(3)a and 24 of the previous constitution.

27 The paradox is that the Fundamental Law invalidates the 1949 constitution, which directly affected the validity of the 1989 constitution: 'We do not recognize the communist constitution of 1949, since it was the basis of a tyrannical rule, therefore we proclaim it to be invalid'. Under para 35 of the CDL-AD(2013)012-e Opinion on the Fourth Amendment to the Fundamental Law of Hungary adopted by the Venice Commission, 'if this meant to have legal consequences, it can only be read as leading to *ex tunc* nullity. . . . This would lead to a legal paradox since an illegitimate or even non-existent Parliament cannot enact a new Constitution'.

28 Article B(3) of the Fundamental Law states that 'the source of public power shall be the people'. By ensuring this, the Fundamental Law implicitly differentiates the constitution-making power from the constitution-amending power. However, the Fundamental Law regulates the process of the total revision in the same way as the amendment process. Not only a constitutional amendment but also a completely new constitution must be adopted by Parliament, and Article S(2) requires the votes of the two-thirds majority 'for the adoption of a new Fundamental Law or any amendment thereof'.

29 Zachary Elkins, Tom Ginsburg and James Melton, *The Endurance of National Constitutions* (Cambridge 2009) 55.
30 Hans Kelsen, *General Theory of Law and State* (Harvard 2009) 124.
31 At that time, Schmitt sought to preserve 'the state from imminent civil war' and to secure 'a peaceful society'. Ellen Kennedy, *Constitutional Failure: Carl Schmitt in Weimar* (Duke 2004) 185.
32 Carl Schmitt, *Constitutional Theory* (Duke 2008) 74.
33 John Rawls, *Political Liberalism* (expanded edn, Columbia 2005) 239.
34 Claude Klein and András Sajó, 'Constitution-making: Process and Substance' in Michel Rosenfeld and András Sajó (eds), *The Oxford Handbook of Comparative Constitutional Law* (Oxford 2012) 440.
35 Yaniv Roznai, *Unconstitutional Constitutional Amendments: A Study of the Nature and Limits of Constitutional Amendment Powers* (LSE, PhD 2014) 58.
36 Monika Polzin, 'Constitutional Identity, Unconstitutional Amendments and the Idea of Constituent Power: The Development of the Doctrine of Constitutional Identity in German Constitutional Law' (2016) 14 *I.CON* 411. Although they did not specify what principles constitute the identity of the constitution, Schmitt mentioned some examples of it, such as the replacement of the system of democratic elections by a system consisting of councils (*Rätesystem*). 420.
37 Ibid., 431.
38 Maurice Adams and Michiel Bot, 'Constitutional Democratic Politics in an Age of Identity' paper presented at the conference *European Constitutional Democracy in Peril: People, Principles, Institutions*, 23–24 June 2016 (on file with the author).
39 José Luis Martí, 'Two Different Ideas of Constitutional Identity: Identity of the Constitution v. Identity of the People' in Alejandro Saiz Arnaiz and Carina Alcoberro LLivina (eds), *National Constitutional Identity and European Integration* (Intersentia 2013) 20.
40 Ibid., 24.
41 Constance Grewe, 'Methods of Identification of National Constitutional Identity' in Alejandro Saiz Arnaiz and Carina Alcoberro LLivina (eds), *National Constitutional Identity and European Integration* (Intersentia 2013) 40.
42 Gary J. Jacobsohn, 'The Formation of Constitutional Identities' in Tom Ginsburg and Rosalind Dixon (eds), *Comparative Constitutional Law* (Edward Elgar 2011) 131.
43 Herman Schwartz, 'Do Economic and Social Rights Belong in a Constitution?' (1995) 10 *The American University Journal of International Law and Policy* 1243.
44 János Kis, 'From the 1989 Constitution to the 2011 Fundamental Law' in Gábor Attila Tóth (ed), *Constitution for a Disunited Nation. On Hungary's 2011 Fundamental Law* (CEU Press 2012) 1–21.
45 1/2010. (VI. 16.) OGY politikai nyilatkozata [Proclamation of the Parliament].
46 Tibor Navracsics 'A New Constitution for Hungary: Locking in the Values of 1989–1990 Transition, At Last' (2011) *The Wall Street Journal* April 19.
47 More on the 2010–2011 constitutional transformation, see Kriszta Kovács and Gábor Attila Tóth, 'Hungary's Constitutional Transformation' (2011) *European Constitutional Law Review* 7, 183.
48 János Kornai, 'Hungary's U-Turn' (2015) 1 *Capitalism and Society* 4.
49 Kriszta Kovács and Kim Lane Scheppele, 'Hungary's Post-Socialist Administrative Law Regimes' in Susan-Rose Ackerman and Peter L. Lindseth (eds) *Comparative Administrative Law* (Elgar 2017) 119–36, 124.
50 More on this see Kriszta Kovács, 'Constitutional Continuity Disrupted' in Balázs Majtényi and Margit Feischmidt (eds) *Nationalizing Post-Postsocialism: Path-Dependency or Structurally Driven Political Turn in Hungary* (Perdue UP forthcoming).
51 See for instance the constitutions of South Africa, Turkey, Germany, Austria and concerning the bill on the constitutional amendment, Romania.

52 The Supreme Court of India is a good example.
53 Order 23/1994. Marta Dezso, *Constitutional Law in Hungary* (Kluwer 2010) 191. But see Andrew Arato, 'Constitution Making in Hungary and the 4/5 Rule' (2011) *Int'l J Const. L. Blog* April 6. According to Arato, it could easily have been said that an amendment is not fully part of the constitution until it has been tested and validated.
54 The constitutional amendment of 16 November 2010 restricted the competencies of the Constitutional Court so that the Court cannot review the constitutionality of certain financial measures. Kovács and Tóth (n45) 183.
55 The justices, for the very first time, undertook an investigation into the constitutional validity of the amendment in terms of the procedure that led to the adoption, even though they did not find the petitions well-grounded in this regard. Gábor Halmai, 'Unconstitutional Constitutional Amendments. Constitutional Courts as Guardians of the Constitution?' (2012) 2 *Constellations* 182–203.
56 As the Venice Commission aptly put it, a consistent pattern of reacting with constitutional amendments to the decisions of the Constitutional Court might be observed in Hungary, and the Fourth Amendment followed this pattern. Opinion 720/2013 on the Fourth Amendment to the Fundamental Law of Hungary, CDL-AD(2013)012, para 81.
57 'The Constitutional Court may only review the Fundamental Law and the amendment thereof for conformity with the procedural requirements laid down in the Fundamental Law with respect to its adoption and promulgation' Article 24(5) of the Fundamental Law.
58 Aharon Barak, 'Unconstitutional Constitutional Amendments' (2011) 44 *Israel Law Review* 321, 333.
59 Ulrich K. Preuss, 'The Implications of "Eternity Clauses": The German Experience' (2011) 44 *Israel Law Review* 429, 430.
60 Lech Garlicki and Zofia A. Garlicki, 'External Review of Constitutional Amendments. International Law as a Norm of Reference' (2011) 44 *Israel Law Review* 343.
61 Rosalind Dixon and David Landau, 'Transnational Constitutionalism and a Limited Doctrine of Unconstitutional Constitutional Amendment' (2015) 3 *I.CON* 606.
62 See more on this in the contribution of Andrew Arato and Gábor Attila Tóth in this volume.
63 '[D]emocratic discussion, deliberation, and decisionmaking under certain conditions are what make the outcomes legitimate for each person. . . . [W]hatever the results of discussions, deliberation, and decisionmaking . . . they are legitimate. The results are made legitimate by being the results of the procedure' Thomas Christiano, *The Rule of the Many. Fundamental Issues in Democratic Theory* (Westview 1996) 35.
64 Ronald Dworkin, *Justice for Hedgehogs* (Harvard 2013) 382–385.
65 One can imagine such a constitutional amendment that would move the constitutional identity outside of the realm of the concept of human dignity and self-governance. For instance, a constitutional amendment on the reinstatement of the death penalty or the abolishment of the Constitutional Court would constitute such changes.
66 Horkay identified the following as shortcomings of the 1989 constitution: 'obstinate adherence to legal certainty', 'superiority of the rule of law over other democratic values', and 'the Constitution's preference of value-neutrality over the popular demand for substantial justice'. Ferenc Horkay Hörcher, 'The National Avowal' in Loránd Csink, Balázs Schanda and András Zs Varga (eds), *The Basic Law of Hungary: A First Commentary* (Clarus 2012) 26. Körösényi shares Horkay's opinion on the legitimacy deficit of the 1989 constitutional revision. J. Pakulski and A. Körösényi, *Toward Leader Democracy* (Anthem 2013) 150.
67 Andrew Arato and Zoltán Miklósi, 'Constitution Making in Hungary 1989–1996' in L. E. Miller and L. Aucoin (eds), *Framing the State in Times of Transition: Case Studies in Constitution Making* (US Institute for Peace 2010) 378–379.

68 CDL-AD(2011)016-e Opinion on the new constitution of Hungary adopted by the Venice Commission, para 144.
69 Catherine Dupré, 'Human Dignity: Rhetoric, Protection and Instrumentalization' in Gábor Attila Tóth (ed), *Constitution for a Disunited Nation: On Hungary's 2011 Fundamental Law* (CEU 2012) 335.
70 Jeremy McBride, 'Trees in the Wood: The Fundamental Law and the European Court of Human Rights' in Gábor Attila Tóth (ed), *Constitution for a Disunited Nation: On Hungary's 2011 Fundamental Law* (CEU 2012) 340.
71 Zsolt Körtvélyesi, 'From "We the People" to "We the Nation"' in Gábor Attila Tóth (ed), *Constitution for a Disunited Nation: On Hungary's 2011 Fundamental Law* (CEU 2012) 111.
72 Miklós Bánkuti, Gábor Halmai and Kim Lane Scheppele, 'From Separation of Powers to a Government without Checks: Hungary's Old and New Constitutions' in Gábor Attila Tóth (ed), *Constitution for a Disunited Nation: On Hungary's 2011 Fundamental Law* (CEU 2012) 237.

10 The rise and fall of constitutionalism in Hungary

Gábor Halmai

In this chapter, I describe the elements and possible reasons for Hungary's recent transition from a liberal to an illiberal system, and will attempt to explain both the unique and the more typical features of this change. I use the term 'constitutional counter-revolution' to describe the Hungarian constitutional restoration.[1] At the same time, my view is that the illiberal turn, which significantly weakened the rule of law safeguards instituted by the 1989–1990 constitutional process, has not resulted in the restoration of either the single-party state or police state structures. I think that the Hungarian constitutional system after 2010 is better characterized as a kind of 'democradura', rather than as a dictatorship.[2]

Let us first discuss the characteristics of the constitution-making process both in 1989 and in 2010.

Revolutionary/non-revolutionary vs. sovereign/post-sovereign constitution-making

The characteristic of system change that Hungary shared with other transitioning countries was that it had to establish an independent nation-state, a civil society, a private economy, and a democratic structure all at the same time.[3] Plans for transforming the Stalin-inspired 1949 Rákosi Constitution into a 'rule of law'-document were delineated in the National Roundtable Talks of 1989 by participants of the Opposition Roundtable and representatives of the state party. Afterwards, the illegitimate parliament only sealed the comprehensive amendment to the constitution, which went into effect on the anniversary of the revolution, and which has since been the basic document of the 'constitutional revolution'.

Revolutionary constitutions – exemplified by the models of the American and French Revolutions – establish an entirely new order rather than merely constraining the reigning power in place.[4] In the order created by such constitutions all forms of exercising public power require an immanent justification, which is provided by the new constitution. The new constitution determines the form and substance of the sovereign exercise of power, and in so doing, it liquidates the previous political order; in other words it severs continuity. The establishment of a new political order is associated with the concept of 'democratic *constituent power*', which designates the people as the subjects of the founding act. This legality manifests itself in democratic procedures and emerges subsequently as the basis for the constitution's legitimacy. This explains why most constitutions only make provisions concerning the amendment of the existing document, while they are silent on the formal requirements of its comprehensive revision, not to mention the adoption of a new constitution. The Spanish Constitution and the constitutions of some states of the U.S. are exceptions to this general observation, since they also regulate the possibility and procedures of a revision. Another exception is the German Grundgesetz of 1949, which, in its Article 146, holds out the prospect of its own replacement by a new constitution to be adopted following German reunification (as we know, ultimately, this promise went unfulfilled in 1990: the six new federal states joined the Federal Republic within the framework of the Grundgesetz). Similarly, the preamble of the comprehensive constitutional amendment act of 1989 in Hungary also promises the adoption of a new constitution. Nevertheless, even though in the Hungarian case, formally speaking, no new constitution was adopted in 1989 – though substantially speaking it did – academic literature qualifies this act not as an amendment or revision, but as a 'constitutional revolution, or new founding'.[5] However, this procedure is called 'chaste constitution-making' by some academics.[6]

The non-revolutionary tradition seeks to legalize an existing system of government. In the case of the German and British constitutional evolutions, which may be regarded as the prototypes of this model, it also strives to constrain royal powers by adopting a new constitution. In contrast to the revolutionary tradition that establishes a new order, the non-revolutionary tradition that seeks to reshape power arrangements does not necessarily require democratization. In fact, democratization may be counterbalanced by strong judicial review, as in England, or by the powers of a constitutional court, as in Germany. But those constitutions that are, in a political sense, non-revolutionary need not even necessarily aim to transform the existing power arrangements. It is conceivable that a new constitutional order is established while the previous power structures continue to prevail. According to Ran Hirschl, the constitutional developments in 1982 in Canada, in 1990 in New Zealand, between 1992 and 1995 in Israel, and indeed, the UK's situation following the adoption of the Human Rights Act in 1998, are precisely such instances of 'no apparent transition'. In these cases the constitutional reforms are neither concomitants of a political-economic transition nor the outcome thereof.[7]

Taking into account the revolutionary/non-revolutionary dichotomy, we can conclude that the constitution-making in Hungary in 1989 can be substantively characterized as a revolutionary act, since it produced a new political order, even though neither the roundtable, which drafted the comprehensive amendment to the old constitution, nor the communist parliament, which rubber stamped the draft, can be considered as a democratic constituent power. Therefore, using the sovereign/post-sovereign binary categories, it was certainly a post-sovereign constitution-making, both procedurally and due to the promise of a new constitution, also substantially.

On the other hand, procedurally, the 2011 Fundamental Law wasn't a revolutionary act, since it was enacted on the basis of the constitution-making rules of the 1949/1989 constitution, with the exception of the special provision of the house rules. However, there was also a new rule incorporated into the constitution in 1994, which required a four-fifths majority for the decision concerning the preparation of a new constitution. Substantially, the new Fundamental Law of Hungary can be treated as revolutionary, as it introduced a new, illiberal type of constitutional system, instead of the liberal constitution of 1989. Even Prime Minister Viktor Orbán responded to European parliament critics regarding the new constitutional order by admitting that his party did not aim at producing a liberal constitution. He said:

> In Europe the trend is for every constitution to be liberal, this is not one. Liberal constitutions are based on the freedom of the individual and subdue welfare and the interest of the community to this goal. When we created the constitution, we posed questions to the people. The first question was the following: what would you like; should the constitution regulate the rights of the individual and create other rules in accordance with this principle or should it create a balance between the rights and duties of the individual? According to my recollection, more than 80 percent of the people responded by saying that they wanted to live in a world where freedom existed, but where welfare and the interest of the community could not be neglected and that these need to be balanced in the constitution. I received an order and mandate for this. For this reason, the Hungarian constitution is a constitution of balance, and not a side-leaning constitution, which is the fashion in Europe, as there are plenty of problems there.[8]

Because of this intention of the government to change the liberal democratic political order, I describe this constitution-making as counter-revolutionary.

Instead of a 'revolutionary/non-revolutionary' dichotomy, Andrew Arato distinguishes between sovereign and post-sovereign constitution-making. By sovereign, he means a constitution-making process conducted by parliament, while the essence of the post-sovereign model is that constitution-making power is not concentrated in a single body or an organ specially constituted and authorized for the purposes of constitution-making, but that each of the organs involved in constitutional politics are bound by laws.[9] According to Arato, the roots of this new form of constitution-making reach back as far as the American Revolution, as well as the post-WWII constitutional processes in France and Germany; its renaissance can also be observed in the 1970s in Spain, in the regime transitions in Central and Eastern Europe in the late 1980s and early 1990s, and in South Africa in the mid-1990s. A basic feature of the process – especially in the latter cases – is the two-step constitution-making, which features intervening free elections and the use of a provisional constitution. Another basic feature is that the principle of constitutionalism does not extend to the final product only, but also to the process whereby the constitution is adopted. Arato believes that where this model is consistently applied, it could be a viable democratic alternative to revolutionary constitution-making, which often results in dictatorships. Where the second step fails to take place, however, this omission can easily doom the entire constitutional process.

In post-communist countries, Arato recognizes three models of constitution-making. The earliest, possibly too early, constitution-making took place in Bulgaria and Romania, where the Parliaments that were created as a result of democratic elections were given the rights of a constituent assembly, as had been the case in France (the National Constituent Assembly between 1789 and 1791) and in Weimar (in 1918). Meanwhile, in the Czech Republic and Slovakia after the dissolution of Czechoslovakia in 1992, constitution-making was carried out by democratically elected legislative bodies, but without the classification of a constituent assembly. The cases of Hungary and Poland represent a third type of constitution-making, where the process was started by an illegitimate conventional legislature whose task was to approve a text that had been agreed upon by the state-party and the new democratic movements before the democratic elections.

Using this dichotomy, which assesses the substance and the process together, the 1989 'pacted'[10] constitution-making in Hungary was designed as a two-step post-sovereign process, the first step being an interim constitution prepared by the National Roundtable Talks and enacted by the illegitimate parliament, followed by a final constitution sometime after the first democratic elections. However, the country has failed to produce a final constitutionalist constitution, even though in the second, center-left-dominated, freely elected parliament, the governing coalition of the socialist MSZP and the liberal SZDSZ alone had constitution-making powers. Therefore, in the context of Hungary, Arato spoke of partial failure in 2010.[11] In 2011, he argued that the adoption of the Fundamental Law was a move against post-sovereign constitution-making.[12] Altogether, we can argue that the new constitution is a result of a sovereign process.

In 1989, Fidesz and Viktor Orbán together with SZDSZ (the Alliance of Free Democrats) played a crucial role in avoiding a kind of semi-presidential system with a former communist president by not signing the agreement of the National Roundtable and by initiating a successful referendum on the process to elect the president. Following Fidesz's election victory in 2010, many argued that Orbán was willing to introduce a presidential system in order to concentrate power in the hands of the presidency. Others claimed that Orbán would not want a presidential system since he prefers a system containing checks and balances against the executive.[13] Proponents of Fidesz, such as Béla Pokol, argued that Fidesz's new constitutional system envisages the Westminster parliamentary model, in which the 'winner takes all' and where the principle of the unity of power prevails. In my view, the Westminster model also works with checks and balances, even if different from that of a presidential system. Therefore one cannot treat Fidesz's new constitutional system as a monistic democracy, which just gives priority to democratic decision-making over fundamental rights.[14]

The institutional arrangement of this model is best embodied by the British doctrine of parliamentary sovereignty, which does not entail the usual institutional elements of a dualist democracy, such as strong judicial review. By contrast, the new Hungarian constitutional system has kept these institutional arrangements, such as the Constitutional Court, but deprived them of their power. They also kept the mixed electoral system, but made it more majoritarian.

Consequently, the new Hungarian constitutional system does not fit into any of the models of government, all of which are based on a different concept of separation of powers. The more traditional models of government forms are based on the relationship between the legislature and the executive. For instance, Arendt Lijphart differentiates between majoritarian (Westminster) and consensual models of democracy, the prototype of the first being the British, while that of the second being the continental European parliamentary and U.S. presidential systems.[15] Giovanni Sartori discusses presidentialism and semi-presidentialism, as well as two forms of parliamentarism – namely, the premiership system in the United Kingdom, Kanzlerdemokratie in Germany, and the assembly government model in Italy.[16] Besides the Westminster and U.S. separation of powers systems, Bruce Ackerman uses the constrained parliamentarism model as a new form of separation of powers, which has emerged against the export of the American system in favor of the model of Germany, Italy, Japan, India, Canada, South Africa, and other nations, where both popular referendums and constitutional courts constrain the power of the parliament.[17] Hungary between 1990 and 2010 belonged to the consensual and constrained parliamentary systems, close to the German Kanzlerdemokratie. But the 2011 Fundamental Law abolished almost all possibility of institutional consensus and constraints on parliamentary power, and the system has since moved towards an absolute parliamentary sovereignty model, without the cultural constraints of the Westminster form of government. Not to mention the fact that in the last few decades, the traditional British model of constitutionalism has also changed drastically with the introduction of a bill of rights by left-of-center governments (and opposed by right-of-center opposition parties) in Canada (1982), New Zealand (1990), the United Kingdom (1998), the Australian Capital Territory (2004), and the State of Victoria (2006). Unlike the traditional commonwealth model of constitutionalism, this codified bill of rights limits legislation, even though the legislature still enjoys the final word.

The biggest change to the absolute parliamentary sovereignty system occurred in the United Kingdom after 1998, and some even talk about the 'demise of the Westminster model'.[18] The greatest deviation from the system of unlimited parliamentary sovereignty was the introduction of judicial review. In just over two decades, the number of applications for judicial review nearly quadrupled to over 3,400 in 2000, when the Human Rights Act of 1998 came into effect in England and Wales.[19] The Human Rights Act has a general requirement that all legislation should be compatible with the European Convention on Human Rights. This does not allow U.K. courts to strike down, or 'disapply', legislation, or to make new law. Instead, where legislation is deemed to be incompatible with

Convention rights, superior courts may make a declaration of incompatibility (under section 4.2). It is then up to the government and parliament to decide how to proceed. In this sense, the legislative sovereignty of the British parliament is preserved. Some academics argue that, although as a matter of constitutional legality parliament may well be sovereign, as a matter of constitutional practice it has transferred significant power to the judiciary.[20] Others go even further to argue that although the Human Rights Act of 1998 is purported to reconcile the protection of human rights with the sovereignty of parliament, it represents an unprecedented transfer of political power from the executive and legislature to the judiciary.[21]

Besides the commonwealth countries mentioned, a similar new model has emerged in Israel, where the Basic Law on occupation, re-enacted in 1994, contains a 'notwithstanding' provision, similar to the Canadian law. This new model of commonwealth constitutionalism is based on a dialogue between the judiciary and the parliament.[22] However, comparative constitutional studies conclude that parliamentary sovereignty tends to be increasingly restrained, either legally or politically, and that the last few decades have witnessed a narrowing scope for the exercise of traditional constituent power conceived as unrestrained, as the sign of the 'will of the people', even in cases of regime change or the establishment of substantially and formally new constitutional arrangements.[23] In contrast to these new trends, in the Hungarian constitutional system, the parliamentary majority decides every single issue without any control mechanism, as the independence of both the ordinary judiciary and the Constitutional Court has been liquidated.

Explanations of Hungary's backsliding to an illiberal state

Since the new constitutional order has weakened checks and balances and guarantees of fundamental rights, the new Hungary (not even a Republic in its name anymore) cannot be deemed a liberal democracy.

The main reasons for the turn of constitutionalism are as follows:

(a) Historically, in Hungary, as in other East-Central European countries, there were some unexpected moments of quick flourishing of liberal democracy followed by an equally quick delegitimization of it. First, between the 1860s/1870s and the end of the 19th century; second, after WWI, except in Hungary, where the short liberal democratic period led by Mihály Károlyi was soon followed by the red terror of commune, and white terror of the right wing. The third such short moment occurred after 1945, especially in Czechoslovakia and Hungary until the communist parties' take over in 1948. And fourth, after 1989, when liberal democracy again seemed to be the 'end of history'.[24]

Some elements of a representative system existed before WWII, after Governor Horthy consolidated his regime, with strong nationalism and anti-Semitism, and without any kind of human rights culture. According to the political theorist István Bibó, who also served as Minister of State in the government of Imre Nagy during the Hungarian revolution of 1956, pre-WWII Hungary was a prime example of a 'deformed political culture', where 'nationhood had to be made, re-fashioned, fought for and constantly protected not only from the predations of imperial powers but also from the indifference and fluctuating sense of national identity as a part of the people themselves'.[25] During the 1920s and 1930s, when Hungary had a far-right government that flirted seriously with fascism, Miklós Horthy governed not only as admiral without a sea, but also as a regent without a king. Horthy relied for some of his authority on his public reverence for the Holy Crown, with which he associated himself whenever possible. He also organized a major national celebration for the Crown in 1937 and took full propaganda advantage of touring the country with the Crown in an open train. While he himself could not claim the title of king, he appeared, nonetheless, in the place of a king governing the country with a toxic mix of nationalism, xenophobia, and disrespect for basic legality and constitutionalism. This means that Hungary had never before had a democratic system, similar to the one of the Third Republic between 1990 and 2010.

Social psychologists in Hungary claim that Hungarian history is full of failures which is also reflected in the national anthem,[26] therefore the self-image of Hungarians is basically negative.[27] Hungary was on the losing side of both WWI and WWII. The victim narrative claims that the country has always been a noble and helpless victim of the malevolent forces of history, for instance by the Trianon Treaty of 1920, in which Hungary lost two-thirds of its territory. The fact that the right-wing governments elected by Hungarians voluntarily joined the losing side, and that Hungary was responsible for a lot of wrongdoings, for instance for the speedy deportation of more than half a million Hungarian citizens of Jewish origin to Auschwitz, has never been mentioned.[28]

The many historical fiascos since the middle ages caused a feeling of inferiority in the sense of Adler, which made it necessary to look for a father figure within the meaning of Freud's father complex. These 'Führers', such as Rákosi, Kádár, and also Orbán in the post-WWII history of the country were able to treat the members of society like their children, and this parent-child transaction made it possible for PM Orbán since 2010 to manipulate people with his government's very effective campaigns through the loyal media and convince them to follow his lead sometimes even against their best interest.[29] The signs of such a parent-child transaction were, for instance, Orbán's attitude towards the paramilitary far right Hungarian Gárda promising them a slap in the face, or treating all their critics as paid agents of enemy powers. This can also be a part of the explanation of why the majority of Hungarians identified themselves with the government's attitude during the refugee crisis. The description of this phenomenon of despotic protectors of the people against their fears goes back to Plato's 'The Republic', in which he warned that a 'towering despot' will inevitably rise in any democracy to exploit its freedoms and seize power fomenting fear and representing himself as the protector, just like Orbán did during the refugee crisis.[30]

(b) Even though the transition to democracy in Hungary was driven by the fact that a large share of the population gave high priority to freedom itself, one of the legacies of the mild version of socialism with the toleration of private businesses, relative social security, and no unemployment in the Kádár-regime ('the happiest barrack in the camp') from the 1960s onwards, was that people expected the new state to produce speedy economic growth, with which the country could attain the living standards of neighboring Austria overnight, without painful reforms. In other words, one can argue that the average Hungarian pursued the West in 1989, though not so much in terms of the Western economic and political system, but rather in terms of the living standards of the West. Claus Offe predicted the possible backsliding effect of the economic changes and decline in living standards, saying that this could undermine the legitimacy of democratic institutions and turn back the process of democratization.[31] This failure, together with the emergence of an economically and politically independent bourgeoisie, the accumulation of wealth by some former members of the communist nomenclature, unresolved issues in dealing with the communist past, the lack of retributive justice against perpetrators of grave human rights violations, and a mild vetting procedure and lack of restitution of the confiscated properties, were reasons for disappointment.

(c) According to some arguments, the prospects for democracy in Hungary (and the other newly independent states of Central and Eastern Europe) following the 1989–1990 transition were diminished by a technocratic, judicial control of politics, as well as the loss of civic constitutionalism, civil society, and participatory democratic government as a necessary counterpoint to the technocratic machinery of legal constitutionalism.[32] This concept argues that the legalistic form of constitutionalism (or legal constitutionalism), while consistent with the purpose of creating the structure of the state and setting boundaries between the state and citizens, jeopardizes the development of participatory democracy.[33] In other words, this view suggests that legal constitutionalism falls short, reducing the constitution to an elite instrument, especially in countries with weak civil societies and weak political party systems that undermine a robust constitutional democracy based on the idea of civic self-government.[34]

The concept of civic or participatory constitutionalism is based on 'democratic constitutionalism' (James Tully), emphasizing that structural problems in new democracies include the relative absence of institutions for popular participation, which is also related to 'counterdemocracy' (Pierre Rosenvallon), as well as robust institutional linkage of civic associations and citizens with formal politics. Critics of this approach say that it does not sufficiently take into account the rise of populism and the lack of civic interest in constitutional matters, and the elite disdain for participatory institutions. Moreover, the approach does not account for the increasing irrelevance of domestic constitutionalism resulting from the tendencies of Europeanization and globalization, especially the internationalization of domestic constitutional law through the use of foreign and international law in constitution-making and constitutional interpretation.[35]

(d) In addition, two initial failures of the 1989 constitutional changes also contributed to Fidesz's ability to change the entire constitutional system after its electoral success in 2010. One of them is the disproportional election system, which translated the 53 percent vote share into 68 percent in 2010 and 45.5 percent into 67 percent of the seats in parliament in 2014. The other failure was the unchanged two-thirds rule for making and amending the constitution.

The present and future of liberal democracy in Hungary

The current Hungarian constitutional system constitutes a new, hybrid type of regime, between a full-fledged democracy and a dictatorship. Even when there is a formal written constitution, a dictatorship is not a constitutional system. Therefore, China, Vietnam, Cuba, Belorussia, the former Soviet Union, and former communist countries cannot be considered to be constitutional systems, even though, as William J. Dobson argues is his recent book, *The Dictator's Learning Curve*, 'today's dictators and authoritarians are far more sophisticated, savvy, and nimble than they once were'.[36] What happened in Hungary is certainly less than a total breakdown of constitutional democracy, but also more than just a transformation of the way that liberal democracy is functioning. Hungary became an illiberal state, which was the openly stated intention of PM Orbán.[37] In this illiberal system, the institutions of a constitutional state (Constitutional Court, ombudsman, judicial or media councils) still exist, but their power is strongly limited. Also, as in many illiberal regimes, fundamental rights are listed in the new Fundamental Law, but the institutional guarantees of these rights are endangered through the lack of independence of the judiciary and the Constitutional Court.

As many scholars noted, there is an incredible range of nondemocratic, nonauthoritarian regimes and their relationship with each other and democracy is often imperfect and unclear. Countries in this 'grey zone' inspired a lot of concepts, which were created to capture the mixed nature of these regimes. Steven Levitsky and Lucas A. Way introduced the term 'competitive authoritarianism' for a distinctive type of 'hybrid' civilian regimes in which formal democratic institutions exist and are widely viewed as the primary means of gaining power, but in which incumbents' abuse of the state places them at a significant advantage vis-á-vis their opponents.[38]

In the democratic changes of the post-1989 East-Central Europe, Jacques Rupnik describes three main trajectories: a) the Central European trajectory is characterized by the consolidation of democracy; b) in the Balkans, democratic transition derailed because of nation-state building; and c) in post-Soviet Eastern Europe (Ukraine, Caucasus), 'hybrid regimes' à la Levitsky-Way have emerged.[39] In a more recent publication, Rupnik also emphasizes the differences of these trajectories as a consequence of their different political culture originating in the Christian or Orthodox culture. He claims that countries with an Orthodox culture (Greece, Romania, Serbia, Bulgaria) have more difficulties accepting traditional liberal democracy, which means that – also considering the experiences of the Arab Spring – instead of Fukuyama's 'end of history' approach we should reconsider Huntington's 'clash of civilizations' scenario.[40]

Let me clarify the paradox of Orbán's alleged defense of Christianity from the 'Muslim hordes' and the Orthodox culture of Hungary. In a speech on 26 July 2012, Orbán explained why authoritarianism is needed to deal with Hungarians: '*Joining forces is not a matter of intentions, but of sheer force. With a half-Asian lot such as ours, there is no other way* [GH: than compulsion or force]'.[41] This assessment is very similar to that of Imre Kertész, the Nobel laureate in literature, who argued that Hungary's ill fate stemmed from her inability to choose between Asia and Western Europe.[42] In other words, Christianity and religion in general serve as a reference point that Orbán's right-wing populism uses instrumentally. Fidesz turned from a liberal party in the early 1990s with a militantly anti-clerical view from the mid-90s into a conservative party turning to an openly positive stance towards religion. Religion, however, was never understood as a significant part of its identity, but rather played a purely instrumental role in Fidesz's political strategy, even after they joined the center-right party family of the European parliament, the European People's Party (EPP).[43] Fidesz uses religious symbols in an eclectic way in which references to Christianity are often mentioned together with the pre-Christian pagan traditions. This refers to the idea of 'two Hungarys': the Western Christian, and the Eastern pagan, tribal one.[44] Orbán once voiced his conviction that the Turul bird, a symbol of ancient Hungarians, is the image into which Hungarians are born, 'the symbol of a national identity of living'.[45] This means that Fidesz interprets this pre-Christianity within the framework of nationalism, and this ethno-nationalism provides sufficient basis of political identification as a type of surrogate religion. In this respect, Fidesz follows the authoritarian traditions of the Horthy regime between the two World Wars, in which the national religion ('nemzetvallás') played a crucial role. Another proof of Christianity being instrumental for Orbán is that the marriage rate is the lowest in East-Central Europe. The difference between Hungary and the deeply Christian Poland, in particular, is especially telling. Hungary's marriage rates are typical of the least religious countries in Europe, which is what the statistics on church attendance also show.[46] One can also have doubts about the seriousness of Christianity considering the fact that when Orbán listed the illiberal regimes he admires from Singapore through China, Turkey, and Russia, all of them are either non-Christian or Orthodox.

Considering its new constitutional system, and its behavior in the refugee crisis, which trajectory is Hungary following right now? As in electoral democracies, a formally competitive election with competing parties was held in April 2014; however, Fidesz needed to strengthen the disproportionality of the election system, to introduce a unique winner compensation, and gerrymandering, which favored the governing party to regain its two-thirds majority. Even though we cannot say that the outcome of this election was determined by the election rules only, we also do not know how much election fraud Fidesz would have used if its simple majority would have been in danger. The Budapest municipal elections held in October 2014 proved that they are ready to engage in fraudulent practices.[47]

In this respect, the hybridity of Hungarian constitutionalism differs from the 'managed democracy' of Putin's Russia, where failing competing parties and candidates, and the results of parliamentary and presidential elections cannot be deemed as uncertain.

The democratic backsliding of Hungary has been demonstrated by many independent ratings. According to Freedom House's *Nations in Transit* ratings, Hungary has weakened more since EU accession than any other member state, with the largest declines in 2010 and 2011. In 2012, Hungary was downgraded both for its electoral process and by losing its 'free' status regarding media freedom – the only country to do so. With downgrades in civil society and local democratic governance in 2012, Hungary's overall democracy score is edging closer to the barrier between consolidated democracies and those classified as 'semi-consolidated', a category that includes Bulgaria, Romania, and the better-performing Balkan states.[48] By the end of 2013, Hungary's democracy score was one full point worse on the 1–7 scale than in 2004, when the country entered the EU. In the 2015 *Nations in Transit* report, which reflects the period 1 January through 31 December, in 2014 Hungary was expelled from the category of 'consolidated democracy regimes' and classified as 'semi-consolidated' due to the worsening of its scores in electoral process, civil society, independent media, local democratic governance, judicial framework independence, and consequently its overall democracy score deteriorated from 2.96 to 3.18.[49] Also, Demos concluded that Hungary was a significant 'backslider' on the dimensions of electoral and procedural democracy, the rule of law, and fundamental rights and freedoms and, worryingly, it scored poorly with respect to citizens' attitudes towards democracy. It was also the poorest performer among EU member states on the measure of active citizenship. Overall, Greece and Hungary emerge as the most worrying backsliders on measures of a healthy democracy.[50]

The attitudes of citizens towards democracy lead us to one of the very reasons for the backsliding. Besides the more means-based, institution-focused elements of an ordinary liberal constitutional democracy in Hungary mentioned earlier, the end-based sociopolitical elements of the term, namely the cultural patterns as reflected both in general and in specific behavior, are lacking. In other words, in Hungary there is not, and never has been, a strong normative commitment to democracy on a behavioral and attitudinal level; therefore, a broad and deep legitimation of constitutional democracy has not been achieved. This means that the significant political actors, at both the elite and mass levels, are not convinced that the liberal democratic regime is the right and appropriate one for the society, better than any other realistic alternative they can imagine.

The major question regarding the future of Hungary is whether democracy and liberalism should go hand in hand, as is the case in the Western world, including the European Union, of which Hungary is currently a member. As with citizens in any other nation-state, Hungarians certainly have the right to oppose joint European measures on immigration and refugees, or even the development of a liberal political system altogether. However, this conclusion must be reached through a democratic process, unlike the constitution-making that took place in 2011, when Hungary's leaders neglected to consult the people on their opinions about the very nature of the constitution. There are still a significant number of people who either consider themselves as supporters of liberal democracy, or at least represent views which are in line with liberal democracy.[51] Liberal or not, the country's next constitution cannot be the exclusive product of elite-driven negotiations. If Hungarians ultimately opt for a non-liberal democracy, as PM Viktor Orbán publicly insisted first in the summer of 2014, and a year later during the refugee crisis, they must accept certain consequences, including parting from the European Union and the wider community of liberal democracies.

*

The described democratic backsliding in Hungary demonstrates that the institutional framework is a necessary but not sufficient element of a successful democratization. Behavioral elements, among them political and constitutional culture, are as important as institutions. The other lesson of this case study is on the one hand that the very definition of democracy is changing, and it is not necessarily liberal, and on the other hand the borders of democratic, authoritarian, or dictatorial regimes are blurred, and there are a lot of different hybrid systems, including the current Hungarian one.[52] Another important aspect of these developments is that, due to a new cold war situation, democratic societies are not only influenced exclusively by the liberal democratic West. The behavior of the Hungarian government, an admirer of Putin's authoritarian Russia, partly supported by the other East European countries during the refugee crisis has taught us that the strengthening of populist and extreme nationalist movements across Europe is incompatible with the values of the liberal democracy, and also that membership of the European Union is not a guarantee for having liberal democratic regimes in all member states. Unfortunately, the refugee crisis also strengthened illiberal regimes all over Europe (Russia and Turkey), and in the case of Hungary, and later of Poland – which from the end of 2015 very much followed the Hungarian playbook to destroy constitutional democracy – even inside the EU. This in spite of the fact that the EU has the authority either to use infringement actions because of the systemic violation of EU laws and principles or to trigger Article 7 of the Treaty. Instead of using Article 7, however, Brussels introduced a very cautious pre-Article 7 mechanism called the Rule of

Law Framework,[53] and started it only later and exclusively against Poland. The possible reason for why the EU was not quite ready to sanction Hungary first and foremost is that the governing Fidesz party delivers votes to EPP, the largest faction in the EP. In this way, EU institutions have proven their lack of capacity to enforce compliance to common values of constitutionalism in a member state.

Notes

1 See G. Halmai, 'From the "Rule of Law Revolution" to an Illiberal Democracy in Hungary', *in Festschrift für Klaus Stern* (Duncker & Humblot, Berlin, 2012); G. Halmai, 'From the "Rule of Law Revolution" to the Constitutional Counter-Revolution in Hungary', *in* Benedek *et al.*, *European Yearbook on Human Rights* (Neuer Wissenschaftlicher Verlag, Wien, 2012); G. Halmai, 'Towards an Illiberal Democracy. Hungary's New Constitution', *Eurozine*, 25 January 2012.

2 See A. Arato, 'Is There a Dictatorship in the E.U.?' (booksandideas.net, 1 May 2012). The term was drawn from Guillermo O'Donnell and Philippe Schmitter, who used it to describe certain Latin American regimes in the 1970s and 1980s. In 2011, Arato and I jointly edited an amicus brief for the Venice Commission on the newly adopted Fundamental Law (Z. Fleck *et al.*, 'Vélemény Magyarország Alaptörvényéről' ['Opinion on Hungary's Fundamental Law'], *Fundamentum*, No. 1, 2011). Generally, the similarities between Arato's and my own assessment of the situation extended even to terminology. See G. Halmai, 'I Speak of a "Counterrevolution" in the Dimension of Constitutionality'. 'Beszélgetés Arató András szociológus-politológussal' ['Conversation with the Sociologist/Political Scientist Andrew Arato'], *Fundamentum*, No. 1, 2011.

3 The terms 'single' and 'dual' transitions are used by A. Przeworski, *Democracy and the Market: Political and Economic Reforms in Eastern Europe and Latin America* (Cambridge University Press, Cambridge, UK, 1991). Later, Claus Offe broadened the scope of this debate by arguing that post-communist societies actually faced a triple transition, since many post-communist states were new or renewed nation-states. See C. Offe, *Varieties of Transition: The East European and East German Experience* (MIT Press, New York, 1997).

4 This *ex nihilo* constitution-making is referred to as 'revolution-based' by Michel Rosenfeld. See M. Rosenfeld, *The Identity of the Constitutional Subject* (Taylor & Francis, Oxford, UK 2009), Chapter 6. Dawn Oliver and Carlo Fusaro in their comparative analysis use another categorization of the birth of new constitutions. They consider the following ways in which new constitutions come into existence: a) granted and patriated constitutions are granted by another state, as happened in the case of New Zealand's constitution in 1852 by the Constitutional Act of the British Parliament, and patriated first in 1947 by the right to amend the 1852 Constitutional Act, and finally by the New Zealand Constitutional Act of 1986; b) independence constitutions, like India's, adopted upon independence in 1948, based on the Constituent Assembly formed for that purpose; c) regime change constitutions of the former communist countries or that of South Africa in 1996; d) post-war constitutions of both Germany and Italy. See D. Oliver and C. Fusaro, 'Changing Constitutions: Comparative Analysis', *in* Dawn Oliver and Carlo Fusaro (eds.), *How Constitutions Change – A Comparative Study* (Hart Publishing, Oxford, UK, 2011), pp. 381–83

5 Cf. S. Holmes and C.R. Sunstein, 'The Politics of Constitutional Revision in Eastern Europe', *in* S. Levinson (ed.), *Responding to Imperfection: The Theory and Practice of Constitutional Amendment* (Princeton University Press, Princeton, NJ, 1995), p. 285.

6 See A. Bozóki, 'Szemérmes alkotmányozás. Rendszerváltás és jogállami forradalom 1989-ben' ['Chaste Constitution-Making. System Change and Rule of

Law Revolution'], in A. Jakab András and A. Körösényi (eds.), *Alkotmányozás Magyarországon és máshol* [*Constitution-Making in Hungary and Elsewhere*] (MTA TKPTI, Új Mandátum Kiadó, 2012), pp. 202–39.

7 See R. Hirschl, *Towards Juristocracy* (Harvard University Press, Cambridge, MA, 2004), pp. 7–10.

8 See 'A Tavares jelentés egy baloldali akció' ('The Tavares report is a leftist action'), Interview with PM Viktor Orbán, 5 July 2013. Kossuth Rádió. <www.kormany.hu/hu/miniszterelnokseg/miniszterelnok/beszedek-publikaciok-interjuk/a-tavares-jelentes-egy-baloldali-akcio>.

9 See A. Arato, *Constitution Making Under Occupation. The Politics of Imposed Revolution in Iraq* (Columbia University Press, New York, 2009), pp. 59–97. Arato himself indicates that the term was first used by Ulrich Preuss in the context of the roundtable talks in the German Democratic Republic that is East Germany. Cf. Arato (n9) 61.

10 The term is used by Michel Rosenfeld, see M. Rosenfeld, *The Identity of the Constitutional Subject* (Routledge, Oxford, UK, 2009).

11 A. Arato, 'Post-Sovereign Constitution-Making in Hungary: After Success, Partial Failure, and Now What?', *South African Journal of Human Rights*, Vol. 26, 2010, p. 19.

12 Cf. G. Halmai, 'Én az alkotmányosság dimenziójában beszélek "ellenforradalomról."' 'Beszélgetés Arató András szociológus-politológussal' ['I speak of "counterrevolution" in the context of constitutionalism. Conversation with the sociologist/political scientist Andras Arato'], *Fundamentum*, No. 1, 2011.

13 See the discussion in the Hungarian weekly, Élet és Irodalom, initiated and concluded by my articles: G. Halmai, 'Búcsú a jogállamtól' ('Farewell to the Rule of Law'), 23 July 2010, and 'Jogállami ellenforradalom – illiberális demokrácia' ('Rule of Law Counter-Revolution and Illiberal Democracy'), 24 September 2010.

14 Bruce Ackerman distinguishes between three models of democracy: monistic, rights fundamentalism, in which fundamental rights are morally prior to democratic decision-making and there impose limits, and dualist, which finds the middle ground between these two extremes, and subjects majoritarian decision-making to constitutional guarantees. See Bruce Ackerman, *We the People: Foundations* (Harvard University Press, Cambridge, MA, 1991), pp. 6–16.

15 A. Lijphart, *Patterns of Democracy. Government Forms and Performance in Thirty-Six Countries* (Yale University Press, New Haven, 1999).

16 G. Sartori, *Comparative Constitutional Engineering. An Inquiry into Structures, Incentives and Outcomes*, 2nd edn (New York University Press, New York, 1997).

17 B. Ackerman, 'The New Separation of Powers', *Harvard Law Review*, Vol. 113, 2000, pp. 633–727.

18 Cf. P. Norton, 'Governing Alone', *Parliamentary Affairs*, 2003, p. 544.

19 See D. Judge, 'Whatever Happened to Parliamentary Democracy in the United Kingdom', *Parliamentary Affairs*, 2004, p. 691.

20 Cf. K.D. Ewing, 'The Human Rights Act and Parliamentary Democracy', *Modern Law Review*, 1999, p. 92.

21 See M. Flinders, 'Shifting the Balance? Parliament, the Executive and the British Constitution', *Political Studies*, 2002, p. 62.

22 See S. Gardbaum, *The Commonwealth Model of Constitutionalism. Theory and Practice* (Cambridge University Press, Cambridge, New York, 2013), about the new model. This model has also come to be known by several other names: (a) 'weak-form of judicial review' (M. Tushnet, 'Alternative Forms of Judicial Review', *Michigan Law Review*, Vol. 101, 2003, p. 2781) or just 'weak judicial review' (J. Waldron, 'The Core of the Case Against Judicial Review', *Yale Law Journal*, Vol. 115, 2006, p. 1354); (b) 'the parliamentary bill of rights model' (J. Hiebert, 'Parliamentary Bill of Rights. An Alternative Model?', *Modern Law Review*, Vol. 69, No. 7, 2006, p. 3), 'the dialogue model', 'the model of democratic dialogue' (A.L. Young, *Parliamentary Sovereignty and the Human Rights Act* (Hart Publishing, Oxford, UK, 2009) chapter 5), or 'dialogic judicial review'

(K. Roach, 'Dialogic Judicial Review and Its Critics', *Supreme Court Law Review*, Vol. 23, second series, 2004, p. 49).

23 See C. Fusaro and D. Oliver, 'Towards a Theory of Constitutional Change', *in* D. Oliver and C. Fusaro (eds.), *How Constitutions Change – A Comparative Study* (Hart Publishing, New York, 2011), pp. 417–18.

24 See the results of the research project 'Negotiating Modernity: History of Modern Political Thought in East-Central Europe', led by Balázs Trencsényi, and supported by the European Research Council, https://erc.europa.eu/"negotiating-modernity"-history-modern-political-thought-east-central-europe.

25 See I. Bibó, *Kelet-európai kis-népek nyomorúsága* [*The Misery of the Small States of Eastern Europe*], 1946.

26 The text of the anthem was written by József Kölcsey in 1823, two years before the Reform Era (1825–1848) started in Hungary. Paradoxically, this was probably the last time in Hungarian history when society was tolerant, open to cultural, religious, and national diversity.

27 'Az írás ott volt a falon, de senki sem volt hajlandó elolvasni és megérteni' ['The scriptum was already on the wall, but nobody dared to read and understand it'], Interview with Professor György Csepeli, 25 September 2015. www.boon.hu/az-iras-ott-volt-a-falon-de-senki-sem-volt-hajlando-elolvasni-es-megerteni/2922802.

28 A sign at an exhibit in the National Museum offers an explanation for opting for the Axis in WWII: 'Aside from the expansive Italian Fascist movement and the foreign policy of the German National Socialist state, there were no other powers from whom a revision of the Trianon Treaty could be expected'. A bronze statue commissioned and installed by the current Hungarian government in the summer of 2014 in Szabadság Square in Budapest features an angel, a male figure with his tunic open to his breast, menaced by an eagle whose talons clutched a bar just overhead. The angel is Hungary, and the eagle is the Nazis, who had entered Budapest on 19 March 1944. See James Traub, 'Hungary's 500-Year-Old Victim Complex', *Foreign Policy*, 28 October 2015. https://foreignpolicy.com/2015/10/28/hungarys-500-year-old-victim-complex-nazis-habsburgs/?utm_source=Sailthru&utm_medium=email&utm_campaign=New%20Campaign&utm_term=%2AEditors%20Picks.

29 This is a long argument of two psychologists, on the reason why Orbán was to keep his power in 2014, despite the population's disappointments with his governance in the previous parliamentary term. See T. Halmai and E. Sebestyén, 'Megvédünk az önállóságtól' ['We protect you from self-determination'], *Élet és Irodalom*, 25 September 2015.

30 See Jason Stanley, 'Democracy and Demagogue', *The New York Times*, 12 October 2015. Stanley argues that Plato's prediction is most dramatically exhibited by Weimar Germany, and recently in the cases of Hungary and Russia.

31 Cf. C. Offe, *Designing Institutions for East European Transitions* (Institut für Höhere Studies, Vienna, 1994), p. 15.

32 See this argument *in* P. Blokker, *New Democracies in Crisis? A Comparative Constitutional Study of the Czech Republic, Hungary, Poland, Romania and Slovakia* (Routledge, Oxford, UK, 2013). Also Wojciech Sadurski argued that legal constitutionalism might have a 'negative effect' in new democracies and might lead to the perpetuation of the problem of both weak political parties and civil society. See W. Sadurski, 'Transitional Constitutionalism: Simplistic and Fancy Theories', *in* A. Czarnota, M. Krygier, and W. Sadurski (eds.), *Rethinking the Rule of Law After Communism* (CEU Press, Budapest, 2005), pp. 9–24.

33 See R. Albert, 'Counterconstitutionalism', *Dalhousie Law Journal*, Vol. 31, No. 1, 2008, p. 4.

34 Cf. Sadurski, 2005, p. 23.

35 See the reviews on Blokker's book by Jiri Priban and Bogusia Puchalska in ICONnect. <www.iconnectblog.com/2013/09/book-reviewresponse-paul-blokker-jiri-priban-and-bogusia-puchalska-on-civic-constitutionalism>.

36 W.J. Dobson, *The Dictator's Learning Curve. Inside the Global Battle for Democracy* (Doubleday, 2012), p. 4.

37 In a speech delivered 26 July 2014 before an ethnic Hungarian audience in neighboring Romania, Orbán proclaimed his intention to turn Hungary into a state that 'will undertake the odium of expressing that in character it is not of liberal nature'. Citing as models he added: 'We have abandoned liberal methods and principles of organizing society, as well as the liberal way to look at the world. . . . Today, the stars of international analyses are Singapore, China, India, Turkey, Russia . . . and if we think back on what we did in the last four years, and what we are going to do in the following four years, then it really can be interpreted from this angle. We are . . . parting ways with Western European dogmas, making ourselves independent from them. . . . If we look at civil organizations in Hungary . . . we have to deal with paid political activists here. . . . [T]hey would like to exercise influence . . . on Hungarian public life. It is vital, therefore, that if we would like to reorganize our nation state instead of the liberal state, that we should make it clear, that these are not civilians . . . opposing us, but political activists attempting to promote foreign interests. . . . This is about the ongoing reorganization of Hungarian state. Contrary to the liberal state organization logic of the past twenty years, this is a state organization originating in national interests'. See the full text of Viktor Orbán's speech here: http://budapestbeacon.com/public-policy/full-text-of-viktor-orbans-speech-at-baile-tusnad-tusnadfurdo-of-26-july-2014/.

38 See S. Levitsky and L.A. Way, *Competetive Authoritarianism. Hybrid Regimes After the Cold War* (Cambridge University Press, New York, 2010), p. 5.

39 See J. Rupnik, 'Europe and the Democratisation of Its Neighbourhood', in *Democracy in Precipice,* Council of Europe Democracy Debates 2011–2012 (Council of Europe Publishing, Strasbourg, 2012), pp. 85–96.

40 Gilles Kepel and Jaques Rupnik, 'Explosive Nachbarn. Demokratie, Revolution und Geopolitik östlich und südlich von Europa', *Lettre International*, 109, Sommer 2015.

41 See B. Szabó, 'Félázsiai származékoknál, mint mi, csak így megy' ['With a Half-Asian Lot such as Ours, There Is No Other Way'], Népszabadság, 27 July 2012.

42 'La Hongrie est une fatalité', *Le Monde,* 10 February 2012.

43 Only 22% of Fidesz voters are followers of churches, and the same percentage of them consider themselves as explicitly non-religious. Political Capital Institute's research, Budapest, 2012.

44 See Zoltán Ádám and András Bozóki, 'The God of Hungarians: Religion and Right-Wing Populism in Hungary', Manuscript, 2015. On file with the author.

45 'Minden magyar a turulba születik' ['All Hungarian Are Born into the Turul Bird'], *Népszabadság*, 29 September 2012.

46 http://uk.businessinsider.com/eurostat-map-of-married-couples-in-europe-2015-10?r=US&IR=T. I am thankful to Kim Lane Scheppele for calling this aspect to my attention.

47 A new law adopted in 10 June 2014 ended the separate city and district council elections in Budapest, and delegated elected district mayors to the city council. According to the original structure, besides the 23 district mayors, 9 additional seats would have been distributed according to a compensation list. The new law abolished the previous system whereby Budapest city council members were directly elected from party lists. Based on the new law, which secured the majority for Fidesz, the 'election' or rather the delegation of the Budapest City Council cannot be considered as free anymore.

48 Sylvana Habdank-Kołaczkowska, 'Authoritarian Aggression and the Pressures of Austerity', Nations in Transit 2013 (Freedom House, 2013).

49 https://freedomhouse.org/report/nations-transit/2015/hungary.

50 J. Birdwell, S. Feve, C. Tryborn, and N. Vibla, Backsliders: *Measuring Democracy in the EU* (Demos, London, UK, 2013), pp. 20–21.

51 See the study of the Republikon Institute saying that in 2013 around 12% of the adult population considered themselves as liberal; there were about 1.5 million people in Hungary who supported liberal values in human rights related questions. In certain issues this support is even bigger: the liberty of abortion and euthanasia as well as the separation of state and church enjoy around 2/3 support, and also about 25–28% of the respondents accept gay marriage. See 'Párhuzamos liberalizmusok: Kik a liberális szavazók?' Republikon Intézet, 2013. http://republikon.hu/media/12016/20130522.pdf. Based on these results, János Kis claims that even if there is no liberal party in the current Parliament, around 8% of the entire adult population would be reachable for liberal politics. See J. Kis, 'Liberalizmus a 3. Köztársaságban' ['Liberalism in the Third Republic'], szuveren.hu and beszelo.hu, 2 October 2014.

52 Asking the question, whether liberal democracy is at risk, Ivan Krastev responds that the big difference from the 1930s is that even extremist parties do not contest the democratic aspect of the liberal democratic consensus; rather, they have a problem with the liberal part of it. See I. Krastev, 'Europe in Crisis: Is Liberal Democracy at Risk?', in *Democracy in Precipice*, Council of Europe Democracy Debates 2011–2012 (Council of Europe Publishing, Strasbourg, 2012), pp. 67–73.

53 Communication from the Commission of 11 March 2014, A New EU Framework to Strengthen the Rule of Law.

Index